European Asylum Law and the Rights of the Child

The child asylum seeker poses unique challenges for reception and refugee status determination systems, not least because the child is entitled to have his or her rights as a child respected as a matter of international and regional human rights law. Over the past decade or so, the European Union has established its own regional system of refugee protection in the form of the Common European Asylum System (CEAS). At the same time, the EU has increasingly engaged with children's rights, as is evident from the Charter of Fundamental Rights, which includes certain rights of the child, and new Article 3(3) of the Treaty on European Union, which commits the Union to promoting the 'protection of the rights of the child'.

This book addresses the question of whether the CEAS complies with the rights of the child. It contrasts the normative standards of international child rights law with the treatment of child asylum seekers and refugees in the CEAS. Ciara Smyth identifies the attributes of the rights of the child that are most relevant to the asylum context and systematically examines whether and to what extent those attributes are reflected in the CEAS legislation. The book goes on to assess whether the CEAS instruments direct Member States to comply with the rights of the child, offering a comprehensive examination of the place of the child within European asylum law and policy.

The book will be of great use and interest to scholars and students of international law, immigration and children's rights studies.

Ciara Smyth is a Lecturer in the School of Law of the National University of Ireland, Galway.

Routledge Research in Asylum, Migration and Refugee Law

Forthcoming titles in this series include:

Refugee Protection and the Role of Law
Conflicting Identities
Edited by Susan Kneebone, Dallal Stevens, Loretta Baldassar

Gender in Refugee Law
From the Margins to the Centre
Efrat Arbel, Catherine Dauvergne, Jenni Millbank

Asylum Law in the European Union
From the Geneva Convention to the Law of the EU
Francesco Cherubini

The Socio-Economic Rights of Asylum Seekers
Liam Thornton

European Asylum Law and the Rights of the Child

Ciara Smyth

Routledge
Taylor & Francis Group

LONDON AND NEW YORK

First published 2014
by Routledge

2 Park Square, Milton Park, Abingdon, Oxon, OX14 4RN
711 Third Avenue, New York, NY 10017, USA

Routledge is an imprint of the Taylor & Francis Group, an informa business

First issued in paperback 2016

Copyright © 2014 Ciara Smyth

The right of Ciara Smyth to be identified as author of this work has been asserted by her in accordance with sections 77 and 78 of the Copyright, Designs and Patents Act 1988.

All rights reserved. No part of this book may be reprinted or reproduced or utilised in any form or by any electronic, mechanical, or other means, now known or hereafter invented, including photocopying and recording, or in any information storage or retrieval system, without permission in writing from the publishers.

Notice:
Product or corporate names may be trademarks or registered trademarks, and are used only for identification and explanation without intent to infringe.

British Library Cataloguing in Publication Data
A catalogue record for this book is available from the British Library

Library of Congress Cataloging-in-Publication Data
Smyth, Ciara, author.
European asylum law and the rights of the child / Ciara Smyth.
pages cm – (Routledge research in asylum, migration and refugee law)
Includes bibliographical references and index.
ISBN 978-0-415-85501-3 (hbk)
ISBN 978-1-138-20205-4 (pbk)
ISBN 978-0-203-79729-7 (ebk)
1. Asylum, Right of–European Union countries. 2. Children's rights–European Union countries. I. Title.
KJE5202.S678 2014
342.2408'3–dc23
2014000659

Typeset in Garamond
by Deer Park Productions

For Geoff

Contents

Acknowledgements   xi
List of acronyms   xii

   Introduction   1

1   Introduction to European asylum law   6
   Introduction 6
   The 1951 Convention regime 6
   Relevant international human rights law 7
   The EU Common European Asylum System 9
     The evolution of the Common European Asylum System 9
     Overview of the key instruments of the CEAS 16
   Conclusion 27

2   Introduction to the rights of the child and their relationship to European asylum law   28
   Introduction 28
   The rights of the child 28
     Note on the 'theory gap' 29
     Overview of the rights in the CRC as they relate to the asylum context 31
     The nature of the legal obligation in the CRC 39
   The relationship between the rights of the child and European asylum law 42
     An indirect channelling 43
     Some complications in the EU–fundamental rights nexus 50
   Conclusion 54

3   The right of the child to seek and qualify for international protection   55
   Introduction 55

The right of the child to seek international protection 56
   The existence of a right of the child to seek international protection 56
   Phase One CEAS: Compliance with the right of the child to seek international protection 58
   Phase Two CEAS: Prospects for enhanced compliance 61
The right of the child to qualify for international protection 63
   The relevance of the rights of the child to eligibility for international protection 63
   Phase One CEAS: Eligibility concepts and the rights of the child 72
   Phase Two CEAS: Eligibility concepts and the rights of the child 91
Conclusion 94

4 The right of the child to be heard   96
Introduction 96
The right of the child to be heard 97
   The right to a hearing 99
   The conduct of the hearing 103
   The evaluation of the child's views 106
Phase One CEAS: Compliance with the right of the child to be heard 108
   The right to a hearing 110
   The conduct of the hearing 116
   The evaluation of the child's views 120
Phase Two CEAS: Prospects for enhanced compliance 125
   The right to a hearing 125
   The conduct of the hearing 129
   The evaluation of the child's views 133
Conclusion 136

5 The right of the child to protection and care   138
Introduction 138
The right of the child to family unity 140
   The concept of derived rights 141
   The prohibition on separating a child from his/her parents 142
Phase One CEAS: Compliance with the right of the child to family unity 145
   The concept of derived rights 145
   The prohibition on separating a child from his/her parents 148
Phase Two CEAS: Prospects for enhanced compliance 151
   The concept of derived rights 151
   The prohibition on separating a child from his/her parents 152
The right of the unaccompanied and separated child to special protection and assistance 153

  *Identification of the child entitled to special protection
    and assistance* 154
  Oversight of care and protection 156
  The provision of alternative care 158
 Phase One CEAS: Compliance with the right of the
 unaccompanied and separated child to special
 protection and assistance 160
  *Identification of the child entitled to special protection
    and assistance* 161
  Oversight of care and protection 163
  The provision of alternative care 165
 Phase Two CEAS: Prospects for enhanced compliance 167
  *Identification of the child entitled to special
    protection and assistance* 167
  Oversight of care and protection 169
  The provision of alternative care 169
 Conclusion 170

6 **Certain socio-economic rights of the child**   172
 Introduction 172
 Health 175
  The right of the child to health 175
  *Phase One CEAS: Compliance with the right of
   the child to health* 183
  Phase Two CEAS: Prospects for enhanced compliance 190
 Standard of living 194
  The right of the child to an adequate standard of living 194
  *Phase One CEAS: Compliance with the right of the child
   to an adequate standard of living* 200
  Phase Two CEAS: Prospects for enhanced compliance 204
 Conclusion 207

7 **The right of the child to liberty**   209
 Introduction 209
 The right of the child to liberty 210
  Permissible detention 211
  Conditions of detention 216
  Procedural protection 221
 Phase One CEAS: Compliance with the right of the
 child to liberty 223
  Permissible detention 223
  Conditions of detention 226
  Procedural protection 227

Phase Two CEAS: Prospects for enhanced compliance 228
   Permissible detention 229
   Conditions of detention 230
   Procedural protection 232
Conclusion 233

Conclusion   234

Index   240

Acknowledgements

I would like to acknowledge the invaluable help of my former colleagues at the Institute of Immigration Law at Leiden University. In particular, I would like to thank Pieter Boeles, Peter Rodrigues and Marcelle Reneman. My colleagues at the National University of Ireland Galway have also played an important part in bringing this book to fruition, especially Donncha O'Connell, Laurent Pech, Marie McGonagle, Padraic Kenna, Charles O'Mahony and Larry Donnelly. I would like to thank the staff of the Irish Refugee Council and, in particular, Sue Conlon and Jaqueline Kelly, for helping to keep me in touch with developments on the ground. I am indebted to Helena King for her proofreading assistance. I would like to acknowledge my friends who have helped me in all sorts of ways to write this book, especially Michelle Scully, Elizabeth Flynn, Fionnuala Dillane, Niamh Doheny and Sinead Curtis. Thank you to my father, Leo Smyth, and sister, Sharon Fitzpatrick, who invariably bear the brunt of things going wrong, and who are unfailingly patient and sympathetic. Thank you, finally, to my husband, Geoff Drea, and to my children, Niamh and Caoimhe, who make everything in life – including struggling with a book – worthwhile.

List of acronyms

APD	Asylum Procedures Directive
CEAS	Common European Asylum System
CRC	Convention on the Rights of the Child
Com. ESCR	Committee on Economic, Social and Cultural Rights
Com. RC	Committee on the Rights of the Child
CJEU	Court of Justice of the EU
DR	Dublin Regulation
EASO	European Asylum Support Office
ECHR	European Convention on Human Rights
ECtHR	European Court of Human Rights
ECJ	European Court of Justice
EU	European Union
UNHCR EXCOM	Executive Committee of the High Commissioner's Programme
FCA	First country of asylum
HRC	Human Rights Committee
ICCPR	International Covenant on Civil and Political Rights
ICESCR	International Covenant on Economic, Social and Cultural Rights
QD	Qualification Directive
RCD	Reception Conditions Directive
SCO	Safe country of origin
STC	Safe third country
TEU	Treaty on European Union
TFEU	Treaty on the Functioning of the EU
UNHCR	United Nations High Commissioner for Refugees

Introduction

A significant proportion of people seeking asylum in EU countries are children.[1] These children may be totally alone, with people who are not their customary caregivers or with members of their immediate family. The child asylum seeker poses unique challenges for reception and refugee status determination systems, not least because the child is entitled to have his or her rights as a child respected as a matter of international and regional human rights law. Since the beginning of the new millennium, the EU has sought to harmonise the law in the area of asylum in the form of a Common European Asylum System (CEAS). The instruments that make up the CEAS often make specific provision for children – as minors, unaccompanied minors and persons with special needs – demonstrating awareness on the part of the EU legislator of the existence and distinct needs of this vulnerable population. However, the existence of age-specific provisions does not necessarily translate to a respect for the rights of the child. Hence, the question arises as to whether the child-specific provisions, the age-neutral provisions, the instruments as a whole and the CEAS as a system are consistent with the rights of the child. This question is particularly pertinent at the moment for two reasons. Firstly, the CEAS is currently moving from its first to its second phase – a process that involved recasting the key instruments in 2013. Secondly, between the two phases, respecting and promoting the rights of the child has emerged as a legal and

---

1 The number of unaccompanied minors seeking asylum in the EU-28 in 2012 was almost 4 per cent (12,785 out of a total of 335,380 applications): http://epp.eurostat.ec.europa.eu/statistics_explained/index.php/Asylum_statistics (accessed 11 November 2013). The number of accompanied minors is more difficult to gauge as such children are typically subsumed into the asylum applications of their parents, making this a largely invisible cohort of asylum seekers. However, it is likely that the numbers of accompanied-minor asylum seekers is statistically significant. For example, as of early September 2013, 1 out of 2 million Syrian refugees were estimated to be children. See 'Number of Syrian refugees tops 2 million mark with more on the way' and 'A million refugee children mark shameful milestone in Syrian crisis', available at www.unhcr.org (accessed 11 November 2013). While this does not necessarily mean that half the Syrian refugee population in the EU comprises children, this example illustrates that a statistically significant proportion of asylum seekers tend to be children.

policy imperative of the EU. It is therefore an opportune moment to undertake a systematic appraisal of the CEAS in the light of the rights of the child. Taking a number of key rights of the child as its point of departure, this book undertakes such an appraisal, with Phase One serving as a base-line and Phase Two serving as a measure of progress.

Chapters 1 and 2 set the scene by providing, respectively, an introduction to European asylum law and to the rights of the child and how the two areas of law interact. The assumption is that the reader may be familiar with one or other areas of law but not necessarily both. Chapter 1 introduces European asylum law. Beginning with the cornerstone 1951 Convention relating to the Status of Refugees, the chapter outlines the international legal regime governing asylum seekers and refugees. It then moves on to examine how international and regional human rights law has developed to supplement the refugee regime with its own *non-refoulement* guarantee in the context of the prohibition of torture and inhuman or degrading treatment or punishment. The bulk of the chapter, however, is devoted to providing an overview of the system of regional protection in the EU, namely, the CEAS. The genesis and evolution of the CEAS is sketched, and the general content of the key instruments – the Dublin Regulation, the Reception Conditions Directive, the Asylum Procedures Directive and the Qualification Directive – is set out.

Chapter 2 introduces the rights of the child. An on-going theoretical debate about whether children are properly rights-holders is briefly summarised, as this helps explains the resistance, frequently observed in the asylum context, to the idea that children have rights. Next, the positive law on the rights of the child is set out. Although children fall within the personal scope of all the international human rights treaties, and indeed many of them contain a child-specific provision or provisions, it is the seminal UN Convention on the Rights of the Child (CRC) that provides the normative blue-print for any discussion relating to children's rights. A brief sketch is drawn of how the various groups of rights in the CRC relate to the asylum context, and of the nature of the general legal obligation under the Convention. The final section of Chapter 2 discusses the relationship between the rights of the child and EU law. This is important because the aim of this book is to evaluate CEAS – a creature, principally, of EU law – in the light of the rights of the child, which presupposes that there is some obligation for EU law to conform to international child-rights law.

Each of the remaining substantive chapters is devoted to a child right that is particularly pertinent to the asylum context. The purpose of each chapter is three-fold: 1) to identify the meaning of the right in general and in the specific asylum context; 2) to assess whether the key attributes of the right in the asylum context, thus identified, are accurately reflected in the relevant Phase One CEAS instruments; 3) to carry out a similar assessment in respect of the Phase Two instruments. Thus, in brief, each chapter is devoted to an elucidation of *meaning* and an assessment of *compliance*. These chapters follow the same basic structure. A first section outlines the normative content of the given right, based primarily on a textual and jurisprudential analysis of the right as it presents in the CRC and as it is interpreted by the Convention's monitoring body – the Committee on the Rights of the Child. In order to provide a fuller picture, however, a comparative analysis is frequently undertaken of the right as it presents in different international human rights instruments as interpreted by their monitoring bodies or courts and in refugee law. A second section assesses whether the relevant provisions of relevant CEAS instruments comply with the right, and a third section assesses the prospects for enhanced compliance in Phase Two of the CEAS. The assessment is based primarily on an analysis of the wording of the instruments as informed by the developing case law of the two European courts and, particularly in respect of Phase Two, by the preparatory documents that informed the negotiation process. State practice, as it emerges from reports by the European Commission, UNHCR and other bodies is used to illuminate how the CEAS instruments are being applied.[2] In chapters that deal with more than one right, this structure is repeated internally within the chapter in respect of each right.

Chapter 3 deals with the right of the child to seek and to qualify for international protection. It begins by clarifying the meaning of this 'right'. First of all, to the extent that anyone has a right to seek asylum, the child too has this right. This means that the child, whether accompanied or unaccompanied, must be allowed to lodge an asylum application. Rules regarding the lodging of asylum applications are laid down in the Asylum Procedures Directive and its recast and are scrutinised accordingly. Second, like anyone else, the child who qualifies for international protection has the right to be granted international protection. But eligibility in the case of children also depends on having the rights of the child recognised as refugee-relevant. It is argued here that various obstacles to recognising the rights of the child as refugee-relevant are created at the intersection of international human rights law and international refugee law. The relevant CEAS instrument – the Qualification Directive – is examined to see whether these obstacles have been transferred to the CEAS and whether the recast directive eliminates some or all of these obstacles.

Chapter 4 outlines the right of the child to be heard, a general principle of the Convention on the Rights of the Child that has significant implications for the asylum procedure. The right is the child-specific equivalent of the general human right to a fair hearing. It comprises the right of the child to a hearing, to be able to participate meaningfully in that hearing and to have his/her views given due consideration in accordance with the age and maturity of the child. It has potentially transformative consequences for the asylum interview, which range from a right to be interviewed to possible exemption from negative credibility inferences. Many provisions of the Asylum Procedures Directive are implicated by the right of the child to be heard.

---

2 However, this book is not a comparative analysis of how member states have implemented the CEAS; rather, is it an evaluation of whether the CEAS complies with the rights of the child.

These are analysed for compliance with the various aspects of the right. The recast directive is then scrutinised to assess the prospects for enhanced compliance in Phase Two.

Chapter 5 concerns the right of the asylum-seeking and refugee child to day-to-day protection and care. In the case of accompanied children, this right is generally met by their parents, underscoring the importance of a cluster of rights that fall under the rubric of 'family unity', such as the concept of derived rights and the prohibition on separating a child from his/her parents against their will. In the case of unaccompanied and separated children, this right to protection and care cannot be met by their parents and hence must be met by the state acting in a surrogate capacity. The state is required to identify such children, to appoint a representative to oversee their best interests and to provide alternative care. Various provisions of the Reception Conditions Directive, the Qualification Directive and the Dublin Regulation speak to these issues and are duly assessed. Finally, the Phase Two instruments are assessed in order to evaluate the prospects for enhanced compliance with these rights.

Chapter 6 concerns certain socio-economic rights of the child, namely, the right of the child to health and to an adequate standard of living. A modified approach to elucidating the content of these rights is advanced because of the distinct legal obligation inherent in socio-economic rights (i.e. progressive realisation rather than full immediate realisation). In brief, the normative content and the 'core' content of each right is delineated on the premise that the relevant CEAS instruments should generally conform to the former, but that in their discretionary and derogation provisions, they should conform at least to the latter. The relevant CEAS instruments are the Reception Conditions Directive and the Qualification Directive. A compliance analysis is undertaken of these directives and repeated in respect of the recast directives.

Chapter 7 relates to the right of the child to liberty. It is an unhappy fact that many asylum-seeking children in the EU, both accompanied and unaccompanied, are deprived of their liberty because of widespread policies of administrative detention of asylum seekers. These policies are sanctioned by the CEAS. This chapter explores the meaning of the right of the child to liberty in the light of recent developments in the jurisprudence of the European Court of Human Rights as regards the administrative detention of children. It evaluates provisions of the Reception Conditions Directive and Asylum Procedures Directive that expressly or implicitly authorise detention. It assesses whether the provisions of the recast directives – which are supposed to radically revise the CEAS position on detention – are consistent with the right of the child to liberty.

The concluding chapter of this book synthesises and comments on the findings relating to European asylum law and the rights of the child and, specifically, on the question of compliance. Some general observations are drawn from the findings in relation to possible causes for any enduring inconsistency between the CEAS and the rights of the child. These observations relate mainly to the EU legislator's engagement with asylum and with children's rights. The assessment of whether the CEAS complies with the rights of the child is important not simply as a critique of the work of the EU legislator in integrating child rights into asylum policy, however, but also for member states, national courts and the Court of Justice of the EU which must attempt to interpret the legislation in a manner that is consistent with the rights of the child.

1 Introduction to European asylum law

Introduction

This chapter provides an introduction to the first of the two areas of substantive law of relevance to this book, namely, European asylum law. The chapter begins by outlining the 1951 Convention regime, which remains the cornerstone of refugee law in Europe. Next, attention is paid to how international human rights law has developed its own, complementary, system of protection. However, the bulk of the chapter is devoted to the system of regional protection in the EU, namely, the Common European Asylum System (CEAS). The genesis and development of the system is outlined. This is important because it helps explain some of the particular features and nuances of the system. Finally, an overview is provided of the content of the key instruments of the CEAS. The chapter is largely descriptive and general (i.e. not specific to children) since it lays the foundation for sustained child-rights analysis in later chapters.

The 1951 Convention regime

Despite the development of a system of regional protection in the EU, the 1951 Convention Relating to the Status of Refugees remains the cornerstone of refugee protection in Europe. The Convention provides a succinct definition of a refugee in Article 1A(2): someone who has a well-founded fear of being persecuted for reasons of race, religion, nationality, membership of a particular social group or political opinion, is outside his/her country of nationality or habitual residence and is unable or unwilling to return to it. Aligned to this definition is the cessation clause in Article 1C, establishing that refugee status may cease for a number of reasons, such as a return to normalcy in the country of origin, and the exclusion clauses in Articles 1D–F, establishing that a person who might otherwise qualify as a refugee can be excluded from the status for a number of reasons, for example, if he/she is considered undeserving due to past criminal behaviour of a serious nature. The bulk of the Convention is devoted to setting out the rights to which refugees are entitled in the country of asylum, which comprise a mix of civil and socio-economic rights. The most important right of the refugee is the right of *non-refoulement* in

Article 33(1): the right not to be sent back to a country where the refugee's life or freedom would be threatened on Convention grounds. The right is not absolute and can be limited under Article 33(2) where the refugee is reasonably regarded as a danger to the security of the country of asylum or where he/she constitutes a danger to the community because he/she has been convicted in the country of asylum of a particularly serious crime. A notable omission from the 1951 Convention is any child-specific provision.[1] A further omission is any direction or guidance about how to undertake refugee status determination or about the kind of procedural guarantees that should be afforded to asylum seekers. In this regard, the Convention is concerned mainly with refugees who have been recognised as such, as distinct from asylum-seekers who are seeking to be recognised.[2] Nevertheless, this gap is plugged somewhat by the development of soft-law standards by the Convention's supervisory body, the United Nations High Commissioner for Refugees (UNHCR), in the form of guidelines, handbooks, notes and the conclusions of its Executive Committee.[3]

Relevant international human rights law

International human rights law has developed its own *non-refoulement* guarantee, which is not limited to refugees and which prohibits sending someone, directly or indirectly, to a country where they face a real risk of torture or inhuman or degrading treatment or punishment. The only explicit *non-refoulement* guarantee in a human rights instrument is found in Article 3 of the UN Convention Against Torture, which is limited to torture (as distinct from lesser forms of ill-treatment). However, the European Court of Human Rights (ECtHR) has developed a *non-refoulement* guarantee jurisprudentially, under the rubric of the prohibition of torture or inhuman or degrading treatment or punishment in Article 3 of the European Convention on Human Rights (ECHR)[4] and the Human Rights Committee has taken a similar approach to the interpretation of Article 7 of the UN International Covenant on Civil and Political Rights (ICCPR).[5] Since the focus of this book is European asylum law, attention will be confined here to the ECHR.[6]

---

1 The only indication that the refugee might be a child is in Article 22 on public education, which establishes an obligation to 'accord to refugees the same treatment as is accorded to nationals with respect to elementary education'.
2 The most comprehensive analysis of the rights to which refugees (note: the status is declaratory, not constitutive) are entitled at the various stages of the process is provided by J. Hathaway, *The Rights of Refugees under International Law*, Cambridge: Cambridge University Press, 2005.
3 Available at: http://www.refworld.org/
4 ECtHR, *Soering v UK*, Appl. No. 14038/88, Judgment of 7 July 1989.
5 Human Rights Committee, *Kindler v Canada*, Communication No. 470/1991, Views of 18 November 1993.
6 For a thorough comparative analysis of the prohibition of *refoulement* in international human rights and refugee law, see K. Wouters, *International Legal Standards for the Protection from Refoulement*, Mortsel: Intersentia, 2009.

There are a number of noteworthy aspects to the Article 3 ECHR jurisprudence. First, unlike the situation under the 1951 Convention, the *non-refoulement* guarantee under Article 3 of the ECHR has been held to be absolute. Therefore, once a real risk of prohibited treatment is made out, neither the individual's past criminal behaviour nor his/her present risk to national security or to the community can serve to limit the right of *non-refoulement*.[7] Second, the phrase 'inhuman or degrading treatment or punishment' is interpreted ever-more expansively by the Court. Where once the Court insisted on a high degree of individuation, amounting almost to a requirement that the individual be personally targeted, now it allows that the risk can stem from generalised violence, if the violence reaches a sufficiently high level of intensity, although this is exceedingly rare.[8] Furthermore, inhuman or degrading treatment or punishment is not confined to acts of violence but may extend to omissions of a socio-economic nature, where the resulting deprivation is sufficiently severe and the responsibility of the State is clearly engaged. This can have important repercussions for States seeking to send unsuccessful asylum-seekers to their own or another country where they risk becoming destitute.[9] Third, a host of procedural rights has coalesced around Article 3 alone and in conjunction with Article 13 (right to an effective remedy) such as the right to be heard and the right to an appeal with suspensive effect.[10]

Finally, it should be noted that in addition to the *non-refoulement* guarantee, the ECHR and the other international human rights instruments contain other rights of potential relevance to the asylum context. Other relevant rights include the right not to be arbitrarily detained, which has implications for asylum detention;[11] the right to private and family life, which has implications for reception conditions;[12] and the prohibition of collective expulsion of aliens, which strengthens the procedural guarantees that must be afforded to asylum seekers.[13] The protection afforded under international human rights law is known as complementary protection since it complements that afforded under the 1951 Convention regime, although unlike the latter, it is non-status conferring. Of course, the rights of the child

---

7 ECtHR, *Chahal v UK*, Appl. No. 22414/93, Judgment (GC) of 15 November 1996. However, diplomatic assurances by the receiving State may be considered to minimise the 'real risk' of torture or inhuman or degrading treatment or punishment. The most high-profile case is: ECtHR, *Othman (Abu Qatada) v UK*, Appl. No. 8139/09, Judgment of 17 January 2012.
8 Contrast ECtHR, *Vilvarajah v UK*, Appl. Nos. 13163/87, 13164/87, 13165/87, 13447/87, 13448/87, Judgment of 30 October 1991 with *Sufi and Elmi v UK*, Appl. Nos. 8319/07 and 11449/07, Judgment of 28 June 2011.
9 ECtHR, *MSS v Belgium and Greece*, Appl. No. 30696/09, Judgment (GC) of 21 January 2011.
10 See Chapter 4.
11 Article 5(1)(f) ECHR and Articles 9 and 10 ICCPR.
12 Article 8 ECHR and Article 17 ICCPR.
13 Protocol 4, Article 4, ECHR and Article 13 ICCPR.

have an important application in the asylum context, as will be outlined in the next chapter.[14]

The EU Common European Asylum System

The CEAS – a project still in the making – aims to gradually harmonise asylum law and policy in the EU Member States. It is a response to the creation of an EU with external but no internal borders. Although the abolition of internal borders was designed to facilitate the free movement of EU citizens, it quickly became apparent that any third country national who managed to gain entry to a Member State could then also move freely within the EU. Hence, it became necessary to harmonise Member States' immigration and asylum systems in order to avoid irregular secondary movements *within* the EU. In the asylum context, it was felt particularly necessary to avoid the dual phenomena of 'refugees in orbit', whereby asylum seekers were passed from one Member State to the next with no State accepting responsibility for processing the claim; and 'asylum shopping', whereby asylum seekers moved within the EU to the Member State they perceived as most likely to grant them refugee status, or lodged successive applications in different Member States to circumvent negative outcomes. Before the introduction of the CEAS, a decade of largely ineffectual intergovernmental cooperation on asylum left Member States and asylum seekers free to exploit and be exploited by these possibilities.[15]

The evolution of the Common European Asylum System

Phase One CEAS (1999–2004)

The original treaty basis for the CEAS was inserted into the Treaty Establishing the European Community (TEC) by the Treaty of Amsterdam, which 'communitarised' asylum by moving it from the intergovernmental third pillar to the Community first pillar.[16] Article 63 provided for the adoption within five

---

14 See J. McAdam, 'Seeking asylum under the Convention on the Rights of the Child: A case for complementary protection', *International Journal of Children's Rights* 14, 2006, 251–274.
15 For the history of pre-CEAS cooperation on asylum, see I. Boccardi, *Europe and Refugees – Towards an EU Asylum Policy*, The Hague: Kluwer Law International, 2002.
16 Some Member States have secured 'opt-outs' from participating in EU legislation governing asylum. See, Protocol on the position of the United Kingdom and Ireland, annexed to the Treaty on European Union and to the Treaty establishing the European Community, which was replaced by Protocol (No. 21) of the Lisbon Treaty on the position of the UK and Ireland in respect of the Area of Freedom, Security and Justice; and Protocol on the position of Denmark, annexed to the Treaty on European Union and the Treaty establishing the European Community, which was replaced by Protocol (No. 22) of the Lisbon Treaty on the position of Denmark.

years of the entry into force of the Treaty of Amsterdam of 'measures on asylum' in accordance with the 1951 Geneva Convention relating to the Status of Refugees. The measures were to comprise minimum standards on the reception of asylum seekers, on qualification for refugee status, on asylum procedures, on temporary protection in the context of a mass influx and on protection for persons who 'otherwise need international protection' – an oblique reference to the concept of complementary protection as it had developed in international human rights law. Furthermore, on the rationale of single-State processing, a mechanism was envisaged for determining which Member State is responsible for processing an asylum claim.[17] More specific guidance on this ambitious legislative agenda was provided in the Presidency Conclusions of the Tampere European Council in 1999.[18]

The communitarisation of asylum occurred at a time when the numbers of asylum seekers in Western Europe were at their highest levels since the Second World War, with the inevitable domestic political fall-out that this entailed.[19] And while this fact underscored the need for supra-national action, ironically it also caused Member States to closely guard their sovereign powers. Article 63 TEC deferred to Member State sensitivity in this regard, with its choice of minimum standards rather than a higher level of harmonisation – the intention being to allow Member States to retain their existing asylum systems subject to a 'floor' of basic standards. In order to further soften the radical communitarisation of asylum, Article 67 TEC provided for a transitional period of five years, during which the right of initiative was shared between the Commission and the Member States, the Parliament's powers were limited to consultation, and the adoption of legislation required unanimity in the Council. In effect, this meant that each Member State exercised a veto over prospective CEAS legislation. The role of the European Court of Justice (ECJ) was also curtailed. Article 68(1) TEC significantly curbed the scope of the preliminary ruling procedure in Article 234 TEC in asylum matters: a question concerning the CEAS could only be referred to the ECJ in cases before a national court or tribunal against whose decisions there was no judicial remedy under national law, *and* where that court or tribunal considered that a reference to the ECJ was necessary to enable it to give a judgment. Hence, the role of the Commission, Parliament and Court was

---

17 Given that certain Member States attract larger numbers of asylum seekers than others, Article 63 also contemplated measures on burden sharing/solidarity between Member States, envisaged as financial solidarity. This was supplemented by Article 64(2), which provided for the adoption of provisional emergency measures to assist Member States faced with a sudden inflow of third country nationals. This provision has never been used.
18 Presidency Conclusions – Tampere, 15 and 16 October 1999, *Bulletin of the European Union No. 10/1999*.
19 Asylum applications in the EU peaked in 2001 with 424,200 applications in the EU-27. See http://epp.eurostat.ec.europa.eu/statistics_explained/index.php/Asylum_statistics (accessed 11 November 2013).

minimised and the role of Member States – in the form of the Council – was maximised.

Other factors further complicated the political landscape in which the Article 63 measures were negotiated. First, despite the fact that the pre-Amsterdam intergovernmental cooperation on asylum had not succeeded in preventing irregular secondary movements of asylum seekers – hence the need for a new approach under Amsterdam – its legacy could not be shaken off. Pre-Amsterdam, a number of Member States began to develop deterrence and deflection policies, which soon spread to neighbouring States for fear that they would be perceived as a 'soft touch' for asylum seekers.[20] These policies became the basis of the intergovernmental *acquis* on asylum.[21] Moreover, the hard-law aspects of the pre-Amsterdam *acquis* (the Schengen and Dublin Conventions) were rooted in a migration-control approach to asylum, in which the distinction between asylum and other forms of migration was not well understood. This control-oriented perspective carried over post-Amsterdam.[22] Second, the events of 11 September 2001 led to a perception that security and protection were mutually incompatible and to an acceleration of the already-existing trend towards criminalising asylum.[23] Third, Phase One CEAS became intertwined with the accession in 2004 of ten new Member States to the EU, because the new Member States were required to adopt the entire asylum *acquis* as it existed at the moment of accession. Although the accession States were not party to the negotiations in the Council, the reality of their lack of asylum capacity meant that the minimum-standards legislation could not be pitched too high.[24]

These political factors, coupled with the transitional legislative arrangements and the minimum-standards brief, had a profound impact on the instruments that followed: a regulation establishing the criteria and mechanisms for determining the Member State responsible for examining an asylum application lodged in one of the Member States (henceforth, the Dublin

---

20 For example, Resolution adopted 30 November 1992 on a harmonised approach to questions concerning host third countries: *Document WG I 1283*; Resolution adopted 30 November 1992 on manifestly unfounded applications for asylum: *Document WG I 1282 REV 1*; Conclusions adopted 30 November 1992 concerning countries in which there is generally no serious risk of persecutions: *Document WG I 1281*.
21 Although it is widely considered that the *acquis* influenced State practice, it is submitted that a more accurate account is that State practice influenced the *acquis*, which was then used by States to validate existing practice. On this point see R. Byrne, G. Noll and J. Vedsted-Hansen, 'Understanding refugee law in an enlarged European Union', *European Journal of International Law* 15, 2004, 355–379.
22 See C. Teitgen-Colly, 'The European Union and asylum: An illusion of protection', *Common Market Law Review* 43, 2006, 1503–1566.
23 See, for example, Commission Working Document, 'The relationship between safeguarding internal security and complying with international protection obligations and instruments', *COM (2001) 743 final*.
24 R. Byrne, G. Noll and J. Vedsted-Hansen, *op. cit.*

Regulation);[25] a directive laying down minimum standards for the reception of asylum seekers (henceforth, the Reception Conditions Directive);[26] a directive on minimum standards on procedures in Member States for granting and withdrawing refugee status (henceforth, the Asylum Procedures Directive);[27] and a directive on minimum standards for the qualification and status of refugees and beneficiaries of subsidiary protection and the content of the protection granted (henceforth, the Qualification Directive).[28] These instruments were generally characterised by Member State flexibility in the form of discretionary provisions and derogations which, on the face of them, were not entirely consistent with either the 1951 Convention relating to the Status of Refugees or international human rights law.[29] On the other hand, the Qualification Directive was lauded for attempting to develop progressively the concept of complementary protection and lend it a distinct status, namely subsidiary protection status.[30] Moreover, some provisions of the other instruments were considered to 'level up' standards in some Member States at least.[31] And, most importantly for present purposes, all the instruments made specific provision for children as minors, unaccompanied minors and persons with special needs, although, as commentators were quick to point out, such

---

25 Council Regulation No. 343/2003 of 18 February 2003. The Dublin Regulation is supplemented by Commission Regulation (EC) No. 1560/2003 of 2 September 2003, the so-called 'Dublin Detailed Rules'. The Dublin Regulation is also supported by the Eurodac Regulation (Council Regulation No. 2725/2000/EC of 11 December 2000 for the establishment of 'EURODAC'), which authorises Member States to take the fingerprints of all asylum seekers and certain irregular migrants and store them in a database, enabling Member States to identify the first EU country of entry or asylum.

26 Council Directive 2003/9/EC of 27 January 2003.

27 Council Directive 2005/85/EC of 1 December 2005.

28 Council Directive 2004/83/EC of 29 April 2004. One further instrument was adopted as part of the CEAS package: Council Directive 2001/55/EC of 20 July 2001 on minimum standards for giving temporary protection in the event of a mass influx of displaced persons and on measures promoting a balance of efforts between Member States in receiving such persons and bearing the consequences thereof. This directive has never been activated and is not part of the analysis in this book.

29 There is a wealth of critical commentary on Phase One CEAS in the literature. For a cross-section, see H. Battjes, 'A balance between fairness and efficiency? The directive on international protection and the Dublin regulation', *European Journal of Migration and Law* 4, 2002, 159–192; H. O'Nions, 'The erosion of the right to seek asylum', *Web Journal of Current Legal Issues* 2, 2006; C. Costello, 'The asylum procedures directive and the proliferation of safe country practices: Deterrence, deflection and the dismantling of international protection?' *European Journal of Migration and Law* 7, 2005, 35–69; J. Pirjola, 'European asylum policy – inclusions and exclusions under the surface of universal human rights language', *European Journal of Migration and Law* 11, 2009, 347–366.

30 H. Storey, 'EU refugee qualification directive: A brave new world?', *International Journal of Refugee Law* 20, 2008, 1–49.

31 See N. El-Enany and E. Thielemann, 'The impact of EU asylum policy on national asylum regimes', in S. Wolff, F.A.N.J. Goudappel and J.W. de Zwann (eds), *Freedom, Security and Justice after Lisbon and Stockholm*, The Hague: T.M.C. Asser Press, 2011.

provisions did not necessarily equate to a protection of the rights of the child.[32]

Phase Two CEAS (2005–2009/2010/2012/2013)

As soon as the Phase One instruments were transposed, an evaluation process began. It consisted of Commission reports on the transposition of the instruments in the Member States,[33] a number of commissioned studies,[34] a Green Paper consultation document on the future of the Common European Asylum System,[35] leading to a Policy Plan on Asylum,[36] and a number of direct consultations with governments and civil society. The general consensus was that Phase One had led to diverse national practices in terms of reception, qualification and procedures, due mainly to the amount of discretion left to Member States and the low level of harmonisation sought. This could be seen

---

32 See, for example, E. Drywood, 'Challenging concepts of the "child" in asylum and immigration law: The example of the EU', *Journal of Social Welfare and Family Law* 32, 2010, 309–323; and E. Zschirnt, 'Does migration status trump the best interests of the child? Unaccompanied minors in the EU asylum system', *Journal of Immigration, Asylum and Nationality Law* 25, 2011, 34–55.
33 'Report from the Commission to the European Parliament and the Council on the evaluation of the Dublin system', *COM (2007) 299 final*; 'Report from the Commission to the Council and to the European Parliament on the application of Directive 2003/9/EC of 27 January 2003 laying down minimum standards for the reception of asylum seekers', *COM (2007) 745 final*; 'Report from the Commission to the European Parliament and the Council on the application of Directive 2004/83/EC of 29 April 2004 on minimum standards for the qualification and status of third country nationals or stateless persons as refugees or as persons who otherwise need international protection and the content of protection granted', *COM (2010) 314 final*; 'Report from the Commission to the European Parliament and the Council on the application of Directive 2005/95/EC of 1 December 2005 on minimum standards on procedures in Member States for granting and withdrawing refugee status', *COM (2010) 465 final*.
34 On the Reception Conditions Directive, 'Comparative overview of the implementation of the Directive 2003/9 of 27 January 2003 laying down minimum standards for the reception of asylum seekers in the EU Member States', Odysseus Academic Network, October 2006; on the Qualification Directive, 'Impact assessment studies on the future development of measures on the qualification and status of third country nationals or stateless persons in need of international protection and on the content of the protection granted, based on Council Directive 2004/83/EC', GHK, Multiple framework service contract JLS/2006/A1/004; On the Asylum Procedures Directive: 'The future development of measures on procedures in Member States for granting and withdrawing refugee status, based on Council Directive 2005/85/EC', GHK, Multiple framework service contract JLS/2006/A1/004.
35 Commission Communication, 'Green paper on the future Common European Asylum System', *COM (2007) 301 final*.
36 Communication from the Commission to the European Parliament, the Council, the European Economic and Social Committee and the Committee of the Regions, 'Policy plan on asylum, an integrated approach to protection across the EU', *COM (2008) 260 final*. For the Council's response to the Commission's plan, see Council of the European Union, 'European pact on immigration and asylum', 24 September 2008, *13440/08 ASIM 72*.

in the varied recognition rates across Member States regarding applicants from the same country of origin, and in the persistence of secondary movements of asylum seekers within the EU, both of which defied the *raison d'être* for a CEAS. It was also generally accepted that persons with special needs, including minors and unaccompanied minors, were not adequately protected in the Phase One instruments. It was clear, therefore, that change was needed.

Indeed, already in 1999 at Tampere, a second phase of the CEAS was envisaged, entailing a greater degree of harmonisation than simply minimum standards. The goal was a common asylum procedure and uniform status for refugees and holders of subsidiary protection status, valid throughout the Union. This phase was outlined in detail at the 2004 Hague European Council which led to a further five-year plan of action.[37] The plan was an ambitious one, envisaging a recasting of four of the five CEAS instruments by 2010. The Commission duly drafted the proposed recasts, but the 2010 deadline for their adoption was not met and a new deadline of 'by 2012' (meaning, the end of 2012) also proved elusive.[38] One element of the plan was delivered on time, however. In recognition of the limits of legal harmonisation in affecting actual harmonisation, the Hague programme also envisaged a number of practical cooperation initiatives that were to lead to a European support office for all forms of cooperation between Member States relating to the CEAS. A regulation establishing a European Asylum Support Office (EASO) was duly adopted in 2010.[39]

The failure to adopt the Phase Two instruments before the entry into force of the Lisbon Treaty resulted in a change to the legal basis for measures on asylum: Article 78 of the Treaty on the Functioning of the EU (TFEU) replaced Article 63 TEC. Henceforth, asylum instruments were to be adopted in accordance with the 'ordinary legislative procedure', i.e. exclusive right of initiative of the Commission and co-decision on the basis of qualified majority voting by the Council and European Parliament.[40] There were also important substantive changes. Thus, the compulsory personal jurisdiction of the CEAS now explicitly extends to both asylum-seekers/refugees and persons seeking/benefitting from subsidiary protection, under the rubric of 'international protection'. Furthermore, eschewing minimum standards, the TFEU provides

---

37 Council of the European Union, 'The Hague Programme: strengthening freedom, security and justice in the European Union', 13 November 2004, *OJ C053, Vol. 48*, 3 March 2005; and 'Council and Commission action plan implementing the Hague Programme on strengthening freedom, security and justice in the European Union', 2005, *OJ C198 Vol. 48*, 12 August 2005.
38 'European pact on immigration and asylum', *op. cit*.
39 Regulation (EU) No. 439/2010 of the European Parliament and of the Council of 19 May 2010 establishing a European Asylum Support Office.
40 This procedure would have been in effect if the Phase Two instruments had been adopted in time, since the transitional legislative arrangements established by Article 67 TEC expired by decision of the Council as of 1 January 2005. *OJ 2004, L 396/45*. This is now a moot point.

for a 'common policy' and a mixture of uniform and common standards.[41] Also of note, Article 267 TFEU (ex Article 234 TEC) on the preliminary ruling jurisdiction of the Court of Justice of the EU (CJEU) applies without restriction to asylum cases, giving the Court the opportunity to shape the interpretation and application of the CEAS instruments significantly.

Notwithstanding these changes, the negotiation of the Phase Two instruments proved to be just as difficult as that of the first phase instruments. A portent of the difficulty lay in the modesty of the Commission proposals: rather than devising a new set of common standards instruments, the Commission opted merely to recast the existing instruments, raising standards by restricting the possibilities for Member State discretion and derogation.[42] Nonetheless, two of the proposals were deemed politically unacceptable and amended versions had to be drafted. [43] The recast Qualification Directive, the least contentious of proposals, was the first to be adopted in 2011.[44] There followed an eighteen-month gap during which even the proposals that were subject to political agreement were not adopted but used as leverage in the negotiation of outstanding proposals.[45] The entire outstanding packing was adopted in

---

41 Article 78 TFEU refers to a 'uniform status of asylum valid throughout the Union', a 'uniform status of subsidiary protection', a 'common system of temporary protection', 'common procedures' and 'standards' on reception, which, presumably, are common standards given the context and the lack of reference to minimum standards.
42 Curiously, the original Commission proposals also retained the words 'minimum standards' in their titles: 'Proposal for a Directive of the European Parliament and of the Council on minimum standards for the reception of asylum seekers (recast)', *COM (2008) 815*; 'Proposal for a Directive of the European Parliament and of the Council on minimum standards for the qualification and status of third country nationals or stateless persons as beneficiaries of international protection and the content of protection granted (recast)', *COM (2009) 551*; 'Proposal for a Directive of the European Parliament and of the Council on minimum standards on procedures in Member States for granting and withdrawing international protection (recast)', *COM (2009) 554*. The final Commission proposal was: 'Proposal for a Regulation of the European Parliament and of the Council establishing the criteria and mechanisms for determining the Member State responsible for examining an application for international protection lodged in one of the Member States by a third country national or a stateless person (recast)', *COM (2008) 820*.
43 'Amended proposal for a directive of the European Parliament and of the Council laying down standards for the reception of asylum seekers (recast)', *COM (2011) 320 final*; 'Amended proposal for a Directive of the European Parliament and of the Council on common procedures for granting and withdrawing international protection status (recast)', *COM (2011) 319 final*.
44 Directive 2011/95/EU of the European Parliament and of the Council of 13 December 2011 on standards for the qualification of third country nationals or stateless persons as beneficiaries of international protection, for a uniform status for refugees or for persons eligible for subsidiary protection, and for the content of the protection granted (recast).
45 See Statewatch Analysis, 'EU immigration and asylum law in 2012: The year of living ineffectually', S. Peers, 28 December 2012. Available at http://www.statewatch.org/analyses/no-210-immigration-asylum-12.pdf (accessed 15 October 2013).

June 2013.[46] The protracted negotiations can be explained by a number of sometimes divergent factors: a Council focused on efficiency and combating 'abuse' versus a European Parliament focused on protection, particularly of vulnerable persons; a sharp increase in the numbers seeking asylum in the EU following a five-year decline;[47] a loss of focus on asylum in the EU as other (economic) imperatives took centre stage on the policy agenda; a continued, highly-politicised, negative focus on asylum in some Member States;[48] and negotiation-fatigue following Phase One.

It should be noted that another five-year legislative programme for the CEAS was established at the 2009 Stockholm European Council for the period 2010–14.[49] This is the third phase of the CEAS. After the second phase instruments have been evaluated, the Commission may propose new legislative instruments to achieve a higher degree of harmonisation still. In view of the above-mentioned negotiation fatigue, however, it is submitted that the Commission is unlikely to exercise its right of initiative.[50]

Overview of the key instruments of the CEAS

In this section, the general content of the key instruments of the CEAS, and their recasts, is sketched. Attention is paid to the child-specific provisions of

---

46 Directive 2013/33/EU of the European Parliament and of the Council of 26 June 2013 laying down standards for the reception of applicants for international protection (recast); Regulation (EU) No. 604/2013 of the European Parliament and of the Council of 26 June 2013 establishing the criteria and mechanisms for determining the Member State responsible for examining an application for international protection lodged in one of the Member States by a third-country national or a stateless person (recast); Directive 2013/32/EU of the European Parliament and of the Council of 26 June 2013 on common procedures for granting and withdrawing international protection (recast).

47 By 2006, the number of asylum applications in the EU-27 had declined from a peak of 424,000 in 2001 to 200,000. However, from that point on there was a gradual increase and by 2011 the number of asylum applications in the EU-27 had reached just over 300,000. It is likely that the number of applications for 2012 and 2013 will be higher still. See http://epp.eurostat.ec.europa.eu/statistics_explained/index.php/Asylum_statistics (accessed 15 October 2013).

48 Kaunert and Leonard refer to 'controversies around asylum and migration [that] have led some Member States to engage in a virtually continuous reform of their asylum and migration legislation'. C. Kaunert and S. Leonard, 'The European Union asylum policy after the Treaty of Lisbon and the Stockholm Programme: Towards supranational governance in a common area of protection?', *Refugee Survey Quarterly* 31, 2012, 1–20, 2.

49 European Council, 'The Stockholm Programme – an open and secure Europe serving and protecting the citizens', 2 December 2009, and Communication from the Commission to the European Parliament, the Council, the European Economic and Social Committee and the Committee of the Regions, 'Delivering an area of freedom, security and justice for Europe's citizens – action plan implementing the Stockholm Programme', 20 April 2010, *COM (2010) 171 final*.

50 Phase Three CEAS also envisages new burden-sharing/solidarity measures and contains a renewed focus on the 'external dimension of asylum' – the EU's relations with regions of origin and transit.

the instruments, but analysis is not confined to these because most provisions of the instruments are age-neutral and apply equally to children.[51] In order to maintain a narrative flow, the citation of provisions is kept to a minimum and case-law of the CJEU on the instruments is referenced but not analysed: in-depth citation and analysis occurs in the substantive chapters of the book.

The Dublin Regulation and recast

The Dublin Regulation (DR) is a specialised form of the 'safe third country' concept. Based on the premise that all EU Member States are safe owing to the minimum standards established in the CEAS, the DR establishes that one – and only one – EU Member State is responsible for processing any given asylum application. It establishes a hierarchy of criteria to determine the Member State responsible. When an applicant lodges a claim for asylum in a Member State, that State goes through the criteria until a match is found, whereupon the asylum seeker can be sent to the responsible State to have his/her claim processed there.

The criteria are based on two principles.[52] The first is the principle of family unity/reunification – the idea that an applicant should have his/her claim processed in the Member State in which he/she has family members. The first three criteria in the hierarchy reflect this principle. The second principle is that of State fault – the idea that the State which bears most responsibility for allowing the applicant to enter the EU should also bear the responsibility for processing the asylum claim.[53] The next four criteria in the hierarchy reflect this principle. In addition to the hierarchy of criteria, there is the so-called 'sovereignty clause', whereby any Member State may opt to take responsibility for the processing of a claim even where it is not responsible under the hierarchy of criteria;[54] and a 'humanitarian clause', whereby a Member State may opt to take responsibility for the processing of a claim for humanitarian reasons, such as reunifying relatives who do not meet the definitional requirements of 'family member' and dependents.[55]

---

51 The term 'age neutral' is something of a misnomer as it glosses over the fact that some provisions of general application can have a disproportionate impact on children.
52 Chapter III, Hierarchy of Criteria.
53 The CJEU pronounced on the operation of one of the fault criteria in *Abdullahi*, Case C-394/12, Judgment (GC) of 10 December 2013.
54 The CJEU held that the sovereignty clause becomes obligatory if transfer to the responsible State would result in a real risk of the applicant being subject to inhuman or degrading treatment contrary to the Charter of Fundamental Rights, and no other State can be identified as responsible under the regulation: *N.S. and M.E*, Joined Cases C-411/10 and C-493/10, Judgment (GC) of 21 December 2011. Reiterated in *Puid*, Case C-4/11, Judgment of 14 November 2013.
55 In *K*, the CJEU gave a strong purposive interpretation to the requirement that Member States 'shall normally' reunite dependents: Case C-245/11, Judgment (GC) of 6 November 2012. Another question has been referred to the Court on the meaning of dependency: *Rajaby*, Case C-158/13, Request for a preliminary ruling lodged on 28 March 2013.

The DR also provides rules for the transfer of applicants between States, including rules regarding the processing of requests, time-limits for making and responding to requests and a default mechanism.[56] An asylum applicant must be notified about the regulation in general and about any decision to transfer him/her to another Member State. However, the regulation is silent on the question of a personal interview and contains only a discretionary provision on the possibility of an appeal, suspensive or otherwise.[57] A further omission is the lack of a provision establishing specific guarantees for persons with special needs, such as minors or unaccompanied minors, such as is found in some of the CEAS directives. However, the first criterion in the hierarchy of criteria is directed to unaccompanied minors. It provides that the State in which a member of the unaccompanied minor's family is legally present is the one responsible for processing his/her asylum claim, provided that this is in the minor's best interests. If the unaccompanied minor has no family member in a Member State, then the State responsible is the one where the claim was lodged, although here the regulation makes no reference to the best interests principle.[58]

Some significant changes are made to the recast DR owing mainly to constraints imposed on the application of the regulation by the two European Courts and to functional problems relating to the processing of requests and transfers.[59] Most of the changes are contained in the new Chapter II, titled 'General principles and safeguards'. First, this chapter introduces a provision stating that where it is impossible to transfer an applicant to the Member State technically responsible because substantial grounds exist for believing that there are systematic flaws in the asylum procedure and in the reception conditions for applicants in that State resulting in a risk of inhuman or degrading treatment contrary to the EU Charter of Fundamental Rights, the determining Member State shall decide on responsibility using the other criteria and, in the last resort, shall assume responsibility for processing the application.[60] Second, Chapter II specifies certain procedural safeguards such as a right to information and to a personal interview. These are supplemented

---

56 Chapter V, Taking charge and taking back.
57 In *Petrosian*, the ECJ ruled that where Member States allow applicants to apply to the courts to suspend a Dublin transfer pending an appeal, the period for the implementation of the transfer begins to run from when the appeal is decided on the merits: Case C-19/08, Judgment of 29 January 2009. In *Abdullahi*, the CJEU ruled that once a Member State agrees to take charge of an application, this decision can only be challenged by pleading systemic deficiencies in the asylum procedure and in the conditions for the reception of applicants for asylum in the receiving Member State. *Op cit*.
58 However, in *MA, BT and DA*, the CJEU held that the best interests of the child also apply to decisions adopted under this provision: Case C-648/11, Judgment of 6 June 2013.
59 ECtHR, *MSS v Belgium and Greece*, Appl. No. 30696/09, Judgment (GC) of 21 January 2011; CJEU, *N.S. and M.E. op cit*.
60 This provision is supplemented by a new early warning mechanism in Article 33 to detect and assist Member States whose asylum systems are becoming dysfunctional; however, it stops well short of providing for the suspension of the regulation in relation to such a State.

in a later chapter by a right to notification of a transfer decision, to interpretation and legal assistance and to an effective remedy with some form of suspensive effect.⁶¹ Third, although Chapter II introduces no new general provision relating to persons with special needs, it does add a new article titled 'Guarantees for minors'. This article provides that the best interests of the child shall be a primary consideration for Member States with respect to all procedures provided for in the regulation, and it provides an illustrative list of factors to be taken into account in assessing the best interests of the child. It further establishes an obligation to appoint a representative to the unaccompanied minor asylum seeker and to undertake family tracing within the EU for the unaccompanied minor, with a view to applying the criterion in the hierarchy relating to unaccompanied minors. That criterion is also expanded in scope, applying now to relatives as well as family members. Other changes include a new provision stating that detention is permissible if the applicant is at risk of absconding before the transfer can be carried out, subject to the guarantees laid down in the recast Reception Conditions Directive.⁶²

The Reception Conditions Directive and recast

The Reception Conditions Directive (RCD) aims to harmonise to a minimum standard how Member States host asylum seekers and their accompanying family members for the duration of the asylum process.⁶³ Chapter II, titled 'General Provisions on Reception Conditions' enumerates most of the standards. It establishes a right to information on reception conditions and to documentation testifying that the asylum seeker has permission to remain in the State while the asylum application is pending. A discretionary article on residence and freedom of movement provides that Member States may allow or curtail freedom of movement. However, restrictions to freedom of movement involve not only limiting the movement of an applicant to a particular area, as might be expected, but also 'confining an applicant to a particular place' – a euphemistic reference to detention. This is permitted broadly 'for legal reasons or reasons of public order', although the detention decision must be amenable to appeal. Basic rights relating to family unity (to be maintained 'as far as possible'), schooling and education of minors ('under similar conditions as nationals'), access to the labour market (if a first instance decision has not been taken within one year) and health care (at a minimum, emergency

---

61 Chapter VI, Section IV, Procedural safeguards.
62 Chapter VI, Procedures for taking charge and taking back, Section V, Detention for the purpose of transfer.
63 In *Cimade and GISTI*, the CJEU held that a Member State is obliged to guarantee the conditions established in the RCD even while calling on another Member State to take charge of or take back the applicant under the Dublin Regulation: Case C-179/11, Judgment of 27 September 2012.

health care and essential treatment of illness) are laid down. Furthermore, Chapter II establishes a basic minimum standard for the provision of 'material reception conditions' which can be provided in kind or in the form of financial assistance or both.[64] Material reception conditions comprise housing, food and clothing and a daily expenses allowance. The standard is one 'adequate for the health of applicants and capable of ensuring their subsistence'. This standard must equally be met in respect of persons with special needs and persons in detention. However, the directive is silent on the level of entitlement this standard entails compared to the social assistance granted to nationals. In a section entitled 'modalities for material reception conditions', various forms of accommodation are outlined and a number of guarantees, such as the protection of family life and the prevention of assault, are provided. However, there is a wide-ranging derogation [...] detention. In such cases the modalities [...] simply cover basic needs.

A chapter on the reduction or [...] the circumstances under which the [...] withdrawn or refused.[65] The circ[...] drawal generally relate to some f[...] asylum seeker, such as abandoning [...] comply with reporting requireme[...] drawal and refusal of reception co[...] due process guarantees and amena[...]

Finally, a chapter is devoted to [...][66] general principle that Member Sta[...] persons into account in the nation[...] illustrative list is provided of suc[...] companied minors, the general pri[...] special needs after an individual [...] unclear whether being a minor o[...] child within the scope of the general principle or whether some further vulnerability has to be demonstrated. It is also unclear whether the absence of an individual evaluation could vitiate the obligation. Aside from the general principle, a specific provision is devoted to the treatment of minors (the best interests of the child must be a primary consideration 'when implementing the provisions of this directive that involve minors' and Member States must ensure access to rehabilitation services for minors who are victims of various types of ill-treatment). There are further guarantees for unaccompanied minors

---

64 A question has been referred to the Court on the intricacies of providing material support in the form of financial allowances: *Saciri and Others*, Case C-79/13, Request for a preliminary ruling lodged on 15 February 2013.
65 Chapter III.
66 Chapter IV.

(an obligation to appoint a representative, to secure a care placement, to 'endeavour' to trace family members and to train those working with unaccompanied minors) as well as for victims of torture and violence (to provide 'the necessary treatment of damages' but, curiously, only 'if necessary').

The recast RCD raises the standards of reception conditions generally. Thus, the provisions in Chapter II relating to family unity, schooling and education of minors, access to the labour market and health care are all subject to moderate improvement. Material reception conditions are still pitched at a standard of living adequate for subsistence and health, but the standard is more closely aligned with, although not necessarily equal to, the minimum standard for nationals and cannot be derogated from in detention. Little change is made to the chapter on the reduction or withdrawal of reception conditions. Aside from these rather modest changes, there are two more radical changes. First, there are four new, detailed articles on detention setting out when detention is permissible, guarantees for detained applicants, conditions of detention and detention of vulnerable persons and of applicants with special reception needs.[67] The latter article provides specific guarantees relating to the detention of minors, unaccompanied minors and families, effectively establishing that detention of these persons is exceptional. Second, the chapter on 'Persons with Special Needs', now renamed 'Provisions for Vulnerable Persons', is altered considerably.[68] It establishes an obligation to assess whether the applicant is an applicant with special reception needs and to monitor his/her situation. The article on minors reiterates the best interests obligation of the original directive but supplements it with an illustrative list of factors to be taken into account in assessing the best interests of the child. Furthermore, this article establishes for the first time that Member States must ensure a standard of living 'adequate for the minor's physical, mental, spiritual, moral and social development'. The article on unaccompanied minors provides a fuller description of the role of the representative and a more robust family tracing obligation than did the original directive. Finally, the provision on victims of torture and violence no longer predicates treatment on whether it is necessary and adds a staff training obligation.

The Asylum Procedures Directive and recast

The Asylum Procedures Directive (APD) establishes basic rules governing the procedure for refugee status determination. In line with State practice, the directive envisages an individual status determination procedure, to be conducted mainly, but not exclusively, by a 'determining authority'.[69] The bulk of the directive is devoted to two aspects of the procedure in particular: the 'basic

---

67 Chapter II, Article 8–11.
68 Chapter IV.
69 Chapter I, General provisions.

principles and guarantees' on which the procedure is founded; and the 'procedures at first instance' which consists mainly of various extraordinary procedures designed to circumvent some or all of the basic principles and guarantees and thereby expedite the procedure. There are also provisions establishing a procedure for withdrawals of asylum applications and an appeals procedure.

Chapter II sets out the basic principles and guarantees to which the asylum seeker is entitled during the procedure. However, some of the basic principles and guarantees place obligations on the determining authority and hence do not apply when an authority other than the determining authority is responsible for processing applications. All adults (though not children) have the right to lodge an asylum application on their own behalf. Applicants have the right to remain in the Member State pending the outcome of the first instance decision, subject to a number of exceptions, such as where the applicant has made a previous application. Minimum requirements are laid down for the examination of applications and regarding the form, content and notification of decisions. Applicants must be informed about the procedure, are entitled to an interpreter in certain circumstances and must be allowed to communicate with UNHCR. All applicants, with some notable exceptions including minors, are entitled to a personal interview. The interview must be conducted under appropriate conditions by competent staff and with the assistance of an interpreter where necessary, and a report of the interview must be provided to the applicant. There is no right to free legal assistance at first instance, but such assistance must be provided on appeal subject to a number of caveats that may be applied at the discretion of Member States. An article titled 'Guarantees for unaccompanied minors' provides not only additional guarantees for this cohort, but an additional obligation too regarding age assessment.[70] The guarantees for unaccompanied minors include: a right to a representative subject to various exceptions; a right to be interviewed – where there is an interview – by a person with knowledge of the 'special needs' of minors and to have a decision taken by a similarly knowledgeable official; and a requirement for Member States to make the best interests of the child a primary consideration when implementing the article. Unlike some of the other directives, there is no provision for minors (as distinct from unaccompanied minors) or other persons with special needs.

Chapter III is titled 'Procedures at first instance' but this is something of a misnomer as it relates mainly to establishing various extraordinary procedures designed to expedite the process. There are five such extraordinary procedures and some overlap. Three are designated as 'specific procedures', and Member States are expressly permitted to derogate from the basic principles and guarantees of Chapter II in the context of these procedures.

---

70 The obligations of asylum seekers in general relate mainly to a duty to cooperate with the asylum authorities, such as an obligation to submit to any reporting requirements or to be searched, photographed and fingerprinted.

They comprise: (1) a 'preliminary examination' procedure for screening subsequent applications, leading to a finding of inadmissibility or a transfer to the regular procedure; (2) a border procedure with minimal guarantees, that Member States are entitled to retain on the basis of a stand-still clause, the purpose of which is to decide on permission to enter the territory; (3) the so-called 'European safe third country procedure', which is essentially an admissibility procedure for applicants coming from (non-EU) European countries designated as 'safe' by the Council. However, the Council's authority to adopt a list of such countries was successfully challenged by the European Parliament on technical grounds and as a result the procedure never became operational.[71] In addition to these 'specific procedures', there is an accelerated procedure for categorising certain applications as *prime facie* without merit and therefore amenable to being accelerated and, if rejected, deemed manifestly unfounded;[72] and an admissibility procedure, which permits Member States not to examine the substance of an application either because it has already done so, because it has granted the applicant some other secure status or because it considers that another country is responsible for processing the claim.

In addition to the first instance procedures just outlined, the directive establishes in Chapter IV a procedure for the withdrawal of refugee status in the circumstances specified in the Qualification Directive (see below). Certain rights of the refugee, such as the right to be heard, and obligations of the determining authority, for example relating to the quality of information on which the decision is based, are established. An appeals procedure is also delineated in Chapter V. It provides a right of appeal against all final first instance decisions.[73] While the appeal must fulfil the right of the applicant to an effective remedy, is it unclear whether it is a *de novo* appeal or a more superficial rationality review.[74] It is left to the Member State to determine whether the appeal has suspensive effect.

The recast APD makes some significant changes but essentially reproduces the plethora of procedures that exist under the original directive. It reduces, but by no means eliminates, the procedures that can be conducted by an

---

71 ECJ, *European Parliament v Council*, Case 133/06, Judgment of 6 May 2008.
72 In *H.I.D., B.A.*, the CJEU ruled that the prioritised or accelerated procedure permits Member States to fast-track an application on the basis that the applicant comes from a 'safe country of origin': Case C-175/11, Judgment of 31 January 2013. In *Diouf*, the CJEU held that the lack of a possibility in domestic law to appeal the decision to process an application in an accelerated procedure did not offend against the right to an effective remedy provided the final decision on the asylum application could be appealed: Case C-69/10, Judgment of 28 July 2011.
73 *Diouf, op cit.*
74 In *H.I.D, B.A.*, the CJEU held that the right to an effective remedy 'before a court or tribunal' was met by an administrative body from whose decisions there was a possibility of judicial review to the High Court, notwithstanding that the body had organisational links to both the first instance status determination body and the relevant government department. *Op cit.*

authority other than the determining authority which, it will be recalled, is an indirect way of limiting the basic principles and guarantees. It generally enhances the basic principles and guarantees of Chapter II, by: increasing standards relating to the personal interview and decision-making; by establishing a right to legal and procedural information free of charge at first instance; and by inserting an article on 'persons in need of special procedural guarantees', which exempts such persons from some of the extraordinary procedures such as the accelerated procedure. The article on unaccompanied minors is also enhanced. Thus, Member States are obliged to make the best interests of the child a primary consideration when implementing not just the article on unaccompanied minors, as previously, but the directive as a whole. Furthermore, unaccompanied minors are partially protected from the scope of some of the extraordinary procedures. The extraordinary procedures subsist for the most part in Chapter III, and the European safe third country procedure is reintroduced by eliminating the need for Council designation of such countries. However, the grounds for invoking the extraordinary procedures and their impact on procedural guarantees is somewhat lessened. The procedure for withdrawals is largely unchanged in Chapter IV, but some significant modifications are made to the appeals procedure in Chapter V. Of particular note, the recast expressly states that the right to an effective remedy requires a full and *ex nunc* examination of both facts and point of law. Furthermore, the recast establishes a right to remain in the territory pending the outcome of the appeal – a right, in other words, to automatic suspensive effect. Certain exceptions are established, for example in relation to manifestly unfounded or inadmissible applications but these are subject to court or tribunal oversight.

The Qualification Directive and recast

The Qualification Directive (QD) aims to provide guidance on the assessment of facts and circumstances in a claim; give legal clarity to certain elements of the refugee definition; provide for the first time a definition of the harms that give rise to subsidiary protection; and outline the rights that attach to refugee status and, for the first time, subsidiary protection status. It is the only Phase One instrument that brings applicants for subsidiary protection within its mandatory personal scope, employing the term 'international protection' to encompass both refugee and subsidiary protection.[75]

---

75 Article 1, Subject matter and scope. Because the QD is the only Phase One instrument to bring applicants for subsidiary protection within its mandatory personal scope, challenges to what are essentially a lack of procedural safeguards for applicants for subsidiary protection, but which cannot be taken under the APD because of its restricted personal scope, are being taken under the QD. See *MM*, Case C-277/11, Judgment of 22 November 2012 and pending case, *HN*, Case C-604/12, Request for a preliminary ruling lodged on 27 December 2012.

Chapter II of the directive provides for the first time hard-law guidance on how to assess applications for international protection, including on how to assess facts and circumstances, on the burden of proof and the principle of the benefit of the doubt.[76] It is innovative in a number of respects. First, it establishes that in assessing whether the acts to which the applicant has been or could be exposed would amount to persecution or serious harm, factors such as age must be taken into account. Second, it settles a long-standing debate between Member States about actors of persecution or serious harm: these are not limited to State actors but extend to *de facto* State entities and non-State actors. Third, in a discretionary provision new to refugee law, 'actors of protection' are listed. This controversial notion is based on the idea that national protection can be given by non-State actors, such as international organisations, where such entities control the State or a substantial part of the State. Fourth, another discretionary provision is devoted to the concept of the 'internal flight alternative' – the idea that if there is part of the country of origin where the applicant would be safe from persecution or serious harm, then this constitutes grounds to deny international protection status. This is so 'notwithstanding technical obstacles to return to the country of origin'.

Chapter III is titled 'Qualification for Being a Refugee'. It elaborates on the inclusion clause in Article 1A(2) of the 1951 Convention relating to the Status of Refugees regarding acts of persecution and reasons for persecution.[77] Notably, it stipulates that acts of persecution may be of a child-specific nature. Chapter III also repeats the cessation and exclusion clauses in Article 1C and Articles 1D, E and F of the Convention, respectively.[78]

Chapter V deals with qualification for subsidiary protection – a concept not contained in the 1951 Convention regime. A person eligible for subsidiary protection is one who does not qualify as a refugee but who is at real risk of 'serious harm'. This term is limited to: a) death penalty or execution; b) torture

---

76 The CJEU pronounced on the shared duty of cooperation and what it means for Member States in practice in *MM, op cit*. A number of cases are pending on acceptable methods of assessing the credibility of a declared sexual orientation in light of the right to personal integrity and privacy: *A*, Case C-148/13, *B*, Case C-149/13 and *C*, Case 150/13, Request for a preliminary ruling lodged on 25 March 2013.
77 Two cases have been heard by the Court on the inclusion provisions of the QD: *Y and Z*, Joined Cases C-71/11 and C-99/11, Judgment (GC) of 5 September 2012 related to religious persecution and *X, Y and Z*, Joined Cases C-199/12 to C-201/12, Judgment of 7 November 2013 related to homosexuals as a particular social group and whether criminalisation of homosexuality can be considered as persecution. A further case is pending: *Shepherd* concerns prosecution or punishment for refusal to perform military service as an act of persecution. Case C-472/13, Request for a preliminary ruling lodged on 2 December 2013.
78 To date, there has been one cessation case: *Abdulla and Others*, Joined Cases C-175/08, C-176/08, C-178/08 and C-179/08, Judgment of 2 March 2010; and three exclusion cases: *El Kott*, Case C-364/11, Judgment of 19 December 2012; *B and D*, Joined Cases C-57/09 and C-101/09, Judgment of 9 November 2010; and *Bolbol*, Case C-31/09, Judgment of 17 June 2010.

or inhuman or degrading treatment or punishment; or c) serious and individual threat to a civilian's life or person by reason of indiscriminate violence in situations of international or internal armed conflict.[79] Chapter V also applies the refugee-law concepts of cessation and exclusion to subsidiary protection status, although the grounds for cessation and exclusion are, respectively, narrower and broader than in the corresponding provisions of Chapter III relating to refugees.

Chapters IV and VI deal with the granting of refugee status and subsidiary protection status, respectively. They also set minimum standards regarding the revocation of, ending of or refusal to renew those statuses. These are the consequences that follow from a finding of cessation or exclusion, a finding that an application was falsified in a material way or a finding that the applicant is a danger to the security or community of the host State.

Chapter VII is titled 'Content of International Protection' and outlines the rights to which beneficiaries of international protection are entitled. It contains a series of 'general rules', such as the requirement that Member States take into account the situation of 'vulnerable persons' when implementing the chapter. An illustrative list of vulnerable persons is provided, and this includes minors and unaccompanied minors. However, as per the RCD, the requirement only applies to persons 'found to have special needs after an individual evaluation of their situation'. Another of the general rules is the principle of the best interests of the child: this must be a primary consideration for Member States when implementing the provisions of the chapters that involve minors. More specific guarantees are provided for unaccompanied minors. These range from the duty to appoint a representative to the duty to secure a care placement for the unaccompanied minor. More general rights include health care and access to employment. The intention was to harmonise the treatment of refugees and beneficiaries of subsidiary protection, subject to objectively reasonable exceptions. However, while beneficiaries of subsidiary protection are entitled to some seven rights on an equal basis to refugees, they receive more qualified rights than refugees do in six key areas.[80]

The recast QD contains relatively few changes, compared to the other recasts. The key changes are to be found in Chapter II on assessing applications

---

79 In *Elgafaji*, the CJEU attempted to reconcile the terms 'individual threat' and 'indiscriminate violence' in Article 15(c): Case C-465/07, Judgment of 17 February 2009. A question has been referred to the Court on whether the phrase 'internal armed conflict' in Article 15(c) should be interpreted consistently with international humanitarian law: *Diakite*, Case C-285/12, Reference for a preliminary ruling lodged on 7 June 2012.

80 Both groups are equally entitled to protection from *refoulement*, the provision of information on their status, access to education for minors under the same conditions as nationals, guarantees for unaccompanied minors, access to accommodation, freedom of movement within the Member State and repatriation assistance. Beneficiaries of subsidiary protection receive more qualified rights in the areas of family unity, residence permits, travel documents, access to employment, entitlement to social welfare and health care.

for international protection and Chapter VII on the content of international protection. Chapter II tightens up the provisions on actors of protection (now the protection must be effective and of a non-temporary nature) and internal protection (now applicable only if the applicant can safely and legally travel to and gain admittance to the 'safe' part of the country). As for Chapter VII, the obligation on Member States to take into account the situation of vulnerable persons when implementing the chapter (but only those found to have special needs after an individual evaluation of their situation) remains unchanged. The recast QD is unlike the recast RCD in this regard – only the latter establishing a requirement to assess whether the applicant has special needs. The scope of the best interests obligation remains unchanged although some direction on factors to consider in assessing the best interests of the child is located in a recital. Finally, whereas the original directive draws a distinction between refugees and persons eligible for subsidiary protection in terms of the amplitude of some six of the rights to which they are entitled, the recast reduces this inequality of treatment to three rights.[81]

Conclusion

It is clear from this brief overview of the key instruments of the CEAS and their recasts that although the bulk of the instruments comprise age-neutral provisions, the instruments also include child-specific provisions. Specifically, the instruments make provision for children as minors, unaccompanied minors and/or persons with special needs. In this regard, the CEAS can be regarded as an advance on the 1951 Convention relating to the Status of Refugees, which contains no child-specific provisions. But what is the quality of the child-specific provisions, and indeed the general provisions, of the CEAS? In order to answer this question, an independent yardstick is needed. Writing in the context of child asylum seekers, Jaqueline Bhabha observes that the United Nations Convention on the Rights of the Child 'plays a critical normative role in establishing agreed benchmarks for the treatment of children'.[82] This underscores the need to clarify, not only how the rights in the Convention on the Rights of the Child apply to asylum-seeking and refugee children, but also the full applicability of the Convention to the CEAS. This is the task of the next chapter.

---

81 The areas of residual inequality are: the right to a residence permit, to travel documents and to social assistance.
82 J. Bhabha, 'Minors or aliens? Inconsistent State intervention and separated child asylum seekers', *European Journal of Migration and Law* 3, 2001, 283–314 at 298.

2 Introduction to the rights of the child and their relationship to European asylum law

Introduction

This chapter provides an introduction to the rights of the child, focusing on the seminal United Nations Convention on the Rights of the Child. It also probes the relationship between international child rights law and European asylum law – a necessary undertaking in light of the aim of this book, which is to assess European asylum law in the light of the rights of the child.

The rights of the child

As humans, children have human rights. Since most human rights instruments apply to all individuals within the territory of a State Party and/or subject to its jurisdiction, children fall within the personal scope of such instruments unless they are expressly or impliedly excluded from the scope of a particular provision.[1] Moreover, many general human rights instruments contain a child-specific provision or provisions, usually providing additional protection to children because of their unique vulnerabilities.[2] However, over and above the guarantees of general human rights law, a specialised body of international law has emerged over the course of almost a century. This *lex specialis* is codified in the Convention on the Rights of the Child (CRC).[3]

---

1 See, for example, Article 2(1) of the ICCPR.
2 In terms of international human rights instruments, see Article 24 of the ICCPR, Article 10(3) of the International Covenant on Economic, Social and Cultural Rights, Article 5 of the Convention on the Elimination of All Forms of Discrimination Against Women and Article 6 of the Convention on the Rights of Persons with Disabilities. In terms of European regional human rights instruments, see Articles 7 and 17 of the Revised European Social Charter and Article 24 of the EU Charter of Fundamental Rights, which is discussed later in this chapter.
3 UN Convention on the Rights of the Child, G.A. res 44/25, annex, 44 UN GAOR Supp. (No. 49) at 167, UN Doc. A/44/49 (1989), entered into force 2 September 1990. Preceded by the UN Declaration on the Rights of the Child, 1959, G.A. Res. 1386 (XIV), 14 UN GAOR Supp. (no. 16) at 19, UN Doc A/4354 (1959) and the Geneva Declaration on the Rights of the Child, adopted 26 September 1924, League of Nations O.J. Spec. Supp. 21 at 43 (1924).

With 193 States Parties, the CRC is the most widely ratified of all UN human rights treaties and is generally regarded as the seminal instrument on the rights of the child. As such, it is the point of departure for any discussion of the rights of the child. However, before coming to the CRC, it is important to mention that behind the edifice of international child rights law runs a seemingly intractable theoretical debate about whether children have rights. This debate relates not so much to the rights children have in positive law, but rather to the foundations of such rights in moral theory. The contours of this debate – one that has repercussions in the asylum context – are briefly sketched, before this chapter turns to a discussion of the CRC.

Note on the 'theory gap'

Theorists debate whether children have the fundamental attributes of rights holders. In liberal theory, rights are predicated on autonomy.[4] To be autonomous is to have the power to govern one's self; it is to have the substantive and procedural capacity to live life free from unwanted intervention by other people or by the State, subject to the usual constraints (rights of others, common good etc.). On one side of the child-rights debate are those who consider that children lack autonomy and, hence, rights.[5] Such theorists advocate child-welfare and protection, with the family being identified as the natural protector of the child. The usual charge levelled against such theorists is that they reify the family and elevate parental rights to an almost absolute norm.[6] On the other side of the debate are those who consider that (some/all) children are in fact autonomous and hence rights-holders. The problem for these theorists is to reconcile the child as rights-holder or agent with the need sometimes to intervene against the child's will to protect the child, since autonomy and paternalism are mutually

---

4 See, for example, B. Arneil, 'Becoming versus being: A critical analysis of the child in liberal theory' in D. Archard and C. Macleod (eds) *The Moral and Political Status of Children*, Oxford: Oxford University Press, 2002; K. Hunt Federle, 'On the road to reconceiving rights for children: A postfeminist analysis of the capacity principle', *DePaul Law Review* 42, 1992{-]1993, 983–1028.
5 See M. Guggenheim, *What's Wrong with Children's Rights*, Cambridge, MA: Harvard University Press, 2005; B. Hafen 'Children's liberation and the new egalitarianism: Some reservations about abandoning youth to their "rights"', *Brigham Young University Law Review* 37, 1976, 605–658.
6 For a succinct exchange of views between the two 'camps' in the debate, see L. Purdy, 'Why children shouldn't have equal rights', *International Journal of Children's Rights* 2, 1994, 223–241; A. McGillivray, 'Why children do have equal rights: in reply to Laura Purdy', *International Journal of Children's Rights* 2, 1994, 243–258; T. Campbell, 'Really equal rights? Some philosophical comments on "Why children shouldn't have equal rights" by Laura M. Purdy', *International Journal of Children's Rights* 2, 1994, 259–263; L. Purdy, 'Why children still shouldn't have equal rights', *International Journal of Children's Rights* 2, 1994, 395–398.

incompatible concepts.⁷ Other schools of thought reject liberalism's focus on autonomy. For example, the interest theory of rights conceives of rights as based on needs or interests: since children have an interest in their protection, they have a right to be protected.⁸ Because this theory is not predicated on autonomy (although autonomy may be presented as an interest of older children in particular) there is no inconsistency in advocating a paternalistic view of rights.⁹ However, the interest theory of rights has attracted criticism for its failure to account for why it is that only humans have rights (since animals and even plants can be said to have interests), and for the mismatch between some interests and some positive law rights (since we have rights that are not in our interests and interests to which we have no right).¹⁰ Some feminist theorists reject autonomy as a fiction, not just for children but for everyone, and try to construct a more relational concept of rights.¹¹ However, the idea of rights as linking rather than separating people provides little assistance when relationships break down and rights become adversarial.¹² Others reject the currency of moral rights altogether, arguing that children's positive law rights are better grounded in fundamental obligations than fundamental rights.¹³ The problem with this thesis is that it is politically and symbolically dissonant: rights simply *are* the language in which moral claims are made nowadays, 'values for a godless age'.¹⁴ In the end, as C.A.J. Coady comments in the context of child rights, '[t]he possibility must be seriously entertained that there is no single analysis of rights that will do justice to all the nuances and functions of rights talk'.¹⁵

Now, it may be countered that this debate has become redundant since the entry into force of the Convention on the Rights of the Child. The Convention

---

7 See, for example, M. Freeman, 'Taking children's rights more seriously', *International Journal of Law and the Family* 6, 1992, 52–71, and J. Eekelaar, 'The importance of thinking that children have rights', *International Journal of Law and the Family* 6, 1992, 221–235.

8 See, for example, E. Ochaita and A. Espinosa, 'Needs of children and adolescents as a basis for a justification of their rights', *International Journal of Children's Rights* 9, 2001, 313–337.

9 Campbell attempts to accommodate autonomy within an interest theory of the rights of the child: T. Campbell, 'The rights of the minor: as person, as child, as juvenile, as future adult', *International Journal of Law and the Family* 6, 1992, 1–23.

10 See J. Donnelly, *Universal Human Rights in Theory and Practice*, New York: Cornell University Press, 2013 (3rd ed.), Chapter 1.

11 See, for example, M. Minow, 'Rights for the next generation: A feminist approach to children's rights', *Harvard Women's Law Journal* 9, 1986, 1–24. For a thorough overview of feminist analyses of children's rights, see F. Olsen, 'Children's rights: Some feminist approaches to the United Nations Convention on the Rights of the Child', *International Journal of Law and the Family* 6, 1992, 192–220.

12 See K. Hunt Federle, 'Rights flow downhill', *International Journal of Children's Rights* 2, 1994, 343–368.

13 See O. O'Neill, 'Children's rights and children's lives', *International Journal of Law and the Family* 6, 1992, 24–42.

14 F. Klug, *Values for a Godless Age. The Story of the United Kingdom's New Bill of Rights*, London: Penguin Books, 2000.

15 C.A.J. Coady, 'Theory, rights and children: A comment on O'Neill and Campbell', *International Journal of Law and the Family* 6, 1994, 43–51, 44.

makes plain that children do have rights, so why bother with where the rights come from? There are a number of reasons to be, at least, aware of the theoretical debate. First, the Convention is drafted at a broad level of generality and contains provisions relating to welfare and protection as well as provisions relating to what might be classically thought of as 'rights', with no direction about how to reconcile the two.[16] Secondly, the debate about whether children have rights continues to this day, despite the fact that the Convention has been in force for almost 25 years.[17] Finally, and most importantly for present purposes, there continues to be a residual ambiguity in law, policy and practice about the status of the child as rights-bearer, Convention notwithstanding. This ambiguity – an unspoken assumption that it is natural and valid not to treat children equally and the converse, that it is legitimate to treat children as if they were adults in miniature – is especially evident in areas, such as asylum, where the State perceives its sovereign interests to be at stake. Hence, it is not unusual for States to deny that asylum-seeking children are children, first and foremost, with rights.[18] The next section counters this practice, at least as a matter of positive law, focusing on the rights in the CRC as they relate to the asylum context and on the nature of the general legal obligation under the Convention.

Overview of the rights in the CRC as they relate to the asylum context

The CRC comprises some 39 substantive rights articles, supplemented by three optional protocols.[19] One article relates explicitly to the asylum context.

---

16 Thus one of the drafters of the CRC and a leading advocate for child rights commented that '[d]ebates over the continuing existence of natural law theory and whether it continues to be viable in one of its various forms will not be settled by studying the CRC'. C. Price Cohen, 'The relevance of theories of natural law and legal positivism' in M. Freeman and P. Veerman (eds), *The Ideologies of Children's Rights*, Boston: Martinus Nijhoff Publishers, 1992. However, from the beginning, the Committee on the Rights of the Child has advocated a harmonious approach to the interpretation of the rights in the Convention, emphasising 'the indispensible, interconnected nature of the Convention's provisions' Com. RC, General Comment No. 1, 'The aims of education', UN Doc. CRC/GC/2001/1, para. 6.
17 See, for example, L. Ferguson, 'Not merely rights for children but children's rights: The theory gap and the assumption of the importance of children's rights', *International Journal of Children's Rights* 21, 2013, 1–32.
18 The most prolific writer in this regard is J. Bhabha. See, for example, 'Arendt's children: do today's migrant children have a right to have rights?', *Human Rights Quarterly* 31, 2009, 410–451, and 'Minors or aliens? Inconsistent State intervention and separated child asylum-seekers', *European Journal of Migration and Law* 3, 2001, 283–314.
19 Optional Protocol to the Convention on the Rights of the Child on the Involvement of Children in Armed Conflicts (2000); Optional Protocol to the Convention on the Rights of the Child on the Sale of Children, Child Prostitution and Child Pornography (2000); Optional Protocol to the Convention on the Rights of the Child on a Communications Procedure (2012). At the time of writing, the 2012 Optional Protocol has yet to enter into force.

This is Article 22, which establishes in paragraph 1 the right of the asylum-seeking and refugee child to appropriate protection and humanitarian assistance in the enjoyment, *inter alia*, of applicable rights in the Convention. What, then, are the applicable rights in the Convention? According to the general principle of non-discrimination in Article 2(1) of the Convention, all the rights in the Convention are in principle applicable to all children. Therefore, the question is less one of which rights are *applicable* to asylum-seeking and refugee children and more one of which rights are *relevant* to this group. But a cursory glance at the rights in the Convention reveals that all the rights in the CRC are potentially relevant to asylum-seeking and refugee children. As space does not permit a discussion of the implications of all the rights in the Convention in the asylum context, the following sections outline in broad brush-strokes how different groups of rights are relevant to the asylum context, with more detailed analysis offered in later chapters. The rights are grouped according to the practice of the Convention's monitoring body – the Committee on the Rights of the Child (Com. RC).[20]

The general principles

Although not specifically designated as such in the text of the Convention itself, four rights in the Convention have long been identified as 'general principles' by the Com. RC.[21] In addition to their own scope of application, the general principles are of horizontal application across all other Convention rights, meaning that they form part and parcel of all substantive rights.

I. NON-DISCRIMINATION

The first general principle is found in Article 2 CRC relating to the prohibition of discrimination. Article 2 has two paragraphs, each with a distinct scope. The first paragraph is a standard 'auxiliary' non-discrimination provision, prohibiting discrimination in relation to other rights in the Convention, like the right to health. As do other such provisions in international human rights law, it prohibits discrimination on a number of grounds, including

---

20 Com. RC, 'General guidelines regarding the form and content of initial reports to be submitted by states parties under Article 44, paragraph 1(a) of the Convention', *UN Doc. CRC/C/5 (1991)* and *UN Doc A/47/41 (1992)* at Annex III; Com. RC, 'General Guidelines for periodic reports', *UN Doc. CRC/C/58 (1996)*; Com. RC, 'Overview of the reporting procedures', *UN Doc. CRC/C/33 (1994)*; Com. RC, 'Treaty-specific guidelines regarding the form and content of period reports to be submitted by states parties under Article 44, paragraph 1(b) of the Convention on the Rights of the Child', *UN Doc. CRC/C/58/Rev.2 (2010)*.
21 The first reference to the 'general principles' can be found in Committee's 1991 General guidelines, *ibid*.

'other status'. Following the initiative of other treaty monitoring bodies[22] and indeed the ECtHR in relation to Article 14 of the ECHR,[23] 'other status' has been interpreted by the Com. RC as extending to nationality and even protection status. Thus the Committee has stated that '[t]he principle of non-discrimination [...] prohibits any discrimination on the basis of the status of a child as being unaccompanied or separated, or being a refugee, asylum seeker or migrant'.[24] Interestingly, the second paragraph of Article 2 is an 'autonomous' non-discrimination provision, prohibiting discrimination or punishment in any matter (including, but not limited to, the enjoyment of Convention rights) on the basis not only of the status but also, *inter alia*, of the *activities* of the child's parents, legal guardians or family members.[25] This has important implications in the asylum context where accompanied children are typically subsumed into the asylum applications of their parents, sometimes suffering negative procedural consequences as a result of their parents' behaviour.

II. THE BEST INTERESTS OF THE CHILD

The next and best-known – though possibly least understood – general principle is that of the best interests of the child in Article 3 CRC. Article 3(1) CRC establishes that '[i]n all actions concerning children, whether undertaken by public or private social welfare institutions, courts of law, administrative authorities or legislative bodies, the best interests of the child shall be a primary consideration'. The best interests principle has traditionally been mired in confusion and controversy, owing to uncertainty about its scope, meaning and weight.[26] Fortunately, the last five years or so have seen an impressive development of 'soft-law' guidance on the best-interests concept,

---

22 Committee on Economic, Social and Cultural Rights, General Comment 20, 'Non-discrimination in economic, social and cultural rights (art. 2, para. 2 of the International Convenant on Economic, Social and Cultural Rights)', *UN Doc E/C.12/GC/2 (2009)*, para. 30; Committee on the Elimination of Racial Discrimination, General Recommendation 30, 'Discrimination against non-citizens', *UN Doc CERD/C/64/Misc 11/rev. 3 (2004)*, particularly paras. 29 and 36, which relate to discrimination in relation to the right to health; Human Rights Committee, General Comment 15, 'The position of aliens under the Covenant', *UN Doc. HRI/Gen/Rev.1 at 18 (1994)*, para. 2.
23 ECtHR, *Gaygusuz v Austria*, Appl. No. 17371/90, Judgment of 16 September 1996.
24 Com. RC, General Comment No. 6, 'Treatment of unaccompanied and separated children outside their country of origin', *UN Doc. CRC/GC/2005/6 (2005)*, para. 18.
25 For analysis of this innovative provision in international law see S. Besson, 'The principle of non-discrimination in the Convention on the Rights of the Child', *International Journal of Children's Rights* 13, 2005, 433–461.
26 For a cross-section of critical commentary on the best interests concept, see R. Mnookin, 'Child custody adjudication: Judicial functions in the face of indeterminacy', *Law and Contemporary Problems* 39, 1975, 226–293; J. Dolgin, 'Why has the best interests standard survived?: The historic and social context', *Child Legal Rights Journal* 16, 1996, Special Report; and S. Parker, 'The best interests of the child – principles and problems', *International Journal of Law and the Family* 8, 1994, 26–41.

in general and in the asylum context, culminating in the adoption by the Com. RC of a general comment on the issue in 2013.[27]

The best interests principle has a broad scope, in terms of actions to which the principle applies, actors obligated and beneficiaries. The principle applies 'in all actions concerning children'. The Com. RC has interpreted the term 'concerning' to encompass not only actions that are explicitly or exclusively directed at children, but also actions that have a direct or indirect impact on children.[28] This means that all refugee law that is applied to children, and not just the child-specific provisions thereof, falls within the scope of the best interests principle. In terms of actors obligated, Article 3(1) enumerates a broad list: 'public or private social welfare institutions, courts of law, administrative authorities or legislative bodies'. This list arguably covers all asylum-related functionaries. In terms of beneficiaries, the wording of Article 3(1) combines the concept of the best interests of the child (singular) with actions relating to children (plural). Clearly, the principle applies each time a decision has to be made concerning an individual child: the various interests of the child have to be assessed and the best interests determined.[29] But the principle also has a collective application. Thus, Com. RC refers to the 'best interests of [...] children as a group or constituency [whereby] all law and policy development, administrative and judicial decision-making and service provision that affect children must take account of the best interests principle'.[30] In the asylum context, this means that refugee law must not only make reference to the best interests principle, but must itself be in the best interests of children. This raises the question of what the best interests concept means.

When it comes to the meaning of the best interests of the child, there can be no grand or universal approaches, since the assessment and determination will depend on the context and circumstances of the individual child. Similarly, when it comes to what is in the best interests of children as a group, much will depend on the particular policy area. However, the meaning of 'best interests' must be guided by the relevant rights of the child.[31] It follows that it is not possible to present a course of action as being in the best interests of the child

---

27 Com. RC, General Comment No. 14, 'The right of the child to have his or her best interests taken as a primary consideration (art. 3, para. 1)', *UN Doc. CRC/C/GC/14 (2013)*. See further, UNHCR, 'Guidelines on Determining the Best Interests of the Child', 2008, which were cited with approval by the ECtHR in *Neulinger and Shuruk v Switzerland*, Appl. No. 41615/07, Judgment of 6 July 2010, para. 52.; UNHCR Executive Committee Conclusion No. 107, 'Children at Risk', 2007; and Com. RC, General Comment No 6, *op cit.*
28 Com. RC, General Comment No. 14, *op cit*, paras. 19 and 20.
29 In this regard, contrast the approach advocated by the Com. RC in General Comment No. 14 with that advocated by UNHCR in its best interests guidelines. *Op cit.*
30 Com. RC, General Comment No. 7, 'Implementing child rights in early childhood', *UN Doc. CRC/C/GC/7/Rev.1 (2006)*, para. 13.
31 Thus, the Com. RC has stated that 'assessment and determination [of the child and children's best interests] should be carried out with full respect for the rights contained in the Convention and Optional Protocols'. General Comment No. 14, *op cit*, para. 32.

if it runs counter to a relevant right of the child.[32] Furthermore, the best interests principle brings a rights-perspective to bear even when the decision at hand does not appear to be based on any right that the child has. Thus, in the asylum context, while the child has no right to be recognised as a refugee solely on the basis of being a child or, it goes without saying, on the basis of the best interests principle *per se*, the best interests principle draws attention to the rights of the child that are relevant to the status-determination context, such as child-specific forms of persecution or the right of the child to be heard.

In short, the principle of the best interests of the child is something of a Trojan Horse of a principle, bringing to bear all the rights of the child that are relevant to the particular context. Linking back to the collective dimension of the best interests principle, the intimate connection between the best interests of the child and the rights of the child effectively means that all asylum law and policy must be 'proofed' to ensure that it is consistent with the relevant rights of the child, or, put differently, that the relevant rights of the child must be integrated into all asylum law and policy. Thus, the Com. RC states that:

> [...] ensuring that the best interests of the child are a primary consideration in legislation and policy development [...] demands a continuous process of child-rights impact assessment (CRIA) to predict the impact of any proposed law, policy or budgetary allocation on children and the enjoyment of their rights, and child-rights impact evaluation to evaluate the impact of implementation.[33]

Finally, as to the weight attached to the principle, the best interests of the child must be 'a primary consideration', although not, notably, the paramount consideration.[34] The danger in the asylum context is that the State's interest in immigration control will habitually override the best interests of the child. Here, the Com. RC has provided useful guidance, stating that 'the child's interests have high priority and [are] not just one of several considerations. Therefore a larger weight must be attached to what serves the child best [than

---

32 According to the Com. RC, 'there is no hierarchy of rights in the Convention; all the rights provided for therein are in the "child's best interests" and no right could be compromised by a negative interpretation of the child's best interests'. General Comment No. 14, *op cit*, para. 4. For a forceful rejection of the proposition that the best interests of the child could conceivably justify violating a right of the child, see Com. RC, General Comment No. 8, 'The right of the child to protection from corporal punishment and other cruel or degrading forms of punishment', *UN Doc. CRC/C/GC/8 (2006)*, para. 26. Reiterated in General Comment No. 13, 'Article 19: the right of the child to freedom from all forms of violence', *UN Doc. CRC/C/GC/13 (2011)*, para. 61.
33 Com. RC, General Comment No. 14, *op cit*, para. 35.
34 This contrasts with the wording of the precursor to Article 3(1) CRC, namely, Principle 2 of the 1959 UN Declaration on the Rights of the Child, which referred to the best interests of the child as 'the paramount consideration'. It also contrasts with other, stronger formulations of the best interests principle in the context of specific rights in the CRC and in other international legal instruments.

competing interests]'.³⁵ Indeed, the Committee has indicated that only rights-based competing interests can be balanced against the best interests of the child, and that 'non rights-based arguments, such as those relating to migration control, cannot override best interests considerations'.³⁶

III. THE RIGHT TO LIFE, SURVIVAL AND DEVELOPMENT

The third general principle is found in Article 6, which establishes the right of the child to life, survival and development. The right to life is no different from that in general human rights law, although its link to survival and development makes explicit the positive dimension of the obligation. The Committee has stated that it expects States parties 'to interpret "development" in its broadest sense as a holistic concept, embracing the child's physical, mental, spiritual, moral, psychological and social development'.³⁷ The right of the child to life, survival and development has two important applications in the asylum context. First, it informs the assessment of whether the child has an international protection need. A threat to an applicant's right to life or survival would normally amount to persecution or serious harm but a threat to a child's development may also reach the requisite threshold. Second, the right bolsters the substantive content of various socio-economic rights of the child, such as the right of the child to health and to an adequate standard of living. How these rights relate to the asylum context is set out below.

IV. THE RIGHT OF THE CHILD TO BE HEARD

The last general principle is the right of the child in Article 12 to express views and be heard. The right to express views applies to 'all matters affecting the child', including, therefore, all asylum matters. The child's view must be given due weight in accordance with the age and maturity of the child – a requirement that has potentially profound implications for such asylum concepts as the assessment of credibility, the burden of proof and the principle of the benefit of the doubt. The right to be heard applies 'in particular [...] in any judicial and administrative proceedings affecting the child', including, therefore, all asylum proceedings. The right of the child to be heard is the child-specific equivalent of the general human right to a fair hearing. It comprises not only the right of the child to a hearing, but also to be able to participate meaningfully in that hearing – a right with obvious consequences for the asylum interview. Finally, like the other general principles, the right of the child to express views and be heard is of horizontal application across all other Convention rights. However, it has a particular application in the assessment and determination of the best interests of the child. In this regard

---

35 Com. RC, General Comment No. 14, *op cit*, para. 39.
36 Com. RC, General Comment No. 6, *op cit*, para. 86.
37 Com. RC, General Comment No. 13, *op cit*, para. 62.

the Com. RC considers that 'there can be no correct application of Article 3 if the components of Article 12 are not respected. Likewise, Article 3 reinforces to functionality of Article 12, facilitating the essential role of children in all decisions affecting their lives'.[38]

Civil rights and freedoms

The Com. RC classifies the traditional freedoms – of expression, thought, conscience and religion, association and assembly and information – under this heading, along with the prohibition of torture and inhuman or degrading treatment or punishment, the right of the child to a name and nationality and the preservation of his or her identity. Other 'classic' civil and political rights, such as the right of the child to life, liberty or due process guarantees, are classified separately by the Committee under the heading of 'General principles' or 'Special protection measures'. The fact that a significant cohort of rights in the CRC are civil and political rights is significant in the asylum context for two reasons. First, international and European refugee law prioritises certain types of harm as being refugee-relevant, namely, violations of civil and political rights. Second, the bias towards these types of rights in refugee law disadvantages children because children are often perceived as not having a civil and political status. This is in part the legacy of the resistance, discussed above, to the idea of children as rights-holders and in part rooted in the Western idealised conception of childhood as apolitical and unburdened by 'adult' concerns.[39] Here, the CRC is of assistance, because it establishes that children do have civil and political rights confirming not only their civil and political status, but also the fact that children suffer egregiously from violations of these rights.[40]

Family environment and alternative care

This rights cluster, the largest grouping of rights in the Convention, can be roughly divided into rights that protect the child by maintaining family unity, such as the right of the child not to be separated from his or her parents against their will in Article 9(1); and rights that protect the child where there is no family, such as the right of the child temporarily or permanently deprived of his or her family environment to special protection and assistance provided by

---

38 Com. RC, General Comment No. 12, 'The right of the child to be heard', *UN Doc. CRC/C/GC/12 (2009)*, para. 74.
39 See P. Aries, *Centuries of Childhood*, New York: Vintage Books, 1962.
40 For example, see *Updated Statistical Analysis of Documentation of Killings in the Syrian Arab Republic*, commissioned by the Office of the United Nations High Commissioner for Human Rights, Human Rights Data Analysis Group, 13 June 2013, available at: http://www.ohchr.org/Documents/Countries/SY/HRDAG-Updated-SY-report.pdf (accessed 24 October 2013), which provides a distribution by age of recorded deaths in Syria between March 2011 and April 2013 and shows that the largest proportion of deaths is in the 0–20 years age category.

the State in Article 20.[41] These rights are of relevance to the day-to-day protection and care of asylum-seeking children. In the case of accompanied children, day-to-day protection and care are generally provided by their parents, underscoring the importance of keeping the family together. Refugee law also operates on the basis of the principle of family unity and on the concept of derived rights – the idea that the child derives its rights from the status of the parents. In the case of unaccompanied or separated children, their day-to-day protection and care cannot be met by their parents and hence must be met by the State acting in a surrogate capacity. Furthermore, the denial of rights relating to family environment and alternative care in the country of origin may be relevant to the assessment of whether the child has an international protection need.

Disability, basic health and welfare, education, leisure and cultural activities

The Com. RC groups these rights under two headings (disability, basic health and welfare under one heading and education, leisure and cultural activities under the other). Here, they are considered together as they all constitute what are typically classified in human rights law as economic, social and cultural rights. They include the right to health and to an adequate standard of living. They are of relevance at two different stages of the asylum procedure: at the reception stage, i.e. from the moment the applicant makes an application for asylum until the moment his or her claim is definitively determined; and once the applicant has been determined to be a person in need of international protection, i.e. a refugee or a beneficiary of subsidiary protection. It is at this latter stage that a 'durable solution' must be found, which, in the EU context, generally consists of local integration and associated rights. However, in the case of children, there is no great distinction between the two stages for, as Goodwin Gill observes, '[t]here is no moment [...] at which the refugee child in flight suddenly becomes ready for a durable solution; on the contrary, as the child will not postpone his or her growth or development, so the need to implement elements of a durable solution is immediate'.[42] The denial of the socio-economic rights of the child in the country of origin may also be relevant to the assessment of whether the child has an international protection need.

Special protection measures

The final cluster of rights in the Convention are special protection measures for particularly vulnerable children, such as child victims of armed conflict, children in detention and asylum-seeking and refugee children. Attention here

---

41 However, some rights in this cluster protect the child *against* the family, such as the right of the child in Article 19 to protection from all forms of physical or mental violence, injury or abuse, neglect or negligent treatment, maltreatment or exploitation, including sexual abuse.
42 G. Goodwin Gill, 'Unaccompanied refugee minors, the role and place of International Law in the pursuit of durable solutions', *International Journal of Children's Rights* 3, 1995, 405–416, 415.

is confined to the latter. Mention has already been made of Article 22(1), which brings asylum-seeking and refugee children squarely within the personal scope of the CRC. That provision also requires that asylum-seeking and refugee children receive appropriate protection and humanitarian assistance in the enjoyment of applicable rights in *other* international human rights or humanitarian instruments ratified by the State Party. The term 'humanitarian instruments' includes the 1951 Convention relating to the Status of Refugees, which establishes the right of the refugee to *non-refoulement* in Article 33(1).[43] The right of *non-refoulement* is the right not to be returned to a country where the refugee's life or liberty is at risk. The term 'other international human rights [...] instruments' includes the Convention Against Torture, the ICCPR and the ECHR, all of which establish a right of *non-refoulement* in the specific context of torture (and in the case of the latter two also inhuman and degrading treatment or punishment) which is absolute and not limited to refugees.[44] Therefore, Article 22(1) serves as a bridge to the right of *non-refoulement*, a cornerstone right in both refugee and international human rights law.

The nature of the legal obligation in the CRC

Having outlined how the various groups of rights in the CRC relate to the asylum context, this subsection turns to the question of the nature of the legal obligation under the Convention: what, in other words, are States Parties undertaking to do when they ratify or accede to the CRC?

The first thing to note is that the CRC is a legally binding instrument of international law, obligating States Parties according to the principle of *pacta sunt servanda*.[45] Article 4 establishes the general legal obligation, namely,

---

43 The 1951 Convention categorises itself as a humanitarian instrument in the preamble, but nowadays it is typically classified as a human rights instrument. See for example, P.R. Chandhi, *Blackstone's International Human Rights Documents*, 5th ed., Oxford: Oxford University Press, 2006. On the declaratory nature of refugee status, see UNHCR, 'Note on Determination of Refugee Status under International Instruments', *EC/SCP/5(1997)*, available at: http://www.unhcr.org/refworld/docid/3ae68cc04.html (accessed 14 February 2012).
44 See Articles 3, 7 and 3 respectively.
45 Some provisions of the Convention may also constitute customary international law. For example, despite the fact that the ECHR makes no reference to the principle of the best interests of the child, the ECtHR has held that 'there is currently a broad consensus – including in international law – in support of the idea that in all decisions concerning children, their best interests must be paramount'. ECtHR, *Neulinger and Shuruk v Switzerland, op cit.*, para. 135. Similarly, the European Committee of Social Rights has stated that 'when ruling on situations where the interpretation of the [Revised European Social] Charter concerns the rights of a child, the Committee considers itself bound by the internationally recognised requirement to apply the best interests of the child principle'. European Committee of Social Rights, *Defence for Children International (DCI) v The Netherlands*, Complaint No. 47/2008, Decision on the merits, 20 October 2009, para. 29. Repeated in similar terms in European Committee of Social Rights, *Defence for Children International (DCI) v Belgium*, Complaint No. 69/2011, Decision on the Merits, 23 October 2012, para. 32.

to 'take all appropriate legislative, administrative, and other measures' to implement Convention rights. How, precisely, a State Party does this is more a matter of domestic than international law, although, at the international level, States cannot use the deficiencies of domestic law as a justification for a violation of a treaty obligation.[46] In practice, the issue largely turns on whether the State Party has a monist or dualist legal system. However, regardless of which legal system is at issue, the Com. RC considers that '[e]nsuring that all domestic legislation is fully compatible with the Convention and that the Convention's principles and provisions can be directly applied and appropriately enforced is fundamental'.[47] The Committee oversees the domestic implementation of the Convention by way of States Parties' periodic reports and, once the 2012 Optional Protocol enters into force, by adjudicating on individual complaints.

As Article 2(1) of the CRC makes clear, States Parties must respect and ensure the rights in the Convention 'to each child within their jurisdiction without discrimination of any kind', irrespective of the child's status. As previously mentioned, the concept of status has been interpreted by the Com. RC as extending to nationality and even protection status. While the prohibition of discrimination does not necessarily mean that distinctions cannot validly be made between children on the basis of their status (provided they are legitimate, necessary and proportionate), there can be no question of excluding asylum-seeking or refugee children from the scope of the Convention *ratione personae*.[48] The fact that some States Parties have excluded non-national children from the personal scope of some articles of the Convention by way of an express interpretative declaration or reservation illustrates that there can be no automatic exclusion.[49] Even where States have entered such reservations, the Committee has consistently opposed them on

---

46 Article 27 of the Vienna Convention on the Law of Treaties 1969 provides, 'A party may not invoke the provisions of its internal law as justification for its failure to perform a treaty'.
47 Com. RC, General Comment No. 5, *op cit.*, para. 1.
48 For example, in its Concluding Observations to Italy in 2011, the Committee reminded Italy 'that the rights stipulated in the Convention should not be limited to children who are citizens of a State party but must extend to all children irrespective of their immigration status'. *UN Doc. CRC/C/ITA/CO/3-4 (2011)*, para. 69.
49 See the interpretative declaration of Belgium on Article 2(1), the interpretative declaration of the Cook Islands on Article 2(1), the declaration of Japan on Article 9(1) and 10, the reservation of Liechtenstein to Article 10, the declaration of the Netherlands on Article 22, the general reservation of Singapore regarding non-nationals, the reservation of Switzerland to Article 10(1), the reservation of Thailand to Article 22, the reservation of the United Arab Emirates to Article 7 and the declaration of the United Kingdom in respect of Hong Kong and the Cayman Islands to Article 22. All interpretative declarations and reservations are accessible at: http://treaties.un.org

the grounds that they are incompatible with the object and purpose of the Convention.[50]

Some rights in the Convention, notably the 'classic' civil and political rights, contain limitation clauses such as are typically found in civil and political rights treaties. Most rights in the CRC, however, do not contain limitation clauses but rather grant States Parties flexibility by way of modifying words or phrases, such as: 'in a manner consistent with the evolving capacities of the child'; 'in a manner consistent with the procedural rules of national law'; and 'States Parties shall use their best efforts to ensure'. Such modifiers are not typically found in international human rights instruments, and this departure from the usual hierarchical language is problematic.[51] Nevertheless, the Committee insists that 'there is no hierarchy of rights in the Convention' – a proposition that has an interesting application in the context of the economic, social and cultural rights in the CRC.[52]

Article 4, previously discussed, establishes not only the general legal obligation but also a distinct legal obligation in respect of socio-economic rights, namely, to 'undertake such measures to the maximum extent of [States Parties'] available resources and, where needed, within the framework of international cooperation'. Modelled on Article 2 of the International Covenant on Economic, Social and Cultural Rights (ICESCR), this provision acknowledges the resource implications of socio-economic rights and predicates fulfilment of these rights on available resources.[53] By contrast, the CRC contains no equivalent to Article 2(3) ICESCR which permits States Parties to limit the extent to which they grant socio-economic rights to non-nationals. The Com. RC has interpreted the omission in the context of unaccompanied and separated children to mean that Article 2(3) of ICESCR has no application to this group of children.[54] Moreover, the Committee observes that '[i]n application of Article 4 of the Convention, the particular vulnerability of unaccompanied and separated children, explicitly recognised in Article 20 of the Convention,

---

50 For example, in its Concluding Observations to the UK in 2002, the Committee stated that it 'remains concerned that the State party does not intend to withdraw its wide-ranging reservation on immigration and citizenship which is against the object and purpose of the Convention'. *UN Doc. CRC/C/15/Add. 18 8 (2002)*, para. 6. In its 2008 Concluding Observations to the UK, the Committee commended the UK for its decision to withdraw its reservation to Article 22 of the Convention – the asylum article. *UN Doc. CRC/C/GBR/CO/4 (2008)*, para. 4.
51 See further, C. Price Cohen, 'Elasticity of obligation and the drafting of the Convention on the Rights of the Child', *Connecticut Journal of International Law* 3, 1987, 71–109.
52 Com. RC, General Comment No. 14, *op cit*, para. 4.
53 Article 2(1) of ICESCR provides: 'Each State party to the present Covenant undertakes to take steps, individually and through international assistance and co-operation, especially economic and technical, to the maximum of its available resources, with a view to achieving progressively the full realization of the rights recognized in the present Covenant by all appropriate means, including particularly the adoption of legislative measures.'
54 Com. RC, General Comment No. 6, *op cit*, para. 16.

must be taken into account and will result in making the assignment of available resources to such children a priority'.[55]

None of the rights in the CRC is subject to derogation in times of public emergency.[56] The issue of whether or not to include a derogation provision such as is found in the ICCPR or the ECHR was discussed by the drafters of the CRC.[57] In the end, no derogation provision was inserted. In this regard, the Com. RC has referred to 'the absolute nature of the obligations deriving from the Convention and their *lex specialis* character'.[58] Indeed, the Committee frequently stresses the fact that certain rights of the child are of particularly urgent application in times of public emergency.[59] The non-derogability of the rights in the CRC can be explained by the transient nature of childhood, the impossibility of postponing the child's development and consequently the lack of proportionality between the reasons for derogation and the impact on the child.

The next section discusses the implications of the fact that the CRC binds *States Parties* for holding the *EU* to the standards enunciated in the Convention.

The relationship between the rights of the child and European asylum law

Having provided an introduction to European asylum law in Chapter 1 and now to the rights of the child, it is important to establish the precise relationship between the two bodies of law. This is important because the aim of this book is to evaluate the CEAS in the light of the rights of the child, which presupposes that there is some obligation for EU law to comply with the rights of the child. Although no discernible legal obligation to this effect existed at the time

---

55 *Ibid.*
56 Note: in international human rights law, the concepts of derogation and limitation are distinct from one another: to derogate from a right means to suspend the operation of the right in times of public emergency; to limit a right means to place a limit on the right for some justifiable reason, such as the protection of the rights of others. The distinction is important because in EU law, derogation generally means limitation.
57 See C. Price Cohen, *op cit*.
58 Com. RC, General Comment No. 6, *op cit*, para. 16.
59 See, for example, Com. RC, General Comment No. 17, 'The right of the child to rest, leisure, play, recreational activities, cultural life and the arts (art. 31)', UN Doc. CRC/C/GC/17 (2013), para. 53 and General Comment No. 15, 'The right of the child to the enjoyment of the highest attainable standard of health (art. 24)', UN Doc CRC/C/GC/15 (2013), para. 40. Furthermore, see the Committee's report of the 2012 Day of General Discussion on the Rights of all Children in the Context of International Migration at para. 55, where 'it was underscored that even in conflict situations States had legal obligations to ensure that their procedures and facilities were compliant with international children's rights and human rights standards, including [...] adherence to principles of *non-refoulement* and the provision of medical, mental health and education services, and birth registration'. Available at: http://www2.ohchr.org/english/bodies/crc/docs/discussion2012/ReportDGDChildrenAndMigration2012.pdf (accessed 24 October 2013).

the Phase One instruments were drafted, arguably a distinct legal obligation has crystallised in recent years with important implications for the Phase Two instruments. The first sub-section below outlines how the rights of the child have been indirectly channelled into EU law through a number of routes over the past decade. Collectively, these various channels form a strong basis for the argument that EU law – and, specifically, the CEAS – must now comply with the rights of the child. Despite this, the EU-fundamental rights nexus is not without its complications. The final subsection explores some of these complications, which are a function of the EU's evolving relationship with human rights in general. Nevertheless, the case is made that in areas of legislative activity that impact on children, like the CEAS, the EU must now comply with the rights of the child.

An indirect channelling

The EU, unlike all of its Member States, is not party to the CRC.[60] This creates a rather complicated legal scenario: EU Member States, as States Parties to the CRC, continue to be bound by the CRC at the international level, notwithstanding that they may have delegated some of their sovereign powers to the EU. Accordingly, when EU Member States appear before the Com. RC as part of the periodic reporting requirement or, in future, in answer to an individual complaint against them, they cannot argue that they are simply acting in accordance with EU law and, hence, are not responsible for violating Convention rights. However, *as a matter of EU law*, neither the EU Member States nor the EU institutions are bound by the CRC.[61] But despite the apparent separateness of the two legal regimes (international child-rights law and EU law), child rights emanating from the CRC are indirectly channelled into EU law in a number of different ways.

The EU Charter of Fundamental Rights

The Charter of Fundamental Rights of the European Union was drafted in 2000 in order to make explicit and, hence more visible, the human rights – or 'fundamental rights' to use the nomenclature of the EU – that were already protected by way of the general principles of EC law (about which more in

---

60 The idea of accession by the EU to the CRC is beginning to be discussed. See, for example, European Parliament, Directorate General for Internal Policies, Policy Department C, 'EU Framework of Law for Children's Rights', 2012.
61 By analogy, one should note the *Bosphorus* ruling of the European Court of Human Rights, which attempted to deal with States Parties' obligations under the ECHR when, as EU Member States, they implement EU law. ECtHR, *Bosphorus v Ireland*, Appl. No. 45036/98, Judgment (GC) of 30 June 2005. The ruling will become redundant once the EU accedes to the ECHR.

the next sub-section).⁶² The Charter became legally binding in 2009 and, in the constitutional structure of the EU, has the same legal value as the Treaties.⁶³ This means that all EU secondary legislation and national measures that implement EU law must conform to the rights in the Charter.⁶⁴ Indeed, all the instruments of the CEAS in both phases pledge conformity with the Charter, each stating in a recital that the instrument 'respects the fundamental rights and observes the principles recognised in particular by the Charter of Fundamental Rights of the European Union'.⁶⁵

The Charter contains a cross-section of civil and political and socio-economic rights, some of which are of particular importance in the asylum context, such as the prohibition of trafficking in human beings, the right to asylum in accordance with the Treaties, the prohibition of collective expulsions and the right of *non-refoulement*. However, for present purposes, the most important article is Article 24, which reads as follows:

1   Children shall have the right to such protection and care as is necessary for their well-being. They may express their views freely. Such views shall be taken into consideration on matters which concern them in accordance with their age and maturity.
2   In all actions relating to children, whether undertaken by public authorities or private institutions, the best interests of the child must be a primary consideration.
3   Every child shall have the right to maintain on a regular basis a personal relationship and direct contact with both his or her parents, unless that is contrary to his or her interests.

According to the explanations on the Charter, which are a source of interpretative guidance to which the Court must have regard, Article 24 is based on based on the CRC, 'particularly Articles 3, 9, 12 and 13 thereof'.⁶⁶ These rights were apparently randomly selected from the CRC, and it is to be regretted that the drafters did not opt for a simple cross-reference to the CRC

---

62 *OJ 2010 C83/02.*
63 Article 6(1), TEU.
64 See Article 51(1) of the Charter. However, the Charter does not give the EU legislator a competence to legislate for the rights therein in the absence of an explicit Treaty competence to legislate. See Article 51(2) of the Charter and Article 6(1) TEU. For a recent case on this point involving the rights of the child, see CJEU, *Alopka*, Case C-86/12, Judgment of 10 October 2013.
65 The CJEU has interpreted this recital to mean that the instrument must be 'interpreted in a manner consistent with the rights recognised in the Charter': *El Kott*, Case C-364/11, Judgment (GC) of 19 December 2012, para. 48.
66 Explanations Relating to the Charter of Fundamental Rights, *2007/C 303/02*. Article 52(7) of the Charter states that the explanations 'shall be given due regard by the courts of the Union and of the Member States'. Article 6(1) TEU also provides that the Charter shall be interpreted 'with due regard to the explanations'.

as a whole.[67] Nevertheless, the rights in Article 24 comprise a potentially powerful medley. Of particular note is Article 24(2) establishing the best interests principle. This is noteworthy because, as has already been outlined, the principle of the best interests of the child is a Trojan Horse of a principle that implicitly encompasses all the rights in the CRC. Hence, it cannot be ruled out that the drafters of the Charter inadvertently incorporated the entirety of the CRC into the Charter via Article 24(2).

On the other hand, there is no guarantee that Article 24 of the Charter will be interpreted consistently with how the Com. RC interprets the CRC. Of particular concern is the fact that the Charter contains a broadly worded horizontal limitation clause in Article 52(1) whereas, as discussed above, only some articles of the CRC have express limitation clauses.[68] Notably, the rights in the CRC that correspond to Article 24 of the Charter contain no limitation clauses, notwithstanding some elasticity of obligation in the language. Furthermore, at least some of the rights in the Charter appear to be derogable notwithstanding the silence of the Charter on the issue. This can be deduced from the intimate link, explained below, between certain ECHR rights, some of which are derogable, and 'corresponding' Charter rights. By contrast, the Com. RC has forcefully stated that none of the rights in the CRC are derogable. Despite a growing jurisprudence on Article 24, the CJEU has yet to pronounce on the precise relationship between the Charter and the CRC.[69] But it seems clear that if a dichotomy opens up between Article 24 of the Charter and the CRC, Member States will not be allowed to insist on the higher international standard if this would threaten the supremacy of EU law.[70] However, even allowing for an autonomous 'Union' interpretation of the rights in Article 24 of the Charter, those rights are now on a constitutional footing in EU law.

---

67 A clear and explicit reference to the CRC had been urged by the European Children's Network (EURONET) in its very first submission to the drafting Convention: *CHARTE 4127/00 CONTRIB 22* of 9 February 2000. However, the Convention was doubtful about the wisdom of referring in the Charter to an instrument external to the Union that could develop independently: *CHARTE 4123/1/00 REV 1 CONVENT 5* of 15 February 2000. For commentary, see C. McGlynn, 'Rights for children? The potential impact of the European Union Charter of Fundamental Rights', *European Public Law* 8, 2002, 387–400.
68 Article 52(1) provides: 'Any limitation on the exercise of the rights and freedoms recognised by this Charter must be provided for by law and respect the essence of those rights and freedoms. Subject to the principle of proportionality, limitations may be made only if they are necessary and genuinely meet objectives of general interest recognised by the Union or the need to protect the rights and freedoms of others.' For critical commentary on this provision, see S. Peers, 'Taking rights away? Limitations and derogations' in S. Peers and A. Ward (eds), *The EU Charter of Fundamental Rights*, Oxford and Portland, OR: Hart Publishing, 2004.
69 For a cross-section of cases in which Article 24 was discussed, see: CJEU, *J. McB*, Case C-400/10, Judgment of 5 October 2010; *Mercredi v Chaffe*, Case C-497/10, Judgment of 22 December 2010; *Zarraga v Pelz*, Case C-491/10, Judgment of 22 December 2010; *O, S and L*, Joined cases C-356/11 and C-357/11, Judgment of 6 December 2012; *MA, BT, DA*, Case C-648/11, Judgment of 6 June 2013; *Alopka, op cit*.
70 CJEU, *Melloni*, Case C-399/11, Judgment (GC) of 26 February 2013, para. 58.

The general principle of respect for fundamental rights in EU law

Long before the advent of the Charter, the ECJ (as it was then) had been 'reading down' fundamental rights protection in its interpretation and application of EC law (as it was then) in the form of the general principles doctrine. The general principles of EC (now EU) law are an unwritten layer of constitutional principles to which secondary EC (now EU) law must conform. They include the general principle of respect for fundamental rights, which is informed by the constitutional traditions common to the Member States and the international human rights treaties to which they are party, especially the ECHR.[71] In the 2006 case of *European Parliament v Council*, the Court held that the CRC is an international instrument to which is has regard in determining the content of the general principle of respect for fundamental rights.[72] Although the Charter of Fundamental Rights is considered to have codified many of the general principles, the general principles doctrine continues to have an autonomous application. This is evident from Article 6 TEU which, in addition to placing the Charter on a legal footing and providing for the accession of the EU to the ECHR, states that fundamental rights constitute general principles of the Union's law. The autonomy of the general principles is also suggested in some post-Lisbon case-law of the Court of Justice.[73]

The European Convention on Human Rights

Child rights are also channelled into EU law through the medium of the ECHR. The ECHR forms part of EU law in two ways: 1) through the general principles of EU law, which derive in part from the international instruments which Member States have ratified and in particular the ECHR; and 2) through certain Charter rights, which 'correspond' to ECHR rights notwithstanding any slight difference in wording. Where a Charter right corresponds to an ECHR right, Article 52(3) of the Charter provides that the meaning and scope of those rights shall be the same. The explanations relating to Article 52(3) provide that 'the meaning and scope of the guaranteed rights are determined not only by the text of those instruments but also by the case-law of the ECtHR and by the CJEU'.[74] Thus, the CJEU is obliged to take account of the jurisprudence of the ECtHR as well as the text of the ECHR in interpreting the corresponding provisions of the Charter – something that the Court of Justice

---

71 For example, ECJ, *Nold v Commission of European Communities*, Case 4/73, Judgment of 14 May 1974.
72 ECJ, *European Parliament v Council*, Case C-540/03, Judgment of 27 June 2006. However, for critical commentary on the judgment from a child-rights perspective, see E. Drywood, 'Challenging concepts of the "child" in asylum and immigration Law: The example of the EU', *Journal of Social Welfare and Family Law* 32, 2010, 309–323.
73 See, for example, *Küchükdeveci*, Case C-555/07, Judgment (GC) of 19 January 2010.
74 Explanations Relating to the Charter of Fundamental Rights, *op cit*.

had acknowledged in a child-rights case even before the entry into force of the Charter.[75]

There is no direct correlation between any right in the ECHR and the CRC. Indeed, drafted decades before the CRC, the ECHR contains only one provision explicitly directed at children, which, ironically, constitutes a child-specific limitation clause.[76] However, over the past number of years the ECtHR has developed a practice of interpreting certain substantive Convention rights in the light of the principle of the best interests of the child. The Court initiated this practice in the context of the right to respect for private and family life in Article 8 of ECHR – family life being the prototypical domain of children.[77] However, in the seminal case of *Neulinger and Shuruk v Switzerland*, the Court held that 'there is currently a broad consensus – including in international law – in support of the idea that *in all decisions concerning children*, their best interests must be paramount'.[78] As the case concerned Article 8, the hint at a broader scope of application for the best interests principle was purely *obiter*. However, the Court put principle into practice in *Rahimi v Greece*, in which it effectively used the best interests principle to (radically) reinterpret the right to liberty provision in the ECHR (specifically, the immigration detention provision in Article 5(1)(f)) in the light of the corresponding, but much more child-friendly, provision in the CRC (Article 37(b)–(d)).[79] The Court in that case also used the best interests principle in its interpretation of Article 3 (prohibition of torture and inhuman or degrading treatment or punishment). The Court has confirmed the applicability of the best interests principle to the interpretation of both of these articles in a number of subsequent cases.[80] The Court has also developed child-friendly jurisprudence in the context of Article 6

---

75 CJEU, *J. McB.*, op cit.
76 Article 5(1)(d) permits a limit on the right to liberty and security in the case of a minor 'for the purpose of his educational supervision or [...] of bringing him before the competent legal authority'.
77 The Court's approach to the best interests principle in the Article 8 context is not without its problems. For example, in the context of expulsion, the Court only brings the best interests principle to bear where there are obstacles to the child leaving with the parent who is threatened with expulsion. Where there are no such obstacles, the Court will not consider where it is in the best interests of the child to reside. For example, contrast ECtHR, *Nunez v Norway*, Appl. No. 55597/09, Judgment of 28 June 2011 with *Antwi and Others v Norway*, Appl. No. 26940/10, Judgment of 14 February 2012, noting the forceful dissent of Judge Sicilianos joined by Judge Lazarova Trajkovska on the issue of the best interests of the child in the latter.
78 ECtHR, *Neulinger and Shuruk v Switzerland*, op cit., para. 135 (emphasis added).
79 ECtHR, *Rahimi v Greece*, Appl. No. 8786/08, Judgment of 5 April 2011. For a thorough discussion of this case, see Chapter 7 below and, further, C. Smyth, 'Is the right of the child to liberty safeguarded in the Common European Asylum System?', *European Journal of Migration and Law* 15, 2013, 111–136.
80 ECtHR, *Kanagaratnam and Others v Belgium*, Appl. No. 15297/09, Judgment of 13 December 2011; ECtHR, *Popov v France*, Appl. No. 39472/07 and 39474/07, Judgment of 19 January 2012.

(right to a fair trial) and Protocol 1, Article 2 (right to education), albeit without the aid of the best interests principle.[81] Notably, all these rights are also present in the Charter. Therefore, when the CJEU comes to interpret these rights in the context of children, it is obliged to do so taking account of the ECtHR's child-friendly jurisprudence. Furthermore, Article 6(2) of the Treaty on European Union (TEU) provides that the Union shall accede to the ECHR.[82] This potentially means that EU law will be subject to the additional scrutiny of the ECtHR and is likely to ensure an even greater consistency of judgments between the two courts on matters of child rights.

Article 3(3) TEU

Since the Lisbon Treaty, 'protection of the rights of the child' is included, for the first time, within the list of general stated objectives of the European Union in Article 3(3) TEU. The legal effect of this provision is unclear, and it should be noted that the horizontal provisions of the Lisbon Treaty (those specified in Title II, Articles 7–17 of the TFEU as having general application) fail to mention children.[83] Nevertheless, at a minimum, Article 3(3) TEU can be interpreted as imposing an obligation on the EU to protect the rights of the child whenever it exercises a competence that implicates the rights of the child.

References to various rights of the child in the CEAS

In addition to the 'constitutional' protection of the rights of the child in EU law, significant protection is also afforded at the level of secondary legislation. As will be recalled from the previous chapter, most provisions of the CEAS instruments are age-neutral. However, all instruments in both phases contain provisions specifically directed towards children: as minors, unaccompanied minors and persons with special needs/vulnerable applicants. Some, but not all, of these provisions are based on certain rights of the child. Furthermore, the CEAS instruments in both phases all stipulate that the best interests of the child must be a primary consideration for Member States when implementing either the instrument as a whole or the provisions thereof that include minors. However, even in the latter situation – where an instrument purports to limit the scope of the principle to the child-specific provisions thereof – it is submitted that the CJEU will interpret the best interests principle expansively,

---

81 On Article 6, see, for example, ECtHR, *SC v United Kingdom*, Appl. No. 60958/00, Judgment of 15 June 2004; on Protocol 1, Article 2, see, for example, ECtHR, *Oršuš and Others v Croatia*, Appl. No 15766/03, Judgment (GC) of 16 March 2010.
82 The draft accession agreement of the EU to the ECHR was finalised in April 2013. At the time of writing, the draft agreement has been sent to the CJEU for its opinion.
83 See H. Stalford and M. Schuurman, 'Are we there yet?' The impact of the Lisbon Treaty on the EU children's rights agenda', *International Journal of Children's Rights* 19, 2011, 381–403.

in accordance with the proper scope of the principle as laid down in the Charter of Fundamental Rights.[84] Hence, the best interests of the child must be a primary consideration whenever Member States implement any provision of any of the instruments and the applicant is a child. Bearing in mind that the best interests of the child must be interpreted consistently with relevant rights of the child, this has potentially far-reaching consequences for Member States if any provisions of the CEAS instruments are contrary to the rights of the child. In such cases, Member States must implement such provisions in a way that is compatible with the best interests of the child (*qua* rights of the right), or risk litigation before the domestic courts and a preliminary reference to the CJEU.[85] In turn, if the Court of Justice finds that the impugned provision cannot be interpreted harmoniously with the best interests of the child, it must find it invalid.[86]

EU policy commitments to the rights of the child

Finally, the EU has made a clear policy commitment to the rights of the child. In 2006, the European Commission published its seminal communication 'Towards an EU Strategy on the Rights of the Child', which was said to be a 'long-term strategy to ensure that EU action actively promotes and safeguards children's rights'.[87] The strategy document is built around seven objectives, one of which is 'mainstreaming children's rights in EU actions', in other words, child-rights proofing draft legislation and policy that may affect them.[88] In 2011, the Commission launched its follow-up document, an 'EU agenda for the Rights of the Child', containing general principles relating to the Union's commitment to the rights of the child, some areas of concrete EU action for children (including vulnerable children such as asylum-seeking children in detention and unaccompanied minors) and a commitment to facilitate children's participation in EU decisions that affect them.[89] The purpose of the Agenda is 'to reaffirm the strong commitment of all EU institutions and of all Member States to promoting, protecting and fulfilling the

---

84 Thus, in a recent asylum case, the Court held that 'although express mention of the best interest of the minor is made only in the first paragraph of Article 6 of [the Dublin Regulation], the effect of Article 24(2) of the Charter, in conjunction with Article 51(1) thereof, is that the child's best interests must also be a primary consideration in all decisions adopted by the Member States on the basis of the second paragraph of Article 6 of [the Regulation]'. CJEU, *MA BT, DA, op cit.*
85 Article 267 TFEU.
86 See *Test Achats,* Case C-236/09, Judgment of 1 March 2011.
87 Communication from the Commission, 'Towards an EU Strategy on the Rights of the Child', *COM (2006) 367 final*, p. 7.
88 *Ibid*, Section III.1.3.
89 Communication from the Commission to the European Parliament, the Council, the European Economic and Social Committee and the Committee of the Regions, 'An EU Agenda on the Rights of the Child', *COM (2011) 60 final*.

rights of the child in all EU policies and to turn it into concrete results'.[90] To that end, according to the Agenda, 'EU policies that directly or indirectly affect children should be designed, implemented and monitored taking into account the principle of the best interests of the child enshrined in the EU Charter of Fundamental Rights and in the UNCRC'.[91] Although these are policy (and hence not legally binding) documents, they are founded on the Charter and the CRC and arguably create a legitimate expectation of fulfilment.

In sum, these six channels by which the rights of the child are routed into EU law form a strong basis for the argument that EU law – and specifically, the CEAS – must now comply with the rights of the child.

Some complications in the EU–fundamental rights nexus

Although the case is made here that the CEAS, in its second phase at least, must comply with the rights of the child, it is important to acknowledge that the EU–fundamental rights nexus is not without its complications.[92] The following subsections focus on two substantive problems of relevance to this book.[93]

Some difficulties in assessing whether EU law complies with fundamental rights

The Union legislator is clearly bound, not only to respect (i.e. not violate) EU fundamental rights when legislating, but also to promote (i.e. fulfil) EU

---

90 *Ibid*, p. 3.
91 *Ibid*.
92 There is a vast scholarly literature on the EU–fundamental rights nexus. For a cross-section, see D. Sarmiento, 'Who's afraid of the Charter? The Court of Justice, national courts and the new framework of fundamental rights protection in Europe', *Common Market Law Review* 50, 2013, 1267–1304; S. Iglesias Sánchez, 'The Court and the Charter: the impact of the entry into force of the Lisbon Treaty on the ECJ's approach to fundamental rights', *Common Market Law Review* 49, 2012, 1565–1611; S. Douglas-Scott, 'The European Union and human rights after the Treaty of Lisbon', *Human Rights Law Review* 11, 2011, 645–682; D. Denman, 'The Charter of Fundamental Rights', *European Human Rights Law Review* 4, 2010, 349–359; T. Ahmed and I. de Jesús Butler, 'The European Union and human rights: An international law perspective', *European Journal of International Law* 17, 2006, 771–801.
93 There are also some procedural concerns about the EU's approach to 'mainstreaming' fundamental rights into the various stages of the legislative process. In brief, although the Commission, Council and Parliament are each responsible for 'Charter-proofing' their own legislative proposals or amendments, in the cut and thrust of negotiations mainstreaming is often compromised and owing to the inscrutability of the informal legislative procedure – the so-called 'trilogues' – it is often hard to discern which institution is responsible for the deviation. See Steve Peers, 'The democratic accountability of the EU's legislative approach', available at: http://www.statewatch.org/analyses/no-203-eu-openness.pdf (accessed 4 November 2013). There are further concerns about the EU's approach to mainstreaming children's rights. For example, there is no *separate* child-rights mainstreaming procedure and limited (albeit growing) child-rights capacity within the institutions. See E. Drywood, '"Child-proofing" EU law and policy: Interrogating the law-making processes behind European asylum and immigration provision', *International Journal of Children's Rights* 19, 2011, 405–428.

fundamental rights when legislating.[94] However, it is not so clear how this obligation plays out when the legislation aims at a low level of harmonisation. As discussed in Chapter 1, the CEAS in both phases aims at precisely such a level of harmonisation. This is evident in the choice of the directive as the key instrument of the CEAS, in the choice of minimum standards legislation (which, nominally at least, become common standards in Phase Two) and in the large number of discretionary and derogation provisions that typify the CEAS legislation. When the CEAS directives are transposed, the standards they contain operate as a 'floor', below which Member States cannot go and above which they are free to choose to go.[95] But the way in which the 'floor' interacts with fundamental rights is not necessarily made explicit and the responsibility is on Member States to transpose/implement/interpret the floor in a way that respects EU fundamental rights, to the extent possible. In the multi-level system of governance of EU law, there are good reasons for this approach.[96] Nevertheless, it complicates any assessment of the compliance of EU law with fundamental rights. In short, in order to comply with the rights of the child, the CEAS instruments must simply be susceptible to an interpretation that permits fundamental rights to be added on. Only if the instruments preclude this move (i.e. by way of mandatory provisions that simply cannot be interpreted consistently with fundamental rights) can they be considered non-compliant, strictly speaking.[97]

However, as De Schutter observes:

> where an EU instrument defines [...] a certain minimal level of protection of certain fundamental rights or creates for the benefit of the Member States certain exceptions, this may create the impression that provided they comply with that instrument or remain within the boundaries set

---

94 Article 51(1) of the Charter provides that the Union's institutions, bodies and agencies must 'respect the [Charter] rights, observe the principles and promote the application thereof'.
95 However, it should be noted that Member States are not entirely free to pitch national standards at a higher level than EU standards. For example, the CEAS directives in both phases all provide that Member States may introduce or retain more favourable provisions or standards *insofar as they are compatible with the directive*. See Article 4 RCD and recast RCD, Article 5 APD and recast APD, Article 3 QD and recast QD.
96 See C. Engel, 'The European Charter of Fundamental Rights, A changed political opportunity structure and its normative consequences', *European Law Journal* 7, 2001, 151–170.
97 The Court of Justice has stated that 'a provision of a Community act could, in itself, not respect fundamental rights if it required, or expressly or impliedly authorised, the Member States to adopt or retain national legislation not respecting those rights'. ECJ, *European Parliament v Council, op cit.*, para. 23. However, as one commentator noted, 'the Court's reading of the Directive [in that case] is rather inventive and seems to demonstrate a determination to give an interpretation to the provisions of the Directive which is in conformity with human rights. This is not without consequences for the Member States. The ECJ calls into being specific obligations for the Member States which are not explicitly laid down in the Directive'. M. Bulterman, 'Case C-540/03, Parliament v Council, Judgment of the Grand Chamber of 27 June 2006', *Common Market Law Review* 45, 2008, 245–259, 253.

by that exception, the Member States are acting in conformity with the requirements of fundamental rights – an impression which, although in certain cases mistaken, may be difficult to dispel.[98]

It can be observed that, in the context of the CEAS, Member States may be inclined to indulge in this mistaken impression because, despite the rhetoric of solidarity, asylum harmonisation is generally perceived as a zero-sum game. In other words, any Member State that raises standards is perceived as losing and vice versa.[99] In this context, it is imperative that the standards of the CEAS should explicitly and faithfully correspond to EU fundamental rights standards. This book proceeds on that premise.

Some ambiguity in the extent to which Member States are bound by EU fundamental rights

As previously mentioned, the States parties to the CRC remain liable at the international level for any violations of the CRC or other international human rights instruments, notwithstanding that they are acting pursuant to EU law. But what is their responsibility for respecting the rights of the child as a matter of EU law? The Charter binds Member States as well as the Union legislator, but in the case of the former, '*only* when they are *implementing* Union law'.[100] This phraseology has caused no little confusion.

Pre-Charter, the ECJ exercised fundamental rights jurisdiction (under the guise of the general principles) over acts of Member States when they were 'acting in the scope of' Community law. There were two distinct lines of cases on the meaning of the 'acting in the scope of' formula: the *Wachauf* line of cases applied to the implementation by Member States of Community law, in other words, the adoption of measures to implement regulations or transpose directives, including discretionary provisions; and the *ERT* line of cases applied to situations where Member States derogated from one of the four fundamental freedoms for reasons of public interest accepted in Community law.[101] However, on a black-letter reading, the reference in the Charter to 'implementing' Union law appears narrower than the Court's formula of 'acting in the scope of' Community law. This is potentially problematic in the context of the CEAS because, as previously observed, the instruments that make up the

---

98 O. De Schutter, 'The implementation of the EU Charter of Fundamental Rights through the open method of coordination', *Jean Monnet Working Paper* 07/04, 2004, 21–22.
99 For an excellent analysis of this problem, see J. Mink, 'EU asylum law and human rights protection: Revisiting the principle of *non-refoulement* and the prohibition of torture and other forms of ill-treatment', *European Journal of Migration and Law* 14, 2012, 119–149.
100 Article 51(1), emphasis added.
101 This line of cases included *Dynamic Medien* in which the Court stated that 'the protection of the child is a legitimate interest which, in principle, justifies a restriction on a fundamental freedom guaranteed by the EC Treaty, such as the free movement of goods'. Case C-244/06, Judgment of 11 February 2008.

CEAS are replete with derogations, discretionary provision and vague injunctions that leave much to be interpreted. When Member States creatively (as they must) execute these provisions, they are clearly 'acting in the scope of' Union law according to the Court's established jurisprudence, but are they 'implementing' Union law *stricto sensu*? If not, then the Charter does not apply and the problem of compliance discussed in the previous subsection replicates itself at the national level.

Commentators have suggested that the unfortunate wording of Article 51(1) was due to a drafting deficiency, a failure on the part of the drafting body to appreciate the nuances of the Court's case-law.[102] This thesis is supported by the explanations relating to the Charter – also drawn up by the drafting body – which seem to equate 'implementing' with 'acting in the scope of'. Thus, the explanation on Article 51(1) uses the 'acting in the scope of' formula and refers to both the *Wachauf* and *ERT* line of cases.[103] The drafting-deficiency thesis is also supported by a purposive interpretation of the Charter, the aim of which was to strengthen and make more visible fundamental rights in the Union.[104] This would appear to rule out any retreat from the Court's pre-Charter jurisprudence relating to Member States' fundamental rights obligations when acting in the scope of Community law. Furthermore, case-law relating to Article 51(1) since the entry into force of the Charter appears to assimilate 'implementing' to 'acting in the scope of', suggesting that the Court is not overly concerned with semantics. *N.S. and M.E.*, for example, concerned a discretionary provision of the Dublin Regulation. Noting that the discretionary provision 'forms an integral part of the Common European Asylum System' and that it 'must be exercised in accordance with the other provisions of that regulation', the Court held that 'a Member State which exercises that discretionary power must be considered as implementing European Union law within the meaning of Article 51(1) of the Charter'.[105] However, a narrow reading of the judgment suggests that only discretionary provisions of the CEAS instruments that are integral to the instrument and/or to the CEAS as a whole can be said to be implementing Union law. A more recent judgment of the Court is less ambiguous: in *Akerberg*, the Court, referring to the explanations relating to Article 51(1) of the Charter, held that:

> Since the fundamental rights guaranteed by the Charter must therefore be complied with where national legislation falls *within the scope of European*

---

102 L. Pech and X. Groussot, 'Fundamental rights protection in the EU post Lisbon Treaty' (14 June 2010). Available at SSRN: http://ssrn.com/abstract=1628552 or http://dx.doi.org/10.2139/ssrn.1628552 (accessed 5 November 2013).
103 Explanations relating to the Charter of Fundamental Rights, *op cit*.
104 Cologne European Council, 3–4 June 1999, Conclusions of the Presidency, Annex IV – European Council Decision on the Drawing up of a Charter of Fundamental Rights of the European Union.
105 CJEU, *N.S and ME,* Joined cases C-411/10 and C-493/10, Judgment of 21 December 2011, paras. 65, 66 and 67, respectively.

Union law, situations cannot exist which are covered in that way by European Union law without those fundamental rights being applicable. The applicability of European Union law entails applicability of the fundamental rights guaranteed by the Charter.[106]

Consequently, although the matter is not entirely settled, it seems that when Member States legislate within the scope of the CEAS, they are bound to comply with the Charter, including the rights of the child contained therein.

Conclusion

In summary, although there continues to be a residual theoretical uncertainty about whether children are properly rights-holders, the positive law position, as most clearly articulated in the CRC, is that children have a range of different rights. All of these rights have an important application in the asylum context. All EU Member States are States Parties to the CRC. Hence, such States are obliged to ensure that their domestic law is fully compatible with the rights in the Convention. However, the EU has not (yet) acceded to the CRC and hence neither the EU legislator nor EU Member States when implementing EU law are directly bound by the Convention. Nevertheless, the rights in the CRC have been channelled indirectly into EU law through various different routes. This supports the proposition that the EU legislator when legislating in areas that affect children and EU Member States when implementing such laws must now comply with the rights of the child. This is so notwithstanding some ambiguities about the precise relationship between EU law and fundamental rights in general. Having established the basic premise on which this book is based, the subsequent chapters deal with a particular right of the child (or group of rights) that is especially pertinent in the asylum context, exploring the meaning of the right as a matter of international and regional human rights law and assessing the extent to which the CEAS instruments in both phases can be said to comply with the right.

---

106 CJEU, *Akerberg*, Case C-617/10, Judgment of 26 February 2013, para. 21 (emphasis added).

3 The right of the child to seek and qualify for international protection

Introduction

This chapter explores the right of the child to seek and qualify for international protection. This 'right' requires some explanation, for two reasons. First, the right (of anyone) to seek international protection, as distinct from the right of *non-refoulement*, is not uncontested in international law.[1] The aim here is not to establish that the child has any greater right to seek international protection than has anyone else, but rather that the right to seek international protection, such as it exists, applies equally to the child. Second, the right to qualify for international protection presupposes that the applicant meets the qualification criteria. The contention here is not that the child has a right to qualify simply by virtue of being a child, but rather that the child has a right to qualify, like anyone else, if he/she meets the qualification criteria. However, a further nuance must be added: it is generally accepted that the qualification criteria are not neutral, but reflect a hidden adult bias. In order to remedy this bias, and make the qualification criteria meaningful for children, it is suggested that the qualification criteria should be sensitive to the rights of the child. Hence, what is meant in this chapter by the right of the child to qualify for international protection is that the child has a right to have his/her rights as a child regarded as refugee-relevant.

This chapter is divided into two substantive sections – the first relating to the right of the child to seek international protection and the second relating

---

1 The right 'to seek and to enjoy in other countries asylum from persecution' in Article 14 of the Universal Declaration of Human Rights finds no equivalent in the legally binding ICCPR. Furthermore, the seminal 1951 Convention relating to the Status of Refugees contains no express right to seek asylum. In this context, the 'right to asylum' in Article 18 of the EU Charter of Fundamental Rights is innovative. It provides: 'The right to asylum shall be guaranteed with due respect for the rules of the Geneva Convention of 18 July 1951 and the Protocol of 31 January 1967 relating to the status of refugees and in accordance with the Treaty establishing the European Community.' The right to asylum in the Charter is considered to cover the right of individuals to seek *and* to enjoy asylum. See M. Gil-Bazo, 'The Charter of Fundamental Rights of the European Union and the right to be granted asylum in the Union's law', *Refugee Survey Quarterly* 27, 2008, 33–52.

to the right of the child to qualify for international protection. Thus, the first section explores the right of the child to seek international protection. It establishes the existence of such a right and then evaluates whether the APD – the relevant CEAS instrument – complies with the right.[2] It scrutinises the recast APD in order to assess the prospects for enhanced compliance in Phase Two CEAS.[3] The second section – by far the larger of the two – examines the right of the child to qualify for international protection. The first subsection sets out the proposition that the rights of the child *tout court* are potentially relevant to establishing an international protection need and exposes the obstacles in international human rights law and refugee law that hinder a general acceptance of this proposition. The next subsection explores whether the qualification criteria in the QD are sensitive to the rights of the child or, conversely, reproduce the obstacles referred to above.[4] The final subsection examines the changes in the recast QD in order to assess the prospects for greater sensitivity to the rights of the child.[5]

The right of the child to seek international protection

The existence of a right of the child to seek international protection

Consistent with the traditional lack of an explicit right to seek asylum in international human rights law, the CRC does not establish any express right of the child to seek asylum. However, Article 22 relating to special measures of protection for refugee and asylum-seeking children provides guarantees for children who are (already) seeking asylum, which implies a prior right to seek asylum. Article 22(1) provides:

> States Parties shall take appropriate measures to ensure that a child who is seeking refugee status or who is considered a refugee in accordance with the applicable international or domestic law and procedures shall, whether unaccompanied or accompanied by his or her parents or by any other person, receive appropriate protection and humanitarian assistance in the enjoyment of applicable rights set forth in the Convention and in other international human rights or humanitarian instruments to which the said States are Parties.

The term 'humanitarian instruments' includes the 1951 Convention relating to the Status of Refugees, which establishes the right of the refugee to

---

2 Council Directive 2005/85/EC of 1 December 2005.
3 Directive 2013/32/EU of the European Parliament and of the Council of 26 June 2013.
4 Council Directive 2004/83/EC of 29 April 2004.
5 Directive 2011/95/EU of the European Parliament and of the Council of 13 December 2011.

non-refoulement and, implicitly (since refugee status is declaratory rather than constitutive), a right to seek asylum.[6] The term 'other international human rights [...] instruments' includes the Convention Against Torture, the ICCPR and the ECHR, all of which establish a right of *non-refoulement* in the specific context of torture (and in the case of the latter two also in the context of inhuman and degrading treatment or punishment) that is absolute and not limited to refugees.[7] Here the right of *non-refoulement* implies a right to seek protection, albeit not necessarily a right to some sort of status. The right of *non-refoulement* in the torture context is reiterated in Article 19 of the EU Charter of Fundamental Rights, and the ECJ held in *Elgafaji* that 'the fundamental right guaranteed under Article 3 ECHR forms part of the general principles of Community law, observance of which is ensured by the Court'.[8]

It is submitted that the link in Article 22(1) CRC between the child who is seeking refugee status and the protection rights in other international human rights or humanitarian instruments establishes that the child has a right to seek asylum, broadly understood as the right to seek some form of protection recognised under international law. This is confirmed in General Comment No. 6 on the treatment of unaccompanied and separated children outside their country of origin, in which the Com. RC stipulates that '[a]sylum-seeking children, including those who are unaccompanied or separated, shall enjoy access to asylum procedures and other complementary mechanisms providing international protection irrespective of their age'.[9]

If the child has a right of access to the procedure, it follows that he/she must have the right to lodge an application for international protection. While this is clearly the position as regards the unaccompanied or separated child, who stands in an unmediated relationship with the asylum procedure, the situation of the *accompanied* child is more ambiguous: is he/she entitled to lodge an independent application or is it enough that his/her claim be subsumed into that of his/her parent?[10] In the case of the former option, the child acquires his/her own status; in the case of the latter, the child derives his/her status from that of his/her parent. In this regard, at least three scenarios can be distinguished: a) the parent is the principal applicant and there are no separate

---

6 The 1951 Convention categorises itself as a humanitarian instrument in the preamble, but nowadays is typically classified as a human rights instrument. See, for example, P.R. Chandhi, *Blackstone's International Human Rights Documents*, 5th ed., Oxford: Oxford University Press, 2006. On the declaratory nature of refugee status, see UNHCR, 'Note on Determination of Refugee Status under International Instruments', *EC/SCP/5 (1997)*, available at: http://www.unhcr.org/refworld/docid/3ae68cc04.html (accessed 14 February 2012).
7 See Articles 3, 7 and 3 respectively.
8 ECJ, *Elgafaji*, Case C-465/07, Judgment of the Court (GC) of 17 February 2009, para. 28.
9 Com. RC, General Comment No. 6, 'Treatment of unaccompanied and separated children outside their country of origin', *UN Doc. CRC/GC/2005/6 (2005)*, para. 66.
10 Or subsumed into both parents' claims.

elements relating to the child's risk of persecution or serious harm; b) the child is the principal applicant in that it is the child (not the parent) who is at risk of persecution or serious harm; c) both parent and child are at risk of persecution or serious harm and there are separate elements to their claims or their claims warrant separate evaluation.[11] Here the wording of Article 22(1) CRC is instructive: the child who is seeking refugee status, whether unaccompanied or *accompanied by his or her parents* must receive *appropriate protection*. Only in the case of scenario a) above is it appropriate to subsume the child's claim into that of his/her parent. It follows that the accompanied child must have the possibility of lodging an independent asylum application or, at the very least, of making separate submissions in the context of his/her parent's claim.[12]

In brief, the right of the child to seek asylum is the right of both the unaccompanied or separated child and the accompanied child.

Phase One CEAS: Compliance with the right of the child to seek international protection

At the outset, it should be noted that the CEAS transforms the hitherto inchoate right to seek asylum into an actionable right. Thus, the DR provides in Article 3(1) that 'Member States shall examine the application of any third country national who applies at the border or in their territory to any one of them for asylum.[13] The application shall be examined by a single Member State, which shall be the one which the criteria set out in Chapter III indicate is responsible'. Although couched in the language of State responsibility, Article 3(1) DR effectively establishes the right of a third country national to have his/her asylum claim examined, in other words, a right to seek asylum.[14] Furthermore, the QD provides that individuals 'shall' be granted refugee or subsidiary protection status if they meet the definitional requirements laid down in the directive.[15] This establishes a practical corollary to the right to seek asylum, namely, the right to be granted international protection. However, despite these significant advances, it is not clear that the

---

11 Of course, there may be cases in which the risk of persecution emanates from the parent, underscoring the importance of the option of making a separate claim. See P. Margulies, 'Children, parents and asylum', *Georgetown Immigration Law Journal* 15, 2000–01, 289–317.
12 These options are foreseen in UNHCR, 'Guidelines on International Protection, Child asylum claims under Articles 1(A)2 and 1(F) of the 1951 Convention and/or 1967 Protocol relating to the Status of Refugees', *HCR/GIP/09/08 (2009)*, para. 9. Hereinafter, 'UNHCR Guidelines on Child Asylum Claims'.
13 Council Regulation No. 343/2003 of 18 February 2003.
14 This right is compromised somewhat by the fact that the DR is not a 'closed system', in the sense that it allows Member States in Article 3(3) to 'retain the right, pursuant to national law, to send the asylum seeker to a third country, in compliance with the provisions of the Geneva Convention'.
15 Article 13 and Article 18 QD.

CEAS conforms to the right of the *child* to seek asylum. In this regard, a number of provisions of the APD are of concern.

Access to the procedure is dealt with in Article 6 APD. Article 6(2) provides that each adult having legal capacity has the right to make an application for asylum on his/her own behalf. As regards minors, Article 6(4) provides that:

> Member States may determine in national legislation:
>
> a the cases in which a minor can make an application on his/her own behalf;
> b the cases in which the application of an unaccompanied minor has to be lodged by a representative as provided for in Article 17(1)(a);
> c the cases in which the lodging of an application for asylum is deemed to constitute also the lodging of an application for asylum for any unmarried minor.

Hence, Member States can opt not to legislate at all on the question of children's access to the procedure. If they do legislate pursuant to Article 6(4), the options outlined therein do not clearly establish a *right* of access to the procedure, either for accompanied or unaccompanied minors.

Thus, as regards *accompanied* minors, it can be observed that between Article 6(4)(a) and (c), there is no reference to a right of the minor either to lodge an application on his/her own behalf or to be included in someone else's application. Moreover, the reference to the marital status of the minor in Article 6(4)(c) but not Article 6(2) places the married minor at particular risk of falling between two stools – excluded from his/her parents' application but not considered as an adult with a right to make his/her own application. The precarious position of married minors in the CEAS will be further commented on in Chapter 5. The lack of a right of an accompanied minor to lodge an independent application can be contrasted with the situation of dependent adults under the directive. Dependent adults cannot be subsumed into someone else's application without their consent and are entitled to a separate decision if their application is based on separate grounds.[16] This is an acknowledgement of the fact that, even in situations of dependency, individuals may have different protection needs. However, this is also true for minor dependants, whose claim may well have a child-specific dimension. The omission of any instruction to Member States to inquire into the possible existence of a child-specific dimension in deciding whether a minor can access the procedure in his/her own right could, in some cases, result in a failure to grant the child *appropriate* protection. As for State practice, the Commission evaluation of the APD states that applications made by parents 'generally' cover dependant minors, and gives examples of three Member States that allow minors over a

---

16 Articles 6(3) and 9(3), respectively.

certain age to lodge an application on their own behalf.[17] While the latter practice is preferable to the former, the imposition of age thresholds is objectionable because it misses the point, which is that even very young children may need to have their claims separately evaluated.

In the absence of a right to lodge an independent application, or of any case-by-case scrutiny of the need to lodge an independent application, the question arises as to whether the accompanied minor can make a claim at a later point or make later submissions in the context of his/her parents' claim. Just one provision of the APD provides, by negative inference, for a later application by an accompanied minor.[18] Article 23(4), relating to the accelerated/manifestly unfounded procedure, lists numerous grounds for acceleration, including ground (o):

> The application was made by an unmarried minor to whom Article 6(4)(c) applies, after the application of the parents or parent responsible for the minor has been rejected and no relevant new elements were raised with respect to his/her particular circumstances or to the situation in his/her country of origin.

Hence, a later application by an accompanied minor, which raises no relevant new elements, is grounds for acceleration and a possible manifestly unfounded determination. *A contrario*, if new elements are raised, the child's subsequent application may be considered in the context of the ordinary procedure. However, the requirement of raising new elements is problematic for two reasons. First, it may be less a case of introducing new elements as having the claim considered from the perspective of the rights of the child – an issue that will be addressed in the next section. Second, the burden of proof appears to be placed squarely on the child – something that is problematic from the point of view of the right of the child to be heard, a right that will be analysed in Chapter 4.

The situation is not much better for *unaccompanied* minors: as between Article 6(4)(a) and (b) the right of an unaccompanied minor to either lodge an application or have one lodged on his/her behalf by a representative is not clearly established. Paragraph 4(b) certainly gives the impression that if the unaccompanied minor him/herself has no right to lodge an application, such

---

17 'Report from the Commission to the European Parliament and the Council on the Application of Directive 2005/85/EC of 1 December 2005 on Minimum Standards on Procedures in Member States for Granting and Withdrawing Refugee Status', *COM (2010) 465 final*, p. 4. Hereinafter, 'Commission evaluation of the APD'.
18 This contrasts with the situation of a dependant adult who makes a later application on his/her own behalf. Such an application can be dealt with in one of three ways: per Article 32(7) in a special procedure for dealing with subsequent applications; per Article 25(2)(g) in the context of an admissibility procedure; and per Article 23(4)(h) in an accelerated/manifestly unfounded procedure.

a right is vested in his/her representative. However, the provisions of Article 17 (Guarantees for unaccompanied minors), which specify the role of the representative, are confined to the representative's tasks in assisting the minor in relation to the examination of the application and in preparing the minor for the personal interview, if there is one.[19] These tasks necessarily follow on from the lodging of an application. But there is no provision explicitly establishing the right of the representative to make an application on behalf of the minor.

In sum, the APD does not clearly establish that the accompanied child has a right to make an application for asylum, either on his/her own behalf or by being included in his/her parents' application. As regards unaccompanied minors, the directive fails to establish clearly that a right to lodge an application is vested either in the child him/herself or in his/her representative. The lack of an explicit right of all minors to lodge an application – one way or another – falls short of the requirements of Article 22 CRC.

Phase Two CEAS: Prospects for enhanced compliance

The recast of the APD makes a number of significant amendments to the provisions on access to the procedure and the making of subsequent applications, which, with some misgivings, can be regarded as an improvement on the current situation.

First, while the provision of the current APD that permits Member States to determine in national legislation whether and when a minor can make an application on his/her own behalf is retained in the recast (Article 7(5)), this is supplemented by new Article 7(3), which provides:

> Member States *shall* ensure that a minor has the right to make an application for international protection either on his/her own behalf, if he/she has the legal capacity to act in procedures according to the national law of the Member State concerned, or through his/her parents or other adult family members, or an adult responsible for him/her, whether by law or by national practice of the Member State concerned, or through a representative.[20]

This provision, which was introduced 'with a view to align the Directive with Article 22(1) of the 1989 Convention on the Rights of the Child',[21] clearly

---

19 See Chapter 4 for a full discussion of the role of the representative in the APD.
20 Emphasis added.
21 Proposal for a Directive of the European Parliament and of the Council on minimum standards on procedures in Member States for granting and withdrawing international protection, *COM (2009) 554 final*, ANNEX, 'Detailed Explanation of the Proposal', p. 4. It is assumed that the detailed explanation of provisions of the 2009 proposal applies to the equivalent provisions of the 2011 proposal to the extent that such provisions remain unchanged. There is no detailed explanation of the 2011 proposal.

establishes that the minor has a *right* to make an application for international protection – one way or another. However, the reference to legal capacity, which was introduced in the amended Commission proposal for a recast in 2011, is unfortunate, as the key issue in determining whether the child should be allowed to make his/her own application is not whether the child has reached the age of legal capacity under national law but rather whether the child has an independent claim, separate elements to his/her claim or elements that warrant separate evaluation.[22]

As regards unaccompanied minors, the reference to the representative in Article 7(3) is welcome, as it (implicitly) establishes the right of the representative to lodge an application on behalf of the minor. Other bodies too are entitled to make an application on behalf of an unaccompanied minor. Thus, Article 7(4) makes a cross-reference to Article 10 of the Returns Directive, which rather obscurely specifies that 'appropriate bodies' other than those involved in enforcing returns must be consulted before a decision is taken to return an unaccompanied minor.[23] Article 7(4) establishes that those bodies 'have the right to lodge an application for international protection on behalf of an unaccompanied minor if, on the basis of an individual assessment of his/her personal situation, those bodies are of the opinion that the minor may have international protection needs'. Unhelpfully, the term 'appropriate bodies' is not defined in either the Returns Directive or the recast APD.

Finally, on the question of whether an accompanied minor can make later submissions or a later application, significant changes are envisaged. Ground (o) is deleted from the list of accelerated/manifestly unfounded grounds in recast Article 31(8). Henceforth, Member States can elect to deal with applications by unmarried minors after an application has already been made on their behalf under a (revised) procedure for dealing with subsequent applications.[24] Under this procedure, the unmarried minor's application is examined by way of a 'preliminary examination', with minimal procedural guarantees, in order to decide whether there are 'facts relating to [his/her] situation which justify a separate application'.[25] Only if a separate application is found to be warranted, is the claim further examined in accordance with the basic principles and guarantees laid down in the directive.[26] If the preliminary

---

22 Amended proposal for a Directive of the European Parliament and of the Council on common procedures for granting and withdrawing international protection status (recast), *COM (2011) 310 final*, Article 7(3).
23 Directive 2008/115/EC of the European Parliament and of the Council of 16 December 2008.
24 Article 40–42.
25 Article 40(6), final sub-para.
26 Article 40(3).

examination finds that a separate application is not warranted, the application is deemed inadmissible.[27]

On the one hand, the processing of later applications by unmarried minors in the context of what is essentially an admissibility procedure is potentially no less prejudicial than in the context of an accelerated/manifestly unfounded procedure.[28] On the other hand, however, the wording of the subsequent application provision is preferable, in that it refers to 'facts [...] which justify a separate application' as opposed to 'new elements'. Nevertheless, the burden of asserting those facts still lies on the child. The recast does not specify what course of action Member States should adopt if they choose not to apply this procedure to late applications by accompanied unmarried minors. In all, this procedure can be regarded as only a modest improvement on the current method of dealing with late applications by accompanied minors.

In sum, the recast APD is an improvement on the current directive in that it provides for a right of all minors to lodge an asylum application, either directly or through a family member or representative. However, where an accompanied minor is included in a family member's application, making a later application may still attract considerable negative consequences.

The right of the child to qualify for international protection

The relevance of the rights of the child to eligibility for international protection

Let us begin with a proposition: the rights of the child *tout court* are potentially relevant to establishing an international protection need. This proposition follows directly from the principle of the best interests of the child, which implicitly encompasses the rights of the child and which applies to all actions concerning children, including, therefore, determining a child's eligibility for international protection (see Chapter 2).[29] However, there is nothing inevitable about this proposition. The cornerstone of international protection – the 1951 Convention relating to the Status of Refugees – contains no provision specific to children and no hint that the definition of

---

27 Article 40(5).
28 Apart from the prejudice to the processing and outcome of the application, making a subsequent application is a ground for reducing or withdrawing reception conditions under Article 20(1)(c) of the recast RCD.
29 See also J. McAdam, 'Seeking asylum under the Convention on the Rights of the Child: A case for complementary protection', *International Journal of Children's Rights* 14, 2006, 251–274.

refugee might be relevant to children.[30] Indeed, as feminist scholars have long pointed out, the 1951 Convention definition is the product of a particular historical and social moment (post Second World War) and protects the central protagonist of that moment: the male activist fleeing totalitarianism.[31] Thus, the definition prioritises types of public harm (i.e. persecution by State authorities) that are perpetrated on the basis of aspects of civil and political identity (i.e. race, religion, nationality, social group and political opinion). Owing to the public/private divide as revealed in feminist theory, non-prototypical refugees, such as women and children, have found it difficult to fit within the dominant paradigm.[32]

Still, great strides have been made over the past 60 years, not least owing to the partial convergence of refugee law and international human rights law, in making the definition of the refugee more relevant. Thus, Haines comments that developments in international law have 'fundamentally transformed the 1951 Convention from a document fixed in a specific moment in history into a human rights instrument which addresses contemporary forms of human rights abuses'.[33] In theory, then, it should be no great task to establish that the rights in the CRC – or more particularly serious violations of those rights – are refugee-relevant. Indeed, this is a task that has been taken up by

---

30 The only indication that the refugee might be a child is in Article 22 on public education, which establishes an obligation to 'accord to refugees the same treatment as is accorded to nationals with respect to elementary education'. The silence of the 1951 Convention on the issue of child refugees is surprising given that there *was* an international awareness of the existence and plight of refugee children at that time, as evidenced by the fact that the International Refugee Organisation (the precursor of UNHCR) included in its 1946 Constitution the group 'unaccompanied children [under the age of 16] who are war orphans or whose parents have disappeared' as one of four categories of persons defined as refugees. Available at: http://www.refworld.org/docid/3ae68bf00.html#_edn10 (accessed 11 November 2013). Furthermore, the *travaux préparatoires* of the 1951 Convention reveal that the U.S. delegation proposed including a similar category in the refugee definition: Ad Hoc Committee on Statelessness and Related Problems (AHC), United States of America: Memorandum on the Definition Article of the Preliminary Draft Convention Relating to the Status of Refugees (and Stateless Persons) (E/AC.32.2), E/AC.32/L.4 (18 January 1950), Art. 1A(3)(b).
31 See, for example, H. Crawley, *Refugees and Gender, Law and Process*, Bristol: Jordan Publishing, 2001.
32 On the public/private divide, see, H. Charlesworth, C. Chinkin and S. Wright, 'Feminist approaches to international law', in R. J. Beck, A. C. Arend, and R. D. Vander Lugt (eds), *International Rules: Approaches from International Law and International Relations*, Oxford: Oxford University Press, 1996; on the application of feminist jurisprudence to the CRC, see F. Olsen, 'Children's rights: Some feminist approaches to the United Nations Convention on the Rights of the Child', *International Journal of Law and the Family* 6, 1992, 192–220; on the difficulties of non-prototypical refugees, see J. Bhabha, 'Demography and rights: Women, children and access to asylum', *International Journal of Refugee Law* 16, 2004, 227–243.
33 Quoted by A. Edwards, 'Age and gender dimensions in international refugee law' in E. Feller, V. Türk and F. Nicholson (eds), *Refugee Protection in International Law, UNHCR's Global Consultations on International Protection*, Cambridge: Cambridge University Press, 2003, 46, n. 1.

the Com. RC,[34] UNHCR[35] and the Executive Committee of the High Commissioner's Programme (UNHCR Excom)[36] in the past five years or so.[37]

However, there is a major obstacle that is not expressly recognised by any of the above bodies. While it is true that international human rights law has had a powerful influence on our understanding of the refugee definition, the concept of *non-refoulement* and the emergence of the notion of complementary protection, the influence has come mainly from one branch of human rights law, namely, the civil and political branch.[38] Thus, the concept of persecution is typically informed by the denial of civil liberties such as freedom of thought, conscience and religion, freedom of association and assembly, freedom from arbitrary arrest and detention. Complementary protection is a response to the extra-territorial dimension of the prohibition of torture and a (very) limited number of other civil and political rights.[39] But the idea that economic, social and cultural rights should have an extraterritorial dimension has traditionally been resisted.[40] Indeed, typically, a rigid distinction is maintained between violations of civil and political rights, which are regarded as refugee-relevant, and economic, social and cultural rights, which are not, the purpose of which is to maintain a clear demarcation between the refugee and the economic migrant. A denial of economic, social and cultural rights can be refugee-relevant, not *per se*, but as evidence of discrimination that may amount to persecution if it leads to 'consequences of a substantially prejudicial nature'.[41] Even then, it

---

34 Com. RC, General Comment No. 6, *op cit*.
35 UNHCR Guidelines on Child Asylum Claims, *op cit*.
36 Executive Committee Conclusion No. 107 (LVIII) – 2007, 'Children at Risk'.
37 Earlier, less focused efforts to make the rights of the child refugee-relevant can be discerned in UNHCR, 'Guidelines on Policies and Procedures in dealing with Unaccompanied Children Seeking Asylum' (1997) and 'Refugee Children, Guidelines on Protection and Care' (1994).
38 See generally, K. Wouters, *International Legal Standards for the Protection from Refoulement*, Mortsel: Intersentia, 2009.
39 For example, the right to life (e.g. ECtHR, *Bader and others v Sweden*, Appl No. 13284/04, Judgment 8 November 2005) and the right to a fair trial (e.g. ECtHR, *Othman (Abu Qatada) v The United Kingdom*, Appl. No. 8139/09, Judgment of 17 January 2012).
40 The ECtHR is generally reluctant to categorise violations of economic, social and cultural rights as inhuman or degrading treatment contrary to Article 3 ECHR, with the result that such violations do not usually fall within the scope of the *non-refoulement* guarantee. However, the Court's case-law on this issue is developing quickly though not always consistently. For a cross-section of cases, see: ECtHR, *D. v UK*, Appl. No. 30240/96, Judgment of 2 May 1997; *N v The United Kingdom*, Appl. No. 26565/05, Judgment (GC) of 27 May 2008; *M.S.S. v Belgium and Greece*, Appl. No. 30696/09, Judgment of 21 January 2011; *Sufi and Elmi v The United Kingdom*, Appl. Nos. 8319/07 and 11449/07, Judgment of 28 June 2011; *S.H.H. v UK*, Appl. No. 60367/10, Judgment of 29 January 2013; *I.K. v Austria*, Appl. No, 2964/12, Judgment of 28 March 2013; *H. and B.*, Appl. No. 7073/10 and 44539/11, Judgment of 9 April 2013.
41 See UNHCR Handbook (1979), *op cit.*, paras. 54 and 55.

must be linked to one of the grounds of persecution, each of which relate to aspects of civil or political identity.

What has this got to do with establishing that the rights of the child are refugee-relevant? A typology of the rights in the CRC will help to illustrate the problem. There are a number of different ways of classifying the rights in the CRC. The dominant approach is classification according to the '3 Ps': 1) the protection of children against discrimination and all forms of neglect and exploitation; 2) the provision of assistance for their basic needs; 3) and the participation of children in decisions affecting their lives.[42] However, the '3 Ps' scheme has attracted criticism because it departs from the usual classification of rights into civil and political rights, on the one hand, and socio-economic rights, on the other, thereby suggesting that the rights of the child are a different species entirely from general human rights and making their acceptance as part of the orthodoxy difficult.[43] While this argument is compelling, in fact not all the rights of the child in the CRC can be categorised along usual lines. Therefore, the typology proposed here is based on the usual classification of rights into civil and political rights and economic, social and cultural rights but it adds a further category of rights, namely, protection rights (see Table 3.1 at the end of this chapter). The bias in refugee law towards violations of civil and political rights will be assessed in relation to each category in turn.

First, as regards civil and political rights, it can be observed that the bias towards these types of rights in refugee law disadvantages children because children are often perceived as not having a civil and political status. This is in part a legacy of the traditional resistance to the idea of children as rights-holders and in part rooted in a Western idealised conception of childhood as apolitical and unburdened by 'adult' concerns.[44] Here, the CRC is of assistance because some 21 of the rights it contains can be classified as 'civil and political' rights. These include such typical civil and political rights as freedom of expression; freedom of thought, conscience and religion; privacy; freedom from arbitrary arrest and detention; and freedom from torture or other cruel, inhuman or degrading treatment or punishment. The fact that all children have these rights confirms not only their civil and political status, but also the fact that children suffer egregiously from violations of these

---

42 See G. Van Bueren, *The International Law on the Rights of the Child*, The Hague/Boston/London: Martinus Nijhoff Publishers, 1998, 15. In fact, Van Bueren identifies four 'Ps', the fourth being 'prevention'. Generally, however, protection and prevention are assimilated, thus leaving three 'Ps'. M. Freeman notes that 'the triad is accepted by virtually every writer on the UNCRC': *Article 3 The Best Interests of the Child, A Commentary on the United Nations Convention on the Rights of the Child*, Leiden: Martinus Nijhoff Publishers, 2007, note 263.
43 A. Quennerstedt, 'Children, but not really humans? Critical reflections on the hampering effect of the "3 Ps"', *International Journal of Children's Rights* 18, 2010, 619–635.
44 See P. Aries, *Centuries of Childhood*, New York: Vintage Books, 1962.

Table 3.1 Typology of rights in the Convention on the Rights of the Child

Rights in the CRC	Civil and political	Economic, social and cultural	Protection	Not a right/ defies tri-partite classification
Article 1: Definition of child				X
Article 2: Right to non-discrimination (a general principle of the Convention)	X	X	X	
Article 3: Best interests of the child (a general principle of the Convention)	X	X	X	
Article 4: Nature of the legal obligation in the CRC				X
Article 5: Rights and responsibilities of parents, family etc.	X (right to family life)		X (responsibilities of parents)	
Article 6: Right to life, survival and development (a general principle of the Convention)	X	X	X	
Article 7: Name, nationality, right to be cared for by parents	X		X	
Article 8: Preservation of identity, nationality, name, family relations	X		X	
Article 9: Right not to be separated from parents against their will	X		X	
Article 10: Family reunification	X		X	
Article 11: Illicit transfer and non-return of children abroad	X		X	

(Continued)

Table 3.1 Typology of rights in the Convention on the Rights of the Child (continued)

Rights in the CRC	Civil and political	Economic, social and cultural	Protection	Not a right/ defies tri-partite classification
Article 13: Freedom of expression	X			
Article 14: Freedom of thought, conscience and religion	X			
Article 15: Freedom of association and assembly	X			
Article 16: Privacy	X			
Article 17: Mass media	X			
Article 18: Common responsibilities of parents; appropriate assistance to parents		X (appropriate assistance to parents)	X (common responsibilities of parents)	
Article 19: Protection from all types of violence			X	
Article 20: Special protection, assistance and alternative care for children deprived of family environment			X	
Article 21: Adoption			X	
Article 22: Right of asylum-seeking/refugee child to appropriate protection and assistance	X	X	X	
Article 23: Rights of the child with disability	X	X	X	
Article 24: Right to health		X		
Article 25: Care placement for physical or mental health		X		
Article 26: Right to social security		X		
Article 27: Right to an adequate standard of living		X		
Articles 28 and 29: Right to education		X		
Article 30: Rights of minority children	X	X		

Article				
Article 31: Right to rest, leisure, play, recreational activities	X			
Article 32: Protection from economic exploitation		X	X	
Article 33: Protection from illicit use of narcotic drugs			X	
Article 34: Protection from exploitation and sexual abuse			X	
Article 35 and Optional Protocol: Prevention of abduction, sale, traffic in children				
Article 36: Protection from all other forms of exploitation			X	
Article 37: Prohibition of torture etc.	X			
Article 37 (cont.): Right to liberty and conditions of detention	X			
Article 38 and Optional Protocol: Prohibition of underage recruitment and participation in hostilities			X	
Article 39: Right to recovery and reintegration of child victim of various forms of ill-treatment		X (Right to health)	X	
Article 40: Juvenile justice	X			
Article 41: Guarantee clause				X
Total number	21	16	23	3

rights.[45] Moreover, as outlined in Chapter 2, none of the rights in the CRC is subject to derogation in times of public emergency.

Second, the bias towards civil and political rights in refugee law disadvantages children because sixteen of the rights in the CRC can be classified as economic, social and cultural rights. Indeed, the CRC was pioneering in its attempt to break down the artificial barrier between civil and political rights, on the one hand, and economic, social and cultural rights, on the other. Consequently, the CRC can be regarded as a real (as opposed to a rhetorical) attempt to bring the doctrine of indivisibility through to its logical conclusion. The economic, social and cultural rights in the CRC include the right to survival and development (which, together with the right to life, is one of the general principles of the Convention), the right to health (which incorporates an obligation to abolish harmful traditional practices such as female genital mutilation), the right to education and the right to an adequate standard of living. UNHCR stresses the importance of such rights to determining whether the child has an international protection need, stating:

> Children's socio-economic needs are often more compelling than those of adults, particularly due to their dependency on adults and unique developmental needs. Deprivation of economic, social and cultural rights, thus, may be as relevant to the assessment of a child's claim as that of civil and political rights. It is important not to automatically attribute greater significance to certain violations than to others but to assess the overall impact of the harm on the individual child.[46]

Third, and perhaps most importantly, 23 of the rights in the CRC do not fit into the traditional divide. These rights are most appropriately classified as protection-related rights and are *child-specific*. They include such rights as protection from physical, mental and sexual violence; special protection for the child deprived of family; appropriate protection and humanitarian assistance for the refugee and asylum-seeking child; protection from exploitation and sexual abuse; protection against trafficking; protection against under-age recruitment; and the right to recovery and reintegration of the child victim of, *inter alia*, armed conflict. While the subject matter of these rights (i.e. protection) is particularly relevant to the question of international protection, the fact that these are not civil and political rights combined with the public/private divide alluded to earlier may prevent decision-makers from perceiving the relevance.

---

45 For a recent example, see 'Report of the Independent International Commission of Inquiry on the Syrian Arab Republic to the UN Human Rights Council', *A/HRC/24/46*, 16 August 2013, which notes that children are victims of, *inter alia*, executions, forced recruitments, arbitrary detention, torture and inhuman or degrading treatment or punishment.
46 UNHCR Guidelines on Child Asylum Claims, *op cit.*, para. 14.

When the bias in refugee law towards civil and political rights is superimposed on the typology of rights in the CRC outlined above (viz. civil and political rights, economic, social and cultural rights and protection rights), it becomes clear that not all the rights of the child in the CRC are likely to be recognised as relevant to international protection. UNHCR attempts to address this dilemma, but, it is submitted, without a clear sense of what the problem is.[47] Thus, in affirming the centrality of 'child-specific rights' (by which it means the standards of the CRC), it distinguishes between 'child-related manifestations of persecution' (i.e. same harm as adults, but differently experienced) and 'child-specific forms of persecution'. As regards the latter, UNHCR provides the following examples: under-age recruitment, child trafficking and labour, female genital mutilation, domestic violence against children and violations of economic, social and cultural rights. Apart from the objection that UNHCR's typology is confusing and inaccurate,[48] it leads UNHCR out of the domain of legal obligation and into the realm of appeals to common-sense discretion. For example, as regards so-called child-related manifestations of persecution, UNHCR warns about the need to adjust the threshold level of harm accordingly, since a level that might not amount to persecution in the case of an adult might well do in the case of a child, owing to his/her 'immaturity, vulnerability, undeveloped coping mechanisms and dependency as well as the differing stages of development and hindered capacities'. A similar appeal to discretion is evident in the quote about economic, social and cultural rights cited above.

It is submitted that this analysis is wrong-headed. It is less a case of lowering the threshold for what constitutes a serious violation of a given right because the applicant is a child and more a case of situating the analysis in the context of the child version of the right; frequently the child version of the right will contain a different level of intrinsic severity than the 'adult' counterpart.[49] To give just one example from the rights analysed in later chapters of this book, the right to liberty/freedom from arbitrary arrest or detention in the CRC is qualitatively different from corresponding rights in the ECHR and the ICCPR. Hence, the obligation to undertake a different threshold analysis derives from the nature of the right itself, not from any (discretionary) common sense about children. Furthermore, once attention is drawn to the CRC as the locus of child-rights, then it is a simple matter to accept that all the rights therein are potentially relevant to eligibility for international protection. The next

---

47 *Ibid*.
48 It falls foul of Quennerstedt's injunction to analyse child rights, insofar as it is possible to do so, according to the vocabulary used for general human rights. A. Quennerstedt, *op cit*.
49 Thus, Goodwin Gill notes that '[i]n certain cases the CRC ensures that children are even better protected than adults'. G. Goodwin-Gill, 'Unaccompanied refugee minors, The role and place of international law in the pursuit of durable solutions', *International Journal of Children's Rights* 3, 1995, 405–416, 411.

section evaluates the extent to which the relevant CEAS instrument evidences an acceptance of this proposition.

Phase One CEAS: Eligibility concepts and the rights of the child

The question for resolution is whether the concepts in the CEAS instruments that relate to eligibility for international protection are sensitive to child-rights and child-rights violations, or conversely, whether they reproduce the bias in refugee law towards civil and political rights. The analysis that follows is of the key concepts relating to inclusion, cessation and exclusion – concepts that are found in the QD. Specifically, an analysis is offered of the refugee definition, the definition of serious harm, sources of harm and protection, the concept of internal protection, cessation and exclusion.[50]

The refugee definition

According to Article 2 QD, the definition of refugee in the directive is the same that in Article 1A(2) of the 1951 Convention, but important guidance is provided in the directive on what constitutes an act of persecution and on the reasons for persecution.

I. ACTS OF PERSECUTION

Article 9 QD (Acts of persecution) provides in paragraph 1:

> Acts of persecution within the meaning of Article 1(A) of the Geneva Convention must:
> a be sufficiently serious by their nature or repetition as to constitute a severe violation of basic human rights, in particular the rights from which derogation cannot be made under Article 15(2) of the European Convention for the Protection of Human Rights and Fundamental Freedoms; or
> b be an accumulation of various measures, including violations of human rights which is sufficiently severe as to affect an individual in a similar manner as mentioned in (a).

Two observations can be made about these provisions. First, the threshold level of harm is high: a severe violation of basic human rights, whether on a

---

50 Unfortunately, space does not permit an analysis of the so-called 'safe country' concepts that are provided for in the APD (safe country of origin, first country of asylum, safe third country, European safe third country), and indeed in the DR, which is predicated on the notion that all EU Member States are safe third countries. These concepts implicitly restrict inclusion. However, the type of analysis conducted here can be readily transferred to the methodology used to determine whether a country is 'safe'.

one-off or cumulative basis. This level is mandatory and inflexible. Second, a particular sub-group of human rights are identified as being particularly relevant to a finding of persecution: rights in the ECHR – hence civil and political rights – and moreover, non-derogable rights in the ECHR.[51] Indeed the CJEU has held that acts which undoubtedly infringe a right in the EU Charter of Fundamental Rights but the gravity of which is not equivalent to the infringement of a non-derogable right in the ECHR cannot amount to persecution within the meaning of Article 9(1) QD.[52] The non-derogable rights in the ECHR comprise the right to life (except in respect of deaths resulting from lawful acts of war), freedom from torture or inhuman or degrading treatment or punishment, the prohibition of slavery and the prohibition of retrospective punishment. Notably, each corresponds to a right in the CRC.[53] But what about the numerous other rights of the child, including other civil and political rights, economic, social and cultural rights and child-protection rights, all of which are non-derogable under the CRC scheme?

Article 9(2) on acts of persecution is of utmost importance in this regard. It states:

> Acts of persecution as qualified in paragraph 1, can, *inter alia*, take the form of:
>
> a   acts of physical or mental violence, including acts of sexual violence;
> b   legal, administrative, police, and/or judicial measures which are in themselves discriminatory or which are implemented in a discriminatory manner;
> c   denial of judicial redress resulting in a disproportionate or discriminatory punishment;
> d   prosecution or punishment for refusal to perform military service in a conflict, where performing military service would include crimes or acts falling under the exclusion clauses as set out in Article 12(2);
> e   acts of a gender-specific or child-specific nature.

The problem of threshold (sufficiently serious/severe violation) is carried over from Article 9(1) by virtue of the *chapeau* in Article 9(2). However, if the acts of persecution are interpreted by reference to the rights in the CRC, as was previously argued for, then the threshold of seriousness is already included in the definition of the right itself. The question, then, is whether any of the acts in Article 9(2) correspond to rights in the CRC. While all of the acts as listed

---

51   Thus, the CJEU has described refugee protection under the QD as relating to 'individual liberties'. CJEU, *Abdulla and Others*, Joined Cases C-175/08, C-176/08, C-178/08 and C-179/08, Judgment of 2 March 2010, para. 90.
52   *Y and Z*, Joined Cases C-71/11 and C-99/11, Judgment of 5 September 2012, para. 61.
53   Article 6(1), Article 37(a), Article 35 (if one classifies trafficking as a modern form of slavery) and Article 40(2)(a), respectively.

are potentially relevant to the claims of children, sub-paragraphs (a), (d) and (e) are of particular interest.

Sub-paragraph (a) covers violence against children (whether physical, mental or sexual). It corresponds to several of the protective rights in the CRC, such as protection against all forms of physical or mental violence, injury or abuse including sexual abuse in Article 19. It cuts across the public/private divide since violence against children is known to be perpetrated in the public sphere (e.g. in State institutions) as well in the private sphere, (e.g. as in the case of domestic violence). Moreover, sub-paragraph (a) also allows for human trafficking – a contentious issue in the refugee context – to be comprehended as persecution, at least when the victim is a child.[54] In this regard, UNHCR notes:

> The trafficking of a child is a serious violation of a range of fundamental rights and, therefore, constitutes persecution. These rights include the right to life, survival and development, the right to protection from all forms of violence, including sexual exploitation and abuse, and the right to protection from child labour and abduction, sale and trafficking, as specifically provided for by Article 35 of the CRC.[55]

Sub-paragraph (e) corresponds, according to the typology advanced earlier, to all the protective rights in the CRC, some of which overlap with economic, social and cultural rights. Furthermore, the reference to gender-specific acts is important because, in the case of the girl-child, there is often an overlap between gender and age in terms of rights violations. The practice of female genital mutilation is a case in point.[56] Unfortunately, such violations are often overlooked because, as Taefi notes, '[g]irls are marginalized within the category of children as female, and within the category of women as minors'.[57] Against this backdrop, the reference to gender- specific and child-specific forms of persecution in the same sub-paragraph is potentially helpful because it can serve to integrate the two concepts.

Finally, sub-paragraph (d) can be interpreted as covering prosecution or punishment for refusal to perform military service by a child under the age

---

54 See UNHCR, 'Guidelines on International Protection: The application of Article 1A(2) of the 1951 Convention and/or 1967 Protocol relating to the status of refugees to victims of trafficking and persons at risk of being trafficked', *HCR/GIP/06/07 (2006)*.
55 UNHCR Guidelines on Child Asylum Claims, *op cit.*, para. 26.
56 Other examples are: forced or early marriages, ritual killing of girls, dowry violence, virginity testing, girl-child infanticide and selective abortions.
57 N. Taefi, 'The synthesis of age and gender: Intersectionality, international human rights law and the marginalisation of the girl-child', *International Journal of Children's Rights* 17, 2009, 345–376, 345. See further, K. Backstrom, 'The international human rights of the child: Do they protect the female child?', *George Washington Journal of International Law and Economics* 30, 1996–1997, 541–582.

of fifteen.[58] This is because the crimes or acts falling under the exclusion clause as set out in Article 12(2) include war crimes 'as defined in the international instruments drawn up to make provision in respect of such crimes'. The Rome Statute of the International Criminal Court classifies as war crimes the enlistment and use of children under the age of fifteen years as combatants, whether in the armed forces of the State or in opposition forces.[59] This reflects the prohibition of the recruitment or direct participation in hostilities of children under the age of fifteen in Article 38 CRC.[60] One criticism can be made, however, of sub-paragraph (d): it has a hidden adult bias. The focus on prosecution or punishment for refusal to perform military service suggests that the persecution emanates from the denial of a right of conscientious objection (another civil liberty). While children may well be conscientious objectors, it is submitted that the greater persecution in their case derives from the threat of military service itself. Thus, according to the Com. RC:

> [U]nderage recruitment (including of girls for sexual services or forced marriage with the military) and direct or indirect participation in hostilities constitutes a serious human rights violation and thereby persecution, and should lead to the granting of refugee status where the well-founded fear of such recruitment or participation in hostilities is based on 'reasons of race, religion, nationality, membership of a particular social group or political opinion' (article 1A(2), 1951 Refugee Convention).[61]

Despite this criticism, it is considered that Article 9(2) QD is generally positive from the point of view of incorporating the rights of the child into the concept of persecution. Moreover, the acts of persecution listed in Article 9(2) are illustrative, not exhaustive, enabling violations of child-rights that do not fit easily within the list to be comprehended as persecution. It is submitted that Article 9(2) neutralises the potentially negative effect of Article 9(1) taken alone.

---

58 A question on the interpretation of Article 9(2)(d) has been referred to the CJEU: *Shepherd*, Case C-472/13, Request for a preliminary ruling lodged on 2 December 2013.
59 Rome Statute of the International Criminal Court, UN Doc. A/CONF.183/9, Article 8(2)(b)(xxvi) relating to international armed conflict and Article 8(2)(e)(vii) relating to armed conflicts not of an international character.
60 The raising of the age for forced recruitment and direct participation in hostilities to eighteen in the case of states parties and the complete ban on recruitment (whether forced or voluntary) of under eighteens by non-state actors in the Optional Protocol to the CRC do not (yet) constitute war crimes, but UNHCR considers the Optional Protocol evidence of a 'strong trend for a complete ban on under-age recruitment'. UNHCR Guidelines on Child Asylum Claims, *op cit.*, p. 10, footnote 42.
61 Com. RC, General Comment No. 6, *op cit.*, para. 59.

II. REASONS FOR PERSECUTION

The reasons for persecution are *per* the 1951 Convention (namely, race, religion, nationality, membership of a particular social group and political opinion), but they are elaborated on in Article 10(1) QD. The question arises whether the reasons thus enlarged on are consistent with the reasons children are persecuted. Attention will be focused here on two of the grounds of persecution that are particularly relevant to children's asylum claims, namely, 'membership of a particular social group' and 'political opinion'.

'Membership of a particular social group' is a ground that is particularly important for children's asylum claims for two reasons: because of the lack of an explicit age ground and because of the difficulties children may experience in having their claims recognised under the other grounds due to a perceived lack of civil or political status. Article 10(1)(d) provides:

> A group shall be considered to form a particular social group where in particular:
>
> — members of that group share an innate characteristic, or a common background that cannot be changed, or share a characteristic or belief that is so fundamental to identity or conscience that a person should not be forced to renounce it; and
> — that group has a distinct identity in the relevant society, because it is perceived as being different by the surrounding society.

These tests are familiar from UNHCR's guidelines on membership of a particular social group, but with one critical difference: whereas UNHCR presents the tests as being alternatives (i.e. the group may be identified *either* by the innate/fundamental characteristics test *or* the social perception test), the QD presents the tests as being cumulative (i.e. two prongs of a single test).[62] This seriously disadvantages claims of persecution on grounds of age. For example, a claim by a fourteen-year old former child soldier may not meet the requirements of the innate characteristics test if an unenlightened approach is taken to age as something that is constantly changing;[63] but it may meet the social perception test if child soldiers are a readily identifiable group in that particular society. Consequently, the applicant will qualify under the second test but not the first, and, it follows, not both taken together. It is unfortunate then, that the two tests are presented in Article 10(1)(d) QD as being cumulative.

---

62 UNHCR, 'Guidelines on International Protection: "Membership of a particular social group" within the context of Article 1A(2) of the 1951 Convention and/or its 1967 Protocol relating to the Status of Refugees', *HCR/GIP/02/02 (2002)*.

63 As one commentator bluntly put it: children's 'main remedy is to grow up'. O. O'Neill, 'Children's rights and children's lives', *International Journal of Law and the Family* 6, 1992, 39.

However, the reference to the phrase 'in particular' may allow for flexibility in this regard.[64]

The 'political opinion' ground is important for children's asylum claims because children can be politically active and, hence, their claims should not be automatically corralled into 'membership of a particular social group'.[65] However, the political opinions of children are unlikely to be recognised if a narrow interpretation is given to the concept of political opinion. Such an interpretation is typified by Grahl Madsen's understanding of the concept as 'opinions contrary to or critical of the policies of the government or ruling party', which suggests an opinion grounded in a political philosophy or ideology (in a Western 'Enlightenment' sense).[66] While some of today's conflicts do fit this stereotype, many identity-based and resource-driven conflicts of the post-Cold War era are less ideological.[67] The protagonists may not be the government or ruling party. And children's involvement in them may be peripheral and practical – acting as couriers or participating in demonstrations, for example – but nonetheless important for that.[68] In such contexts, political activity *is* political opinion, but only if political opinion is construed broadly, for example, along the lines suggested by Goodwin Gill, i.e. 'any opinion on any matter in which the machinery of the State, government and policy may be engaged'.[69] Indeed, one might go further and suggest that political opinion is anything that engages – in whatever large or small way – the dominant power structures (both State and non-State) in society.

In short, in order for the full gamut of children's political opinion to be comprehended as political opinion proper, it is important that the term be given a broad construction. In this regard, Article 10(1)(e) QD states: 'The concept of a political opinion shall in particular include the holding of an opinion, thought or belief on *a matter related to the potential actors of persecution* mentioned in Article 6 and to their *policies or methods*, whether or not that

---

64 In the only judgment to date on the issue, the Court was not required to pronounce on whether the tests in Article 10(1)(d) could be alternatives because the putative social group – homosexuals – met both tests anyway, the first test on principle and the second test on the facts: *X, Y and Z*, Joined Cases C-199/12 to C-201/12, Judgment of 7 November 2013. However, in her opinion on the case, Advocate General Sharpston considered the tests to be cumulative: Opinion of A. G. Sharpston, delivered on 11 July 2013, para. 34.
65 Writing in the North American context, Bhabha notes that children whose claims to international protection are based on their own activism are less likely to be recognised than children whose claims are based on their vulnerability as children. J. Bhabha, 'Minors or aliens? Inconsistent State intervention and separated child asylum-seekers', *European Journal of Migration and Law* 3, 2001, 283–314.
66 A. Grahl-Madsen, *The Status of Refugees in International Law*, Leyden: Sijthoff, 1972, 220.
67 Contrast the political opinions that have led to the 'Arab Spring' with some of the recent and on-going conflicts in sub-Saharan Africa.
68 UNHCR Guidelines on Child Asylum Claims, *op cit.*, p. 18.
69 G. Goodwin Gill, *The Refugee in International Law*, 2nd ed., Oxford: Oxford University Press, 1996, 49.

opinion, thought or belief has been acted upon by the applicant'.[70] It is submitted that this provision does three noteworthy things. First, it grounds the concept of political opinion in the political culture of origin (as opposed to any Western conception of political opinion). Second, it links the opinion to the potential actors of persecution. Article 6 QD establishes that actors of persecution (or serious harm) are not confined to State actors but extend to parties or organisations controlling the State or a substantial part of it and to non-State actors if the authorities are unable or unwilling to provide protection.[71] This is highly significant in the context of children's asylum claims because of the often private nature of the harm suffered, for example, at the hands of parents, carers and authority figures in the community. Where children take a view on the workings of the actors of persecution, this is a political opinion. Finally, Article 10(1)(e) connects the political opinion to the policies *or* methods of the potential actors of persecution, establishing that the opinion need not be ideological. Seen from the perspective of why children tend to be persecuted, Article 10(1)(e) can be regarded as a positive provision.

Equally important is the assertion in Article 10(2) that the grounds of persecution need not be actually possessed by the applicant, 'providing that such a characteristic is attributed to the applicant by the actor of persecution'. This is critical in the context of children's asylum claims, as frequently the persecution will be meted out because of the assumption that the child shares, for example, the religious beliefs or political opinion of the parent(s), clan or ethnic group. This is underscored by Recital 27 of the directive, which notes that '[f]amily members, merely due to their relation to the refugee, will normally be vulnerable to acts of persecution in such a manner that could be the basis for refugee status'.

There is one further provision of the QD that is relevant to the present analysis. Article 9(3) QD establishes that 'there must be a connection between the reasons mentioned in Article 10 and the acts of persecution as qualified in [Article 9(1)]'. This is not new – a causal connection is implicit in the wording of Article 1A(2) of the 1951 Convention, which provides that a refugee is someone who has a well-founded fear of being persecuted 'for reasons of' race, religion etc. However, Article 9(3) takes a position on a hitherto unresolved debate about non-State actors of persecution and whether the link to the ground is confined to the actor of persecution or can equally be drawn to the reason the State failed to protect.[72] As previously noted, the QD

---

70 Emphasis added.
71 Prior to the QD, there was a considerable divergence in State practice between EU Member States on the question of whether persecution by non-State actors was refugee-relevant. See, for example, ECtHR, *T.I. v United Kingdom*, Appl. No. 43844/98, Judgment of 7 March 2000.
72 UNHCR rather blurs the issue, stating, 'As with adult claims to refugee status, it is necessary to establish whether or not the child's well-founded fear of persecution is linked to one or more of the five grounds listed in Article 1A(2) of the 1951 Convention. It is sufficient that the Convention ground be a *factor relevant to the persecution*, but is not necessary that it be the sole, or even dominant, cause.' Emphasis added. UNHCR Guidelines on Child Asylum Claims, *op cit.*, para. 40.

is commendably progressive on the issue of non-State actors of persecution. However, Article 9(3) appears to be a retrograde step in this regard because, on its face, it precludes satisfying definitional requirements by making a connection between the persecution and the reason the State failed to protect.[73] An example will help to illustrate the problem. An insurgent group may recruit children because it desperately needs combatants (of any age), but the State may be unwilling to protect the children or a sub-group of them for reasons of race, religion, nationality, social group or political opinion. Article 9(3) QD effectively means that such claims are not refugee-relevant, unless, as seems unlikely, a highly creative approach is taken to the grounds.

To conclude, the provisions of the QD relating to the reasons for persecution are a mixed bag from the point of view of the rights of the child. 'Membership of a particular social group' appears to require a two-pronged cumulative test. 'Political opinion', on the other hand, is defined broadly. Helpfully, the grounds of persecution need not actually be held by the actor but, unhelpfully, it seems that the nexus to the grounds can only be drawn to the persecution, not the reason the State failed to protect. In sum, the reasons for persecution as outlined in the QD contain both positive and negative aspects from the perspective of the rights of the child.

The definition of 'serious harm'

According to Recital 24 QD, '[s]ubsidiary protection should be complementary and additional to the refugee protection enshrined in the Geneva Convention'. The question is whether the definition of 'serious harm' for the purposes of subsidiary protection status expands the circumstances in which child-rights violations are recognised as relevant to international protection. Article 2(e) QD defines a person eligible for subsidiary protection as someone in respect of whom 'substantial grounds have been shown' for believing that, if returned to his/her country of origin, he/she 'would face a real risk of suffering serious harm'. Serious harm is defined in Article 15 as:

a   death penalty or execution; or
b   torture or inhuman or degrading treatment or punishment of an applicant in the country of origin, or
c   serious and individual threat to a civilian's life or person by reason of indiscriminate violence in situations of international or internal armed conflict.

---

73   It is interesting to note that the courts in no less than ten Member States have ruled that the nexus requirement is also fulfilled where there is a connection between the acts of persecution and the absence of protection against such acts. See 'Report from the Commission to the European Parliament and the Council on the Application of Directive 2004/83/EC of 29 April 2004 on Minimum Standards for the Qualification and Status of Third Country Nationals or Stateless Persons as Refugees or as Persons who Otherwise Need International Protection and the Content of the Protection', *COM (2010) 314 final*, § 5.2.1, p. 8. Hereinafter, 'Commission evaluation of the QD'.

As has been noted by commentators, there is a large degree of overlap between the harms in (a) and (b) and the acts of persecution as defined in Article 9 QD.[74] In this regard, ground (c) appears to be the most fertile, although some of its limitations should be noted.

First, Article 15(c) applies in situations of international or internal armed conflict. As the link between armed conflict and child-rights violations is well established, this provision is potentially useful for children in such situations.[75] However, Article 15(c) does not apply in peacetime. Consequently, ordinary 'common or garden' violations of children's human rights are not cognisable, which is a clear protection gap. Moreover, if the term 'internal armed conflict' is interpreted consistently with the concept of non-international armed conflict in international humanitarian law, then this excludes violations of children's rights that occur in situations of internal disturbance and tension and in situations of low-level insurgency.[76] Hence, the focus on armed conflict excludes many potential child-rights violations. On the other hand, the focus on armed conflict compensates for the prioritisation of non-derogable rights in the definition of persecution – the implication there being that violations of rights that can be legitimately derogated from in times of emergency (such as armed conflicts) are less readily identifiable as persecution.

Second, the threat must be to a civilian's life or person, as distinct from a combatant's. This makes no allowance for the phenomenon of under-age recruitment. Yet, as has already been observed, children fleeing such recruitment may struggle to make out a link to a Convention ground and consequently may have difficulties in being recognised as refugees. The value-added of subsidiary protection should kick in here, but this is precluded by the restriction of the personal scope of Article 15(c) to civilians.

---

74 See, for example, C. Teitgen-Colly, 'The European Union and asylum: An illusion of protection', *Common Market Law Review* 43 (2006): 1503–1566.
75 See, for example, United Nations, 'Impact of Armed Conflict on Children: Report of the expert of the Secretary General, Ms Graça Machel, submitted pursuant to General Assembly Resolution 481/157', *UN Doc. A/51/306 (1996)*.
76 A preliminary reference has been made to the CJEU on the question of whether Article 15(c) QD offers protection only in a situation of 'internal armed conflict' as interpreted by international humanitarian law and, in particular, by reference to Common Article 3 of the four Geneva Conventions of 1949: *Diakite*, Case C-285/12, Reference for a preliminary ruling lodged on 7 June 2012. With respect, given that Common Article 3 does not contain a definition of internal armed conflict, a more apt question is whether Article 15(c) QD should be interpreted by reference to Protocol II Additional to the Geneva Convention 1977. Article 1 thereof defines non-international armed conflict as armed conflict that takes place 'in the territory of a High Contracting Party between its armed forces and dissident armed forces or other organized armed groups which, under responsible command, exercise such control over a part of its territory as to enable them to carry out sustained and concerted military operations and to implement this Protocol [excluding, however] situations of internal disturbances and tensions, such as riots, isolated and sporadic acts of violence and other acts of a similar nature, as not being armed conflicts'.

Finally, there is the apparent contradiction between an *individual* threat and *indiscriminate* violence. This was addressed by the Court of Justice in *Elgafaji*, although the Court may well have confused as much as it illuminated.[77] The question the Dutch Council of State referred to the Court was whether Article 15(c) QD had a distinct scope from that of Article 3 ECHR, which is generally regarded as being reflected in Article 15(b) QD. The confusion arose from a 2008 ruling by the ECtHR in *NA. v The United Kingdom*, in which the Court stated that it:

> has never excluded the possibility that a general situation of violence in a country of destination will be of a sufficient level of intensity as to entail that any removal to it would necessarily breach Article 3 of the Convention. Nevertheless the Court would adopt such an approach only in the most extreme cases of general violence, where there is a real risk of ill-treatment simply by virtue of an individual being exposed to such violence on return.[78]

If a situation of indiscriminate violence could engage Article 3 ECHR, then what is the value-added of Article 15(c) QD? In attempting to answer this question, the CJEU distinguished between Article 15(b) QD, which corresponds to Article 3 ECHR, and Article 15(c), which the Court said is different and must be interpreted in such a way that it has its own field of application. However, the Court was constrained by the statement in Recital 26 QD that '[r]isks to which a population of a country or a section of the population is generally exposed do normally not create in themselves an individual threat which would qualify as serious harm'. In attempting to square the circle, the Court held:

> the word 'individual' must be understood as covering harm to civilians irrespective or their identity, where the degree of indiscriminate violence characterizing the armed conflict taking place [...] reaches such a high level that substantial grounds are shown for believing that a civilian, returned to the relevant country or, as the case may be, to the relevant region, would, solely on account of his presence on the territory of that country or region, face a real risk of being subject to the serious threat referred to in Article 15(c) of the Directive.[79]

Such is the parallel between this passage and the above-quoted passage from *NA.* that it is unclear where the stated difference in scope between Article 15(b)

---

77 ECJ, *Elgafaji, op cit.*
78 ECtHR, *NA. v The United Kingdom*, Appl. No. 25904/07, Judgment of 17 July 2008, para. 115.
79 Paras. 35 and 43.

and Article 15(c) actually lies.[80] The CJEU went on to say that such a degree of indiscriminate violence would be 'exceptional'; in a more normal situation (i.e. a lesser degree of indiscriminate violence), the general situation in the country would not be sufficient to meet the requirements of Article 15(c) and an applicant would have to demonstrate some personal targeting or heightened risk.[81] But in such a situation, one wonders why an applicant would not have been recognised as a refugee. Consequently, the value-added of Article 15(c) over and above Article 15(b) and over and above the refugee definition is unclear. This is attested to in a UNHCR study of State practice in relation to Article 15(c).[82] While this fact presents no greater barriers for children than it does for adults, nevertheless it further reduces the usefulness of Article 15(c) for children.[83]

In sum, the limitation in the material scope and personal scope of Article 15(c) to, respectively, situations of armed conflict and civilians, coupled with the overlap with either Article 15(b) QD or the refugee definition means that Article 15(c) offers little 'value added' to child claimants.

Sources of harm and protection

Article 6 QD specifies the identity of potential actors of persecution or serious harm, while Article 7 lists potential actors of protection. Article 6 has already been favourably commented on for its broad personal scope, which includes non-State actors of persecution or serious harm. This helps break down the public/private divide and makes children's claims more cognisable.

However, the *quid pro quo* for the acceptance in Article 6 that actors of persecution or serious harm can be non-State actors is the statement in Article 7 that actors of protection can also be non-State actors. A central part of the definition of a refugee in Article 1A(2) of the 1951 Convention is that the applicant is unable or unwilling to avail him/herself of the protection of

---

80 The ECtHR has since stated that it 'is not persuaded that Article 3 of the Convention, as interpreted in NA., does not offer comparable protection to that afforded under the [Qualification] Directive'. ECtHR, *Sufi and Elmi v The United Kingdom, op cit.*, para. 226.
81 *Elgafaji, op cit.*, paras. 37–39.
82 UNHCR, 'Safe at Last? Law and Practice in Selected EU Member States with Respect to Asylum Seekers Fleeing Indiscriminate Violence, A UNHCR Research Project' (2011), in which Article 15(c) protection is described as an 'empty shell' (p. 29). However, UNHCR notes that this is partly due to restrictive interpretations by States of Article 15(c). Lambert, on the other hand, argues that Article 15(c) provides scope for broadening protection: H. Lambert, 'The next frontier: Expanding protection in Europe for victims of armed conflict and indiscriminate violence', *International Journal of Refugee Law* 25, 2013, 207–234.
83 Contrast the judgment in *Elgafaji* with UNHCR's suggested interpretation of Article 15(c) in 'UNHCR Statement on Subsidiary Protection Under the EC Qualification Directive for People Threatened by Indiscriminate Violence', January 2008. For academic commentary, see R. Errera, 'The CJEU and subsidiary protection: Reflections on *Elgafaji* – and after', *International Journal of Refugee Law* 23, 2010, 93–112.

the State. Traditionally, this has been interpreted to mean that the State must be shown to be unable or unwilling to provide effective protection.[84] However, in view of such factors as the prevalence of internal conflicts in which control over significant parts of the territory may be exercised *de facto* by opposition forces, the international preference for internal rather than international displacement, and the rise of transitional *interim* administrations, it began to be questioned whether effective protection could not be provided by non-State entities. This idea is formalised in Article 7 QD which provides:

1. Protection can be provided by:
   a. the State; or
   b. parties or organizations, including international organizations, controlling the State or a substantial part of the territory of the State.
2. Protection is generally provided when the actors mentioned in paragraph 1 take reasonable steps to prevent the persecution or suffering of serious harm, *inter alia*, by operating an effective legal system for the detection, prosecution and punishment of acts constituting persecution or serious harm, and the applicant has access to such protection.
3. When assessing whether an international organization controls a State or a substantial part of its territory and provides protection as described in paragraph 2, Member States shall take into account any guidance which may be provided by relevant Council acts.

Before coming to the issue of non-State actors of protection, it is worth analysing Paragraph 2 from a child-rights perspective. Paragraph 2, which applies whether State or non-State actors of protection are at issue, equates protection with preventive measures including the operation of an effective legal system for the detection, prosecution and punishment of acts of persecution or serious harm provided the applicant can access such protection. While, of course, the existence of a criminal justice response is important in assessing whether a child has an international protection need, it is only part of the picture. For example, a child who claims to be a victim of persecution at the hands of his/her family, in addition to being protected in the narrow criminal justice sense, will also need special protection, assistance and alternative care (under Article 20 CRC). Similarly, a child who has been trafficked, in addition to the right to judicial redress, has a further right to recovery and reintegration (under Article 39 CRC). While such protection-related rights of the child are not precluded by the example in Article 7(2), neither are they suggested by it.

Furthermore where the actor of protection is a non-State actor, it is unlikely that such an actor would have the capacity to provide for the child's protection needs. This observation links with one of the main criticisms of the concept of non-State actors of protection from the perspective of international law,

---

84 See UNHCR Guidelines on Child Asylum Claims, *op cit.*, paras. 97–100.

which is that non-State entities typically possess less than full international legal personality because they lack all the attributes of statehood.[85] Furthermore, non-State entities are often temporary constructs and thus inherently unsuited to providing for the long-term protection needs of children. A related finding is made by the Commission in its evaluation of the QD.[86] It notes that different Member States have different criteria for holding non-State entities to be actors of protection, with some Member States insisting that the actors of protection have the attributes of a State, and others proposing transient and relatively powerless organisations as actors of protection.

In sum, while the recognition in the QD of non-State actors of persecution or serious harm is welcome from the point of view of the rights of the child, the recognition in the directive of non-State actors of protection is inimical to the rights of the child. Furthermore, the conflation of protection with a criminal justice response fails to reflect the more holistic approach to child protection that is evident in the CRC.

Internal protection

The concept of internal protection (also known as the internal flight alternative) is found in Article 8 QD. Internal protection is the notion that if part of the country of origin can be identified as safe for the applicant, then there is no need for international protection in the form of refugee or subsidiary protection. Before analysing Article 8 it is proposed firstly to outline how an analysis of internal protection should proceed. The approach advocated here follows the emerging jurisprudence of the ECtHR on internal flight in the Article 3 ECHR context.[87] Next, it is proposed to work out the implications of such analysis where the applicant is a child.

---

85 See I. Brownlie, *Principles of Public International Law*, 6th ed., Oxford: Oxford University Press, 2003, Chapter 3 (Subjects of the Law).
86 Commission evaluation of the QD, *op cit.*, § 5.1.4, p. 6.
87 The key ECtHR cases in which internal protection was rejected as being contrary to Article 3 ECHR are: *Salah Sheekh v The Netherlands* Appl. No. 1948/04, Judgment 11 January 2007 and *Sufi and Elmi v the United Kingdom, op cit.* The key cases in which internal protection was found not to violate Article 3 ECHR are: *A.a.o v Sweden*, Appl. No. 71680/10, Judgment of 27 June 2013 and *K.A.B. v Sweden*, Appl. No. 886/11, Judgment of 5 September 2013. Before the emergence of ECtHR jurisprudence on internal flight, a number of divergent approaches was advocated by UNHCR, on the one hand, and academic commentators, on the other. See UNHCR, 'Guidelines on International Protection: "Internal Flight or Relocation Alternative" Within the Context of Article 1A(2) of the 1951 Convention and/or 1967 Protocol relating to the Status of Refugees', *HCR/GIP/03/04' (2003)*. For criticism, see J. Hathaway and M. Foster, 'Internal protection/relocation/flight alternative as an aspect of refugee status determination', in E. Feller, V. Türk and F. Nicholson (eds), *Refugee Protection in International Law, UNHCR's Global Consultations on International Protection*, Cambridge: Cambridge University Press, 2003, 357–417. A thorough overview of the debate in the context of the QD is provided in J. Eaton, 'The internal protection alternative under European Union law: Examining the Recast Qualification Directive', *International Journal of Refugee Law* 24, 2012, 765–792.

Arguably, the internal protection analysis should comprise three steps. It can be assumed that the applicant has a well-founded fear of persecution or is at real risk of serious harm in the part of the country from which he/she fled, otherwise it would not be necessary to canvass the possibility of internal protection. Consequently, the first step is to assess whether the applicant would be free of the original persecution or serious harm in the proposed area of relocation. Second, unlike in the case of an 'ordinary' rejection, the applicant is not being sent home, but rather to another area of the country of origin. So, the next step is to assess whether the relocation puts him/her at risk of any other persecution or serious harm, including being subjected to dire humanitarian conditions contrary to Article 3 ECHR (and, hence, also Article 15(b) QD).[88] The third, critical, step relates to the feasibility of the concept in the specific circumstances of the case. In particular, can the applicant practically, safely and legally get to the proposed area of relocation, and once there, can he/she stay there? In other words, is the proposed area of relocation *accessible* and *sustainable*? Because if it is not, then the likelihood is that the applicant will end up back in the original area of the country in which he has a well-founded fear of persecution or a real risk of serious harm, contrary to the prohibition of (indirect) *refoulement*.[89]

When applied to child applicants, the analysis of persecution and serious harm in steps one and two should take account of child-rights violations. As regards the accessibility and sustainability requirements, these take on a whole new complexion when the applicant is a child, particularly when he/she is an unaccompanied minor. In this regard, how will the child get to the proposed area of relocation? Does he/she have family members there? Are they willing to look after him/her? If not, who will provide the alternative care and assistance to which the child is entitled? On the last question, UNHCR observes that '[i]f the only available relocation option is to place the child in institutional care, a proper assessment needs to be conducted of the care, health and educational facilities that would be provided and with regard to the long-term life prospects of adults who were institutionalized as children'.[90] In terms of the three-step approach advocated here, this follows from the requirement to assess any risk of persecution or serious harm that could arise as a result of the relocation, as well as the requirement of sustainability.

Consequently, the assessment of internal protection is a complex one; all the more so in the case of children and particularly unaccompanied minors.

---

88 ECtHR, *Sufi and Elmi v the United Kingdom, op cit*. See in particular para. 272. The second step proposed here is also consistent with the CJEU's case-law on cessation – the cessation analysis being similar to the internal protection analysis in that the former is disjointed in time, the latter disjointed in space, both arguably requiring two sets of analyses of persecution/serious harm. See CJEU, *Abdulla and Others, op cit*.
89 ECtHR, *Salah Sheekh v The Netherlands, op cit*. See, in particular, para. 141.
90 UNHCR Guidelines on Child Asylum Claims, *op cit*., para. 57, p. 21.

To what extent is this complexity reflected in the QD? Article 8 QD (Internal protection) provides:

1. As part of the assessment of the application for international protection, Member States may determine that an applicant is not in need of international protection if in a part of the country of origin there is no well-founded fear of being persecuted or no real risk of suffering serious harm and the applicant can reasonably be expected to stay in that part of the country.
2. In examining whether a part of the country of origin is in accordance with paragraph 1, Member States shall at the time of taking the decision on the application have regard to the general circumstances prevailing in that part of the country and to the personal circumstances of the applicant.
3. Paragraph 1 may apply notwithstanding technical obstacles to return to the country of origin.

On the positive side, Article 8(1) refers to the absence of a well-founded fear of persecution or real risk of serious harm. It is submitted that the categorical nature of this requirement ('no well-founded fear', 'no real risk') mandates a thorough assessment of the original fear/risk and any new fear/risk. A further mandatory requirement is that the applicant can reasonably be expected to stay in the proposed area of relocation. Although it is probably best to avoid grounding obligations in reasonableness requirements, nevertheless this requirement can be regarded as corresponding to the sustainability requirement in step three of the proposed analysis. Furthermore, Article 8(2) requires that the safety assessment be made, not only in light of general circumstances in the proposed area of relocation, but also of the personal circumstances of the applicant. It is submitted that this ensures that child-rights arguments can come to the fore.

On the negative side, Article 8(3) expressly excludes an analysis of accessibility. In this regard, it can be questioned whether, for example, locating family members or identifying a care placement for an unaccompanied minor is part of the assessment of safety under Article 8(2) or a mere 'technical obstacle to return' under Article 8(3). The Commission evaluation of the QD underscores these concerns, reporting that:

> Technical obstacles are generally defined as: lack of valid travel documents, impossibility to travel to the country of origin and lack of cooperation of authorities in the country of origin and physical inability of the applicant [due to] illness or pregnancy. Applicants falling within the scope of this paragraph are often not given any legal status or only tolerated status with limited social rights.[91]

---

91 Commission evaluation of the QD, *op cit.*, § 5.1.5, p. 7.

Consequently, depending on the approach adopted by Member States, Article 8 can be interpreted in a way that either takes account of child accessibility requirements, or disregards them. The latter scenario risks violating the *non-refoulement* obligation.

In conclusion, the concept of internal protection must be applied with care in order to conform to the requirements of international human rights and refugee law. From a child-rights perspective, a child-sensitive analysis of the accessibility and sustainability of the proposed area of relocation is key. It is submitted that this is not adequately foreseen in Article 8 QD.

Cessation

Cessation of refugee or subsidiary protection status occurs when international protection is no longer needed. The focus here will be on cessation of refugee status, since it raises substantially the same issues as cessation of subsidiary protection status. Under Article 11 QD, which generally mirrors the cessation clauses in Article 1C of the 1951 Convention, refugee status can be ceased on a number of grounds, the most common of which is the 'ceased circumstances' ground.[92] This is reflected in Article 11(1)(e) QD which provides for cessation when the refugee 'can no longer, because the circumstances in connection with which he or she has been recognized as a refugee have ceased to exist, continue to refuse to avail himself or herself of the protection of the country of nationality'. In making the decision, Article 11(2) obliges Member States to 'have regard to whether the change in circumstances is of such a significant and non-temporary nature that the refugee's fear of persecution can no longer be regarded as well-founded'.

The question that arises from a child-rights perspective is whether the change of circumstances that vitiates the need for refugee protection may or must take account of the child-rights situation. The answer seems obvious: if a risk of child-rights violations was an aspect of the claim that gave rise to refugee protection, then the changed circumstances must be shown to have eradicated such a risk. This logic was endorsed by the CJEU in the only case on cessation to come before the court to date. Thus, in *Abdulla*, the Court held that 'cessation thus implies that the change in circumstances has remedied the

---

92 The other grounds listed in Article 11(1) are: (a) the refugee has voluntarily re-availed himself or herself of the protection of the country of nationality; (b) having lost his or her nationality, has voluntarily reacquired it; (c) has acquired a new nationality and enjoys the protection of the country of his or her new nationality; (d) has voluntarily re-established himself or herself in the country which he or she left or outside which he or she remained owing to fear of persecution; (f) being a stateless person with no nationality, he or she is able, because the circumstances in connection with which he or she has been recognised as a refugee have ceased to exist, to return to the country of former habitual residence. This last ground is essentially a 'ceased circumstances' ground for stateless persons.

reasons which led to the recognition of refugee status'.[93] However, the CJEU went further. It held that not only must the circumstances that led to the original grant of refugee status have ceased, but it must be verified 'that the person has no other reason to fear being "persecuted" within the meaning of Article 2(c) of the Directive [i.e. the refugee definition]'.[94] Since the definition of refugee in the QD is reasonably amenable to child-rights violations (see above), it follows that such violations can be argued in the cessation context. An example will illustrate the potential importance of this. If an unaccompanied minor was persecuted by a regime that has since been toppled, the original fear of persecution has ceased. However, if he/she became separated from his/her family during flight and family tracing has proved unsuccessful, then it must be assessed whether the vulnerability caused by being alone would lead to fresh persecution if returned to the country of origin, for example, if the child were to end up on the street or in institutional care. Seen from this perspective, the ruling in *Abdulla* is a positive one.

Exclusion

Exclusion from refugee or subsidiary protection status occurs, most commonly, when a person is not deserving of international protection because of past conduct. The intention here, as in the previous sub-section, is to focus on exclusion from refugee status. In particular, the focus will be on Article 12(2) QD, which reflects, with some minor additions, the terms of Article 1F of the 1951 Convention.[95] Article 12(2) QD provides:

> A third country national or stateless person is excluded from being a refugee where there are serious reasons for considering that:
>
> a   he or she has committed a crime against peace, a war crime, or a crime against humanity, as defined in the international instruments drawn up to make provision in respect of such crimes;
> b   he or she has committed a serious non-political crime outside the country of refuge prior to his or her admission as a refugee; which means the time of issuing a residence permit based on the granting of refugee status; particularly cruel actions, even if committed with

---

93   CJEU, *Abdulla and Others, op cit.*, para. 69.
94   *Ibid.*, para. 76.
95   There are two other exclusion clauses in the QD that do not relate to the question of deservedness: Article 12(1)(a), which mirrors Article 1D of the 1951 Convention and which essentially excludes UNRWA refugees from refugee status, and Article 12(1)(b), which reflects Article 1E of the 1951 Convention and which excludes *de facto* citizens of the host State from refugee status. Article 12(1)(a) was pronounced on by the CJEU in *Bolbol*, Case C-31/09, Judgment of 4 March 2010 and *El Kott*, Case C-364/11, Judgment of 19 December 2012.

an allegedly political objective, may be classified as serious non-political crimes;
c he or she is guilty of acts contrary to the purposes and principles of the United Nations as set out in the Preamble and Articles 1 and 2 of the Charter of the United Nations.

The application of Article 12(2) QD to children raises particular difficulties because it involves complex issues relating to the age of criminal responsibility, intent and circumstances vitiating individual criminal liability such as duress, coercion and self-defence. This can best be illustrated by referring, again, to the issue of child soldiers. Very often such children have been involved in committing war crimes – a ground of exclusion under Article 12(2)(a). However, as has already been outlined, the recruitment and participation of children under the age of fifteen in hostilities is itself a war crime. Consequently, to exclude such children from refugee status is to exclude them for being victims of a war crime. Furthermore, Article 39 CRC provides, 'States Parties shall take all appropriate measures to promote physical and psychological recovery and social reintegration of a child victim of: any form of [...] armed conflicts. Such recovery and reintegration shall take place in an environment which fosters the health, self-respect and dignity of the child'. Accordingly, the response envisaged in the CRC to the phenomenon of child soldiers is the physical and psychological recovery and social reintegration of such children, which – it is clear – is diametrically opposed to excluding them from refugee status.[96]

Because of the complexity of applying Article 1F of the 1951 Convention (and hence also Article 12(2) QD) to children, UNHCR recommends that, as with any exclusion analysis, a three-step analysis be undertaken: 1) **Does the act in question correspond to one of the grounds of exclusion?**; 2) **Can the act be attributed to the child?**; 3) **Are the consequences of exclusion from refugee status proportional to the seriousness of the act committed?**[97] The last step follows from UNHCR's long-held position that inclusion comes before exclusion and, hence, that States have at their disposal all the necessary information about the applicant's well-founded fear of persecution in order to be able to balance that against the seriousness of the crime. But furthermore, UNHCR recommends that:

> In the case of a child, the exclusion analysis needs to take into account not only general exclusion principles but also the rules and principles that address the special status, rights and protection afforded to children

---

96 See further, M. Gallagher, S.J., 'Soldier boy bad: Child soldiers, culture and bars to asylum', *International Journal of Refugee Law* 13, 2001, 310–353.
97 UNHCR Guidelines on Child Asylum Claims, *op cit.*, para. 62. See also, UNHCR, 'Guidelines on International Protection: Application of the Exclusion Clauses: Article 1F of the 1951 Convention relating to the Status of Refugees', *HCR/GIP/03/05 (2003)*.

under international and national law at all stages of the asylum procedure. In particular, those principles related to the best interest of the child, the mental capacity of children and their ability to understand and consent to acts that they are requested or ordered to undertake needs to be considered.[98]

The CJEU pronounced on Article 12(2) in Joined Cases C-57/09 and C-101/09 (*B and D*).[99] The case involved exclusion on the basis of the alleged participation by two adults in serious non-political crimes and acts contrary to the purposes of the UN. The judgment of the Court is highly relevant to the question of exclusion of minors – in both positive and negative ways.

According to the Court, the requirement in Article 12(2) that there must be 'serious reasons for considering' that the person has committed the crime presupposes 'a full investigation into all the circumstances of each individual case'.[100] Individual responsibility 'must be assessed in the light of both objective and subjective criteria'.[101] In this regard, the Court stated that 'the competent authority must, *inter alia*, assess the true role played by the person concerned in the perpetration of the acts in question; his position within the organization; the extent of the knowledge he had, or was deemed to have, of its activities; any pressure to which he was exposed; or other factors likely to have influenced his conduct.'[102] This much of the judgment is highly positive from a child-rights perspective.

However, the Court was also asked to pronounce on whether a proportionality test was required for the purposes of Article 12(2). It categorically rejected the idea that inclusion comes before exclusion, asserting the converse, and forcefully rejected the notion of a proportionality test:

> Since the competent authority has already, in its assessment of the seriousness of the acts committed by the person concerned and of that person's individual responsibility, taken into account all the circumstances surrounding those acts and the situation of that person, it cannot […] be required, if it reaches the conclusion that Article 12(2) applies, to undertake an assessment of proportionality, implying as that does a fresh assessment of the level of seriousness of the acts committed.[103]

With respect to the Court, this logic is not entirely convincing: if exclusion comes before inclusion, as argued by the Court, then the 'fresh assessment' is not of the level of seriousness of the acts committed but rather of the persecution

---

98 UNHCR, *ibid*, para. 63.
99 CJEU, *B and D,* Joined Cases C-57/09 and C-101/09, Judgment of 9 November 2010.
100 *Ibid.* para. 93.
101 *Ibid.* para. 96.
102 *Ibid.* para. 97.
103 *Ibid.* para. 109.

feared when considered in the light of the seriousness of the acts committed.[104] But if the exclusion-therefore-no-inclusion scheme is applied to a child soldier, what is of greater concern is that it is not obvious that a decision-maker would grasp that precisely what vitiates individual responsibility is that the child him/herself is also a victim of the excludable act *because it is an act of persecution.*

In conclusion, Article 12(2) QD as interpreted by the Court in *B and D* is both positive and negative from the perspective of the rights of the child. The Court's insistence on a full investigation into the circumstances of the individual case is positive, since it enables factors such as mental capacity, consent and duress to be explored. However, the Court's rejection of the chronology of inclusion before exclusion and of a proportionality test may mean that the coincidence of the crime as an excludable act *and* as an act of persecution is missed.

Phase Two CEAS: Eligibility concepts and the rights of the child

This section explores whether the rights of the child are better integrated into eligibility concepts in the recast QD than they are in the original directive.

The refugee definition

I. ACTS OF PERSECUTION

It was found that the QD in Article 9(1) conceives of acts of persecution through the lens of civil and political rights and sets a high threshold for persecution, but that this is mitigated by the illustrative list of acts of persecution in Article 9(2), which can be interpreted to include child-rights violations. To what extent does the recast QD alter this situation?

Articles 9(1) and (2) are unchanged in the recast. However, a significant amendment is made to one of the recitals. Recital 18 reiterates the principle in existing Recital 12 that the best interests of the child should be a primary consideration of Member States when implementing the Directive, but adds that '[i]n assessing the best interests of the child, Member States should in particular take due account of the principle of family unity, *the minor's wellbeing and social development, safety and security considerations* and the views of the minor in accordance with his or her age and maturity'.[105] The italicised phrases facilitate the recognition that economic, social and cultural rights and protection rights can be refugee-relevant.

---

104 Kosar argues that a holistic reading of the QD requires adjudicators to address inclusion in the interview even where they plan to apply the exclusion clause: D. Kosar, 'Inclusion before exclusion or vice versa: What the Qualification Directive and the Court of Justice do (not) say', *International Journal of Refugee Law* 25, 2013, 87–119.
105 Emphasis added.

II. REASONS FOR PERSECUTION

The reasons for persecution as elaborated on in Article 10(1) QD are of mixed benefit to child claimants. On the problematic side, the provision on 'membership of a particular social group' presents the innate characteristics test and the social perception test as two prongs of a single test, making the test difficult to meet. Furthermore, Article 9(3) requiring a connection between the reasons for persecution and the acts of persecution effectively excludes persecution by non-State actors where the link to the reasons for persecution emanates from the failure of State protection. To what extent are these problems remedied in the recast QD?

As regards the 'membership of a particular social group' ground, the cumulative nature of the innate characteristics and social perception tests is retained. However, more guidance is provided on gender-related aspects of a social group, which is helpful to claims involving violations of the rights of the girl-child.[106] Furthermore, the problematic provision in Article 9(3) requiring a connection between the reasons for persecution and the acts of persecution is amended in recast Article 9(3), which adds that the connection can equally be drawn between the reasons for persecution and 'the absence of protection against such acts'. This allows child-rights violations perpetrated by non-State actors for private reasons to be refugee-relevant if the failure of State protection can be linked to one of the listed reasons.

In sum, two significant improvements are made in relation to the reasons for persecution, but the problematic cumulative test for the existence of a social group remains.

The definition of 'serious harm'

The definition of 'serious harm' in the QD was criticised for being too narrow. In particular, Article 15(c) omits serious child-rights violations that occur in peacetime and one of the most serious child-rights violations that occurs in time of conflict, namely underage recruitment. As interpreted by the CJEU in *Elgafaji*, its value-added to Article 15(b) is uncertain. In this regard, it is striking that the Commission decided that 'in view of the interpretative guidance provided by [the *Elgafaji*] judgment and of the fact that the relevant provisions were found to be compatible with the ECHR, an amendment of Article 15(c) is not considered necessary'.[107] Consequently, there is no change to Article 15(c) in the recast QD.

---

106 Article 10(d) and Recital 30.
107 Proposal for a Directive of the European Parliament and of the Council on minimum standards for the qualification and status of third country nationals or stateless persons as beneficiaries of international protection and the content of the protection granted, *COM (2009) 551*, 'Explanatory Memorandum', p. 6.

Sources of harm and protection

While Article 6 QD relating to sources of harm was considered praiseworthy for its inclusion of non-State actors of persecution, Article 7 was criticised for including non-State actors in the list of actors of protection. It was argued that this is not viable in the context of child protection, because non-State actors generally lack the capacity and durability needed to provide for the myriad protection needs of children. In this regard, an important phrase is added to recast Article 7(2): protection against persecution or serious harm 'must be effective and of a non-temporary nature'. The CJEU has given the term 'non-temporary' a robust interpretation in the cessation context, equivalent to permanency, suggesting by analogy that protection by a non-State actor should be durable or long-lasting.[108] Providing effectiveness is assessed in relation to child-protection needs, then it is submitted that this provision remedies the deficiencies of original Article 7.

Internal protection

Article 8 QD was criticised in particular for its third paragraph, which states that the concept of internal protection 'may apply notwithstanding technical obstacles to return in the country of origin'. In the particular context of unaccompanied minors, this leads to the risk that highly relevant factors, such as the ability to locate family members or identify a care placement, might be disregarded in applying the concept. The recast QD contains some significant improvements in this regard. Article 8(1)(b) now provides that the concept applies if the applicant has access to protection against persecution or serious harm in the part of the country of origin identified as safe and 'he or she can safely and legally travel to and gain admittance to that part of the country and can reasonably be expected to settle there'. Furthermore, recast Recital 27 provides, *inter alia*, '[w]hen the applicant is an unaccompanied minor, the availability of appropriate care and custodial arrangements, which are in the best interest of the unaccompanied minor, should form part of the assessment as to whether that protection is effectively available'.

Cessation

The cessation provisions in Article 11(1) and (2) QD were found not to be problematic from a child-rights perspective. Therefore, the fact that they are unchanged in the recast is also unproblematic. Interestingly, a new paragraph is added to Article 11 in the recast: the ceased circumstances provision 'shall not apply to a refugee who is able to invoke compelling reasons arising out of previous persecution for refusing to avail himself or herself of the protection

---

108 *Abdulla and Others, op cit.*, para. 73.

of the [country of origin]'.[109] This provision is a variation on Article 1C(5) of the 1951 Convention, second sub-paragraph, which was limited in scope to refugees who were recognised under various *ad hoc* arrangements in the 1920s and 1930s. The impulse was humanitarian: to provide an exception to cessation in compelling cases. The inclusion of this provision, but without any limitation in personal scope, in Article 11(3) of the recast is significant from the point of view of the child claimant. One can readily envisage the use of the 'compelling reasons' exception when the persecution suffered or feared has had a lasting impact on the child (now perhaps an adult). Moreover, the exception could be raised when the child has spent a significant part of his/her life in the country of refuge and has lost all effective ties with the country of origin.[110] Consequently, recast Article 11(3) is a welcome provision.

Exclusion

Article 12(2) QD, which reflects the terms of Article 1F of the 1951 Convention, is insufficiently nuanced to take account of the many considerations involved in applying the exclusion clauses to children. The likely exclusion of child soldiers is a poignant illustration of this. The interpretation of Article 12(2) QD by the CJEU in *B and D* is unhelpful in this regard. It is all the more unfortunate, then, that Article 12(2) of the recast QD remains unchanged.

Conclusion

This chapter posed the question of whether the CEAS complies with the right of the child to seek and qualify for international protection. It began by exploring the right of the child to seek international protection. It established that the accompanied as well as the unaccompanied child has this right and therefore must be able to lodge an asylum application. It scrutinised the relevant provisions of the APD and found that the directive fails to explicitly establish the right of all minors to lodge an application. The recast remedies this defect, establishing a right of all minors, directly or indirectly,

---

109 Article 11(3).
110 On the basis of their research into the development and prospects of children living in asylum centres in The Netherlands, Kalverboer *et al.* report that all children in the six to twelve year age bracket who have spent five years or more in the asylum country 'feel attached to their host society after five years and feel like strangers in the country of their parents. They are acquainted with expressing themselves freely. Being involuntarily sent back to a country where such rights are not guaranteed provides a culture shock. Most children in this age range almost exclusively speak the language of their host country'. Older children are also reported to be attached to the host society, but the attachment is more ambivalent. M. Kalverboer, A. Zijlstra and E. Knorth, 'The developmental consequences for asylum-seeking children living with the prospect of five years or more of enforced return to their home country', *European Journal of Migration and Law* 11, 2009, 41–67, 60.

to lodge an application. However, in the case of the accompanied minor, the recast leaves it to the Member State to determine whether the child can make an independent application, while also permitting Member States to attach negative procedural consequences to 'subsequent applications' by minors who were previously incorporated into their parents' applications. In sum, the right of the child to seek international protection is not categorically met in the CEAS.

This chapter also explored the right of the child to qualify for international protection, meaning the right of the child to have his/her rights as a child recognised as refugee-relevant. It was argued that the tendency to interpret eligibility concepts in refugee law through the exclusive lens of civil and political rights constitutes a real obstacle to recognising the full gamut of child rights as potentially refugee-relevant. The QD was examined to establish the extent to which it reproduces or overcomes this obstacle. It was found that in many significant ways the directive is (or is capable of being interpreted in a way that is) sensitive to child rights, but that in about as many significant ways it is not. However, the recast QD corrects many of the problems identified, such as: clarifying gender-related aspects of 'membership of a particular social group'; clarifying the permissibility of connecting the ground to *either* the persecution *or* the reason the State failed to protect; establishing that protection by non-State actors must be effective and non-temporary; inserting more rigorous standards relating to the use of internal protection, particularly as regards unaccompanied minors; and including a new reason to refrain from ceasing refugee status that seems readily applicable to children. Consequently, the number of problematic provisions from a child-eligibility perspective are considerably reduced. The remaining problematic provisions are: the double test for 'membership of a particular social group'; the reducing of 'protection' to a criminal justice response; the limited material and personal scope of 'serious harm' for the purposes of subsidiary protection; and the failure to accommodate a child-rights perspective into the exclusion provisions. However, without minimising any of these remaining problems, it is submitted that the recast QD is generally compliant with the right of the child to have his/her rights recognised as refugee-relevant.

4 The right of the child to be heard

Introduction

Chapter 3 set out the right of the child to seek and qualify for international protection. But even assuming that the child is given access to the procedure and that the eligibility concepts are child-rights sensitive, there is still a problem: the typical asylum *procedure* is not designed for children. The adult-orientation is apparent in the central feature of the asylum process – an individual status determination procedure usually based on an interview. Asylum officers are required to elicit information from the applicant, who, in turn, is required to render an accurate and nuanced account, communicated verbally and often through the medium of a translator, of his/her reasons for not being able to return to his/her country of origin. The burden of proof rests principally on the applicant. This process implies that the applicant possesses reasonably sophisticated communication skills and the ability to understand and analyse his/her predicament. However, it is clear, even from a superficial knowledge of the stages of child development, that depending on their age and maturity, not to mention the possible traumatic nature of their experience, children may not be able to communicate their story in this way. Given that children are unlikely to meet the requirements of the procedure they risk not being interviewed at all. So, the question arises: what rights do children have that could make the adult-oriented asylum procedure more sensitive and amenable to children? The key right of the child in this regard is the right to be heard in Article 12 CRC. This chapter is devoted to an exploration of the meaning of this right, its implications in the asylum context and whether or not the relevant provisions of the key CEAS instrument in this regard, the APD and its recast, are consistent with the right to be heard.[1]

---

1 Directive 2005/85/EC of 1 December 2005 and Directive 2013/32/EU of the European Parliament and of the Council of 26 June 2013, respectively.

The right of the child to be heard

Article 12 CRC provides:

1   States Parties shall assure to the child who is capable of forming his or her own views the right to express those views freely in all matters affecting the child, the views of the child being given due weight in accordance with the age and maturity of the child.
2   For this purpose the child shall in particular be provided the opportunity to be heard in any judicial and administrative proceedings affecting the child, either directly, or through a representative or appropriate body, in a manner consistent with the procedural rules of national law.

The right of the child to be heard in Article 12 is interpreted by the Com. RC as a general principle of relevance to the interpretation and implementation of all the rights in the CRC.[2] This right was *sui generis* in international human rights law at the time of the drafting of the Convention, but it has since been restated in Article 24 of the EU Charter of Fundamental Rights.[3] Despite its originality, Article 12 CRC cannot be considered in isolation. It bears a relationship to a cluster of rights in general (i.e. non child-specific), human rights law that can be categorised broadly under the heading of the right to a fair hearing.[4] This relationship is evolving.

Thus, at the time of the drafting of the Convention, Article 12 CRC was conceived as an *alternative* to the procedural rights associated with a fair hearing. Under domestic law, children were typically precluded from enjoying the same procedural rights as adults because of a perceived lack of intellectual/emotional capacity and a resulting lack of legal capacity.[5] The presumption of a lack of capacity was also evident in international law. Hence, the CRC contains no right of legal personality and consequently no right of access to the courts, to a fair hearing or to an effective remedy. For the same reason, it contains no individual complaints procedure, although this situation is due to change shortly. This presumption was also discernible in the case-law of the

---

2   Com. RC, General Comment No. 5, 'General measures of implementation of the Convention on the Rights of the Child (arts. 4, 42 and 44, para 6)', *UN Doc. CRC/GC/2003/5 (2003)*.
3   Article 24(1) CFR provides, *inter alia*: '[Children] may express their views freely. Such views shall be taken into consideration on matters which concern them in accordance with their age and maturity.'
4   The right to a fair hearing is established in Article 14 ICCPR, Article 6 ECHR and Article 47 of the EU Charter of Fundamental Rights. The associated right to an effective remedy is established in Article 2 ICCPR, Article 13 ECHR and is part of Article 47 of the EU Charter. The right to a fair hearing may be implicit in other substantive rights that involve a strong evaluative element, such as the prohibition of torture and lesser forms of ill-treatment.
5   See, for example, C. Smith, 'Children's rights: Judicial ambivalence and social resistance', *International Journal of Law, Policy and the Family* 11, 1997, 103–139.

ECtHR[6] and in EU law.[7] The original rationale for Article 12 must be understood in this context: Article 12 was included in the CRC as a substitute for the procedural rights normally associated with a fair hearing, its function being to give the child a voice and (modestly) to challenge the image of the child as a passive object of other people's decisions.

However, in the intervening years, the traditional resistance to the idea of children as having the capacity to enforce their rights has been steadily eroded. Thus, an optional protocol to the CRC allowing for an individual complaints mechanism was adopted by the General Assembly in 2012,[8] and the Com. RC considers the right to an effective remedy to be implicit in the CRC,[9] including in Article 12 itself.[10] In 2009, the Com. RC produced a General Comment (No. 12) on the right of the child to be heard, which gives it a dynamic, contemporary interpretation.[11] There are indications in the case-law of the ECtHR[12] and the CJEU[13] that the European courts, too, are revising their attitudes to the issue of children's (lack of) capacity. Ironically,

---

6 See, for example, ECtHR, *Golder v UK*, Appl. No. 4451/70, Judgment (Plenary Court) of 21 February 1975, in which it was held to be lawful to impose restrictions on access to the courts by minors.

7 Until relatively recently, it was doubted by commentators whether children were subjects of EU law in their own right (as opposed to being beneficiaries of rights derived from their parents). See H. Stalford, 'Constitutionalising equality in the EU: A children's rights perspective', *International Journal of Discrimination and the Law* 8, 2005, 53–73; and H. Stalford and E. Drywood, 'Coming of age?: Children's rights in the European Union', *Common Market Law Review* 46, 2009, 143–172.

8 Optional Protocol to the Convention on the Rights of the Child on a Communications Procedure, *UN Doc. A/RES/66/138*, 27 January 2012. The protocol will enter into force once it secures ten ratifications or accessions; at the time of writing there have been eight.

9 Com. RC, General Comment No. 5, *op cit.*, para. 24.

10 According to the Com. RC, Article 12 implies a right to an effective remedy if the child is not given the opportunity to be heard or his/her views are not given due weight: General Comment No. 12, 'The right of the child to be heard', *UN Doc. CRC/C/GC/12 (2009)*, para. 46.

11 *Ibid.*

12 The right of the child to participate has become an established element of the jurisprudence of the ECtHR relating to Article 6 ECHR on the right to a fair trial. See, for example, ECtHR, *T. v The United Kingdom*, Appl. No. 24724/94, Judgment of 16 December 1999, and ECtHR, *S.C. v The United Kingdom*, Appl. No. 60958/00, Judgment of 15 June 2004. For the Council of Europe position, see 'Guidelines of the Committee of Ministers of the Council of Europe on child-friendly justice', adopted by the Committee of Ministers on 17 November 2010 at the 1098th meeting of the Ministers' Deputies (hereinafter, 'Council of Europe Guidelines 2010').

13 For example in *Chen*, the Court rejected the proposition that a young child cannot activate free movement and residence rights, holding that 'a young child can take advantage of the rights of free movement and residence guaranteed by Community law. The capacity of a national of a Member State to be the holder of rights guaranteed by the Treaty and by secondary law on the free movement of persons cannot be made conditional upon the attainment by the person concerned of the age prescribed for the acquisition of legal capacity to exercise those rights personally'. ECJ, *Chen*, Case C-200/02, Judgment of 19 October 2004, para. 20. See further, CJEU, *Zambrano*, Case C-34/09, Judgment of 8 March 2011.

now that children are increasingly recognised as possessing the same procedural rights as adults, the right to be heard in Article 12 CRC may constitute an additional, rather than an alternative, set of guarantees. The following subsections outline the key aspects of the right of the child to be heard: the right to a hearing, the conduct of the hearing and the evaluation of the child's views.[14] Attention is paid throughout to the implications of the right in the asylum context.

The right to a hearing

Article 12 CRC establishes the right of the child to be heard, but does this right extend to the asylum context and, if so, what child is entitled to a hearing? In other words, what is the scope *ratione materiae* and *personae* of the right of the child to be heard? On the first question, it is useful to begin by establishing the existence of a general (i.e. non child-specific) right to be heard in the asylum context. To this end, the provisions of international refugee law, European human rights law and EU law are briefly canvassed.

The 1951 Convention is silent on matters procedural, but the definition of a refugee strongly suggests an individual status determination interview. The importance of an interview is also clear from the official soft-law sources of guidance and is reflected in State practice.[15] In terms of European human rights law, although the ECtHR has declined to apply Article 6 ECHR (right to a fair trial) to immigration or asylum cases,[16] procedural rights relevant to the asylum context have been developed jurisprudentially under the rubric of Article 3 (prohibition of torture and inhuman and degrading treatment or punishment) alone and in conjunction with Article 13 (right to an effective remedy).[17] Thus, the Court regularly reiterates the need for rigorous and close scrutiny of claims of a violation of Article 3 in the context of expulsion, involving an assessment not only of the general situation, but also of the

---

14 The approach is necessarily selective: there are many rights that are corollary to the right of the child to be heard relating, for example, to free legal assistance or representation, to adequate time to prepare one's case and to an effective remedy. But in so far as these rights have no particular child-specific implications, it is submitted that there is little value to be added here to existing commentaries on the content and application of such rights in the context of the CEAS. See later footnotes for citations of such commentaries.
15 See, for example, UNHCR, Handbook and Guidelines on Procedures and Criteria for Determining Refugee Status, Reissued Geneva, December 2011 (hereinafter, 'UNHCR Handbook').
16 ECtHR, *Maaouia v France*, Appl. No. 39652/98, Judgment of 5 October 2000.
17 Procedural rights have also been established under the rubric of Protocol 4, Article 4 (prohibition of collective expulsion of aliens) in conjunction with Article 13. The leading case is ECtHR, *Conka v Belgium*, Appl. No. 51564/99, Judgment of 5 February 2002. A more recent but also ground-breaking case is *Hersi Jamaa and Others v Italy*, Appl. No. 27765/09, Judgment (GC) of 23 February 2012.

personal circumstances of the applicant.[18] This suggests a hearing. In a line of Article 3 cases involving Turkey (where UNHCR undertakes the refugee status determination) the Court has attached significant weight to UNHCR's assessment of the asylum claim because, unlike the respondent State, UNHCR had actually interviewed the applicant.[19] Indeed, the need for the applicant to give evidence in person, thereby allowing the decision-maker to see, hear and assess his/her demeanour, is underscored in many Article 3 cases.[20] As regards the right to an effective remedy, the Court has stated that an effective remedy in the context of an arguable claim of an Article 3 violation requires an individualised assessment.[21] Again, an individualised assessment suggests a personal hearing. In *I.M. v France*, the Court found a violation of Article 13 and 3 because, *inter alia*, an asylum applicant was only given a brief 30-minute hearing, which did not allow for the complexities of his application to be properly communicated or explored.[22] In sum, the Court's case-law clearly points to a right to be heard in these contexts. Given the overlap with the asylum context, including the risk of *refoulement*, it is reasonable to infer that asylum seekers also have such a right.

As regards EU law, Article 42(2)(a) of the EU Charter of Fundamental Rights codifies the general principle of EU law that every person has a right to be heard before any individual adverse measure is taken against them. Although there has been much uncertainty about the proper scope of this Article,[23] a recent judgment of the CJEU has clarified that it applies to the asylum context.[24] Thus, in *M.M*, the Court held that 'the right [...] of the applicant for asylum to be heard must apply fully to the procedure in which the competent national authority examines an application for international

---

18 See, for example, ECtHR, *Saadi v Italy*, Appl. No. 37201/06, Judgment of 28 February 2008 and ECtHR, *Baysakov and Others v Ukraine*, Appl. No. 54131/08, Judgment of 18 February 2010.
19 See ECtHR, *Jabari v Turkey*, Appl. No. 40035/98, Judgment of 11 July 2000, paras. 40 and 41; ECtHR, *Abdolkhani and Karimnia v Turkey*, Appl. No. 30471/08, Judgment of 22 September 2009, paras. 82 and 113; ECtHR, *Charahili v Turkey*, Appl. No. 46605/07, Judgment of 13 April 2010, paras. 57 and 59; ECtHR, *M.B. and others v Turkey*, Appl. No. 36009/08, Judgment of 15 June 2010, para. 33; and ECtHR, *Ahmadpour v Turkey*, Appl. No. 12717/08, Judgment of 15 June 2010, para. 39.
20 For example, ECtHR, *E.G. v The United Kingdom*, Appl. No. 41178/08, Judgment of 31 May 2011, in particular para. 72 and ECtHR, *R.C. v Sweden*, Appl. No. 41827/07, Judgment of 9 March 2010, in particular para. 52.
21 See ECtHR, *Gebremedhin v France*, Appl. No. 25389/05, Judgment of 26 April 2007, para. 58. See further ECtHR, *Jabari v Turkey, op cit.*, para. 50.; ECtHR, *Abdolkhani and Karimnia v Turkey*, Appl. No. 30471/08, Judgment of 22 September 2009, para. 108; and ECtHR, *Baysakov and Others v Ukraine, op cit.*, para. 71.
22 ECtHR, *I.M. v France*, Appl. No. 9152/09, Judgment of 2 February 2012, particularly para. 155.
23 See I. Rabinovici, 'The right to be heard in the Charter of Fundamental Rights of the European Union', *European Public Law* 18, 2012, 149–173.
24 CJEU, *M.M.*, Case C-277/11, Judgment of 22 November 2012.

protection pursuant to rules adopted in the framework of the Common European Asylum System'.²⁵ Furthermore, Article 47 of the EU Charter of Fundamental Rights provides for a right to an effective remedy and to a fair trial, codifying existing general principles of EU law that encompass the right to be heard.²⁶ Unlike Article 6 ECHR, Article 47 of the Charter is not limited to the determination of civil rights and obligations and therefore applies to the asylum context.²⁷

In short, international refugee law, European human rights law and EU law now clearly point to a general right to be heard in the asylum context. It follows that the child-specific equivalent of the right to be heard contained in Article 12 CRC also applies to the asylum context. This is reinforced by the wording and drafting history of Article 12 itself. Article 12(1) establishes the right to express views in 'all matters affecting the child'. The drafters of the Convention resisted inserting a list of matters on which children could express views and rejected limiting the scope of Article 12 to the *rights* of the child, with the result that the right to be heard has a broad subject-matter scope.²⁸ However, since 'all matters' includes *at least* the rights of the child (as evidenced by the fact that Article 12 is a general principle of the Convention), it is worth drawing a connection to Article 22(1) CRC, which establishes the right of the child seeking refugee status to appropriate protection. If the child seeking refugee status has the right to appropriate protection, it follows that all decisions relating to protection, whether relating to admissibility or to the substantive claim, whether taken in a 'regular' or 'extraordinary' procedure, whether at first instance or on appeal, are 'matters affecting the child' for the purposes of Article 12(1). Furthermore, Article 12(2) states that the child shall *'in particular* be provided the opportunity to be heard in any judicial and administrative proceedings affecting the child'.²⁹ Clearly, asylum procedures can be classified as either judicial or administrative proceedings or both, often depending on the instance. Accordingly, the Com. RC states that Article 12(2) 'applies to all relevant [...] proceedings affecting the child, without limitation,

---

25 *Ibid.* at para. 89.
26 Relevant general principles include the principle of effectiveness and effective judicial protection. See generally, T. Tridimas, *The General Principles of EU Law*, 2nd ed., Oxford: Oxford University Press, 2006, in particular Chapters 8 and 9.
27 Explanations Relating to the Charter of Fundamental Rights *(2007/C 303/02)*, Explanation on Article 47, p. 29.
28 On the drafting history of Article 12, see L. Krappmann, 'The weight of the child's view (Article 12 of the Convention on the Rights of the Child)', *International Journal of Children's Rights* 18, 2010, 501–513.
29 Emphasis added. Similarly, the Council of Europe Guidelines 2010, which advocate the right of the child to be heard and to express views, apply to 'all ways in which children are likely to be, for whatever reason and in whatever capacity, brought into contact with all competent bodies and services in implementing criminal, civil or administrative law'. *Op. cit.*, para. 2.

including [...] unaccompanied children, asylum seeking and refugee children'.[30]

Having established that the material scope of Article 12 CRC extends to the asylum context, the question now arises as to which asylum-seeking children fall within its personal scope. The wording of Article 12(1) makes clear that the right extends to every child who is capable of forming his or her own views. According to the Com. RC:

> This phrase should not be seen as a limitation, but rather as an obligation for States Parties to assess the capacity of the child to form an autonomous opinion to the greatest extent possible. This means that States Parties cannot begin with the assumption that a child is incapable of expressing his or her own views. On the contrary, States Parties should presume that a child has the capacity to form his or her own views and recognize that she or he has the right to express them; it is not up to the child to first prove her or his capacity.[31]

In view of this presumption of capacity, the Committee considers that the imposition of fixed-age thresholds on the right of the child to express his or her views is inappropriate: a presumption of capacity constitutes the point of departure, and this can only be rebutted in the individual case.[32] As regards the meaning of capacity, the Com. RC challenges the predominant adult notion of capacity as being equivalent to a complete understanding of the matter at hand and an ability to express oneself fluently through the medium of language. It is enough that the child has sufficient understanding to be able to have a view on the matter and an ability to communicate his or her view by some means. Thus, the Committee provides that 'full implementation of Article 12 requires recognition of, and respect for, non-verbal forms of communicating including play, body language, facial expressions, and drawing and painting, through which very young children demonstrate understanding,

---

30 Com. RC, General Comment No. 12, *op. cit.*, para. 32.
31 *Ibid.*, para. 20.
32 The resistance to 'bright line' age thresholds can be traced back to the movement for children's liberation in the 1960s and 1970s. See, for example, H. Rodham, 'Children under the law', *Harvard Education Review* 43, 1973, 487–514 and L. Houlgate, *The Child and The State: A Normative Theory of Juvenile Rights*, Maryland: John Hopkins University Press, 1980. For more recent literature on the topic, see R. Hodgkin and P. Newell, *Implementation Handbook for the Convention on the Rights of the Child*, 3rd ed., UNICEF, 2007, and M. Lücker-Babel, 'The right of the child to express views and be heard: An attempt to interpret Article 12 of the UN Convention on the Rights of the Child', *International Journal of Children's Rights* 3, 1995, 391–404. It is interesting to note that the version of Article 12 that appears in Article 24 of the EU Charter of Fundamental Rights omits any reference to 'the child who is capable of forming his or her own views'. Article 24(1) simply says that '[children] may express their views freely', i.e. all children, regardless of capacity.

choices and preferences'.³³ The Committee also draws attention to the importance of Article 12 for children who experience difficulties in making their views heard, such as children with disabilities, migrant children and other children who do not speak the majority language. These children must be facilitated in expressing their views. Hence, the *problem* of child participation is reconceived: the problem is not the child; the problem is the adult-oriented nature of the process, which excludes the child.

However, a *caveat* must be entered at this point. The Com. RC considers that the reference to expressing views 'freely' in Article 12(1) and to the 'opportunity' to be heard in Article 12(2) means that expressing views is a choice for the child, not an obligation.³⁴ Consequently, it is for the child to decide whether he or she wishes to exercise or waive the right to be heard: the child cannot be forced to be heard against his/her will. Linked to this, a child should not be interviewed more often than is necessary, particularly where the subject matter is distressing. This is because of the risk of re-traumatisation.³⁵ This was confirmed by the CJEU in the context of the right of the child to be heard in Article 24 of the EU Charter of Fundamental rights. In *Zarraga v Pelz*, the Court linked the right of the child to be heard in Article 24(1) with the best interests of the child in Article 24(2), noting that 'hearing the child cannot constitute an absolute obligation, but must be assessed having regard to what is required in the best interests of the child in each individual case'.³⁶

In sum, the right of the child to be heard is fully applicable to the asylum context and is a right of every child who has the capacity – broadly construed – to form and express his/her own views and who wishes to communicate those views.

The conduct of the hearing

Article 12(1) establishes the right of the child with the requisite capacity to express views 'freely', while Article 12(2) relating to the right of the child in particular to be heard in any judicial or administrative proceedings provides that this may be done 'either directly, or through a representative or an appropriate body'. These provisions have a number of important implications for the conduct of the hearing.

The right to a representative

According to the Com. RC, once the child has decided to be heard he or she has to decide whether to be heard directly or through a representative.³⁷

---

33 Com. RC, General Comment No. 12, *op. cit.*, para. 21.
34 *Ibid.*, para. 16. The same point is made in the Council of Europe Guidelines 2010, *op. cit.*, para. 46.
35 *Ibid.*, para. 24. In a similar vein, the Council of Europe Guidelines 2010 warn against 'secondary victimisation', *ibid.*, para. 11.
36 CJEU, *Zarraga v Pelz,* Case C-491/10, Judgment of 22 December 2010, para. 64.
37 Com. RC, General Comment No. 12, *op. cit.*, para. 35.

While a direct hearing may be preferable, where this is not desired by the child arrangements must be put in place for a representative. In the case of an accompanied minor, the most obvious representative is the child's parent. The representation of a child by his/her parent is consistent with Article 5 CRC, which requires states to respect the right and responsibility of parents to provide direction and guidance to the child in the exercise of his/her Convention rights in accordance with the evolving capacities of the child. However, the Committee draws attention to potential conflicts between the child and his/her most obvious representative and underscores the need in such circumstances for an independent representative. In the case of an unaccompanied minor, the role of the representative should be acquitted by a guardian or adviser, which presupposes the formal appointment of such a professional and a clear articulation of his/her enabling role, *viz à viz* the right of the child to be heard.[38] The representative should be independent of the status determination body in order to avoid any conflict of interest. Furthermore, a clear distinction should be drawn between the representative (*qua* guardian or adviser) and a *legal* representative: the former is a child-care professional whose role is to oversee the child's best interests and to speak for the child where necessary; the latter is a legal professional whose role is to provide the child with legal advice and/or representation. The Com. RC considers that the unaccompanied child is entitled to both.[39]

The adaptation of the hearing

In terms of the hearing itself, the right of the child to express views 'freely' requires that the hearing be conducted in an age-appropriate manner. Thus, the CJEU stated in *Zarraga v Pelz* that the right of the child to be heard in Article 24 of the Charter 'require[s] the court to take all measures which are appropriate to the arrangement of such a hearing, having regard to the child's best interests and the circumstances of each individual case, in order to ensure the effectiveness of [Article 24], and to offer the child *a genuine and effective opportunity to express his or her views*'.[40] Similarly, but more concretely, the Com. RC observes that:

> A child cannot be heard effectively where the environment is intimidating, hostile, insensitive or inappropriate for his or her age. Proceedings

---

38 The Com. RC provides useful guidance in this regard in its General Comment No. 6, 'Treatment of unaccompanied and separated children outside their country of origin', *UN Doc CRC/GC/2005/6 (2005)*. See further, Defence for Children International-ECPAT the Netherlands, 'Core Standards for Guardians of Separated Children in Europe: Goals for Guardians and Authorities', Leiden, 2011.
39 *Ibid.*, para. 36. The Committee further states, at para. 72, that the guardian and legal representative should be present during all interviews.
40 CJEU, *Zarraga v Pelz*, *op. cit.*, para. 66 (emphasis added).

must be both accessible and child-appropriate. Particular attention needs to be paid to the provision and delivery of child-friendly information, adequate support for self-advocacy, appropriately trained staff, design of court rooms [and] clothing of judges and lawyers [...].[41]

Indeed, there is a wealth of soft-law guidance on how to adapt the status determination interview to the needs of children, which ranges from guidance on the layout of hearing rooms to child-friendly questioning.[42] On the issue of child-friendly questioning, the Com. RC notes from experience that 'the situation should have the format of a talk rather than a one-sided examination',[43] an observation consistent with the findings of research into the interviewing of children for the purposes of refugee status determination.[44] However, a balance must be struck between the need for a 'soft' approach to interviewing children and the need for a comprehensive hearing. The interviewer must enable the child to be heard by using child-friendly interview techniques, including lines and modes of questioning that are appropriate to the child, while facilitating a full ventilation of the claim by giving the child the opportunity to rebut any presumptions and challenge any negative inferences that are likely to be held against him/her when making the decision. After all, the child has a right pursuant to Article 22(1) to 'appropriate protection' – something the child is unlikely to get if the claim is not thoroughly explored.

In order that the hearing be conducted in an age-appropriate manner, staff involved in the hearing must be trained and competent to work with children. By now, it should be apparent just how difficult it is to interview children

---

41 Com. RC, General Comment No. 12, *op. cit.*, para. 34. The Council of Europe Guidelines 2010 provide similar guidance on 'organisation of the proceedings, child-friendly environment and child-friendly language'. *Op. cit.*, paras. 54–63.
42 See generally, UNHCR, 'Guidelines on International Protection, Child Asylum Claims under Articles 1(A)2 and 1(F) of the 1951 Convention and/or 1967 Protocol relating to the Status of Refugees', *HCR/GIP/09/08 (2009)* (hereinafter, 'UNHCR Child Guidelines'); Separated Children in Europe Programme, 'Statement of Good Practice', 4th revised ed. (2009); UNHCR, 'Guidelines on Policies and Procedures in dealing with Unaccompanied Children Seeking Asylum' (1997). More detailed guidance can often be found in administrative guidance or practice instructions to asylum institutions at the national level. See, for example, Canadian Immigration and Refugee Board, 'Child Refugee Claimants: Procedural and Evidentiary Issues' (1996); US Department of Justice, Immigration and Naturalisation Service, 'Guidelines for Children's Asylum Claims' (1998); Finnish Migration Board, Directorate of Immigration, 'Guidelines for Interviewing (Separated) Minors' (2002). For academic commentary on the importance of such guidance, see J. Bhabha and W. Young, 'Not adults in miniature: Unaccompanied child asylum seekers and the new U.S. guidelines', *International Journal of Refugee Law* 11, 1999, 84–125.
43 Com. RC, General Comment No. 12, *op. cit.*, para. 43.
44 For example, O. Keselman *et al.*, 'Mediated communication with minors in asylum seeking hearings', *Journal of Refugee Studies* 21, 2008, 103–116; and more generally, G. Smith, 'Considerations when interviewing children', *Children's Legal Rights Journal* 12, 1991, Special Report 1–7.

sensitively but thoroughly for the purposes of status determination. It is not something that can be done in the absence of specialised training.[45] The need for training is especially pronounced in the case of children who, because of their age, stage of development, disability or psychological state, cannot express themselves easily. Indeed, it is quite likely that the intervention of specialists will be required in respect of such children.[46] Thus, in its General Comment No. 12, the Com. RC notes that it is incumbent on States Parties to provide training on Article 12 and its application in practice to all professionals working with, and for, children, including lawyers, judges, police, social workers, psychologists, caregivers, residential and prison officers, civil servants, public officials and asylum officers. The obligation of staff training derives from Article 3(3) CRC, which provides: 'States Parties shall ensure that the institutions, services and facilities responsible for the care or *protection* of children shall conform with the standards established by competent authorities, particularly in the areas of safety, health, in the number and *suitability of their staff*, as well as *competent supervision*'.[47]

The evaluation of the child's views

Article 12(1) CRC states that 'the views of the child [must be] given due weight in accordance with the age and maturity of the child'. According to the Com. RC, 'simply listening to the child is insufficient; the views of the child have to be seriously considered when the child is capable of forming his or her own views'.[48] Consequently, nominal or token consultation with the child is inconsistent with the requirements of Article 12. However, giving 'due weight' to the child's views is complicated in the asylum context, because there seems at first to be little correlation between a child's views and

---

45 The need for specialised training for eligibility officers working with children has been stressed by the Com. RC in a number of concluding observations to EU Member States. For example, in its Concluding Observations to Austria in 2005, the Committee recommended that Austria 'ensure that all interviews with unaccompanied and separated asylum seeking children are carried out by professionally qualified and trained personnel'. *UN Doc. CRC/C/15/Add.251 (2005)*, para. 48. Similarly, in its Concluding Observations to Finland in 2000, it recommended 'that the State Party ensure adequate resources for the training of the officials who receive refugee children, in particular in child interviewing techniques'. *UN Doc. CRC/C/15/Add.132 (2000)*, para. 52. Training materials on interviewing asylum-seeking children have been developed in a number of different fora. For example, Separated Children in Europe Programme (SCEP), 'Training Guide', UNHCR and Save the Children, 2001.
46 See F. Gutierrez, 'Psychological evaluation of children and families in the immigration context', *Children's Legal Rights Journal* 19, 1999, 17–25.
47 Emphasis added. See also Council of Europe Guidelines 2010, *op. cit.*, paras. 14 and 15 on the training of professionals working with and for children.
48 Com. RC, General Comment No. 12, *op. cit.*, para. 28.

his/her eligibility for international protection.⁴⁹ In this regard, the views of the child as to whether he/she would prefer to remain in the host State or return home are largely irrelevant, just as they are in the case of an adult. However, the views of the child about the reasons for flight, the conditions in the country of origin and the risks on return are highly relevant from an evidential stand-point, just as they are in the case of an adult. Consequently, Article 12 CRC requires 'due weight' to be given to the child's view of his/her protection needs, in accordance with his/her age and maturity: the greater sum of the age and maturity of the child, the more weight to be given to the child's views, and vice versa.⁵⁰ The latter situation (i.e. minimal weight to the views of the child because of a deficit of age and maturity) does not prevent the decision-maker from taking a decision on the matter; rather, it requires the decision-maker to assume more responsibility for ascertaining the facts, for example, by having greater regard to objective factors. In the asylum context, this has repercussions for the burden of proof. Although the burden of proof is normally shared between the applicant and the examiner in asylum cases, UNHCR has long held that 'it may be necessary for an examiner to assume a greater burden of proof in children's claims, especially if the child concerned is unaccompanied.'⁵¹

Furthermore, giving 'due weight' to the views of the child in the asylum context has significant implications for the use of automatic, negative credibility inferences. This is the practice of using prototype credibility indicators,

---

49 For a discussion of the idea that Article 12 CRC is more relevant to certain kinds of legal and administrative proceedings than others, see D. O'Donnell, 'The right of children to be heard: Children's right to have their views taken into account and to participate in legal and administrative proceedings', *Innocenti Working Paper*, UNICEF, 2009.

50 This casts doubt on the suggestion in the UNHCR Handbook that '[i]t can be assumed that – in the absence of indications to the contrary – a person of 16 or over may be regarded as sufficiently mature to have a well-founded fear of persecution. Minors under 16 years of age may normally be assumed not to be sufficiently mature. They may have fear and a will of their own, but these may not have the same significance as in the case of an adult'. *Op. cit.*, para. 215. This approach effectively conflates age with maturity and conflicts with the Com. RC's recommendation about the presumption of capacity. For critical commentary of the UNHCR Handbook in this regard, see J. Bhabha, 'Minors or aliens? Inconsistent State intervention and separated child asylum-seekers', *European Journal of Migration and Law* 3, 2001, 297–298.

51 UNHCR Child Guidelines, *op. cit.,* para. 73. See further UNHCR Handbook, *op. cit.,* para. 219. Furthermore, according to para. 196 of the Handbook, 'while the burden of proof in principle rests on the applicant, the duty to ascertain and evaluate all the relevant facts is shared between the applicant and the examiner. Indeed, in some cases, *it may be for the examiner to use all the means at his disposal to produce the necessary evidence in support of the application*'. Emphasis added. In *Hatami v Sweden*, the ECtHR pronounced on the need for flexibility in dealing with the claims of traumatised persons or victims of rape or torture who may have difficulties in recounting their experiences. ECtHR, *Hatami v Sweden*, Appl. No. 32448/28, Judgment of 23 April 1998, para. 106. Arguably, the same principle applies to minors.

such as a lack of internal consistency, to infer that the applicant does not have a fear of persecution or serious harm.[52] In this regard, it is worth quoting at some length from the UNHCR Guidelines:

> Children cannot be expected to provide adult-like accounts of their experiences. They may have difficulty articulating their fear for a range of reasons, including trauma, parental instructions, lack of education, fear of State authorities or persons in positions of power, use of ready-made testimony by smugglers, or fear of reprisals. They may be too young or immature to be able to evaluate what information is important or to interpret what they have witnessed or experienced in a manner that it easily understandable to an adult. Some children may omit or distort vital information or be unable to differentiate the imagined from reality. They also may experience difficulty relating to abstract notions such as time or distance. Thus, what might constitute a lie in the case of an adult may not necessarily be a lie in the case of a child.[53]

Accordingly, it is submitted that giving 'due weight' to the views of the child in accordance with age and maturity – in the above sense of attributing the proper quality, substance or credence to the child's views – is simply not possible if the weight to be given to testimony has been pre-determined by rules establishing negative credibility inferences. This is particularly the case when such rules are founded on assumptions about how *adults* conduct themselves credibly (or incredibly) – assumptions that are quite unsound in the case of children.

Phase One CEAS: Compliance with the right of the child to be heard

According to Article 12 CRC, the right of the child to be heard pertains to 'any judicial and administrative proceedings affecting the child'. A large number of asylum proceedings (or 'procedures' to use the nomenclature of the CEAS) can be identified as relevant to this right. Two sets of procedures are not covered by the APD: procedures for determining the Member State responsible under the DR, and the procedures in the RCD for the reduction or withdrawal of reception conditions. The bulk of procedures, however, are governed by the APD, which will be the focus of this section.

---

52 For a critical analysis of the central role of credibility assessment in EU asylum systems, see UNHCR, 'Beyond proof: credibility assessment in EU asylum systems', Brussels, May 2013. Hereinafter, 'UNHCR, Beyond Proof'.
53 UNHCR Child Guidelines, *op. cit.*, para. 72.

The procedures in the APD may, with some shoe-horning, be classified as follows:

- what might be called the 'regular' first instance procedure, which must generally, subject to some derogations, comply with the 'basic principles and guarantees' set out in Chapter II of the directive;
- what might be called 'extraordinary' first instance procedures, to which some or all of the 'basic principles and guarantees' as set out in Chapter II of the directive are not required to apply.[54] These consist of an admissibility procedure,[55] an accelerated procedure[56] and the so-called 'specific procedures'.[57] There are two specific procedures currently in operation:
  - a preliminary examination procedure for screening subsequent applications to determine whether they should be admitted to the regular procedure or summarily rejected;[58] and
  - a border procedure, which Member States can retain on the basis of a stand-still clause, for deciding on permission to enter the territory;[59]
- procedures for the withdrawal of refugee status, which establish a unique set of procedural rules but also cross-reference a limited number of the provisions of the 'basic principles and guarantees' of Chapter II;[60] and
- appeal procedures, which are governed by some of the 'basic principles and guarantees' of Chapter II and some rules specifically geared to the appellate stage.[61]

---

54 The term 'extraordinary' is something of a misnomer, as the chapter relating to first instance procedures (Chapter III) is largely taken up with establishing extraordinary procedures. Thus, as Costello opines, 'exceptional procedures become the norm'. C. Costello, 'The European Asylum Procedures Directive in legal context', *New Issues in Refugee Research*, UNHCR Research Paper No. 134, 2006, 1–35, 8.
55 Article 25.
56 Article 23(4). The grounds for acceleration may also constitute grounds for a manifestly unfounded determination under Article 28(2). The procedural consequences of acceleration are left to the discretion of Member States, subject to the caveat that the procedure is in accordance with the basic principles and guarantees of Chapter II of the directive. However, some of the derogations in Chapter II apply to some of the grounds for acceleration.
57 Article 24. Member States are expressly permitted to derogate from the basic principles and guarantees of Chapter II in the context of the specific procedures.
58 Articles 32–34.
59 Article 35(2)–(5). Hereinafter, the 'border-entry procedure'. This procedure should be distinguished from the 'regular' border procedure in Article 35(1), the purpose of which is to decide at the border or transit zones on applications made at such locations. The latter is not classified as a 'specific procedure'. There was originally a third 'specific procedure' under the directive, namely, the European safe third country concept in Article 36. However, since ECJ, *European Parliament v Council*, Case C-133/06, Judgment of 6 May 2008, this concept is no longer operative and therefore will not be analysed in the context of Phase One CEAS; it will be analysed in the context of Phase Two.
60 Articles 37 and 38.
61 Article 39.

Not surprisingly, the procedural guarantees in the APD have been described as 'highly qualified and differentiated',[62] making an assessment of compliance with the right of the child to be heard a complex exercise – itself a portent of the difficulties the child is likely to face in participating in the procedure.

The right to a hearing

Based on the general presumption of capacity, children should be given the opportunity of a hearing in all asylum procedures to which they are subject. To what extent is the right of the child to a hearing respected in the APD?

Article 12 (Personal interview) of Chapter II of the APD provides in paragraph 1 that:

> Before a decision is taken by the determining authority, the applicant for asylum shall be given the opportunity of a personal interview on his/her application for asylum with a person competent under national law to conduct such an interview.
> [...]
> Member States may determine in national legislation the cases in which a minor shall be given the opportunity of a personal interview.

As outlined in Chapter 3 above, Article 6(4) APD on access to the asylum procedure permits but does not require Member States to determine whether a minor can be an 'applicant for asylum'. Where a Member State provides that a minor can be an applicant for asylum, the first sentence of Article 12(1), being a mandatory provision, should arguably take precedence over the subsequent optional provision. Hence, where a minor is an applicant for asylum, he/she must be given the opportunity of a personal interview. However, where a minor is not an applicant for asylum – because the Member State has omitted to legislate for this possibility or because the minor's claim is subsumed into that of his/her parent or lodged by a representative – then the minor has no automatic right to a personal interview. The European Commission's evaluation of the APD contains no information on whether or which Member States grant minors the opportunity of a personal interview.[63] However, a UNHCR report on the application of key provisions of the APD from 2010 notes that '[t]he research found that in the absence of a specific requirement in the APD, national legislation on the circumstances in which a child shall be given the

---

62 C. Costello, *op. cit.*, p. 1.
63 'Report from the Commission to the European Parliament and the Council on the Application of Directive 2005/85/EC of 1 December 2005 on Minimum Standards on Procedures in Member States for Granting and Withdrawing Refugee Status', *COM (2010) 465 final* (hereinafter, 'Commission evaluation of the APD').

opportunity of a personal interview in the asylum procedure is divergent, and in some cases absent.'[64]

In addition to the ambivalence in the APD regarding whether the child has a right to be interviewed, the directive provides for what has been described as an 'extensive catalogue of situations in which the personal interview can be omitted'.[65] Therefore, even if the child is granted, in principle, a right to be interviewed under national law, the Member State may still omit the interview on numerous grounds. While there are at least ten such grounds in the APD, the focus here will be on those grounds that seem likely to be applied or are particularly detrimental to children.[66]

One such ground is Article 12(3), which provides for the omission of the personal interview where it is 'not reasonably practicable, in particular where the competent authority is of the opinion that the applicant is unfit or unable to be interviewed owing to enduring circumstances beyond his/her control'. This provision seems apt to be applied to young children whose age is an enduring circumstance beyond their control and which, if the procedure is not adapted to children, could render them unfit or unable to be interviewed.[67] Furthermore, the reference to the 'competent authority' as opposed to the usual 'determining authority' means that a body that is not the normal status-determination body can make the critical decision that the applicant is unfit or unable to be interviewed. So, what kind of body is this 'competent authority'? Some insight is provided by Article 4(2), which provides that an authority that is not the determining authority may administer six different types of procedure, including two types of border procedure.[68] Hence, a body that administers any of these procedures is a 'competent authority' for the purposes of the directive. The idea, for example, that a border guard should

---

64 UNHCR, 'Improving Asylum Procedures, Comparative Analysis and Recommendations for Law and Practice (A UNHCR research project on the application of key provisions of the Asylum Procedures Directive in selected Member States)', Brussels, 2010, 23 (hereinafter, 'UNHCR APD Report').
65 Ibid., p. 21.
66 Four grounds for omitting a personal interview arise in the context of the ordinary procedure: in Article 12(2)(a), Article 12(2)(b), Article 12(3) and Article 20. Five grounds arise in the context of the accelerated/manifestly unfounded procedure: in Article 12(2)(c) which cross-references Article 23(4)(a), (c), (g), (h) and (j). One ground arises in the context of the preliminary examination of subsequent applications in Article 35(3)(d). Finally, Article 25 relating to the admissibility procedure is silent on the question of a personal interview.
67 No feedback on the operation of this provision is provided in the Commission's evaluation of the directive. Commission evaluation of the APD, op. cit.
68 The six procedures are: the DR procedure, a procedure for dealing with so-called 'national security cases', a preliminary examination procedure for processing subsequent applications, a border procedure for deciding on claims made at the border or in transit zones, a border procedure to decide on permission to enter, and a procedure for dealing with 'European safe third country' cases.

be vested with the power to decide whether a child is fit or able to be interviewed is highly troubling.

Another problematic provision is Article 12(2)(c), which allows the personal interview to be omitted in certain unfounded cases that may also be the basis for an accelerated procedure and a manifestly unfounded determination.[69] Five grounds are enumerated: 1) the application is not relevant or of minimal relevance to qualification as a refugee; 2) the applicant comes from an objectively designated safe country of origin or a safe third country; 3) the applicant has made inconsistent, contradictory, improbable or insufficient representations, which make his/her claim clearly unconvincing; 4) the applicant has submitted a subsequent application that does not raise any new elements; and 5) the applicant is making an application merely in order to delay or frustrate the enforcement of a removal decision. Four of these grounds are particularly problematic in the context of minors. Grounds 1) and 2) are problematic because, as was outlined in Chapter 3, owing to the adult-oriented nature of the definition of persecution and serious harm, a child-specific protection need may not be immediately perceived as relevant to international protection. Ground 3) is problematic because children's accounts are prone to being non-linear, disjointed and sometimes – in consequence of the cultural relativism of the adjudicator – improbable. And ground 4) is problematic because children who fail to be recognised on account of the reasons just outlined or because their claims were inappropriately subsumed into those of their parents (per Chapter 3) may have no choice but to submit a subsequent application. Aside from these child-specific objections, omitting a personal interview where the application involves a claim of torture or inhuman or degrading treatment or punishment is also likely to offend against Article 13 ECHR in conjunction with Article 3.[70]

A final area in which a personal interview can (apparently) be omitted and which is particularly detrimental to children is the admissibility procedure. Article 25 on inadmissible applications exempts the State from having to examine the substance of the application in seven circumstances.[71] Article 25 is silent on the question of a personal interview. However, two of the grounds

---

69 According to the Commission evaluation of the directive, nine Member States avail of the option to omit the personal interview in the context of accelerated procedures: CY, CZ, DE, EL, FI, IT, LU SI, UK. Commission evaluation of the APD, *op. cit*, § 5.1.4, p. 6.
70 See ECtHR, *I.M. v France*, *op. cit.*, in which the Court found a violation of Article 13 in conjunction with Article 3 in circumstances where the applicant's asylum claim was processed in an accelerated/manifestly unfounded procedure in which he was given only a brief, half-hour interview. The judgment applies *a fortiori* to the practice of omitting a personal interview altogether.
71 The circumstances are: another EU Member State is a first country of asylum; a non-EU Member State is a first country of asylum; a non-EU Member State is a safe third country; the applicant has a status equivalent to refugee status; the applicant has a right to remain pending a decision on the granting of a status equivalent to refugee status; the applicant has lodged an identical application after a final decision; the application is a subsequent application by a dependent who formerly consented to be part of an application made on his/her behalf.

of inadmissibility, namely, 'safe third country' and the lodging of an identical application, overlap with two of the grounds in Article 12(2)(c) regarding the omission of the personal interview. Therefore, a personal interview is not a prerequisite for a finding of inadmissibility on either of these grounds, at least. The admissibility procedure is particularly detrimental to children because it conflicts with the right of the child to *appropriate* protection in Article 22 CRC. This mandates an assessment of the child's protection needs, which, in turn, requires that a child's claim be considered substantively, as opposed to being screened to exclude a substantive examination on formal or procedural grounds. Moreover, deeming a child's claim to be inadmissible conflicts with the principle of the best interests of the child as laid down in Article 3(1) CRC. As outlined in Chapter 2 above, the best interests principle mandates an individualised assessment of all relevant facts in order to identify from the available options which is in the child's best interest. Since the admissibility procedure excludes from consideration the facts relating to the substance of the claim, it circumvents a best-interests assessment.

Having dealt with the matter of the personal interview at first instance, there are two remaining procedures that must be evaluated in the light of the right of the child to be heard: the procedure for withdrawing refugee status and the appeals procedure.

Although Article 14 of the Qualification Directive (QD) establishes the grounds on which refugee status can be withdrawn, grounds such as cessation and exclusion,[72] the procedure is governed by the APD. As regards the right to be heard, Article 38(1)(b) APD provides that where a Member State is considering withdrawing refugee status, the person concerned is entitled to submit, in a personal interview *or* in a written statement, reasons why his/her refugee status should not be withdrawn. Consequently, there is no right to a personal interview. Article 38(1)(b) goes on to state that where a personal interview is conducted, it must be in accordance with Article 12. Article 12, as we have already seen, authorises Member States to determine in national legislation the cases in which a minor shall be given the opportunity of a personal interview.[73] However, in a number of cases concerning withdrawal of refugee status for reasons of exclusion and cessation, the CJEU has strongly indicated the need for a personal interview on the basis of the wording of the exclusion and cessation clauses in the QD.[74] This is significant in the context of children because, as was discussed in Chapter 3 above, minors are not exempt from having their refugee status withdrawn, and, moreover, the application of exclusion and

---

72 Council Directive 2004/83/EC of 29 April 2004.
73 The Commission evaluation of the directive is silent on the issue of the personal interview in the context of withdrawal procedures. Commission evaluation of the APD, *op. cit*.
74 The key exclusion case in this regard is CJEU, *B and D*, Case C-57/09 and C-101/09, Judgment of the Court (GC) of 9 November 2010. See, in particular, para. 91. The cessation case is CJEU, *Abdulla and Others*, Joined cases C-175/08, C-176/08, C-178/08 and C-179/08, Judgment of the Court (GC) of 2 March 2010. See in particular para. 70.

cessation grounds to minors raises particular difficulties from a child-rights perspective, underscoring the need for a personal interview.

Finally, as regards appeal procedures, Article 39(1) on the right to an effective remedy provides that asylum applicants have the right to an effective remedy before a court or tribunal against an illustrative list of first-instance asylum decisions, a provision that has been interpreted broadly by the Court as applying to all decisions that entail rejection of the application for asylum for substantive reasons or for formal or procedural reasons that preclude any decision on the substance.[75] Consequently, the material scope of the right to an effective remedy under the directive is broad. However, Article 39 is silent on the question of whether the remedy must include a hearing or whether a paper review is sufficient. Certain provisions of the directive appear to militate against an appeal hearing, while others appear to imply a hearing.

For example, Article 7 provides that, subject to certain exceptions, applicants must be allowed to remain in the Member State until a first instance decision has been made. *A contrario*, there is no right to remain after the first instance decision has been made and, it follows, no right to an appeal hearing. However, Article 7 must be interpreted in the light of Article 39(3), which allows Member States, in accordance with their international obligations, to decide on the question of suspensive effect. But Member States' international obligations (in particular, the right to an effective remedy under Article 13 ECHR) mandate a remedy with automatic suspensive effect when there is an arguable claim of irreparable harm.[76] Furthermore, the case-law of the ECtHR on Article 13 strongly suggests the need for an appeal hearing.[77] Unsurprisingly, in view of the ambiguity in the directive on the question of an appeal hearing, State practice is mixed: although the Commission evaluation has nothing to say on the question of an appeal hearing, the UNHCR report on the directive notes that only six of the twelve countries surveyed provide the appellant with the possibility of a hearing.[78]

In sum, the qualified right of the child to a personal interview, which is undermined by the catalogue of situations in which a personal interview may be omitted – some of which are apt to be applied or are particularly detrimental

---

75 CJEU, *Diouf*, Case C-69/10, Judgment of 28 July 2011, para. 42.
76 For a cross-section of cases, see ECtHR, *Jabari v Turkey*, *op. cit.*; ECtHR, *Conka v Belgium*, *op. cit.*; ECtHR, *Gebremedhin v France*, Appl. No. 25389/05, Judgment of 26 April 2005; ECtHR, *Abdolkhani and Karimnia v Turkey*, *op. cit.*; ECtHR, *Baysakov and Others v Ukraine*, *op. cit.*; ECtHR, *M.S.S. v Belgium and Greece*, Appl. No. 30696/09, Judgment of 21 January 2011. For commentary, see M. Reneman, 'An EU right to interim protection during appeal proceedings in asylum cases?', *European Journal of Migration and Law* 12, 2010, 407–434.
77 For instance, in the context of an allegation that expulsion will violate Article 3, the ECtHR has stressed the need for a full and *ex nunc* assessment of the claim. It is hard to see how this could be done in the absence of an appeal hearing. See, for example, ECtHR, *Salah Sheekh v The Netherlands*, Appl. No. 1948/04, Judgment of 11 January 2007 and ECtHR, *NA. v The United Kingdom*, Appl. No. 25904/07, Judgment of 17 July 2008.
78 UNHCR ADP Report, *op. cit.*, p. 91.

to children – suggests that the right of the child to a hearing is not guaranteed in the first-instances procedures as established in the APD. The right of the child to a hearing is no better secured in the withdrawals procedure or in the appeals procedure. However, it is submitted that the discretion given to Member States regarding a personal interview or appeal hearing is likely to be fettered by the CJEU and the ECtHR.

There is one final issue to address in this subsection: whether the APD conceives of the hearing of the applicant as a right of the applicant or a duty of the applicant. Article 12 CRC establishes that a child cannot be forced to be heard against his/her will. However, the APD is ambiguous as to whether the hearing of the applicant is a right or a duty. Article 12 (Personal interview) refers to the 'opportunity of a personal interview', presenting the interview as a right, not an obligation. However, various other provisions of the directive suggest the contrary, providing for negative procedural consequences if the applicant does not appear for or engage with the personal interview.[79] There is no exemption for minors, and, indeed, Article 17 on guarantees for unaccompanied minors, having established the right to a representative in paragraph 1, goes on to provide that 'Member States may require the presence of the unaccompanied minor at the personal interview, even if the representative is present'.[80] Consequently, the APD does not prohibit and may even facilitate the interviewing of children against their will.[81]

---

79 Thus, Article 12(6) provides: 'Irrespective of Article 20(1) Member States, when deciding on the application for asylum, may take into account the fact that the applicant failed to appear for the personal interview, unless he/she had good reasons for the failure to appear.' Article 20, in turn, sets out the procedure to be followed in the case of implicit withdrawal or abandonment of the application. It provides in paragraph 1(a) that failure to appear for interview constitutes a ground for implicit withdrawal or abandonment of an application. Article 33 (Failure to appear) allows Member States to apply the preliminary examination procedure for subsequent claims to an applicant who fails to appear before the competent authority at a specified time. Finally, failure to engage with the hearing may fall under any one of a number of grounds for accelerating the claim under Article 23(4), such as ground (d), withholding relevant information, or ground (g), making insufficient representations, all of which also constitute grounds for a manifestly unfounded determination.

80 Similarly, Article 16 relating to the scope of legal assistance and representation provides in the second sub-paragraph of paragraph 4 that 'Member States may require the presence of the applicant at the personal interview, even if he/she is represented under the terms of national law by [...] a legal adviser or counselor, and may require the applicant to respond in person to the questions asked'.

81 The EU Fundamental Rights agency conducted research into the treatment of separated asylum-seeking children in the EU and found that '[t]he interview process itself was invariably an unpleasant experience for children, who often complained, especially in Austria and Belgium, that it was a long and detailed interrogation with the same questions asked repeatedly'. EU Fundamental Rights Agency, 'Separated, asylum-seeking children in European Union Member States' (Summary Report/Conference Edition) 2010, 100 (hereinafter, 'FRA separated asylum-seeking children report').

The conduct of the hearing

The right of the child in Article 12 CRC to be heard 'either directly or through a representative' and to express views 'freely' has significant implications for the conduct of the hearing. In particular, the child has a right to a representative and to an appropriately modified hearing. To what extent are these rights met in the APD?

The right to a representative

Article 17 APD (Guarantees for unaccompanied minors) provides in paragraph 1(a) that Member States must 'take measures to ensure that a representative represents and/or assists the unaccompanied minor with respect to the examination of the application'. Article 17(1)(b) establishes that the representative plays an information and support role in relation to preparing the minor for the personal interview. With this in mind, the representative must be permitted to be present at the interview and to ask questions or make comments within the framework set by the person who conducts the interview. The representative, who can be the same person as the representative appointed under the RCD, is defined in Article 2(i) as:

> [A] person acting on behalf of an organization representing an unaccompanied minor as legal guardian, a person acting on behalf of a national organization which is responsible for the care and well-being of minors, or any other appropriate representation appointed to ensure his/her best interests.

On the one hand, these provisions can be regarded as positive since they establish the right of an unaccompanied minor to a representative. But on the other, it is not entirely clear that the role of the representative is to represent – in the Article 12 CRC sense – the child. The 'and/or' formulation in Article 17(1)(a) and the limited role of the representative at interview as outlined in Article 17(1)(b) suggest that the role can be reduced to one of an assistant. Furthermore, no standards are explicitly established regarding the qualifications of the representative or his/her independence from the status-determination body. The net result is uncertainty about what the representative is supposed to do in the procedure. This is reflected in the Commission evaluation of the APD, which reports that, while all Member States do provide for representation of unaccompanied minors in the procedure, generally in the form of a guardian, the guardianship systems vary considerably between Member States in terms of institutional arrangements, authorities involved and the guardians' role and qualifications.[82] Other reports have made similar findings. For example,

---

82 Commission evaluation of the APD, *op. cit.*, § 5.1.6, p. 8.

in a report into separated children seeking asylum in the EU, the Fundamental Rights Agency found that 'most of the children interviewed were not fully aware of whether they had a guardian, who that person was or which responsibilities were attached to the guardianship function'.[83] Consequently, there is a need for a fuller definition of the role and responsibilities of the representative in the APD.

Furthermore, Article 17(2) and (3) APD between them permit Member States to derogate from the obligation to appoint a representative on four grounds: three on the basis of the constructive emancipation of the minor (i.e. the child is likely to 'age out' before a first instance decision, is or has been married, or is over 16 if such a derogation exists in national law at the time of the adoption of the directive), and one by eliminating the right to a representative where the minor has access to a free legal advisor. The constructive emancipation of the minor is objectionable for reasons that will be discussed in Chapter 5, while conflating the role of representative and legal representative betrays an unfortunate lack of understanding of the distinct roles of – and right to – both.

These are not the only derogations. Although Article 17(1) on the right to a representative is explicitly stated to apply to 'all procedures provided for in this Directive', it is unclear how this provision interacts with Article 24, which allows Member States to derogate from the basic principles and guarantees of Chapter II (including Article 17) in the context of the specific procedures. Of the two specific procedures that are operational, namely, the preliminary examination of subsequent applications and the border entry procedure, only the latter envisages a role for the representative of the unaccompanied minor.[84]

Finally, the obligation to appoint a representative only applies to unaccompanied minors. No provision of the APD refers to the need for an accompanied minor who lodges an application on his/her own behalf or makes representations in relation to his/her parent's claim to be represented by someone – either the parent or, in case of a conflict of interest, an independent representative. However, Article 13 (Requirements for a personal interview) does allow, exceptionally, for the presence of family members at interview where the determining authority considers it necessary. Hence Article 13 could be used as an enabling provision. This would not, however, address the need for an independent representative where there is a conflict of interest.

---

83 FRA separated asylum-seeking children report, *op. cit.,* p. 33. See further, UNHCR APD Report, *op. cit.*, p. 36. Inadequate representation of unaccompanied minors by EU Member States has been a consistent theme of the Com. RC over the past decade. For example, in 2012 alone, three of the four EU Member States that reported to the Committee were criticised on this score: Concluding Observations to Austria, *UN Doc. CRC/C/AUT/CO/3-4 (2012)*, para. 54; Concluding Observations to Cyprus, *UN Doc. CRC/C/CYP/CO/3-4 (2012)*, para. 46(a); Concluding Observations to Greece, *UN Doc. CRC/C/GRC/CO/2-3 (2012)*, para. 62.
84 Article 35(3)(f) cross-references Article 17(1)–(3).

In brief, the provisions of the APD relating to the appointment of a representative for unaccompanied minors are drafted at a level of generality that does not guarantee that the requirements of Article 12 CRC will be met. Furthermore, the obligation to appoint a representative to an unaccompanied minor can be derogated from in various circumstances, at least some of which are problematic. Finally, the APD fails to establish the right of an accompanied minor to an independent representative in situations of conflict of interest. In sum, therefore, it can be said that the APD goes some, but not all, of the way toward meeting the requirements of Article 12 CRC regarding the right of the child to be heard, if necessary through a representative.

The adaptation of the hearing

As regards the first instance procedure, Article 17 APD (Guarantees for unaccompanied minors) stipulates in paragraph 4 that personal interviews of unaccompanied minors (where they take place) and decisions on the applications of unaccompanied minors must be conducted/taken by a person 'with the necessary knowledge of the special needs of minors'. On the one hand, this is an important recognition of the fact that interviewing minors and assessing their claims is a qualitatively different exercise than in the case of adults. On the other hand, in view of the myriad ways that the interview needs to be adapted in order to be 'child-friendly', it is submitted that Article 17(4) is a rather inadequate expression of what is at stake. While one would not necessarily expect guidelines on child-friendly interviewing to appear in legislation, one might legitimately expect to find a direction to Member States to provide such guidance in their domestic legislation, along with some broad indications of the content of such guidance.[85] As regards training, while the reference in Article 17(4) to 'the necessary knowledge of the special needs of minors' implicitly presupposes staff training, Article 17 establishes no explicit training requirement much less any direction as to the content of such training. Indeed, there are only two references to training in the entire APD – one in a recital[86] and one, ironically, relating to authorities *other than* the usual 'determining authority'.[87] The Commission evaluation notes that institutional arrangements for training, including follow-up training, are in place in just eight

---

85 UNHCR has called for EU-wide guidelines on the personal interview of all children. UNHCR APD Report, *op. cit.*, p. 36.
86 Recital 10 provides: 'It is essential that decisions on all applications for asylum be taken on the basis of the facts and, in the first instance, by authorities whose personnel has the appropriate knowledge or receives the necessary training in the field of asylum and refugee matters.'
87 Article 4(3) states: 'Where [alternative] authorities are designated [...], Member States shall ensure that the personnel of such authorities have the appropriate knowledge or receive the necessary training to fulfill their obligations when implementing this Directive.'

Member States and that 'other Member States tend to rely on *ad hoc* training and the length, intensity and content of training vary considerably'.[88]

Furthermore, unsatisfactory though it is, there is no corollary to Article 17 for accompanied minors. Consequently, those accompanied minors who are entitled to lodge an asylum application on their own behalf and who are permitted to be interviewed do not benefit from any child-specific guarantees relating to the hearing.

There are, however, a number of important general (i.e. non child-specific) standards established in the directive regarding staff competence, the examination of applications and the conduct of the personal interview, which are equally applicable to minors. Thus, Article 4 (Responsible authorities) requires in paragraph 1 that the designated determining authority must conduct an 'appropriate examination' of applications. Article 8 (Requirements for the examination of applications) provides in paragraph 2 that personnel examining applications and taking decisions have knowledge of the relevant standards in asylum and refugee law. Article 12 (Personal interview) provides in paragraph 1 that the personal interview (where there is one) must be conducted by 'a person competent under national law to conduct such an interview'. Article 13 (Requirements for a personal interview) establishes in paragraph 3 that personal interviews must be conducted 'under conditions which allow applicants to present the grounds for their application in a comprehensive manner', and to this end sub-paragraph (a) obliges Member States to 'ensure that the person who conducts the interview is sufficiently competent to take account of the personal or general circumstances surrounding the application, including the applicant's cultural origin and vulnerability, insofar as it is possible to do so'. The qualified wording of this last provision aside ('*sufficiently* competent', 'personal *or* general circumstances', 'insofar as it is possible to do so'), these are important general standards that could benefit minors equally.

However, some or all of the general standards can be derogated from – explicitly or implicitly – in various circumstances, all of which potentially apply to minors. First, it is not clear from the wording of Article 12(1) that the personal interview must be conducted by the determining authority.[89] If not, then the standards that are established in respect of the determining authority in Articles 4 and 8 are not applicable. Second, Article 4(2) of the APD provides that an authority other than the usual 'determining authority' may be established for processing cases under six categories, including the

---

88 Commission evaluation of the APD, *op. cit.,* § 5.1.3, p. 5.
89 Article 12(1) first sub-paragraph provides: 'Before a decision is taken by the determining authority, the applicant for asylum shall be given the opportunity of a personal interview on his/her application for asylum with a person competent under national law to conduct such an interview.' It is not obvious that the 'person competent under national law' must be from the determining authority.

specific procedures (i.e. the preliminary examination of subsequent applications and the border-entry procedure) and the border procedure to decide at the border or in transit zones on applications made at those locations. Here again, the standards established in Articles 4 and 8 are not applicable. Article 4(3) does oblige Member States to 'ensure that the personnel of such [alternative] authorities have the appropriate knowledge or receive the necessary training to fulfil their obligations when implementing this directive'. However, this is clearly a lesser, or, at least, a less detailed, standard than that laid down in Article 8, in particular. Thirdly, as regards the specific procedures, even if Member States do not appoint an alternative authority to administer such procedures, they are permitted in Article 24 to derogate from the basic principles and guarantees of Chapter II, including Articles 8, 12, 13 and 17 discussed above.

Neither the provisions on withdrawal of refugee status nor the provisions relating to the appeals procedures make any reference to the need to adapt the hearing, if there is one, to facilitate the participation of minors. As regards the withdrawal procedure, it can be further observed that this can be administered by an authority other than the determining authority, which means that the standards pertaining to the determining authority do not apply. As for the appeals procedure, the lack of any provision on a hearing, much less on the conduct of the hearing, appears to have facilitated the growth of widely divergent approaches to holding and conducting appeals in Member States.[90]

In conclusion, the APD contains a limited acknowledgement of the need to adapt the interview for unaccompanied, though not accompanied, minors. While this is bolstered by a number of important general standards regarding staff competence, the examination of applications and the conduct of the personal interview, some or all of those standards may be derogated from in various circumstances. The provisions of the directive relating to the procedure for the withdrawal of refugee status and the appeals procedure contain no acknowledgement of the need to adapt the hearing for minors. Consequently, the APD falls short of the requirements of Article 12 CRC relating to the right of the child to express views 'freely'.

The evaluation of the child's views

Article 12(1) CRC establishes that the views of the child must be given due weight in accordance with the age and maturity of the child. Giving due weight to the child's view of his/her protection needs may require the Member State to assume a greater share of the burden of proof and desist from applying automatic negative credibility inferences. To what extent is this foreseen in the APD?

---

90 See, EU Fundamental Rights Agency, 'Access to effective remedies: The asylum-seeker perspective', Thematic Report, (2010), 35.

Burden of proof

The APD does not contain any clear statement relating to the burden of proof. However, Article 4 of the QD (Assessment of facts and circumstances) is of relevance, although it does not use that exact term. Article 4(1) provides that 'Member States *may* consider it the duty of the applicant to submit as soon as possible all elements needed to substantiate the application for international protection. In cooperation with the applicant, it *is* the duty of the Member State to assess the relevant elements of the application'.[91] The CJEU has categorised this as a two-stage assessment, the first stage concerning the establishment of factual circumstances and the second stage relating to a legal appraisal of the evidence.[92] While the second stage is solely the responsibility of the Member State, the Court has declined to infer the converse, namely, that the first stage is solely the responsibility of the applicant. Thus in *M.M.*, the Court held that 'if, *for any reason whatsoever*, the elements provided by an applicant for international protection are not complete, up to date or relevant, it is necessary for the Member State concerned to cooperate actively with the applicant [...] so that all the elements needed to substantiate the application may be assembled'.[93] Hence, the burden of proof in the QD may be characterised as shared and flexible.[94] This is consistent with the approach of the ECtHR to the burden of proof in Article 3 ECHR cases.[95] A shared and flexible burden of proof bodes well for giving 'due weight' to the views of the child.

However, while certain provisions of the APD appear to reinforce the concept of a shared and flexible burden of proof established in the QD, others appear to undermine it.[96] For reasons of space, the focus here will be on the

---

91 Emphasis added.
92 CJEU, *M.M*, Case C-277/11, Judgment of 22 November 2012.
93 *Ibid.*, para. 66 (emphasis added). Furthermore, in *Abdulla*, the Court stated in relation to Article 4(1) and (2) of the QD that '[i]t must be acknowledged that the level of difficulty encountered, first, in gathering the relevant elements for the purposes of the assessment of the circumstances may, solely from the perspective of the relevance of the facts, prove to be higher or lower from one case to another'. CJEU, *Abdulla and Others, op. cit.*, para. 86.
94 For academic commentary see G. Noll, 'Evidentiary assessment in refugee status determination and the EU Qualification Directive', *European Public Law* 12, 2006, 295–317, and more generally, G. Noll (ed.), *Proof, Evidentiary Assessment and Credibility in Asylum Law*, Leiden/Boston: Martinus Nijhoff Publishers, 2005.
95 See, for example, ECtHR, *Singh v Belgium*, Appl. No. 33210/11, Judgment of 2 October 2012.
96 Certain paragraphs of Article 12 ADP, for example, reinforce the concept of a shared and flexible burden of proof. Paragraph 3 of Article 12 permits the personal interview to be omitted where the applicant is 'unfit or unable to be interviewed owing to enduring circumstances beyond his/her control'. Paragraph 4 establishes that this 'shall not prevent the determining authority from taking a decision on an application for asylum', while paragraph 5 states that the absence of a personal interview 'shall not adversely affect the decision of the determining authority'. If the lack of a personal interview is not to adversely affect the decision, it follows that the determining authority must assume greater responsibility for investigating the claim.

'safe country' concepts in the APD, which, among other provisions of the directive, appear to place the burden of proof solely on the applicant.[97] The provisions of the APD that relate to safe country of origin (SCO), safe third country (STC) and first country of asylum (FCA) concepts establish a presumption based on objective factors that the country of origin or a third country is safe for the applicant, thereby placing the burden on the applicant to rebut that presumption. The stakes are high: in the case of SCO, if the applicant cannot rebut the presumption of safety, the claim may be accelerated, designated manifestly unfounded and a personal interview may be omitted;[98] in the case of STC, the claim may *additionally* be deemed inadmissible;[99] and in the case of FCA, the claim may be deemed inadmissible.[100] Each of these safe country concepts will be dealt with in turn.

As regards SCO, the APD establishes that Member States should be able to 'presume [a designated country's] safety for a particular applicant, unless he/she presents serious counter-indications'[101] and should operate 'on the basis of a rebuttable presumption of safety of that country'.[102] The presumption will be rebutted if the applicant submits 'serious grounds for considering the country not to be a safe country of origin in his/her particular circumstances and in terms of his/her qualification as a refugee [...]'.[103] One case regarding the SCO concept has come before the CJEU to date: in *HID, BA*, the Court upheld a national practice of prioritising claims from a designated SCO so long as *the applicants* were given sufficient time to 'gather and present the necessary information in support of their application, thus allowing the determining authority to carry out a fair and comprehensive examination'.[104] Unlike the earlier case of *MM*, the Court in *HID, BA* did not refer to a shared responsibility to establish factual circumstances, confirming what already

---

97 Two further provisions are of concern. Article 23(4)(o) was mentioned in Chapter 3 above. It relates to accompanied minors who lodge an application after their parents' claim is rejected and appears to place the burden entirely on the minor to raise new elements with respect to his/her particular circumstances or to the situation in his/her country of origin. Article 34 on procedural rules governing preliminary examinations of subsequent applications also appears to permit placing the burden of proof solely on the applicant. Specifically, Member States are permitted to establish rules in national law obliging the applicant concerned to 'indicate facts and substantiate evidence which justify a new procedure'.
98 Article 23(4)(c)(i), Article 28(2) and Article 12(2)(c) APD, respectively.
99 Article 25(1)(c). The claim may also be accelerated and deemed manifestly unfounded under Article 23(4)(c)(ii) and 29(2) and be decided without a personal interview under Article 12(2)(c).
100 Article 25(1)(b).
101 Recital 17.
102 Recital 19.
103 Article 31(1). The Commission evaluation of the APD reports that only four Member States do not have a SCO procedure in place and that '[w]ide divergences are identified between Member States which have SCO procedures in place'. *Op. cit.*, § 5.2.5, p. 12.
104 H.I.D., B.A., Case C-175/11, Judgment of 31 January 2013, para. 75.

seemed apparent from the wording of the above provisions, namely, that a different test applies in the context of the SCO concept. The problem of shifting the burden of proof in this way is that it is a slippery slope. Thus, in its report on the APD, UNHCR notes that although *in law* only one of the States surveyed shifted the entire burden of proof to the applicant (most States simply increasing the burden of proof on the applicant), 'UNHCR is concerned that *in practice, however, some States may place the burden of proof entirely on the applicant*, sometimes in the context of an accelerated procedure, without adequately recognizing the necessity of a shared examination of the claim'.[105]

As regards STC, Article 27 provides in paragraph 2(c) that Member States must lay down in national legislation rules 'in accordance with international law' providing for an individual examination of the safety of the third country for the particular applicant, which, 'at a minimum, permit the applicant to challenge the application of the safe third country concept on the grounds that he/she would be subjected to torture, cruel, inhuman or degrading treatment or punishment'. The reference to international law in conjunction with the reference to torture, cruel, inhuman or degrading treatment or punishment suggests that international law can be reduced to the requirements of international human rights law. However, international law also includes international refugee law, which establishes a prohibition of *refoulement* that is broader in scope than the right of *non-refoulement* in the torture context.[106] Consequently, Article 27(2)(c) is highly ambiguous, mandating rules in accordance with international law but then establishing a minimum standard that falls short of the requirements of international law. Where Member States avail of the minimum option – and four do according to the Commission – this means that the presumption of safety on all other objective grounds is conclusive, and hence that there is *no way* for the applicant to discharge the burden of proof in relation to those grounds.[107] Unfortunately, the key judgment of the CJEU in relation to the DR (which is a specialised form of STC) – *N.S. and M.E.* – lends credence to this reductionist approach, collapsing the broader refugee law understanding of *non-refoulement* into the narrower human rights

---

105 UNHCR APD Report, *op. cit.,* p. 71 (emphasis added).
106 If *non-refoulement* in refugee law is interpreted strictly in line with Article 33(1) of the 1951 Refugee Convention, then a person cannot be returned to a country where his or her life or liberty is likely to be threatened on account of his/her race, religion, nationality, membership of a particular social group or political opinion. It can be observed that a threat to life or liberty encompasses but is broader than a risk of torture or inhuman or degrading treatment or punishment. If, however, in accordance with State practice, *non-refoulement* is interpreted in the light of the definition of a refugee in Article 1A(2) of the 1951 Convention, then it includes contemporary interpretations of persecution. According to Article 9 QD, acts of persecution within the meaning of the Geneva Convention comprise 'a severe violation of basic human rights'. It can be observed that 'basic human rights' are broader than simply the prohibition of torture and inhuman or degrading treatment or punishment.
107 Commission evaluation of the APD, *op. cit.,* § 5.2.4, pp. 11–12.

understanding of the concept.¹⁰⁸ On the other hand, the ECtHR held in its key judgment on the DR – *MSS v Belgium and Greece* – that 'the applicant should not be expected to bear the entire burden of proof' in establishing the risk of *refoulement* in a safe third country where such a risk is well known to the authorities.¹⁰⁹

Finally, as regards FCA, Article 26 APD infers that the country is safe from the simple fact that the applicant was recognised as a refugee there or 'otherwise enjoys sufficient protection in that country, including benefiting from the principle of *non-refoulement*'. Article 26 is silent on whether or how an applicant can rebut the presumption that the FCA is safe.

These safe country concepts are fundamentally at odds with the notion of a shared and flexible burden of proof, which, in turn, enables 'due weight' to be given to the views of the child. The safe country concepts apply equally to minors – accompanied and unaccompanied – under the directive. Indeed, in *H.I.D., B.A.*, one of the applicants in the case was aged only ten at the material time in the main proceedings, something that failed to elicit any comment from the Court, although, admittedly, this fact should have been brought to light in the referring question.¹¹⁰

Automatic negative credibility inferences

An issue related to the burden of proof is the use of automatic negative credibility inferences, which establish a presumption that the application is manifestly unfounded and justify the processing of the application in an accelerated procedure. Article 23(3) APD permits Member States to 'prioritise or accelerate' any asylum claim, while Article 23(4) specifies sixteen different grounds on which Member States may fast-track applications, all of which may also constitute the basis for a manifestly unfounded determination under Article 28(2). Ostensibly, a claim can only be deemed manifestly unfounded, *per* Article 28(1), 'if the determining authority has established that the applicant does not qualify for refugee status pursuant to [the QD]'. In reality, however, the grounds taint the credibility of the applicant and/or the substance of the claim, making a negative decision a formality. This is confirmed in the Commission evaluation of the APD, which found that eleven Member States automatically reject an application as manifestly unfounded if the determining authority establishes a circumstance falling under Article 23(4) APD.¹¹¹

---

108 CJEU, *N.S and M.E.*, Joined Case C-411/10 and C-493/10, Judgment (GC) of 21 December 2011. See, in particular, para. 94. The Court's approach can be negatively contrasted with the Opinion of Advocate General Trstenjak delivered on 22 September 2011, para. 127.
109 ECtHR, *M.S.S. v Belgium and Greece, op. cit.*, para. 352. See also para. 359.
110 *H.I.D., B.A., op. cit.* The fact that one of the applicants was a minor was not mentioned by the Court and can be gleaned only from the Opinion of the Advocate General: Opinion of Advocate General Bot, 6 September 2012.
111 Commission evaluation of the APD, *op. cit.*, § 5.2.1, p. 10.

A recent judgment of the ECtHR casts doubt on the compatibility of such practices, at least in the context of Article 3 ECHR claims, with the right to an effective remedy in Article 13 ECHR.[112]

While many of the sixteen grounds in Article 23(4) APD can be criticised for being irrelevant to the core of the claim and consequently to the credibility of the applicant on the main issue, the following ground, (g), is particularly problematic for children: the making of 'inconsistent, contradictory, improbable or insufficient representations which make [the applicant's] claim clearly unconvincing in relation to his/her having been the object of persecution referred to in [the QD]'.[113] This ground seems apt to be applied to children, particularly younger, immature or less articulate children.[114]

In summary, the consistency of the APD with the obligation to evaluate the child's views in Article 12(1) CRC is highly doubtful. The directive does not establish that due weight be given to the views of the child in accordance with age and maturity. On the contrary, several provisions, for example, those relating to the burden of proof in the context of the safe country concepts and to the sanctioning of automatic credibility inferences, appear to undermine the testimony of the child.

Phase Two CEAS: Prospects for enhanced compliance

The recast APD simplifies to a limited extent the plethora of confusing procedures that currently exist. For example, the 'specific procedures' are no longer designated as such and hence are no longer exempt from complying with the basic principles and guarantees of the directive on that account. However, it is fair to say that the recast falls short of the kind of radical revision that would make the APD transparent and easily comprehensible. Against this backdrop, the question arises as to whether the right of the child to be heard is any better served in the recast than it is at present.

The right to a hearing

Under the current directive, whether or not a minor has a right to a personal interview is left to the discretion of Member States. Even where such a right is established in domestic law, the APD provides for an 'extensive catalogue of situations' in which the personal interview can be omitted, some of which

---

112 ECtHR, *I.M. v France, op. cit.*
113 The practice of drawing negative credibility inferences based on peripheral as opposed to core aspects of the claim is strongly criticised by UNHCR in its report on credibility assessment in EU asylum claims. The report does not deal with the issue of assessing credibility in the context of child asylum claims, but UNHCR plans to devote a specific follow-up report to the issue in 2013–14. UNHCR, Beyond Proof, *op. cit.*, 16.
114 It is likely that this ground requires too much of adults too. See H. Evans Cameron, 'Refugee status determination and the limits of memory', *International Journal of Refugee Law* 22, 2010, 469–511.

seem likely to be applied or are particularly detrimental to children. Furthermore, the APD envisages that refugee status may be withdrawn without a personal hearing and fails to establish clearly a right to an appeal hearing. Consequently, the APD is highly ambivalent on the right of the child to a hearing. Is the situation improved in the recast APD?

The most important thing to note is that the provision that gives discretion to Member States as to whether to give the opportunity of a personal interview to a minor is unchanged in the recast.[115] However, the catalogue of situations in which Member States can opt to omit the personal interview is significantly reduced. In terms of the situations identified as likely to be applied or particularly detrimental to children, the situation is substantially improved.

First, while Article 14(2) of the recast establishes that a personal interview can be omitted where the applicant is unfit or unable to be interviewed, this provision is tightened up in several respects. It is now only the determining authority that can decide that the applicant is unfit or unable to be interviewed. Furthermore, when in doubt, the determining authority must consult a medical expert to establish whether the condition that makes the applicant unfit or unable to be interviewed is of a temporary or enduring nature. Finally, owing to various other innovations in the recast, which effectively facilitate the claims of minors, analysed below, the risk of systematically applying this ground to minors is significantly reduced.

Second, the provision in the current directive allowing the personal interview to be omitted in the context of an accelerated/manifestly unfounded procedure is omitted from the recast. Furthermore, recalling that four of the five grounds for acceleration/ manifestly unfounded finding in the current directive are apt to be applied or particularly detrimental to children, one of those grounds is deleted from the procedure entirely (safe third country),[116] while two others (application not relevant to qualification for international protection; inconsistent, contradictory etc. representations) are no longer applicable to unaccompanied minors because this group of children is susceptible only to a reduced list of grounds.[117] Nevertheless, these exemptions fall short of what was envisaged in the amended Commission proposal for a recast, namely, complete exemption of unaccompanied minors from the accelerated/manifestly unfounded procedure.[118] Furthermore, the accelerated/manifestly unfounded procedure can now be administered at the border, and where unaccompanied minors are processed

---

115 Article 14(1) sub-para. 4.
116 Article 31(8) reduces the grounds for acceleration/manifestly unfounded from sixteen to ten.
117 Article 25(6)(a). The grounds in the reduced list are: the applicant comes from a safe country of origin; the applicant has introduced a subsequent application that is not inadmissible; the applicant is a danger to national security or public order or has been forcibly expelled for these reasons.
118 Article 25(6) of the Amended proposal for a Directive of the European Parliament and of the Council on common procedures for granting and withdrawing international protection status (Recast), *COM (2011) 319 final*.

in such a procedure, two further grounds are added to the reduced list normally applicable to unaccompanied minors.[119] Notwithstanding these critical comments, the fact that a personal interview is now required in the context of the accelerated/manifestly unfounded procedure is positive from the point of view of the right of the child to be heard.

Third, the recast refines the admissibility procedure, adding a new article specifying that 'Member States shall conduct a personal interview on the admissibility of the application'.[120] An exception to this requirement is crafted in respect of the preliminary examination of subsequent applications (which is now explicitly linked to the admissibility procedure). As outlined in Chapter 3 above, an application by an unmarried minor who lodges an application after an application has already been made on his/her behalf by a parent may be dealt with under this procedure for subsequent applications.[121] However, in such cases, the exception to the personal interview does not apply. In other words, accompanied minors in this situation must be afforded a personal interview. The fact that a personal interview must generally be conducted in the context of the admissibility procedure is positive from the point of view of the right of the child to be heard. However, bearing in mind that the admissibility procedure is particularly detrimental to children, it is to be regretted that children are not exempted from the procedure altogether in the recast. This shortcoming is compounded because it is now possible for the admissibility procedure to be conducted at the border, although when unaccompanied minors are processed in the context of such a procedure the grounds for inadmissibility are reduced from five to two.[122]

No change is envisaged to the procedure for withdrawing refugee status, and hence no right to a personal interview in such circumstances is envisaged.

Finally, as regards a possible appeal hearing, although this issue is not squarely addressed in the recast certain provisions imply an appeal hearing. Thus, Article 46, reiterating the right to an effective remedy, provides in paragraph 3 for a full examination of both facts and law, including an *ex nunc* examination of the claim, at least on appeal. This suggest a full (re)hearing of

---

119 Article 25(6)(b). The additional grounds are: the applicant has misled the authorities by presenting false documents; and, in bad faith the applicant has destroyed or disposed of identity or travel documents that would have helped establish his or her identity or nationality. These can only be applied 'in individual cases where there are serious grounds for considering that the applicant is attempting to conceal relevant elements which would likely lead to a negative decision and provided that the applicant has been given full opportunity, taking into account the special procedural needs of unaccompanied minors, to show good cause for [these] actions [...] including by consulting with his or her representative'.
120 Article 34(1).
121 Article 40(6)(b).
122 Article 15(6)(b). The grounds are: the applicant has introduced a subsequent application; and, safe third country. When the safe third country concept is applied to unaccompanied minors it is subject to a best-interests assessment: Article 15(6)(c).

the claim. This suggestion is bolstered by the use of the term 'hearing' in the recast article on free legal assistance and representation, which provides that the right to free legal assistance and representation on appeal shall include 'at least, the preparation of the required procedural documents and *participation in the hearing* before the court or tribunal of first instance on behalf of the applicant'.[123] Furthermore, the apparent discretion afforded to Member States in the APD on the question of suspensive effect – a significant practical obstacle to participation in any appeal hearing – is addressed in the recast. In line with the jurisprudence of the ECtHR, Article 46(5) establishes an automatic right to remain pending the expiry of the time limit for lodging an appeal or, thereafter, the outcome of the appeal. However, pursuant to Article 46(6), Member States may provide that certain decisions, such as manifestly unfounded decisions, entail no automatic right to remain pending appeal. In such cases, a court or tribunal must have jurisdiction to rule on a right to remain pending the outcome of the appeal, either on the request of the applicant or on its own motion, and the Member State must allow the applicant to remain pending the outcome of that ruling. Furthermore, when applying Article 46(6) to unaccompanied minors, Member States must provide them with additional guarantees such as interpretation, legal assistance and a requirement that the court or tribunal examine the negative decision of the determining authority in terms of fact and law.[124]

The final issue to be addressed in this subsection is whether the recast APD is better than its predecessor in establishing that the interview, at least for minors, is a right and not an obligation. Unfortunately, the relevant provisions of the recast are mostly unchanged in this regard.[125] Article 25 (Guarantees for unaccompanied minors), for example, still provides that Member States may compel the minor to be present at interview.[126]

In sum then, although the right of a minor to a hearing is no more clearly established in the recast than it is in the APD, if the minor is entitled to a hearing pursuant to domestic law then the possibilities for further curtailing that right are significantly reduced in the recast. Of course, a clear articulation of the right of the child to be heard would be preferable. Finally, the recast appears to permit Member States to compel a minor to be interviewed, contrary to Article 12 CRC.

---

123 Article 20(1).
124 Article 25(6) final sub-para.
125 There are two exceptions. First, Article 23(4)(g) APD, which establishes that making 'insufficient representations' is a manifestly unfounded ground, is amended: recast Article 31(8)(e) no longer refers to 'insufficient representations'. Second, Article 33 APD on failure to appear is omitted from the recast. All the other provisions establishing or implying negative procedural consequences for failing to appear at or engage with the interview subsist in the recast.
126 Para. 1(b), second sub-para.

The conduct of the hearing

The right to a representative

The APD establishes the right of an unaccompanied minor to a representative in Article 17. However, the definition and role of the representative is vague and the obligation to appoint a representative can be derogated from on four grounds. To what extent is this situation improved in the recast?

The definition of 'representative' undergoes substantial change in the recast. Article 2(n) defines the representative as:

> A person or organization appointed by the competent bodies in order to assist and represent an unaccompanied minor in procedures provided for in this Directive with a view to ensuring the best interests of the child and exercising legal capacity for the minor where necessary. Where an organization acts as a representative, it shall designate a person responsible for carrying out the duties of the representative in respect of the minor, in accordance with this Directive.

This definition is superior to the existing definition in specifying that the role of the representative is to assist *and* represent the child in the procedure, and in establishing that the aim of the representation is to exercise legal capacity for the child where necessary. These changes better align the role of the representative with the right of the child to be heard in Article 12 CRC. Furthermore, recast Article 25 (Guarantees for unaccompanied minors) is more elaborate on the qualities of the representative than existing Article 17. It specifies that the representative 'shall perform his or her duties in accordance with the principle of the best interests of the child and shall have the necessary expertise to that end'. In an improvement on the amended Commission proposal, it establishes that organisations or individuals whose interests conflict with those of the unaccompanied minor cannot be representatives.[127] The obligation to appoint a representative can still be derogated from, but the grounds for derogation are reduced to one, namely, where the minor is likely to 'age out' before a first instance decision is taken. Unfortunately, the obligation to appoint a representative is limited to unaccompanied minors in the recast, just as it is currently. Consequently, the accompanied minor has no right to an independent representative.

The adaptation of the hearing

In the article on guarantees for unaccompanied minors, the APD establishes that the personal interview of an unaccompanied minor and decision on his/

---

127 A requirement of impartiality, which was included in the 2009 Commission proposal, was omitted from the 2011 amended proposal. Its reappearance in the recast as adopted is therefore to be welcomed.

her application must be conducted by a person 'with the necessary knowledge of the special needs of minors'. Accompanied minors, by contrast, benefit only from the general guarantees established in respect of staff competence, the examination of applications and the personal interview, which are rather vague, open to derogation and have led to uneven practice.

In the recast, the above-mentioned guarantee for unaccompanied minors subsists unchanged, but higher, and in some cases child-specific, standards are established in relation to staff competence and training, the examination of applications and the personal interview. These are significant from the point of view of adapting the hearing for *all* minors who get a hearing. However, a number of explicit and implicit derogations are established or retained in respect of these standards. For clarity, the new standards will be set out first, before addressing the various derogations.

Article 4 of the recast (Responsible authorities) contains two significant additions. First, a new requirement is laid down in paragraph 1 that the determining authority 'is provided with appropriate means, including competent personnel, to carry out its tasks in accordance with this Directive'. Second, for the first time the issue of staff training is explicitly addressed. Paragraph 3 provides that 'Member States shall ensure that the personnel of the determining authority are properly trained. To that end, Member States shall provide for relevant training which shall include the elements listed in Article 6(4)(a)–(e) of [the EASO Regulation]. Member States shall also take into account the training established and developed by the European Asylum Support Office'. Of particular note for our purposes, Article 6(4)(b) of the EASO Regulation provides for training on issues related to the handling of asylum applications from minors and vulnerable persons with specific needs, while sub-paragraph (c) provides for training on interview techniques.[128] While it is unfortunate – especially in view of the fast pace of developments in the area of the right to an effective remedy in general and the right of the child to be heard in particular – that a reference in the amended Commission proposal to initial *and* follow-up training was omitted from the recast, it is submitted that the final provision will nevertheless have a significant impact on the right of the child to an appropriately adapted hearing.[129]

Recast Article 10 (Requirements for the examination of applications) reiterates in paragraph 3 the requirement in current Article 8 that decisions by the determining authority on applications be taken after an appropriate examination. However, a new paragraph is added on the steps that have to be

---

128 Regulation (EU) No. 439/2010 of the European Parliament and of the Council of 19 May 2010 establishing a European Asylum Support Office. The EASO Work Programme for 2013 undertakes to update its training and modules on interviewing children: http://easo.europa.eu/wp-content/uploads/BZAC12001ENC-web.pdf (accessed 12 August 2013).

129 Article 4(3) of the Amended proposal for a Directive of the European Parliament and of the Council on common procedures for granting and withdrawing international protection status (Recast), *COM (2011) 319 final*.

taken in this regard. Sub-paragraph (d) obliges Member States to ensure that 'the personnel examining applications and taking decisions have the possibility to seek advice, whenever necessary, from experts on particular issues such as [...] child-related [...] issues'. Recast Article 14 (Personal interview) specifies, where existing Article 12 is silent, that interviews on the substance of the application for international protection shall be conducted by the determining authority.[130] This means that the Article 4 competence and training standards are fully applicable to staff conducting such personal interviews. Recast Article 15 (Requirements for a personal interview) contains some apparently minor, but actually significant, amendments to the obligation in existing Article 13 that the person who conducts the interview be sufficiently competent to take account of the personal or general circumstances surrounding the application where possible. Notably, the word 'sufficiently' is deleted, with the result that the requirement of competence is not qualified in any way; the disjunction 'or' is replaced by the conjunction 'and', with the result that both personal and general circumstances must be taken into account; and the qualification 'insofar as it is possible to do so' is omitted.[131] Furthermore, a new sub-paragraph is added whereby Member States are obliged to 'ensure that interviews with minors are conducted in a child-appropriate manner'.[132] Finally, a new article (Content of a personal interview) is added in recast Article 16, which provides:

> When conducting a personal interview on the substance of an application for international protection, the determining authority shall ensure that the applicant is given an adequate opportunity to present elements needed to substantiate the application in accordance with Article 4 of the [QD] as completely as possible. This shall include the opportunity to give an explanation regarding elements which may be missing and/or any inconsistencies or contradictions in his/her statements.

As this provision applies equally to minors, it provides an important counterbalance to 'soft' requirements of a child-friendly hearing, and hence is a significant addition. In sum, while these amendments fall short of a direction to Member States to establish guidelines on child-friendly interviewing, the mix of improved general standards and additional child-specific standards makes for a better likelihood of a child-friendly hearing.

It is unfortunate then that the recast permits many of these provisions to be derogated from in various circumstances. First, Article 4 (Responsible authority) permits Member States to establish an alternative authority for DR cases and, significantly, for 'granting or refusing permission to enter' in the framework of the border procedure established in Article 43 'subject to the conditions as set

---

130 Para. 1.
131 Para. 3(a).
132 Para. 3(e).

out therein and on the basis of the opinion of the determining authority'.[133] Article 43, in turn, provides for an admissibility procedure for applications made at the border or in transit zones and an accelerated/manifestly unfounded procedure. The alternative authority is not subject to the training requirements of Article 4(3), but rather to the lesser requirements of Article 4(4), which provides that that personnel 'have the appropriate knowledge or receive the necessary training to fulfil their obligations when implementing this Directive'. Moreover Articles 10 and 16, outlined above, do not apply, since they explicitly relate to the determining authority. In the Commission proposal, unaccompanied minors were exempt from border procedures. However, in the recast as adopted, unaccompanied minors are susceptible to them albeit on reduced grounds.[134]

Second, Article 14 (Personal interview) specifies that interviews on the substance of the application for international protection must be conducted by the personnel of the determining authority.[135] *A contrario*, interviews that are not on the substance of the application need not be conducted by the personnel of the determining authority. This raises the question: what is (and is not) the substance of the application? Recitals 43–45 of the recast APD shed some light on this question, stating that all applications should be examined on the substance except, respectively, in the case of FCA, STC and European STC – the latter a currently defunct concept that is set to be reintroduced in the recast (of which more below). Accordingly, as regards FCA, STC and European STC, interviews need not be conducted by the personnel of the determining authority. It follows that whatever standards are established in respect of the determining authority – notably in Articles 4, 10 and 16, outlined above – will not apply. No alternative standards are specified. However, the obligation to ensure that interviews with minors are conducted in a child-appropriate manner as set out in Article 15 is still applicable, as this obligation is not expressly linked to the determining authority. Also of some succour, not all the safe country concepts apply to all unaccompanied minors: the FCA concept applies to unaccompanied minors in the context of an admissibility procedure, but not where the procedure is administered at the border;[136] the STC concept can only be applied to an unaccompanied minor if it is in his or her best interests;[137] and the European STC concept is fully applicable to unaccompanied minors.

Third, Article 14 adds a new sub-paragraph to the provision on the personal interview, which provides:

> Where simultaneous applications for international protection by a large number of third country nationals or stateless persons make it impossible

---

133 Para. 2(b).
134 Article 25(6)(b).
135 Para. 1.
136 Article 25(6)(b).
137 Article 25(6)(c).

in practice for the determining authority to conduct timely interviews on the substance of each application, Member States may provide the personnel of another authority be temporarily involved in conducting such interviews. In such cases, the personnel of that other authority shall receive in advance the relevant training which shall include the elements listed in Article 6(4)(a) to (e) of [the EASO Regulation] [...].[138]

No exception is made for minors or other applicants in need of special procedural guarantees. It is hard to see how another authority brought in at short notice to conduct personal interviews could possibly be competent to interview minors, notwithstanding the provision of training. In this regard, it is doubly unfortunate that Article 10 outlined above on instruction and advice on child-related matters is stated to apply to the determining authority and not, therefore, to any alternative authority.

No changes on question of the conduct of the hearing are made to the procedure for withdrawing refugee status or to the appeals procedure. Hence, these procedures remain impervious to any child-specific modifications.

In short, the recast APD contains substantial improvements with regard to the adaptation of the hearing for *all* minors at first instance. However, these improvements are diminished because Member States are permitted to derogate from the new standards in various circumstances. While unaccompanied minors are shielded (somewhat) from some (though by no means all) of the derogations, accompanied minors are not. No improvements are made to the procedure for the withdrawal of refugee status or the appeals procedure. Therefore, the recast APD can best be characterised as a modified improvement on its predecessor in terms of adapting the hearing for minors.

The evaluation of the child's views

The 'due weight' requirement in Article 12(1) CRC impacts on the burden of proof in asylum claims, requiring a shared and flexible burden of proof. It is also inconsistent with the use of automatic negative credibility inferences. The APD was found to undermine the shared and flexible burden of proof established in the QD in certain contexts, such as the safe country concepts. The APD was also found to sanction the use of automatic negative credibility inferences. To what extent does the recast APD improve this situation?

Burden of proof

On the question of the burden of proof in the application of safe country concepts, the situation is largely unchanged. Thus, as regards the SCO and STC concepts, the burden of rebutting the presumption of safety continues to be placed on the

---

138 Para. 1, 2nd sub-para.

applicant in Article 36(1) and 38(2)(c), respectively, although the latter no longer permits Member States to confine the rebuttal to the case of torture, cruel, inhuman or degrading treatment or punishment. Hence, the applicant can rebut the presumption of safety on any grounds. As for the FCA concept, Article 35 of the recast adds a new stipulation, that '[t]he applicant shall be allowed to challenge the application of the first country of asylum concept in his/her particular circumstances'. While this is an improvement on the silence of the current provision with its implication that the presumption of safety of the FCA is conclusive, nevertheless, the burden seems to be placed solely on the applicant.

These provisions are contrary to the requirement of a shared and flexible burden of proof in the case of child applicants. However, they are not all equally applicable to unaccompanied minors. The amended Commission proposal provided that unaccompanied minors were exempt from the operation of the accelerated/manifestly unfounded procedure (and hence the SCO concept). However, this exemption did not survive the negotiation process, with the result that the SCO concept is fully applicable to unaccompanied minors as a ground for acceleration,[139] including in the context of a border procedure.[140] By contrast, the STC concept only applies to an unaccompanied minor if it is in his/her best interests.[141] Again, under the Commission proposal, unaccompanied minors were exempted altogether from the admissibility procedure on grounds of STC.[142] The inclusion of a reference to the best interests concept in the recast was the *quid pro quo* that enabled the European Parliament to agree to forego the exemption. Considering, however, that the recast contains a broad statement that the best interests of the child are a primary consideration for Member States when implementing the directive – meaning, presumably, all the provisions thereof – the additional reference to best interests in the context of STC is at best superfluous and at worst undermining of the broad statement of principle.[143] Finally, the FCA concept is fully applicable to unaccompanied minors,[144] except when conducted as part of a border procedure, in which case the concept cannot be applied to unaccompanied minors.[145]

Furthermore, in a definite retrograde step from the point of view of the appropriate burden of proof in children's claims, Article 39 of the recast APD reintroduces the concept of the European STC. Modelled on existing (but inoperative) Article 36, Article 39 provides in paragraph 1:

> Member States may provide that *no, or no full, examination* of the application for international protection and *of the safety of the applicant in his/her*

---

139 Article 25(6)(a)(i).
140 Article 25(6)(b)(i).
141 Article 25(6)(c).
142 Amended Commission proposal, *op. cit.*, Article 25(6).
143 Article 25(6) first sub-para.
144 Article 33(2)(b).
145 Article 25(6)(b) omits any reference to FCA.

particular circumstances as described in Chapter II, shall take place in cases where a competent authority has established on the basis of the facts, that the applicant for international protection is seeking to enter or has entered illegally into its territory from a safe third country according to paragraph 2.[146]

If the minimum option of no examination of the safety of the applicant in his/her particular circumstances is adopted by Member States, this effectively establishes a conclusive presumption of safety, which the applicant is powerless to rebut. However, it seems unlikely that Member States will be free to pursue this minimum option in the light of the judgments of the ECtHR and the CJEU in *MSS v Belgium and Greece* and *N.S.*, respectively. But even the higher option – a perfunctory examination of the safety of the applicant – appears to place the burden solely on the applicant. Neither unaccompanied nor accompanied minors are exempt from the European STC concept. And yet, unaccompanied minors would appear to be highly susceptible to the European STC concept as they generally enter the EU illegally, being unlikely to meet the formal requirements for legal entry into the EU owing to their age and unaccompanied status.[147]

Negative credibility inferences

On the issue of the use of negative credibility inferences, the situation in the recast APD is somewhat improved. In a positive move, the grounds for an accelerated/ manifestly unfounded procedure are reduced from sixteen to ten. Unfortunately, existing ground (g) (i.e. inconsistent, contradictory, improbable or insufficient representations, claim clearly unconvincing…) subsists, with only slight modifications.[148] However, this ground for acceleration/manifestly unfounded is no longer applicable to unaccompanied minors.[149] But, as previously mentioned, this concession pales in significance when compared with the amended Commission proposal for a recast, which exempted unaccompanied minors from the accelerated/manifestly unfounded procedure altogether.[150]

In sum, there are some modest improvements in the provisions of the recast APD that impact on giving 'due weight' to the views of the unaccompanied – though not the accompanied – child. In its original proposal for a recast APD, the Commission envisaged much greater exemptions from the safe country

---

146 Emphasis added.
147 See European Migration Network, 'Policies on Reception, Return and Integration arrangements for, and numbers of, Unaccompanied Minors – an EU comparative study', 2010, Chapter 5 (Entry procedures including border controls).
148 Article 31(8)(e).
149 Article 25(6)(a).
150 Amended Commission Proposal, *op. cit.*, Article 25(6).

concepts and the accelerated/manifestly unfounded procedure for unaccompanied minors under the rationale that 'unaccompanied minors may be unable, *due to their age*, to articulate and substantiate their request for international protection'.[151] While this coincides exactly with what is being expressed in this chapter, it is not followed through to its logical conclusion, which is that *all* minors, *due to their age*, should be exempted from *all* such procedures. In this regard, the patchwork of exemptions and partial exemptions for unaccompanied minors in the recast as adopted are wholly lacking in transcendent principle.

Conclusion

This chapter posed the question of whether the right of the child to be heard is met in the CEAS. The normative content of the right of the child to be heard was presented along three lines: the right to a hearing, the right to an appropriately adapted hearing and the right of the child to have his/her views given due weight in accordance with age and maturity. Phase One CEAS, in the form of the APD, was found to comply with none of these elements. Thus, whether or not the child is entitled to an asylum interview is left to Member States and, even if domestic law does allow the child to be interviewed, the directive permits Member States to omit the interview on numerous grounds, some of which are apt to be applied to or are particularly detrimental to children. Decisions relating to withdrawals can be taken without a hearing, and the directive is silent on the question of an appeal hearing. Unaccompanied, though not accompanied, minors are entitled to a representative, but the representative's role is unclear and the right can be derogated from in various situations. Where an interview occurs, the directive provides that the 'needs' of unaccompanied, though again not accompanied, minors must be taken into account – a stipulation that is omitted in the provisions relating to withdrawals and appeals. Finally, as regards giving due regard to the views of the child, not only does the directive not legislate for this, it contains several provisions relating to the burden of proof and automatic negative credibility inferences that appear to disregard the views of the child. In short, Phase One CEAS does not comply with the right of the child to be heard.

Some improvements can be discerned in Phase Two. However, the improvements are generally qualified in some way. Thus, the opportunities for Member

---

151 Proposal for a Directive of the European Parliament and of the Council on minimum standards on procedures in Member States for granting and withdrawing international protection (Recast), *COM (2009) 554 final*, ANNEX, 'Detailed Explanation of the Proposal', pp. 11–12 (emphasis added). It is assumed that the detailed explanation of provisions of the 2009 proposal applies to the equivalent provisions of the 2011 proposal to the extent that such provisions remain unchanged. There is no detailed explanation of the 2011 proposal.

States to omit the interview are curtailed, but the child still has no right to an interview; a general right to an appeal hearing is implied, but not explicitly stated; significant improvements are made regarding the representative for the unaccompanied minor, but still no provision is made for the possibility that the accompanied minor might need a representative; notable improvements are made with regard to the adaptation of the hearing for all minors, but these improvements are detracted from because the recast is peppered with derogation provisions, expressed and implied, and furthermore, no child-friendly modifications are made to the withdrawals or appeals procedure; some amendments improve the likelihood that 'due weight' will be given to the views of the child, but these apply neither to all children nor to all objectionable concepts. In sum, relatively speaking, Phase Two CEAS is better than Phase One in terms of the right of the child to be heard, but considered on its own merits in the light of the normative requirements of the right, it cannot be said to be in compliance.

5 The right of the child to protection and care

Introduction

This chapter explores the conformity of the CEAS with the rights of the child relating to protection and care. A general source for this right is the best-interests principle, which includes the obligation 'to ensure to the child such protection and care as is necessary for his or her wellbeing'.[1] Furthermore, a specific right of asylum-seeking and refugee children to protection and assistance is established in Article 22 CRC, which provides in the first paragraph that:

> States Parties shall take appropriate measures to ensure that a child who is seeking refugee status or who is considered a refugee in accordance with applicable international or domestic law and procedures shall, whether unaccompanied or accompanied by his or her parents or by any other person, receive appropriate protection and humanitarian assistance in the enjoyment of applicable rights set forth in this Convention and in other international human rights or humanitarian instruments to which the said States are Parties.

Chapter 3 above analysed this provision from the point of view of appropriate protection in the enjoyment of applicable rights set forth in *other* international human rights or humanitarian instruments, such as the 1951 Convention relating to the Status of Refugees. Here the focus in on applicable rights in the CRC. Furthermore, whereas Chapter 3 interpreted the term 'protection' in the classic refugee law sense of protection from *refoulement*, here the term is interpreted in the more mundane (but equally important) sense

---

1 Article 3(2) CRC and Article 24(1), EU Charter of Fundamental Rights, first sentence. According to the chairperson of the Com. RC, '[w]e can consider paragraph 2 [of Article 3 CRC] as providing the fullest explanation of the best interests principle'. J. Zermatten, 'The best interests of the child principle: Literal analysis and function', *International Journal of Children's Rights* 18, 2010, 483–499, 490.

of day-to-day protection and care of the child.[2] Hence, the question arises as to what rights in the Convention relate to the protection (in this specific sense) and care of the asylum-seeking and refugee child? The answer to this question is too broad to be useful: a great many rights in the CRC relate to protection and care, all of which are, in principle, applicable to all children by virtue of the general principle of non-discrimination laid down in Article 2.[3] However, we can refine the search by asking the further question: who, primarily, protects and cares for the child? In the normal course of events, children are primarily protected and cared for by their parents. Therefore the rights in the Convention that relate to keeping the family together – family unity, in other words – are key. However, in refugee-type situations it is not unusual for children to become separated from their parents. In such situations, the State must step in and take over the parental role. Therefore, the rights in the Convention that relate to surrogate protection and care are key.

Accordingly, this chapter is divided into two substantive sections. The first section deals with the protection and care of the accompanied child. It explores the various rights of the child relating to family unity, focusing on the concept of derived rights and the prohibition on separating a child from his or her parents against their will. It examines the extent to which the relevant CEAS instruments conform to these rights and evaluates the prospects for better conformity in Phase Two. The second section deals with the protection and care of the unaccompanied or separated child. It sets out the right of the child who is deprived of family to be identified as such, to a guardian or similar representative and to alternative care. It evaluates the extent of conformity of the relevant CEAS instruments in their first and second phases with this cluster of rights. The relevant CEAS instruments are the RCD and its recast, which contain provisions relating to the *interim* protection and care of asylum-seeking children;[4] and the QD and its recast, which contain provisions relating to the

---

2 This clarification is important because, as Goodwin Gill notes, '[i]n refugee discourse, protection is a term of art, whose meanings are not always clear'. G. Goodwin Gill, 'Unaccompanied refugee minors, the role and place of international law in the pursuit of durable solutions', *International Journal of Children's Rights* 3, 1995, 405–416, 415.
3 Article 2(1) CRC provides: 'States Parties shall respect and ensure the rights set forth in the present Covenant to each child within their jurisdiction without distinction of any kind, irrespective of the child's or his or her parent's or legal guardian's race, color, sex, language, religion, political or other opinion, national, ethnic or social origin, property, disability, birth or other status.' The term 'other status' has been interpreted by the Com. RC as extending to 'the status of a child as being unaccompanied or separated, or being a refugee, asylum seeker or migrant': General Comment No. 6, 'Treatment of unaccompanied and separated children outside their country of origin', *UN Doc CRC/GC/2005/6*, para. 18.
4 Council Directive 2003/9/EC of 27 January 2003 and Directive 2013/33/EU of the European Parliament and of the Council of 26 June 2013, respectively.

long-term protection and care of children who are beneficiaries of international protection.[5] Some provisions of the DR and its recast are also relevant.[6]

The right of the child to family unity

In general human rights terms, the right to family unity derives from the right to respect for private and family life, such as is established under Article 8 of the ECHR and Article 17 of the ICCPR.[7] A similar right is established in Article 16 of the CRC, which provides:

1   No child shall be subjected to arbitrary or unlawful interference with his or her privacy, family, home or correspondence, nor to unlawful attacks on his or her honor and reputation.
2   The child has the right to the protection of the law against such interference or attacks.

However, this is only one of a host of rights in the Convention either directly or indirectly relating to the concept of family unity, broadly understood.[8] Thus, Article 7(1) CRC provides that the child, as far as possible, has the right to know and be cared for by his/her parents. Article 8(1) establishes the right of the child to preserve his or her identity, including family relations, without unlawful interference. Article 9 prohibits the separation of the child from his/her parents against their will, unless it is determined that separation is necessary for the best interests of the child. Article 9 further establishes the right of the child who is separated from one or both parents to maintain personal relations and direct contact with them, unless contrary to the child's best interests. Notably, this provision was the inspiration for Article 24(3) of the EU Charter of Fundamental Rights.[9] Furthermore, Articles 10 and 22(2) CRC relate to the right to family reunification – a right based on the logic of family unity.

Given the number of provisions of the CRC relevant to the right of the child to family unity, it is proposed to outline the normative content of

---

5   Council Directive 2004/83/EC of 29 April 2004 and Directive 2011/95/EU of the European Parliament and of the Council of 13 December 2011, respectively.
6   Council Regulation No. 343/2003 of 18 February 2003 and Regulation (EU) No. 604/2013 of the European Parliament and of the Council of 26 June 2013, respectively.
7   Article 8(1) ECHR provides: 'Everyone has the right to respect for his private and family life, his home and his correspondence.' Article 17(1) ICCPR provides: 'No one shall be subjected to arbitrary or unlawful interference with his privacy, family, home or correspondence, nor to unlawful attacks on his honour and reputation.'
8   Thus, family unity in international child rights law has a broader rights base than family unity in general human rights law. On the relationship between the terms 'family', 'family unity', 'family life' and 'family reunification', see D. Stevens, 'Asylum-seeking families in current legal discourse: a UK perspective', *Journal of Social Welfare and Family Law* 32, 2010, 5–22.
9   Article 24(3) of the Charter of Fundamental Rights provides: 'Every child shall have the right to maintain on a regular basis a personal relationship and direct contact with both his or her parents, unless that is contrary to his or her interests.'

the right under two headings: the concept of derived rights and the prohibition on separating a child from his/her parents.

The concept of derived rights

Family unity is established as a kind of meta-norm in the CRC, not only for ideological reasons related to the importance of the family in society but also for more functional reasons associated with child-rearing *responsibilities*. This is evident in the fifth preambular paragraph of the Convention, which asserts that States Parties are '[c]onvinced that the family, as the fundamental group of society and the natural environment for the growth and well-being of all its members and particularly the children, should be afforded the necessary protection and assistance so that it can fully assume its responsibilities within the Community'. This statement is based on the pragmatic consideration that, in view of the inevitable dependence of the child on his/her parents or guardian, many of the rights in the Convention must be realised by or through the parents or guardian, albeit with the assistance of the State.[10] Thus, the Convention establishes in Article 18 the principle that parents or guardians have the primary responsibility for the child and the realisation of his/her rights, with the State exercising a secondary role.[11] This principle is expressed in more applied terms in numerous other articles of the Convention.[12] In this regard, family unity is the mechanism through which the child realises his/her rights, the extent of the State obligation depending on the circumstances of the parents. In the refugee-law context, the term used to express this dynamic is 'derived rights', whereby the child who is accompanied by his/her parents or guardian derives his/her entitlements from their status.[13]

Having established the centrality of family unity to the Convention scheme, two definitional questions arise, namely, what is the family and who

---

10 For critical commentary, see D. Gomien, 'Whose right (and whose duty) is it? An analysis of the substance and implementation of the Convention on the Rights of the Child', *New York Law School Journal of Human Rights* 7, 1989–1990, 161–175.
11 Article 18 provides *inter alia*: '1. [...] Parents, or as the case may be, legal guardians, have the primary responsibility for the upbringing and development of the child. The best interests of the child will be their basic concern. 2. For the purpose of guaranteeing and promoting the rights set forth in the present Convention, States Parties shall render appropriate assistance to parents and legal guardians in the performance of their child-rearing responsibilities and shall ensure the development of institutions, facilities and services for the care of children.'
12 For example, Article 27 CRC relating to the right of the child to an adequate standard of living provides that the primary responsibility for securing an adequate standard of living for the child lies with the parents or other persons responsible for the child, but that the State is under an obligation to assist the parents or others responsible for the child in this regard. See further Articles 3(2), 5, 14(2), 23(2) and (3), 24(2)(e) and (f) and 26(2).
13 The term 'family asylum' is sometimes used. See C. Bierwirth, 'The protection of refugee and asylum-seeking children, the Convention on the Rights of the Child and the work of the Committee on the Rights of the Child', *Refugee Survey Quarterly* 24, 2005, 98–124, 102.

is the child? Somewhat surprisingly, the term 'family' is not defined in the Convention. The CRC uses a wide variety of terms to refer to family relationships.[14] Moreover, the Convention offers no definition of the term 'guardian' and seems to accept that the role of primary carer can be played, *de facto* or *de jure*, by a range of different adults who may or may not have blood ties with the child.[15] This suggests that the concept of family should be construed widely. Such an interpretation is supported by the broad, purposive understanding of 'family' adopted by the ECtHR in its interpretation of Article 8 ECHR, which parallels Article 16 CRC.[16] In contrast to the lack of a definition of the family in the CRC, the child is clearly defined in Article 1 as 'every human being below the age of eighteen years unless under the law applicable to the child, majority is attained earlier'.

In sum, the child (i.e. anyone under the age of eighteen unless a lower age of majority is provided for in domestic law) is entitled to derive rights from the status of his/her parents, guardian or other family members, as appropriate. This follows from the functional rationale for family unity that underpins many of the rights in the CRC.

The prohibition on separating a child from his/her parents

Although Article 7(1) CRC relates to the right of the child to know and be cared for by his/her parents and Article 8(1) relates to the right of the child to preserve family relations, it is Article 9 that does all the heavy lifting when it comes to supplying a 'core' right of the child to family unity. The first two paragraphs of Article 9 are of particular importance and will be analysed in turn. They provide:

1   States Parties shall ensure that a child shall not be separated from his or her parents against their will, except when competent authorities subject to judicial review determine, in accordance with applicable law and procedures, that such separation is necessary for the best interests of the

---

14 The following terms can be found in the Convention: 'parents', 'family members', 'legal guardians', 'parents or other members of the family', 'other individuals/persons legally responsible for the child', 'persons having responsibility for the maintenance of the child', 'others having financial responsibility for the child', 'members of the extended family or community as provided by local custom', 'others responsible for the child' and 'any other person who has the care of the child'.
15 *Ibid*.
16 The ECtHR has recognised the following relationship to constitute 'family': husband, wife and dependent children, including illegitimate and adopted children (*B. v UK*, Appl. No. 8940/82, Judgment of 8 July 1987); siblings (*Moustaquim v Belgium*, Appl. No. 12313/86, Judgment of 18 February 1991); grandparents (*Vermeire v Belgium*, Appl. No. 12849/87, Judgment of 29 November 1991); and importantly, 'young adults who had not yet founded a family of their own [and] their parents and other close family members' (*Osman v Denmark*, Appl. No. 38058/09, Judgment of 14 June 2011, para. 54).

child. Such determination may be necessary in a particular case such as one involving abuse or neglect of the child by the parents, or one where the parents are living separately and a decision must be made as to the child's place of residence.
2 In any proceedings pursuant to paragraph 1 of the present article, all interested parties shall be given an opportunity to participate in the proceedings and make their views known.

Article 9(1) is a complex provision establishing a general rule and a limitation, the latter illustrated by two examples. A number of observations may be made on the operation of this provision. First, the best interests of the child functions differently in Article 9 CRC than it does when it operates as a general principle in Article 3 CRC. The general principle of the best interests of the child involves an evaluation of all available options with a view to deciding which is best; thus identified, the best interests of the child must be a primary, but not necessarily the paramount, consideration. By contrast, there is a presumption in Article 9 CRC that family unity with the parents is in the best interests of the child. This presumption is rebutted where it is shown that separation is necessary for the best interests of the child. Here the best interests of the child becomes the paramount consideration (cf. 'necessary'). The illustrative examples of when separation may be necessary for the best interests of the child – child abuse and custody arrangements when the parents are living separately – indicate that the reasons for separation are limited to those relating to the relationship between and personal circumstances of the child and his/her parents. Consequently, extraneous considerations relating to the interests of the State or the rights of others are immaterial.[17]

Second, whether separation is necessary for the best interests of the child must be determined in accordance with applicable law and procedures. This is akin to the requirement under Article 8 ECHR that the right to family life cannot be interfered with 'except such as is in accordance with law and is necessary in a democratic society'.[18] Such a decision can only be taken by 'competent authorities'. While this term could apply equally to a court or an administrative body, the key requirement for the deciding body is competence. In his commentary on Article 9, Doek argues that the competent authority must be competent not only in the legal sense (of being formally mandated for the task), but also in the substantive sense (of being qualified

---

17 See J. Bhabha and W. Young, 'Not adults in miniature: Unaccompanied child asylum seekers and the new U.S. guidelines', *International Journal of Refugee Law* 11, 1999, 84–125.
18 Indeed, in its jurisprudence on Article 8 EHCR as it relates to the separation of children from their parents, the ECtHR's approach is very similar to that required by Article 9 CRC. See, for example, *A.D. and O.D. v United Kingdom*, Appl. No. 28680/06, Judgment of 16 March 2010.

for the task).¹⁹ This double-competence requirement is consistent with emerging 'soft-law' standards relating to the formal determination of the best interests of the child.²⁰

Third, the decision of the competent authority must be subject to judicial review. However, this is not limited to an initial review of the placement on appeal but extends to a periodic review. In this regard, Doek links Article 9 with Article 25 CRC concerning placement of the child for the purposes of care, protection or treatment of his physical or mental health, noting that separation from the parents by a competent authority is a placement.²¹ Article 25 obliges States to undertake 'a periodic review of the treatment provided to the child and all other circumstances relevant to his or her placement.' Article 9(2) specifies further procedural guarantees: all interested parties must be allowed to participate in the proceedings and make their views known. The interested parties are not limited to the parents, but extend to the child him/herself. This is evident when Article 9(2) is read in conjunction with Article 12 CRC, a general principle of the Convention which, as outlined in Chapter 4 above, establishes the right of the child who is capable of forming his or her own views to express those views freely in all matters affecting the child, the views of the child being given due weight in accordance with the age and maturity of the child.

In sum, Article 9 establishes that the separation of a child from his or her parents is highly exceptional, relating only to reasons associated with the child–parent relationship; otherwise, the State is under an obligation not to separate a child from his/her parents or, put differently, to facilitate the unity of the child with his/her parents. When, exceptionally, separation is contemplated, it is subject to requirements of lawfulness, periodic judicial review and participation of the child in the decision.²²

---

19 J. Doek, *A Commentary on the United Nations Convention on the Rights of the Child, Article 8, The Right to Preservation of Identity and Article 9, The Right Not to be Separated From his or her Parents*, Leiden/Boston: Martinus Nijhoff Publishers, 2006.
20 See UNHCR, 'Guidelines on Determining the Best Interests of the Child', 2008, which were cited with approval by the European Court of Human Rights in *Neulinger and Shuruk v Switzerland*, Appl. No. 41615/07, Judgment of 6 July 2010, para. 52.
21 J. Doek, *op. cit.*
22 It follows from the prohibition in Article 9 CRC of separating a child from his or her parents against their will that where separation inadvertently occurs – in flight, for example – every effort should be made to reunite a separated child with his or her parents, unless this is not in the best interests of the child for the reasons already discussed. This is underscored by Article 22 relating to refugee children, paragraph 2 of which establishes an obligation to undertake family tracing with a view to family reunification. However, the issue of family reunification is not dealt with in this chapter because, other than the DR, which establishes a number of criteria for determining the Member State responsible based on the location of family members, the regulation of family reunification of 'third country nationals' including refugees in EU law, is extraneous to the CEAS. See, in this regard, Council Directive 2003/86/EC of 22 September 2003 on the right to family reunification.

Phase One CEAS: Compliance with the right of the child to family unity

The concept of derived rights

The functional dimension of the right of the child to family unity finds expression in the refugee law context in the concept of derived rights, whereby children derive their rights from their parents' status. This concept is well recognised in both the RCD and the QD.

Thus, the personal scope of the RCD extends to asylum applicants and their family members if the latter are 'covered by such application for asylum according to the national law'.[23] In order to understand the meaning of this provision, it is necessary to cross-reference the APD, which provides in Article 6(4) that Member States may determine in national legislation the cases in which a minor can make an application on his/her own behalf, and the cases in which an application by an adult is deemed to cover the application of any unmarried minor child. In the case of the former, the child is the asylum applicant and is directly entitled to the rights in the RCD; in the case of the latter, the concept of derived rights applies, as outlined in Chapter 3 above. State practice reveals that most Member States subsume the child's application into that of his/her parents'.[24]

Similarly, the QD establishes in Article 23(2) that 'Member States shall ensure that family members of the beneficiary of refugee or subsidiary protection status, who do not individually qualify for such status, are entitled to claim the benefits referred to in Articles 24–34'. However, of some concern, the next subparagraph provides that Member States may 'define the conditions' applicable to the benefits of family members of beneficiaries of subsidiary protection. This provision, which authorises the placing of limits on the derived rights of children of beneficiaries of subsidiary protection, is contrary to the functional dimension of the right to family unity. The extent to which Member States have availed of it is unclear.[25]

---

23 Article 3(1) (Scope).
24 The Commission notes that applications made by parents 'generally' cover dependent minors: 'Report from the Commission to the European Parliament and the Council on the Application of Directive 2005/85/EC of 1 December 2005 on Minimum Standards on Procedures in Member States for Granting and Withdrawing Refugee Status', *COM (2010) 465 final*, § 4.3.1.1. Hereinafter, 'Commission evaluation of the APD'.
25 No information on the operation of this provision is provided in the Commission evaluation of the QD: 'Report from the Commission to the European Parliament and the Council on the Application of Directive 2004/83/EC of 29 April 2004 on Minimum Standards for the Qualification and Status of Third Country Nationals or Stateless Persons as Refugees or as Persons who Otherwise Need International Protection and the Content of the Protection', *COM (2010) 314 final*. Hereinafter, 'Commission evaluation of the QD'.

However, the major problem with the concept of derived rights as provided for in both the RCD and the QD lies in the definition of the term 'family members'. Article 2(d) of the RCD provides:

> '[F]amily members' shall mean, in so far as the family already existed in the country of origin, the following members of the applicant's family who are present in the same Member State in relation to the application for asylum:
>
> i   spouse or unmarried partner of the asylum seeker or his or her unmarried partner in a stable relationship [...];
> ii   the minor children of the couple referred to in point (i) or of the applicant, on condition that they are unmarried and dependent and regardless of whether they were born in or out of wedlock or adopted as defined under the national law.

Article 2(h) of the QD supplies exactly the same definition of family members of the refugee or beneficiary of subsidiary protection status. This definition can be criticised for a number of reasons.

First, the definition freezes membership of the family at the moment the family left the country of origin. This means that any children born during transit or after arriving in the EU do not qualify as family members, and consequently do not benefit from derived rights under the directives. This is rather startling, especially in view of the fact that pregnant women are included in the illustrative list of 'vulnerable persons' in Article 17 RCD and in Article 20(3) QD whose specific situation Member States must take into account in implementing various provisions of the directives. It can be observed that the vulnerability of pregnant women is unlikely to be diminished post-partum if their children are excluded from the scope of application of the directives.

Second, minor children are only comprehended within the definition if they are unmarried and dependent. This is a way of constructing the emancipation of children and, as *de facto* adults, of denying them their Convention rights. It is inconsistent with the scheme of the CRC, which defines the child as anyone under the age of eighteen unless majority is attained earlier under domestic law, and which conceives of child marriage as itself a cause for concern. In this regard, it is worth quoting from the Com. RC's General Comment No. 4 on adolescent health and development:

> [I]n some States Parties married children are legally considered adults, even if they are under 18, depriving them of all the special protection measures they are entitled [sic] under the Convention. The Committee strongly recommends that States Parties review and, where necessary, reform their legislation and practice to increase the minimum age for

marriage with and without parental consent to 18 years, for both girls and boys.[26]

Given these concerns, it follows that it may be in the best interests of the married/independent child to be included in the parents' family unit and to derive his/her rights accordingly. But this possibility is precluded by the definition of family in the directives.

Third, the definition of family member omits any reference to a guardian or responsible adult in situations where there are no parents, meaning that the child is not entitled to derive rights from the status of that person. Presumably, such a child could make his/her own application for international protection under the APD, thereby becoming directly entitled to the rights in the RCD and the QD (if found eligible).[27] However, such a child would not be considered to be an 'unaccompanied minor' and thus entitled to special protection and assistance. This is because the term 'unaccompanied minor' is defined in the RCD and the QD as 'persons below the age of eighteen who arrive in the territory of the Member State *unaccompanied by an adult responsible for them whether by law or by custom*, and for as long as they are not effectively taken into the care of such a person'.[28] Therefore, there is an inconsistency between the definition of family member in the directives and the definition of an unaccompanied minor, the net effect of which is that the child who is accompanied by an adult who is not a parent but who is responsible for him/her whether by law or custom is considered not to be an unaccompanied minor by virtue of that relationship, but is not entitled to derive any rights from the relationship. However, somewhat inconsistently, the RCD does envisage that such children should be lodged with the adult family member responsible for them, as will be outlined below.

Fourth, the definition of family member is constructed solely from the adult perspective, encompassing spouse or partner and (some) minor children. The lack of a definition of family member from the perspective of the child effectively means that a child cannot be the central claimant from whom other family members, such as parents or siblings, derive their rights. This signals a resistance to the idea of the child as a person with distinct protection needs, and to the concept of asylum as an appropriate remedy for the child in his/her own right – ideas that were developed in Chapters 3 and 4 above.

---

26 UN Doc. *CRC/GC/2003/4 (2003)*, para. 20. The Committee on the Elimination of Discrimination against Women has made a similar recommendation in its General Recommendation No. 21, 'Equality in marriage and family relations', 13th session, 1994. The Convention on the Elimination of All Forms of Discrimination Against Women States in Article 16(2): 'The betrothal and the marriage of a child shall have no legal effect, and all necessary action, including legislation, shall be taken to specify a minimum age for marriage [...].'
27 Article 6(4) APD provides that Member States may determine in national legislation the cases in which a minor can make an application on his/her own behalf and the cases in which an application by an adult is deemed to cover the application of any unmarried minor child – the term 'child' presumably meaning child of the adult.
28 Article 2(h) RCD and Article 2(i) QD. Emphasis added.

In conclusion, although the concept of derived rights is amply provided for in both the RCD and QD, the latter authorises placing restrictions on the derived rights of family members of beneficiaries of subsidiary protection. Furthermore, both directives define family members narrowly, such that certain categories of children – those born after the family left the country of origin and married and presumptively independent children – are precluded from deriving any rights from their parents' status. Children in the company of a guardian or responsible adult who is not a parent are in a particularly invidious position: precluded from being considered as unaccompanied minors but not entitled to derive any rights from the relevant adult's status. Finally, there is no definition of family member from the point of view of the child, meaning that the child cannot be the person from whom other family members derive their rights. In sum, the RCD and QD recognise the concept of derived rights but severely curtail the personal scope of those rights.

The prohibition on separating a child from his/her parents

Article 9 CRC establishes an absolute prohibition on separating a child from his/her parents unless, subject to various procedural guarantees, the separation is necessary for the best interests of the child. To what extent is this right reflected in the relevant CEAS instruments? The relevant instruments are the RCD, the QD and the DR. These will be considered in turn.

As regards the RCD, various provisions of Chapter II (General Provisions on Reception Conditions) speak to the issue of family unity. Article 8 provides, *inter alia*, 'Member States shall take appropriate measures to maintain *as far as possible* family unity as present within their territory, *if applicants are provided with housing by the Member State concerned*'.[29] Article 14(2) stipulates that Member States must ensure the protection of family life where housing-in-kind is provided. Article 14(3) establishes the particular entitlement of the child to family unity, stating that 'Member States shall ensure, *if appropriate*, that minor children of applicants or applicants who are minors are lodged with their parents or with the adult family member responsible for them whether by law or by custom'.[30] However, Article 14(8) permits Member States to 'exceptionally' derogate from the Article 14 guarantees in four circumstances, one of which is when the asylum seeker is in detention.[31] In such circumstances, different rules may apply for a reasonable period, which must be as short as possible. In other words, in such circumstances, the duty to provide housing that assures protection of family life and to accommodate children with their parents may be limited.

---

29 Emphasis added.
30 Emphasis added.
31 The other circumstances are: when an initial assessment of the specific needs of the applicant is required; when material reception conditions are not available in a certain geographical area; and when housing capacities normally available are temporarily exhausted.

These various provisions can be criticised from the point of view of the right of the child not to be separated from his/her parents on a number of grounds. First, the qualifying terms ('as far as possible'; 'if applicants are provided with housing by the Member State concerned'; 'if appropriate') are problematic. Article 9(1) CRC provides that the only situation in which the separation of a child from his/her parents is permitted is if the separation is necessary for the best interests of the child. Consequently, predicating family unity on what is 'possible' (presumably, in terms of administrative convenience) and 'appropriate' (meaning unclear) is contrary to the requirements of Article 9. By the same token, limiting the State's obligation to situations of direct provision of accommodation overlooks the fact that, where an accommodation allowance is provided, it must be sufficient to pay for family accommodation.[32]

Second, the derogation provision in Article 14(8) implicitly allows the child to be lodged separately from one or both parents for a number of management and administrative reasons. Since the only legitimate reason for separating a child from his or her parents is where separation is necessary for best interests – understood solely in terms of the relationship between and personal circumstances of the child and his/her parents – the derogation provision is contrary to Article 9(1) CRC. Article 14(3), which establishes the specific entitlement of the child to family unity, would seem to come within the scope of application of Article 18 of the directive, which provides that '[t]he best interests of the child shall be a primary consideration for Member States when implementing the provisions of the Directive that involve minors'. Therefore, any derogation from Article 14(3) would also be subject to a best-interests assessment. However, as previously explained, the general principle of the best interests of the child (which is reflected in Article 18 RCD) is weaker than the specific best-interests obligation in the context of forced separation, making Article 18 RCD of little succor in this context.

Third, Article 9(1) and (2) CRC mandates that any separation decision be taken by competent authorities subject to periodic judicial review, and that all interested parties, including the child, be given the opportunity to make their views known and have their views considered. Nothing in the text of the directive suggests that such procedural requirements must be satisfied.[33]

---

32 A question has been referred to the CJEU on whether various provisions of the directive, including the provision establishing the particular entitlement of the child to family unity, must be met when material support is provided in the form of a financial allowance: *Saciri*, Case C-79/13, Request for a preliminary ruling lodged on 15 February 2013.
33 Chapter V RCD on appeals does provide that negative decisions relating to the granting of benefits under the Directive or decisions taken under Article 7 must be amenable to appeal, including, at last instance, an appeal before a judicial body. The reference to negative decisions, although somewhat obscure, most probably relates to Chapter III of the directive (Reduction or Withdrawal of Reception Conditions), while Article 7 – itself an opaque provision – relates to detention. Therefore, it seems unlikely that negative decisions relating to family unity fall within the scope of Chapter V, unless the separation is as a result of a reduction or withdrawal of reception conditions or detention.

Fourth, it is unclear how the narrow definition of family member in Article 2(d) RCD, which has already been commented upon, maps on to the provisions relating to family unity. If Member States restrict the provisions on family unity to the family as defined in the directive, then children born after the parent(s) arrived in the EU and married and independent children will not benefit from the provisions on family unity. In sum, the family unity provisions of the RCD fall short of the strict requirements of Article 9 CRC not to separate the child from his/her parents against their will.

The QD and the DR also contain provisions relating to the issue of family unity of a child with his/her parents. The concept of family unity is provided for in Article 23 of the QD, with paragraph 1 providing that 'Member States *shall ensure* that family unity can be maintained'.[34] While, unlike the RCD, there is no separate statement of the child's entitlement to family unity, it is submitted that this is inconsequential in view of the categorical terms of Article 23(1). However, if this provision is interpreted in light of the narrow definition of 'family member' in Article 2(h) QD, then not all children will benefit.

As regards the DR, Article 4(3) provides that the situation of an accompanied minor who meets the definition of family member in the directive is indissociable from that of his/her parent or guardian for the purposes of the regulation and establishes that this applies equally to children born after the asylum seeker arrived in the territory of the Member States. While the definition of family member in the DR is the same as that in the RCD and the QD, and therefore excludes married and independent children, the reference to children born after arrival is novel and to be welcomed. On the whole, Article 4(3) amounts to a reasonably robust family unity guarantee.[35]

In sum, the RCD is problematic from the point of view of the right of the child not to be separated from his/her parents. This is because the family unity provisions are amenable to being applied (and derogated from) in a manner that undermines family unity. The QD and the DR are much more robust in this regard, although an unfortunate feature of all the instruments, to varying degrees, is the narrow definition of 'family member'.

---

34 Emphasis added.
35 While Article 4(3) DR is positive from a family unity point of view, the assimilation of the situation of the child to the parent or guardian is potentially problematic in that it obscures any inquiry into whether transfer to another EU Member State is safe for the child. Inquiries into the safety of other EU Member States are becoming more common since the CJEU established that there can be no conclusive presumption of safety under the DR: *N.S. and M.E.*, Joined Cases C-411/10 and C-493/10, Judgment (GC) of 21 December 2011. That ruling followed the seminal ECtHR judgment in *M.S.S. v Belgium and Greece* in which both respondent States were held liable for violating Article 3 ECHR in the context of the DR. Appl. No. 30696/09, Judgment (GC) of 21 January 2011. However, it should be noted that subsequent attempts to apply the *M.S.S.* precedent have been largely unsuccessful: *Mohammed Hussein et al. v the Netherlands and Italy*, Appl. No. 27725/10, Judgment of 2 April 2013 (involving a DR transfer to Italy); *Mohammed v Austria*, Appl. No. 2283/12, Judgment of 6 June 2013 (involving a DR transfer to Hungary).

Phase Two CEAS: Prospects for enhanced compliance

The concept of derived rights

The central problem with both the RCD and the QD on the issue of derived rights is the restrictive definition of 'family member'. Do the recast RCD and QD solve this problem?

As regards the recast RCD, it can be observed that, first, the family is still limited to the family as it existed in the country of origin, thereby excluding children born after arrival or in transit.[36] Second, the exclusion of married and dependent children from the definition of family is partly remedied by the removal of the dependency, although not the marital-status, criterion.[37] This exclusion is mitigated somewhat by new Recital 22, which provides that, when deciding on housing arrangements, Member States should take due account of the best interests of the child 'as well as of the particular circumstances of any applicant who is dependent on family members or other close relatives, such an unmarried minor siblings already present in the Member State'. Although somewhat tenuous, this could provide the legal basis for including married children who are dependent on their parents within the family unit. Third, for the first time, 'family member' is defined from the perspective of the (unmarried) child as 'the father, mother or another adult responsible for the applicant whether by law or by the practice of the Member State concerned'. Although this definition does not extend to siblings, again, Recital 22 mitigates the exclusion. Fourth, the definition of 'unaccompanied minor' is revised. Article 2(e) defines an unaccompanied minor as a minor 'unaccompanied by an adult responsible for him or her whether by law or by the practice of the Member State concerned', thereby aligning this definition with that of family member from the perspective of the child and correcting the current gap that exists between the two definitions.

Identical changes are made in the recast QD with one notable exception: there is no equivalent to Recital 22 RCD and consequently no legal basis, however tenuous, for married children and siblings to be considered as part of the family unit for the purposes of derived rights. The recast does, however, delete the problematic sub-paragraph in current Article 23(2) that permits Member States 'to define the conditions' applicable to the benefits accruing to the family members of beneficiaries of subsidiary protection.

To summarise, there are some significant improvements in the definition of family member in the recast RCD and QD, but children born in transit or

---

36 Article 2(c).
37 The amended Commission proposal for a recast RCD (*COM (2011) 320 final*) included some married minor children within the definition of family (i.e. those who are not accompanied by their spouses and in whose best interests it is to be considered as family members) but this aspect of the proposal did not survive the negotiation process with the result that married children are still excluded from the family unit.

after arrival are still excluded from the definition as are, to a greater or lesser extent, married children and siblings. In this regard, Phase Two CEAS constitutes a significant but qualified improvement on Phase One from the point of view of the derived rights of the accompanied child.

The prohibition on separating a child from his/her parents

With the exception of the narrow definition of family member, the provisions of the QD and DR that speak to the prohibition on separating a child from his/her parents were found to be broadly consistent with the requirements of Article 9 CRC. Furthermore, the previous subsection outlined how the definition of family member has been (somewhat) expanded in the recast QD. Identical changes have been made to the definition of family member in the recast DR.[38] Attention now turns to the RCD, which was the central cause for concern from the point of view of the prohibition on separating a child from his/her parents.

A number of problems were identified in the critique of the family unity provisions in the RCD, seen from the perspective of Article 9 CRC: the use of qualifying phrases in the provisions relating to family unity, the possibility of derogating from the guarantees relating to family unity, the lack of any procedural safeguards in decisions interfering with family unity and the narrow definition of 'family member'. As the latter has just been discussed, the focus here will be on the other problems and on whether they are remedied in the recast of the directive.

The general provision on 'families' in Article 8 of the RCD, which obliges Member States to take appropriate measures to maintain family unity 'as far as possible', but only 'if applicants are provided with housing by the Member State concerned', remains unchanged (in Article 12 of the recast). However, the specific right of minors to family unity is moved from the article on 'Modalities for material reception conditions' to the article on 'Minors' (Article 23 of the recast). The significance of this move is that it is no longer subject to the derogation provision that implicitly permits the separation of the child from his/her parents in various circumstances. Furthermore, the qualifying term 'if appropriate' is removed and a new sentence is added relating to best interests. Thus, Article 23(5) reads:

> Member States shall ensure that minor children of applicants or applicants who are minors are lodged with their parents, their unmarried minor siblings or with the adult family member responsible for them whether by law or the national practice of the Member States concerned, provided this is in the best interests of the minors concerned.

---

38 Article 2(g) DR.

Furthermore, an enhanced provision on best interests (Article 23(2) of the recast) provides that in assessing best interests, Member States must take due account of, *inter alia*, the minor's well-being and social development, taking into particular consideration the minor's background. When these two paragraphs of Article 23 are read together, and in light of the procedural requirements for undertaking a best interests determination that are articulated in various soft-law documents (see Chapter 2 above), they present a strong case for family unity. As such, the recast RCD can be considered to meet the requirements, including the procedural demands, of Article 9 CRC.

The right of the unaccompanied and separated child to special protection and assistance

Having explored the right of the asylum-seeking/refugee child to family unity, which is the principal means of ensuring the protection and care of the child, this section turns to the protection and care of the asylum-seeking/refugee child who is unaccompanied or separated and therefore bereft of family.

Article 22 CRC relating to the right of the asylum-seeking or refugee child to protection and assistance contains a second paragraph, which provides that the child who is without parents or other members of the family 'shall be accorded the same protection and care as any other child permanently or temporarily deprived of his or her family environment for any reason, as set forth in the present Convention'. In turn, Article 20 CRC provides:

1   A child temporarily or permanently deprived of his or her family environment, or in whose best interests cannot be allowed to remain in that environment, shall be entitled to special protection and assistance provided by the State;
2   States Parties shall in accordance with their national laws ensure alternative care for the child;
3   Such care could include, *inter alia*, foster placement, *kafalah* of Islamic law, adoption or if necessary placement in suitable institutions for the care of children. When considering solutions, due regard shall be paid to the desirability of continuity in a child's upbringing and to the child's ethnic, religious, cultural and linguistic background.

The right of the child without family to special protection and assistance is well established in international and regional human rights law. For example, it is implicit in Article 24 ICCPR relating to the right of the child to special measures of protection,[39] and is found in the Revised European Social

---

39   Thus, the Human Rights Committee in its General Comment 17 on Article 24 ICCPR 'considers it useful that reports by States Parties should provide information on the special measures of protection adopted to protect children who are abandoned or deprived of their

Charter.[40] In extreme cases, inadequate care and protection of an unaccompanied child may amount to inhuman treatment contrary to Article 3 ECHR.[41] Furthermore, there is a large body of soft-law guidance about the right of the child without family to special protection and assistance in general,[42] and about its specific application to unaccompanied minors.[43] However, as the function of some of the guidance is to elaborate best practice or 'desirable orientations for policy and practice', it arguably goes beyond the minimum requirements of the CRC.[44] Consequently, only such guidance as can be directly inferred from the provisions of the CRC will be used in identifying the normative content of the right of the child without family to special protection and assistance. Three questions arise in relation to this right: a) What child is entitled to special protection and assistance?; b) Who should oversee the special protection and assistance?; c) What alternative care must be provided for the child? In answering these questions, the normative content of the right will be sketched.

Identification of the child entitled to special protection and assistance

This first issue relates to the personal scope of Article 20 CRC, taken in conjunction with Article 22 CRC. Article 20 refers to the child 'who has been temporarily or permanently deprived of his or her family environment'. Article 22 refers to the child who is without 'parents or other members of the family'. The issue to be resolved is whether the right to special protection and assistance is limited to the child who is without any relatives whatsoever (i.e. the child who is unaccompanied or totally alone), or extends to the child who is without parents or other primary care-givers but is in the company of other adult family members (i.e. the separated child). The answer to this question is of considerable consequence because a narrow interpretation means that the State is not primarily responsible for the separated child.

---

family environment in order to enable them to develop in conditions that most closely resemble those characterizing the family environment'. *UN Doc HRI/GEN/1/Rev.1 (1994)* at 23, para. 6.

40 Article 17 of the Revised European Social Charter establishes an obligation to 'provide protection and special aid [...] for children and young persons temporarily or definitively deprived of their family's support'.
41 See ECtHR, *Mayeka Mitunga v Belgium*, Appl. No. 13178/03, Judgment of 12 October 2006, and ECtHR, *Rahimi v Greece*, Appl. No. 8687/08, Judgment of 5 April 2011.
42 For the most recent guidance see UN General Assembly, 'Guidelines for the Alternative Care of Children', *A/RES/64/142*, 2010.
43 For a cross-section of guidance, see Separated Children in Europe Programme, 'Statement of Good Practice', 4th revised ed., 2009 (hereinafter 'SCEP Statement of Good Practice); Com. RC, General Comment No. 6, *op. cit.*; UNHCR 'Guidelines on Policies and Procedures in dealing with Unaccompanied Children Seeking Asylum', 1997.
44 General Assembly, 2010, *op. cit.*, p. 2.

In its General Comment No. 6 on the treatment of unaccompanied and separated children outside their country of origin, the Com. RC adopts a pragmatic middle ground: Article 20 applies to both groups, but in the case of the separated child guardianship should regularly be assigned to the accompanying adult family member, 'unless there is an indication that it would not be in the best interests of the child to do so', and the child should live with the accompanying adult family member 'unless such action would be contrary to the best interests of the child'.[45] Hence, day-to-day protection and assistance are generally delegated to relatives but subject to State oversight. It follows that when a child is accompanied by a relative who is not a parent or primary care-giver, a process must be put in place to establish the nature of the relationship and the suitability and willingness of the relative to continue to care for the child.[46] This raises the larger issue of identification of unaccompanied minors.

Article 20 CRC presupposes a mechanism for identifying whether a child is deprived of his or her family environment. Although there is no article in the Convention explicitly establishing such a mechanism, Article 8(1) is of relevance in this regard, providing: 'States Parties undertake to respect the right of the child to preserve his or her identity, including nationality, name and family relations as recognized by law without unlawful interference.' Although originally intended to relate to 'disappeared' children,[47] the Com. RC considers that Article 8(1) extends to a duty to identify separated or unaccompanied children upon arrival at ports of entry or as soon as their presence in the country becomes known to the authorities.[48] This 'prioritised identification' process includes age assessment, prompt registration by means of an initial interview to collect bio-data and ascertain identity and on-going recording of further information, including information pertaining to international protection needs. As regards age assessment, the Committee recommends that it should not be confined to a physical assessment but should also encompass an assessment of the child's psychological maturity; moreover, it should be conducted in a manner that respects the physical integrity of the child and be governed by the principle of the benefit of the doubt.[49] Indeed,

---

45 Com. RC, General Comment No. 6, *op. cit.*, paras. 34 and 40 respectively. The SCEP Statement of Good Practice goes further, requiring the appointment of an *independent* guardian (para. D3.1) and stating that '[w]here children live with or are placed with relatives, these relatives must be assessed for their ability to provide suitable care and undergo necessary recruitment checks.' SCEP, *op. cit.*, § D8.1.1.
46 UNHCR's 1997 Guidelines provide practical guidance on how to carry out this assessment in Annex II. *Op. cit.* See also, EctHR, *Rahimi v Greece*, *o.p cit.*, paras. 70–73, in which the ECtHR reprimanded the government for failing to establish any mechanisms for verifying the relationship between a fifteen-year-old boy and his supposed cousin.
47 See J. Doek, *op. cit.*
48 Com. RC, General Comment No. 6, *op. cit.*, para. 31.
49 *Ibid.*, para. 31(i).

there is a large amount of soft-law guidance and literature on the proper conduct and limitations of age assessment.[50]

In short, the child who is entitled to special protection and assistance in the CRC is the child who is separated from his/her parents or primary caregivers, notwithstanding that the child may be with other relatives. There must be a mechanism for identifying such children, since otherwise the right to special protection and assistance would be largely deprived of application.

Oversight of care and protection

It follows from the personal scope of Article 20 that special protection and assistance has a surrogate function: it should, in so far as possible, take the place of parental protection and assistance. Accordingly, legal responsibility for the child should be vested in a designated individual who has the right and responsibility to make decisions *in lieu* of the parents. This suggests the appointment of a guardian. Surprisingly, in view of the many references in the CRC to the concept of guardianship, the Convention contains no provision on when a guardian should be appointed to a child. However, Article 18 is of utmost importance in this regard, providing, *inter alia*:

1   [...] Parents or, as the case may be, legal guardians, have the primary responsibility for the upbringing and development of the child. The best interests of the child will be their basic concern.
2   For the purpose of guaranteeing and promoting the rights set forth in the present Convention, States Parties shall render appropriate assistance to parents and legal guardians in the performance of their child-rearing responsibilities and shall ensure the development of institutions, facilities and services for the care of children.

The Com. RC considers that Article 18(2), in conjunction with Article 20(1), forms the basis of an obligation to appoint a guardian or adviser to the unaccompanied or separated child.[51] According to the Committee, the guardian or adviser should have the necessary expertise in the field of childcare so as to

---

50   See, for example, UNHCR, 'Guidelines on International Protection, Child Asylum Claims under Articles 1(A)2 and 1(F) of the 1951 Convention and/or 1967 Protocol relating to the Status of Refugees', *HCR/GIP/09/08* (2009), para. 75; SCEP, Statement of Good Practice, *op. cit.*, para. D5; H. Crawley, *When is a Child Not a Child? Asylum, Age Disputes and the Process of Age Assessment,* London: Immigration Law Practitioners' Association, 2007; K. Halvorsen, 'Report: Separated Child in Europe Programme Workshop on Age Assessment and Identification', Bucharest, 2003 (on file with author).
51   Com. RC, General Comment No. 6, *op. cit.*, paras. 33–38. Article 3(2) CRC is also of relevance in this regard: 'States Parties undertake to ensure the child such protection and care as is necessary for his or her well-being, taking into account the rights and duties of his or her parents, legal guardians, or other individuals legally responsible for him or her, and, to this end, shall take all appropriate legislative and administrative measures.'

ensure that the interests of the child are safeguarded and that the child's legal, social, health, psychological, material and educational needs are appropriately covered. Hence, the guardian's role is essentially to ensure that in all actions concerning the child, the best interests of the child are a primary consideration. This clearly follows from Article 18(1) above. Moreover, in view of the pivotal role of the guardian in securing the child's protection and assistance, the Com. RC considers that the exercise of guardianship should be regularly monitored.[52] This obligation derives from Article 3(3) CRC, which provides:

> States Parties shall ensure that the institutions, services and facilities responsible for the care or protection of children shall conform with the standards established by competent authorities, particularly in the areas of safety, health, in the number and *suitability* of their staff, as well as *competent supervision*.[53]

Finally, it should be noted that the obligation to appoint a guardian to secure the protection and assistance of unaccompanied minors may be classified as part of the State's positive obligations under Article 3 ECHR. In *Mayeka Mitunga v Belgium*, in which a five-year-old unaccompanied minor was detained for two months in an adult detention centre, the Court reprimanded the government for the haphazard care it provided to the child, stating that '[t]he fact that the [child] received legal assistance, had daily telephone contact with her mother or uncle and that staff and residents at the centre did their best for her cannot be regarded as sufficient to meet all her needs as a five-year-old. The Court further considers that the uncoordinated attention she received was far from adequate'.[54] Although the Court did not expressly refer to a guardian, it is clear on the facts that the 'uncoordinated attention' that the child received was the result of her not having been appointed one. In *Rahimi v Greece*, a case concerning the detention and subsequent abandonment by the State of a 15-year-old unaccompanied minor, the Court was less circumspect on the issue of guardianship.[55] It found that the failure of the Greek authorities to appoint a guardian to the child, with the result that he was left homeless and destitute until he happened to be taken charge of by an NGO, constituted inhuman and degrading treatment contrary to Article 3 ECHR.[56]

---

52 *Ibid.*, para. 35.
53 Emphasis added.
54 ECtHR, *Mayeka Mitunga v Belgium, op. cit.*, para. 52.
55 ECtHR, *Rahimi v Greece, op. cit.*
56 For critical commentary of the Court's finding in this regard, see M. Bossuyt, 'The Court of Strasbourg acting as an asylum court', *European Constitutional Law Review* 8, 2012, 203–245. Bossuyt's argument is that 'The Court does not state that the conditions of accommodation and care as ensured by NGOs in themselves violate Article 3 of the Convention, but that the accommodation and care were ensured, not by the Government, but by NGOs'. Bossuyt goes on to query why accommodation and care of asylum seekers

To summarise, special protection and assistance under Article 20 is surrogate parental protection. As such, this form of protection should principally be delegated to a guardian or adviser, who has the right and responsibility to oversee the child's best interests. The exercise of guardianship should itself be overseen. The failure to appoint a guardian or adviser may lead to a situation amounting to inhuman or degrading treatment.

The provision of alternative care

Article 20, first paragraph, establishes that the child deprived of his/her family environment is entitled to special protection and care, while paragraphs two and three set out the requirement to provide alternative care for the child. But what, in practical terms, is the nature of the alternative care that must be provided? The answer lies in the scheme of Article 20 itself.

Discussions about alternative care for unaccompanied minors often focus on the *type* of care arrangement that should be put in place.[57] But Article 20 CRC does not mandate any particular type of care arrangement. In this regard it can be observed that the obligation in Article 20 diminishes in strength from paragraph (1) (the child 'shall be entitled to special protection and assistance provided by the State'), through paragraph 2 (States Parties 'shall' ensure alternative care, but 'in accordance with their national laws') to paragraph 3 ('Such care could include foster placement, *kafalah* of Islamic law, adoption or if necessary placement in suitable institutions for the care of children'). Hence, there is a right to special protection and assistance; there is a right to some form of alternative care; but there is no right to any specific modality of care placement. In this regard, the Com. RC notes that:

> A wide range of options for care and accommodation arrangements exist and are explicitly acknowledged in Article 20(3) [...] When selecting from these options, the particular vulnerabilities of such a child, not only having lost connection with his or her family environment, but further finding him or herself outside of his or her country of origin, as well as the child's age and gender, should be taken into account.[58]

Consequently, it is permitted and indeed appropriate to provide different care arrangements for different children, according to their protection needs, age, gender and so forth.[59] What is most important – and this applies regardless

---

cannot be ensured by NGOs. (p. 233). With respect, this is missing the point, which is that the respondent State did not refer the applicant to an NGO, but, rather, abandoned him to his fate, and that he happened to be rescued by an NGO.

57 See, for example, the SCEP Statement of Good Practice, *op. cit.*
58 Com. RC, General Comment No. 6, *op. cit.*, p. 13.
59 Hence, the claims that are sometimes made, that children must be placed in families or that it is prohibited to place older children in adult accommodation, cannot be sustained.

of the type of care arrangement – is that the placement should be identified following a best-interests assessment. Assessing what is in the best interests of the child requires soliciting the views of the child and giving due weight to the views of the child in accordance with his/her age and maturity. While the best-interests assessment is an individualised appraisal, certain observations can be made about what is in the best interests of children generally when it comes to alternative care. For example, it is generally in the best interests of children that changes of residence be kept to a minimum and that siblings be kept together. This follows from the second sentence of Article 20(3) mandating continuity in the child's upbringing and due regard to the child's ethnic, religious, cultural and linguistic background. A further, related requirement is that, whatever the type of care arrangement identified for the child, it must serve to protect the child. This requirement derives from a schematic interpretation of Article 20 as a whole: the right to alternative care in paragraphs 2 and 3 being a functional expression of the broader right to protection (and assistance) in paragraph 1. Indeed, the term 'protection' links Article 20 with a cluster of CRC rights that relate to child protection and the prevention of abuse. Article 19(1) is particularly important in this regard, providing:

> States Parties shall take all appropriate legislative, administrative, social and educational measures to protect the child from all forms of physical or mental violence, injury or abuse, neglect or negligent treatment, maltreatment or exploitation, including sexual abuse, while in the care of parents(s), legal guardians or any other person who has the care of the child.[60]

While the guardian has an important role in overseeing the child's protection, in reality, whether the child is protected on a day-to-day basis will depend on the care placement allocated to the child. In this regard, any such placement must ensure that the child is protected from threats in the wider environment as well as threats that emanate from the care placement itself. As regards the latter, it is necessary that persons working in the care placement be qualified to care for children and that care arrangements be monitored and regularly

---

For example, according to the SCEP Statement of Good Practice, '[e]very separated child should have the opportunity to be placed within a family if it is in their best interests to do so. [...] Separated children over 16 years of age who are not placed within families should be found appropriate residential placements and must not be treated as "de facto" adults and placed in an adult hostel or reception center settings'. Here, the gulf between best practice and the minimum requirements of the CRC becomes apparent. *Op. cit.*, § D8.1.

60 Other relevant rights are established in Article 32 (right of the child to be protected from exploitation), Article 33 (right of the child to be protected against the illicit use of narcotic drugs), Article 34 (the right of the child to protection from sexual exploitation and abuse), Article 35 (the obligation to prevent the abduction of, sale of or traffic in children), Article 36 (the right of the child to protection against all other forms of exploitation) and in the Optional Protocol on the Sale of Children, Child Prostitution and Child Pornography.

reviewed.[61] This follows from the requirements of Article 3(3) CRC, previously mentioned, regarding standards and supervision of child care services. Accordingly, the Committee notes that:

> Irrespective of the care arrangements made for unaccompanied or separated children, regular supervision and assessment ought to be maintained by qualified persons in order to ensure the child's physical and psychosocial health, protection against domestic violence or exploitation, and access to educational and vocational skills and opportunities.[62]

In summary, while Article 20(2) and (3) do not mandate any particular type of care arrangement, they do require that the child placement follows a best-interests assessment. Furthermore, the care arrangement must protect the child, both from without and from within. This has implications for staff training and monitoring.

Phase One CEAS: Compliance with the right of the unaccompanied and separated child to special protection and assistance

Of all the child-rights issues that arise in the asylum process, the rights of unaccompanied minors have been most thoroughly researched and subject to policy and legislation.[63] This is a result of not only the extreme vulnerability of unaccompanied minors, but also of the perception that this group constitutes a 'problem' population.[64] This sub-section explores whether

---

61 For a compelling account of what happens when States fail to ensure the protective dimension of the care placement, see S. Mullally, 'Separated children in Ireland, responding to "terrible wrongs"', *International Journal of Refugee Law* 23, 2011, 632–655.
62 Com. RC, General Comment No. 6, *op. cit.*, para. 40, p. 14.
63 For recent research, see Frontex, 'Unaccompanied Minors in the Migration Process', 2010 (hereinafter 'Frontex report'); European Migration Network, 'Policies on Reception, Return and Integration arrangements for, and numbers of, Unaccompanied Minors – an EU comparative study', 2010 (hereinafter, 'EMN report'); EU Agency for Fundamental Rights, 'Separated, asylum-seeking children in European Union Member States, Report', 2010 (hereinafter, 'FRA report'); and Eurasylum, 'The protection of the rights and special needs of irregular minors and asylum seeking children, A thematic discussion paper prepared for the EU Agency for Fundamental Rights', 2008. For policy initiatives, see, Communication from the Commission to the European Parliament and the Council, 'Action Plan on Unaccompanied Minors (2010–2014)', *COM (2010) 213 final* (hereinafter, 'Commission Action Plan on Unaccompanied Minors'), and Council Conclusions on Unaccompanied Minors, 3018th Justice and Home Affairs Council meeting, Luxembourg, 3 June 2010. As regards legislation, in the area of unaccompanied minors seeking asylum, it can be observed that more provisions of the CEAS are devoted to unaccompanied minors than to any other child-rights issue.
64 For example, the Frontex report opens with the following observation: 'The phenomenon of unaccompanied minors claiming asylum in the EU has become a more visible problem.

such scrutiny has led to a convergence between the treatment of unaccompanied minors and their rights. The relevant instruments of the CEAS are the RCD and the QD.

Identification of the child entitled to special protection and assistance

As previously established, it is the child who is separated from his/her parents or primary caregivers as well as the child who is totally alone that is entitled to special protection and assistance. There must be a mechanism for the identification of such children. This question does not arise in the context of the QD because, chronologically, identification precedes recognition. However, it does arise in the context of the RCD which, therefore, is the focus of this section.

Unaccompanied minors are defined in Article 2(h) RCD as:

> [P]ersons below the age of eighteen who arrive in the territory of the Member State unaccompanied by an adult responsible for them whether by law or by custom, and for as long as they are not effectively taken into the care of such a person; it shall include minors who are left unaccompanied after they have entered the territory of Member States.[65]

The key provision of the directive relating to the protection and assistance of unaccompanied minors is Article 19. Article 19(1) obliges Member States to 'as soon as possible take measures to ensure the necessary representation of unaccompanied minors', while Article 19(2) entitles unaccompanied minors who make an application for asylum to be placed in one of four care placements 'from the moment they are admitted to the territory'.

At first glance, the definition of 'unaccompanied minor' can be criticised for excluding the concept of the separated child.[66] This is because the term 'unaccompanied minor' strongly suggests a child who is not in the company of anybody, in other words, a child who is totally alone. However, on closer scrutiny, it is not clear that Article 2(h) in conjunction with Article 19 RCD does exclude the concept of the separated child. First, Article 2(h) refers to the child 'unaccompanied by an adult responsible for them whether by law or by custom', a formulation that suggests a verification of the relationship between the child and the accompanying adult. Further, the child will be considered unaccompanied 'for as long as they are not effectively taken into

---

The increasing extent and weight of the problem was also identified in the Frontex Annual Risk Assessment (ARA) 2009.' *Ibid.*, Executive summary, p. 3.
65 The same definition of an unaccompanied minor is provided in Article 2(i) QD.
66 For such criticism, see A. Enenajor, 'Rethinking vulnerability: European asylum policy harmonisation and unaccompanied asylum seeking minors', *Childhoods Today* 2, 2008, 1–24.

the care of such a person', the term 'effectively' indicating an oversight process. Second, one of the four care placements listed in Article 19(2) is a placement with adult relatives. This implies that some unaccompanied minors, at least, are separated, as opposed to being totally alone. Therefore, although the RCD uses the terminology 'unaccompanied minors', on closer scrutiny it encompasses separated children too.

An arguably bigger problem with Article 19 RCD is that, despite the hints at verification and oversight, it does not establish any mechanism for identifying unaccompanied minors. Since the scope of the directive is limited to persons who lodge an application for asylum,[67] chronologically, the issue of identification is something that should be addressed in the APD.[68] However, that directive also fails to establish any mechanism for identifying unaccompanied minors.[69] Thus, the issue is left entirely to the discretion of Member States.[70] This lacuna in the CEAS has a knock-on effect on *when* the unaccompanied minor asylum seeker becomes entitled to special protection and assistance. Article 19(1) of the RCD establishes an obligation to appoint a representative 'as soon as possible', while Article 19(2) requires Member States to secure a care placement for unaccompanied minors who make an application for asylum 'from the moment they are admitted to the territory'. But these provisions are inconsistent with each other (an application for asylum is often predicated on having a representative and hence cannot be made the moment the unaccompanied minor is admitted to the territory)[71] and inconsistent with reality (unaccompanied minors do not always present at the border for the purposes of being admitted to the territory).

A related omission from the RCD is any reference to age assessment for identification purposes. Indeed, the only reference to the concept of age assessment is made in Article 17(5) of the APD, which provides that 'Member States may use medical examinations to determine the age of unaccompanied minors within the framework of the examination of an application for asylum'. This raises the question of why age assessment is perceived as useful in the context of status determination of unaccompanied minors, but not in

---

67 Article 3(1) RCD provides, *inter alia*, '[t]his Directive shall apply to all third country nationals and stateless persons who make an application for asylum'. The CJEU confirmed that the directive applies from the moment an asylum application is made in *Cimade and GISTI*, Case C-179/11, Judgment of 27 September 2012.
68 Directive 2005/85/EC of 1 December 2005.
69 Article 6 on access to the procedure simply provides, at para. 5: 'Member States shall ensure that authorities likely to be addressed by someone who wishes to make an application for asylum are able to advise that person how and where he/she may make such an application and/or may require these authorities to forward the application to the competent authority.'
70 For a description of the different approaches of Member States, see the EMN Report, *op. cit.*, n.83.
71 Thus, Article 6(4)(b) APD permits Member States to determine in national legislation the circumstances in which an application for asylum by an unaccompanied minor has to be lodged by a representative.

the context of special protection and assistance for unaccompanied minors. It is hard to avoid the conclusion that it is perceived as an exclusionary, rather than an inclusionary, tool.[72] This impression is reinforced by the fact that Article 17(5) assimilates age assessment with medical examinations. Medical examinations cover a range of age-assessment techniques, such as bone density tests, assessment of dental age and anthropometric measurements, which, apart from being of scientifically dubious merit, take no account of the child's psychological maturity. Furthermore, although Article 17(5) does establish a consent requirement, there are negative procedural consequences for refusing to undergo a medical examination.[73] Finally, the article makes no reference to the principle of the benefit of the doubt. But the main point is that age assessment as envisaged in the CEAS is not a tool for identifying unaccompanied minors. The lack of any mechanism for identifying unaccompanied minors is inconsistent with Article 20 CRC in conjunction with Article 8(1).

To sum up, while the RCD makes provision for the special protection and assistance of unaccompanied minors, it, along with the APD, fails to establish any mechanism for identifying such children. This is problematic because, clearly, if unaccompanied minors are not identified as such they cannot benefit from the rights afforded to them under the directive.

Oversight of care and protection

Special protection and assistance for the unaccompanied minor necessitates the appointment of a guardian or adviser who acts in the best interests of the child and whose role is overseen by a higher authority. Failure to appoint a guardian or adviser may lead to a situation that amounts to inhuman or degrading treatment.

The first thing to note is that both the RCD and the QD oblige Member States to appoint a guardian or representative to the unaccompanied minor.

---

72 This underlying rationale for age assessment has been highlighted in a number of recent reports. See, for example, Separated Children in Europe Programme (SCEP), 'Review of current law, policies and practices relating to age assessment in 16 European Countries', 2011; EMN report, *op. cit.*, pp. 73–83; and FRA report, *op. cit.*, Summary report/Conference Edition. The latter report found that '[m]ost children expressed fear and were critical of age assessment procedures, and in some countries had little information on these procedures. In others, children considered age assessment essentially unfair and most children wished that officials would simply believe them. Some children seemed troubled and perplexed by the fact that their statements about their age were challenged, as well as being distressed about the possibility of being perceived as liars'. Summary/Conference version, p. 36.

73 Article 17(5)(c) provides that any decision to reject the application of a minor who has refused to undergo age assessment 'shall not be based *solely* on that refusal'. Emphasis added. According to the Commission evaluation of the APD, '[w]here a person refuses to consent, he/she is treated as an adult (CZ, HU, NL, RO, PL and SK), the credibility of his/her statements is affected (AT and LU), or he/she may not rely on the benefit of the doubt principle (LT)'. *Op. cit.*, § 5.1.6, p. 8.

Consequently, there is no question of a possible violation of Article 3 ECHR. The issues raised by the guardianship provisions of the directives are more nuanced, relating to the quality of the arrangements envisaged.

As regards the RCD, Article 19(1) provides that:

> Member States shall as soon as possible take measures to ensure the necessary representation of unaccompanied minors by legal guardianship or, where necessary, representation by an organization which is responsible for the care and well-being of minors, or by any other appropriate representation. Regular assessments shall be made by the appropriate authorities.

This provision, which is substantially the same as the definition of a representative in Article 2(i) of the APD, has already been analysed in Chapter 4 above. In brief, the difficulty with this provision is that it is drafted at such a broad level of generality that it is unclear who the representative is, what his/her qualifications should be or what his/her role involves. The lack of clarity about the role of the representative is evident in the Commission evaluation of the RCD, which confuses the representative with a legal representative.[74] While unaccompanied minors are *also* entitled to a legal representative during the asylum process (as outlined in Chapter 4), this is separate from the right to a guardian or adviser. On the other hand, the obligation to conduct regular assessments of the representative speaks to the oversight requirement in the CRC and, hence, can be regarded as positive.

As for the QD, Article 30 provides that the representation must be by legal guardianship, by an organisation responsible for the care and well-being of minors, 'or by any other appropriate representation *including that based on legislation or Court order*'.[75] The italicised part of this provision, which does not appear in the corresponding provision of the RCD, establishes that the representative may be appointed in a more formal manner. It is submitted that this is an appropriate reflection of the fact that the unaccompanied minor is now a beneficiary of international protection who is entitled to a durable solution. Although the QD does not supply any guidance about the qualifications of the representative, Article 30(2) does clarify the role of the representative, providing that 'Member States shall ensure that the minor's needs are duly met in the implementation of this Directive by the appointed guardian or representative. The appropriate authorities shall make regular assessments'.

---

74 'Report from the Commission to the Council and to the European Parliament on the Application of Directive 2003/9/EC of 27 January 2003 Laying Down Minimum Standards for the Reception of Asylum Seekers', *COM (2007) 745 final*, § 3.5.2, p. 9. Hereinafter, 'Commission evaluation of the RCD'.
75 Emphasis added.

Put differently, the representative's role is to ensure that the minor benefits from all the rights to which he/she is entitled under the directive.

In sum, both the RCD and the QD quite correctly mandate the appointment of a representative to the unaccompanied minor and provide for some form of oversight. However, the RCD, in particular, is ambiguous about the representative and silent on his/her proper role as an over-seer of the child's care and protection.

The provision of alternative care

Although Article 20(2) and (3) CRC do not mandate any particular type of care arrangement, they do require that the child placement follows a best-interests assessment, while the various protection rights in the Convention require that the placement serves to protect the child. This necessitates staff training and monitoring. How do the relevant provisions of the RCD and the QD measure up in this regard?

As regard the RCD, Article 19(2) is the key provision. It provides:

> Unaccompanied minors who make an application for asylum shall, from the moment they are admitted to the territory to the moment they are obliged to leave the host Member State in which the application for asylum was made or is being examined, be placed:
> a   With adult relatives;
> b   With a foster family;
> c   In accommodation centers with special provision for minors;
> d   In other accommodation suitable for minors.
> Member States may place unaccompanied minors aged 16 or over in accommodation centers for adult asylum seekers. As far as possible, siblings shall be kept together, taking into account the best interests of the minor concerned and, in particular, his or her age and degree of maturity. Changes of residence of unaccompanied minors shall be limited to a minimum.

The range of care placements for unaccompanied minors in the first sub-paragraph, together with the references to various aspects of a best-interests assessment in the second sub-paragraph (i.e. siblings kept together, changes of residence limited to a minimum), correspond broadly with Article 20(2) and (3) CRC. However, the optional derogation whereby Member States can opt to place minors aged sixteen or over in accommodation centres for adult asylum seekers has elicited much criticism from NGOs and academic commentators on principle, although, in practice, only three Member States use the derogation.[76] Nevertheless, it is submitted that the derogation is not

---

76 For NGO criticism see, for example, ECRE, 'Comments from the European Council on Refugees and Exiles on the Amended Commission Proposal to recast the Reception

necessarily contrary to the requirements of Article 20 CRC and other relevant protection articles of the Convention, provided it is applied subject to a best-interests assessment. Article 18 of the directive (Minors) looks promising in this regard, stipulating that '[t]he best interests of the child shall be a primary consideration for Member States when implementing the provisions of this Directive that involve minors'. Since the derogation provision undisputedly involves minors, it follows that the best interests of the child must be a primary factor in deciding whether or not to apply the provision to any given minor.

Less positively, however, Article 19(2) RCD is weak on the protective function of the care placement. The lack of any reference to child protection is unfortunate, especially in light of the well-established trend across the EU of disappearances of unaccompanied minors from care.[77] Furthermore, Article 19(2) is silent on the requirement that alternative care be subject to regular supervision and assessment. Article 19(1) (discussed in the previous subsection), relating to representation of unaccompanied minors, does provide that 'regular assessments shall be made by the appropriate authorities', but these assessments are *of* the representative; they are not assessments of the care placement *by* the representative – a point not fully understood in the evaluation process.[78] In fact, there is nothing in the text of Article 19(1) to suggest that the representative is empowered to exercise a supervisory role over the care placement, to challenge the quality of care provided in the placement or, if necessary, to remove the child from that placement and secure for him/her an alternative placement. There is a requirement in Article 19(4) RCD that persons 'working with unaccompanied minors shall have had or receive appropriate

---

Conditions Directive (*COM (2011) 320 final)*', 2011, p. 25. For academic criticism, see E. Zschirnt, 'Does migration status trump the best interests of the child? Unaccompanied minors in the EU asylum system', *Journal of Immigration Asylum and Nationality Law* 25, 2011, 34–55. Zschirnt argues at p. 46 that the derogation provision 'still conflicts with the CRC's provision that children should be separated from adults in their accommodation'. However, while there is a provision in the CRC that the child should be separated from adults in *detention* (Article 37(c)), there is no obligation in the CRC to separate children from adults in accommodation generally.

77 All recent reports and policy documents on unaccompanied minors report on this phenomenon. *Op. cit.* The Com. RC has expressed its concern in its concluding observations to Nordic countries, in particular, at the disappearance of unaccompanied minors from care. See Com. RC, Concluding Observations to Denmark in 2011, *UN Doc. CRC/C/DNK/CO/4*, para. 58; to Norway in 2010, *UN Doc. CRC/C/NOR/CO/4*, para. 50; to Norway in 2005, *UN Doc. CRC/C/15/Add.262*, para. 41; and to Sweden in 2005, *UN Doc. CRC/C/15/Add.248*, § 7.

78 For example, the Odysseus Report, which fed into the Commission's evaluation of the RCD, states: 'It has not been possible to gather sufficient information concerning the question of finding out whether enough monitoring is effected by legal guardians in conformity with the requirements of Article 19(1) of the Directive'. Academic Network for Legal Studies on Immigration and Asylum in Europe, 'Comparative Overview of the Implementation of the Directive 2003/9 of 27 January 2003 laying down Minimum Standards for the Reception of Asylum Seekers in the EU Member States', October 2006, p. 83.

training concerning their needs'. While this is an important acknowledgement of the need for suitably qualified staff, the fact that the training could be a one-off or take place after appointment casts doubt on the seriousness of this provision.

As regards the QD, Article 30(3) contains the same list of possible placements that are outlined in the RCD, but with an explicit obligation to take the views of the child into account in accordance with age and maturity, and without any derogation provision in respect of over sixteens. Like the RCD, Article 30(4) iterates the desirability of keeping siblings together, subject to the best interests of the child and his or her age and degree of maturity, and of limiting changes of residence to a minimum. This is all consistent with the requirements of the CRC. However, like the RCD, the QD makes no reference to child protection in the context of the care placement and contains the same weak provision on training for those working with unaccompanied minors.[79]

In short, while the RCD and QD provide for a range of care placements for unaccompanied minors and contain provisions that implicitly relate to the best interests of the child, both directives fail to articulate the protective function of the care placement. This is unsatisfactory in view of the well-known dangers that care placements pose for unaccompanied minors.

Phase Two CEAS: Prospects for enhanced compliance

Identification of the child entitled to special protection and assistance

Although identification of the unaccompanied minor does not arise in the context of the QD, the lack of an identification mechanism is problematic in the context of the RCD. The recast RCD has the same temporal scope as the original directive, applying once an application is made.[80] Unsurprisingly, then, the recast introduces no new mechanism for the identification of unaccompanied minors prior to this point. There is a new article relating to the assessment of the special reception needs of vulnerable persons (the illustrative list of which includes unaccompanied minors), but this is of little assistance because it provides that the assessment 'shall be initiated within a reasonable time *after* an application for international protection is made'.[81] Obviously, it is necessary to identify the unaccompanied minor before that point or conceivably an application for international protection will not be made.

---

79 Article 30(6).
80 Article 3(1) recast RCD.
81 Article 22(1), second sub-para. Emphasis added. Similarly, Article 24 of the recast APD provides that 'Member States shall assess within a reasonable period of time after an application for international protection is made whether the applicant is an applicant in need of special procedural guarantees'.

Is the recast APD of any greater succor in this regard?[82] The recast does contain one amended and one new article geared towards ensuring that persons likely to make an application for international protection but who cannot access the usual determining authority be provided with the necessary information, interpretation and counselling.[83] Although potentially useful, these provisions contain no elements specific to the identification of unaccompanied minors.

The failure to introduce a mechanism for the identification of unaccompanied minors in Phase Two CEAS is puzzling. The Commission's Action Plan on Unaccompanied Minors provides that whenever unaccompanied minors are detected they should be separated from adults for their own protection, to sever relations with traffickers or smugglers and prevent (re)victimisation.[84] 'From the first encounter', the Action Plan states, 'attention to protection is paramount, as is early profiling of the type of minor'.[85] However, the Action Plan acknowledges that there is generally a gap between the moment when an unaccompanied minor is detected by the authorities and the moment when the CEAS, with its various protections for unaccompanied minors seeking asylum, is triggered. But then, when it comes to legislative action, the Action Plan simply states that:

> The EU should adopt higher standards of protection for unaccompanied minors completing negotiations on the revision of the asylum *acquis* [...]. The Commission will ensure that EU legislation is correctly implemented and, on the basis of an impact assessment, evaluate whether it is necessary to introduce targeted amendments or a special instrument setting down common standards on reception and assistance for all unaccompanied minors [...].[86]

While it may well be the case that a special instrument governing all unaccompanied minors (those seeking international protection and otherwise) is needed – an issue that is beyond the scope of the present work – it is unclear why, in the meantime, Phase Two CEAS was not used to improve the position of unaccompanied minors at the identification stage. Admittedly, not all unaccompanied minors, thus identified, would necessarily apply for international protection, but some would. The implicit suggestion in the Action Plan, that the revision of the asylum *acquis* tackles the problem of the gap between identification and application, is misleading.

---

82 Directive 2013/32/EU of the European Parliament and of the Council of 26 June 2013.
83 Article 6, 'Access to the procedure', and Article 8, 'Information and counselling in detention facilities and at border crossing points', respectively.
84 Commission Action Plan on Unaccompanied Minors, *op. cit.*, § 4.1.
85 *Ibid.*, p. 9.
86 *Ibid.*, pp. 9 & 10.

In sum, neither the recast RCD nor the recast APD contains any new mechanism for the identification of unaccompanied minors. The omission constitutes a significant practical barrier to the enjoyment by unaccompanied minors of applicable rights.

Oversight of care and protection

On a more positive note, a considerable improvement is made to the provisions of the RCD relating to the representative. A new definition of representative is supplied in Article 2(j), identical to the one in the recast APD, already analysed in Chapter 4 above. Furthermore, the first paragraph of the article relating to unaccompanied minors (now Article 24) is significantly amended. It establishes that the role of the representative is to represent and assist the unaccompanied minor to benefit from the rights and comply with the obligations under the directive. It mandates that the unaccompanied minor be informed immediately about the appointment of the representative and provides that the representative can be changed only when necessary, thus tackling the phenomenon of unaccompanied minors being confused about whether they have a representative and who that person might be. Article 24(1) further establishes that the representative can have no conflict of interest with the unaccompanied minor; that he/she is obliged to perform his/her duties in accordance with the principle of the best interests of the child (which is stated to include the minor's well-being and social development and safety and security considerations); and that he/she 'shall have the necessary expertise to that end'. Finally, the regular assessments by the appropriate authorities must include an assessment of 'the availability of the necessary means for representing the unaccompanied minor'. This detailed provision addresses the concern, outlined earlier, that the identity, qualifications and role of the representative are not adequately delineated.

Inconsistently, no similar changes relating to the representative were proposed by the Commission for the recast QD and hence there is no definition of 'representative' in the recast QD and no similar description of his/her role.

The provision of alternative care

Article 19(2) RCD has attracted criticism because it authorises Member States to derogate from the obligation to accommodate unaccompanied minors over the age of sixteen separately from adults. However, it was considered that, providing the derogation provision is subject to a best-interests assessment (as it seems to be under Article 18 of the directive), the derogation is unproblematic. The real difficulty with the RCD – one that is also apparent in the QD – is the lack of any reference to the protective function of the care placement. The recast RCD, in particular, envisages some significant changes in this regard.

Article 24(2) of the recast RCD on unaccompanied minors provides that the derogation from the obligation to secure a child placement for over sixteens can only be used 'if it is in their best interests, as prescribed in Article 23(2)'. Hence, the derogation provision is expressly subject to a best-interests assessment. Article 23(2), in turn, provides that in assessing the best interests of the child, due account must be taken of, *inter alia*, safety and security considerations. This goes some way towards integrating a protective dimension into the care placement. Unfortunately, there is still no reference to the need for supervision and monitoring of the care placement. A slight improvement is, however, made to the provision requiring training of staff working with unaccompanied minors. Such staff must have had 'and shall continue to receive' appropriate training concerning the needs of unaccompanied minors – a recognition of the need for previous *and* on-going training.

The recast QD makes no reference to the protective dimension of the care placement. However, an identically worded provision to Article 23(2) of the recast RCD on assessing the best interests of the child appears in a recital to the QD.[87] Like the recast RCD, there is still no reference to supervision or monitoring of the care placement, but the training provision is amended in the recast QD to include an on-going dimension.[88]

In sum, the recast RCD and recast QD take some steps towards strengthening the protective dimension of the care placement, although both stop short of an explicit acknowledgement of the need for protection in care or of the need to establish an oversight mechanism.

Conclusion

This chapter dealt with two rights: the right of the child to family unity and the right of the child without family to special protection and assistance by the State. In the case of the former, the normative content of the right was delineated along two lines: the concept of derived rights and the prohibition on separating a child from his/her parents against their will. The question for resolution was whether the relevant CEAS legislation conforms to these dimensions of the right. Taking the Phase One instruments first, it emerged that conformity varies according to instrument. However, allowing for variations between instruments, it was found that the instruments generally acknowledge the major attributes of the right to family unity. However, they curtail the scope of the family unity provisions by defining the child and/or the family in a rigidly narrow way. This is compounded by differential treatment of beneficiaries of subsidiary protection and by expressly or impliedly permitting aspects of the right to family unity to be derogated from. In Phase Two, the definition of the child and the family is broadened somewhat, with the result that there is a modest gain in terms of who benefits from the rights associated with family unity. Moreover, the differential treatment of beneficiaries of

---

87 Recital 18.
88 Article 31(6).

subsidiary protection is removed in respect of derived rights, and the right to family unity is less amenable to express or implied limitations generally. Therefore, Phase Two CEAS constitutes a distinct improvement on Phase One in terms of the right of the child to family unity.

As regards the right of the child without family to special protection and assistance, it was found that this right comprises three essential elements: the right of the unaccompanied or separated child to be identified as such, to be appointed a guardian or adviser to oversee the child's best interests, and to be provided with alternative care. The second and third elements are provided for in the Phase One instruments but the first is not, with the result that the unaccompanied or separated child may not get to benefit from the rights to which he/she is entitled under the instruments. Furthermore, the provisions of the instruments relating to the guardian or representative lack the specificity necessary to communicate the role and essential attributes of that person. Finally, while the instruments outline a range of care placements for unaccompanied minors, they fail to make clear that the central role of the placement is to protect the child. Consequently, the existence of detailed provisions relating to the protection and care of unaccompanied minors in Phase One CEAS belies the fact that the standards they contain do not conform to international standards. Some improvements were discerned in Phase Two. Notably, the provisions of the instruments relating to the role and qualities of the guardian are much improved, and the protective dimension of the care placement is indirectly strengthened; however, there is still no explicit reference to protection in the context of care. Moreover, the improvements are undermined by a continued failure in Phase Two to establish a mechanism for the identification of the unaccompanied or separated child. In sum, Phase Two CEAS constitutes a modest improvement on Phase One in terms of the right of the child without family to special protection and assistance.

6 Certain socio-economic rights of the child

Introduction

This chapter explores the conformity of the CEAS with two key socio-economic rights: the right of the child to health and the right of the child to an adequate standard of living.[1] As is the case for the rights discussed in the previous chapter, these rights also fall under the general rubric of Article 22(1) CRC (the right of the asylum-seeking and refugee child to protection and assistance in the enjoyment of applicable Convention rights) but it is appropriate to deal with them as a discrete category. This is because they are socio-economic rights, a fact that poses a complication for the assessment. This is because of the nature of the legal obligation relating to socio-economic rights. Article 4 CRC provides:

> States Parties shall undertake all appropriate legislative, administrative and other measures for the implementation of the rights recognized in the present Convention. *With regard to economic, social and cultural rights, States Parties shall undertake such measures to the maximum extent of their available resources* and, where needed, within the framework of international cooperation.[2]

It is well established, if increasingly open to challenge, that there is a difference between the legal obligation inherent in most socio-economic rights, as compared with most civil and political rights.[3] While the latter are generally

---

1 Space does not permit an examination of other socio-economic rights of the child that arise in the asylum context, such as the right of the child to education. However, it is submitted that the methodology developed here for assessing the conformity of the CEAS with the socio-economic rights of the child applies beyond the two sample rights that are dealt with in this chapter.
2 Emphasis added.
3 The mantra of 'indivisibility' has been part of the UN rhetoric on rights at least since the Vienna World Conference on Human Rights in 1993.

immediately realisable, socio-economic rights are generally progressively realisable.[4] Article 4 CRC reflects this distinction, conceiving of socio-economic rights in the Convention in maximal terms as goals to be achieved progressively.[5] At any given moment, they are determined by the amount of available resources. The question of whether middle and high income countries – such as the EU Member States that have adopted the CEAS – can reasonably argue a lack of resources is complex and beyond the scope of this work.[6] However, it is an inescapable fact that such countries have proven strongly resistant in practice to extending the full gamut of socio-economic rights to non-nationals (including children). If the CRC sets maximal standards regarding the socio-economic rights of the child and the CEAS establishes minimum standards, at least in its first phase, how is it possible to measure the latter by the former?

---

4 For example, Article 2(1) of the ICESCR provides: 'Each State Party to the present Covenant undertakes *to take steps*, individually and through international assistance and co-operation, especially economic and technical, *to the maximum of its available resources, with a view to achieving progressively the full realization of the rights recognized in the present Covenant* by all appropriate means, including particularly the adoption of legislative measures.' Emphasis added. Similarly, the EU Charter of Fundamental Rights maintains the distinction between the two sets of rights. Thus Article 52(5) provides that 'principles' (as distinct from rights or freedoms) are to be 'implemented by legislative and executive acts of the Union and acts of Member States when implementing Union law' and are 'judicially cognizable only in the interpretation of such acts and in the ruling on their legality'. The general assumption in the literature is that 'principles' correspond to socio-economic rights and that the legal effect of Article 52(5) is to make such rights non-justiciable. See X. Groussot and L. Pech, 'Fundamental Rights Protection in the EU Post Lisbon Treaty', *Foundation Robert Schuman Policy Paper*, European Issue No. 173, 2010.
5 McGoldrick has pointed out a subtle textual difference between Article 2(1) ICESCR and Article 4 CRC, noting: '[w]ith respect to economic, social and cultural rights, article 4 clearly indicates that they are not immediate obligations but the absence of any reference to 'achieving progressively' as in article 2 of the ICESCR may imply that the relevant obligations are of a more immediate nature if the resources are demonstrably available'. D. McGoldrick, 'The United Nations Convention on the Rights of the Child', *International Journal of Law and the Family* 5, 1991, 132–169, 138.
6 In this regard, it is interesting to note that the CRC contains no equivalent of Article 2(3) of the ICESCR, which states that '[d]eveloping countries, with due regard to human rights and their national economy, may determine to what extent they would guarantee the economic rights recognized in the present Covenant to non-nationals'. The Com. RC has interpreted the omission to mean that developing countries are not permitted to limit the Convention rights of non-nationals. The same must be true *a fortiori* of developed countries. General Comment No. 6, 'Treatment of unaccompanied and separated children outside their country of origin', *UN Doc CRC/GC/2005/6 (2005)*, para. 16. On the other hand, the Committee on Economic, Social and Cultural Rights (Com. ESCR) has acknowledged 'the realities of the real world and the difficulties involved for *any* country in ensuring the full realization of economic, social and cultural rights'. General Comment 3, 'The nature of States Parties obligations (Art. 2, par.1)', *HRI/GEN/1/Rev.6 at 14 (1990)*, para. 9 (emphasis added).

A number of observations may be made on this dilemma. First, it is submitted that it is not within the gift of the EU legislator to curtail the definition of socio-economic rights according to presumptions about resources in Member States when it has no jurisdiction over those resources. Accordingly, it is argued that the standards regarding socio-economic rights established in the CEAS should correspond to the standards established in international human rights law, while, of course, leaving a margin of discretion to Member States to sculpt those rights in accordance with available resources. Indeed, the CEAS is characterised by the large amount of discretion it allows to Member States in the wording and derogation provisions of its instruments. Second, discretion must know some bounds. Just because a right is socio-economic in nature cannot mean that there is no absolute minimum entitlement. Indeed, efforts have been on-going for at least 25 years to identify the minimum entitlement inherent in socio-economic rights in the absence of which there is a violation.[7] These efforts have centred around identifying the 'core content' of socio-economic rights, the term 'core' being understood as the essence of a right that is impervious to resource constraints and immediately realisable. As a general proposition, it is submitted that the provisions of the CEAS instruments should broadly conform to the normative content of the socio-economic right under consideration, but that in their discretionary and derogation provisions they should conform *at least* to the core content of the right. The first section of this chapter deals with health, outlining the normative and core content of the right of the child to health and contrasting the provisions of the relevant CEAS instruments with both dimensions of the right. The second section deals with standard of living and follows a similar structure. The relevant CEAS instruments are the RCD and its recast;[8] and the QD and its recast.[9]

---

[7] For an early initiative, see 'The Limburg Principles on the Implementation of the International Covenant on Economic Social and Cultural Rights', *UN Doc E/CN.4/1987/17*, Annex, reprinted in the *Human Rights Quarterly* 9, 1987, 122–135. See also 'Maastricht Guidelines on Violations of Economic, Social and Cultural Rights', *Netherlands Quarterly of Human Rights* 15, 1997, 244–252 and *Human Rights Quarterly* 20, 1998, 691–704. The Committee on Economic, Social and Cultural Rights (Com. ESCR) has delineated the core content of many of the rights in the ICESCR in its general comments and will have further opportunities to do so now that the 2008 Optional Protocol relating to a complaints procedure has entered into force. For commentary, see, B. Griffey, 'The "reasonableness" test: Assessing violations of State obligations under the Optional Protocol to the International Covenant on Economic, Social and Cultural Rights', *Human Rights Law Review* 11, 2011, 275–327.

[8] Council Directive 2003/9/EC of 27 January 2003 and Directive 2013/33/EU of the European Parliament and of the Council of 26 June 2013, respectively.

[9] Council Directive 2004/83/EC of 29 April 2004 and Directive 2011/95/EU of the European Parliament and of the Council of 13 December 2011, respectively.

Health

The right of the child to health

The right of the child to health is set out in Article 24 CRC, which provides, in relevant part:

1 States Parties recognize the right of the child to the enjoyment of the highest attainable standard of health and to facilities for the treatment of illness and rehabilitation of health. States Parties shall strive to ensure that no child is deprived of his or her right of access to such health care services.
2 States Parties shall pursue full implementation of this right and, in particular, shall take appropriate measures:
 [...] (b) To ensure the provision of necessary medical assistance and health care to all children with emphasis on the development of primary health care [...]

Article 24 CRC builds on the right to health in Article 12 of the ICESCR, which sets out the right of everyone to the enjoyment of the highest attainable standard of physical and mental health, and which includes, among the steps necessary for the realisation of the right, provision for the healthy development of the child. Furthermore, at the regional level, a number of instruments explicitly or implicitly protect the right to health.[10]

Also of relevance to the right of the child to health is Article 39 CRC, which provides:

> States parties shall take all appropriate measures to promote physical and psychological recovery and reintegration of a child victim of: any form of neglect, exploitation or abuse; torture or any other form of cruel, inhuman or degrading treatment or punishment; or armed conflicts. Such recovery and reintegration shall take place in an environment which fosters the health, self-respect and dignity of the child.

This right of the child victim to recovery and reintegration is novel in international and regional human rights law, finding no equivalent, for example, in the ICESCR or in the Convention Against Torture.[11]

---

10 A right to protection of health and to medical assistance are provided in Articles 11 and 13 respectively of the Revised European Social Charter and a right to health care is provided in Article 35 of the EU Charter of Fundamental Rights. Health issues may also arise in the context of Article 2 and 3 ECHR. See respectively ECtHR, *Cyprus v Turkey,* Appl. No. 25781/94, Judgment of 10 May 2001 and ECtHR, *Pretty v UK*, Appl. No. 2346/02, Judgment of 29 April 2002.
11 The closest equivalent in the Convention Against Torture is Article 14(1) which provides: 'Each State Party shall ensure in its legal system that the victim of an act of torture obtains redress and has an enforceable right to fair and adequate compensation, including the

The normative content of the right

Beginning with Article 24 CRC, it is useful, given the complexity of the article, to analyse it according to its constituent elements.

The first sentence of Article 24(1) can be divided into two parts. The first of these parts establishes the right of the child to the 'highest attainable standard of health'. A similar provision is found in Article 13 ICESCR, but explicitly relates to both physical and mental health. However, nothing should be made of the omission in the CRC as the Com. RC has consistently interpreted the right to health as pertaining both to physical and mental health.[12] But the larger question remains, what is health? In its General Comment No. 15 on the right of the child to health, the Committee adopts the definition of health contained in the Constitution of the World Health Organisation, namely, a state of complete physical, mental and social well-being and not merely the absence of disease or infirmity.[13] It follows that the right to health is not confined to the right to *health care*, but rather embraces a wide range of socio-economic factors that promote conditions in which people can lead a healthy life, and extends to the *underlying determinants of health*, such as food and nutrition, housing, access to safe and potable water and adequate sanitation, safe and healthy working conditions, and a healthy environment.[14] As a result of this broad understanding of the right to health, States Parties are required not only to provide health care facilities, goods and services, but to meet other rights relevant to creating the conditions precedent to the highest attainable standard of health, such as the right to an adequate standard of living and the right of the child to life, survival and development.

The next part of Article 24(1), first sentence, relates to 'facilities for the treatment of illness and rehabilitation of health'. This provision is not limited to curative facilities; rather it mandates 'quality health services, including

---

means for as full rehabilitation as possible.' Also of note is the obligation, often couched in 'soft' or conditional terms, in international and regional law governing anti-trafficking to facilitate the rehabilitation of victims of trafficking. See, for example, Protocol to Prevent, Suppress and Punish Trafficking in Persons, Especially Women and Children, supplementing the UN Convention against Transnational Organised Crime, 2000, Article 6.

12 See Com. RC, General Comment No. 4, 'Adolescent health and development in the context of the Convention on the Rights of the Child', *UN Doc. CRC/GC/2003/4 (2003)*, para. 39(c) and (i); General Comment No. 6, *op. cit.*, para. 48; General Comment No. 9, 'The right of children with disabilities', *UN Doc. CRC/C/GC/9 (2007)*, para. 51; General Comment No. 13, 'Article 19: The right of the child to freedom from all forms of violence', *UN Doc. CRC/C/GC/13 (2011)*, para. 52; General Comment No. 15, 'The right of the child to the enjoyment of the highest attainable standard of health (art. 24)', *UN Doc. CRC/C/GC/15 (2013)*, paras. 38 and 39.

13 *Ibid.*, para. 4.

14 For more on the terminology of the right to health, see V. Leary, 'The right to health in international human rights law', *Health and Human Rights* 1, 1999, 25–56.

prevention, promotion, treatment, rehabilitation and palliative care services'.[15] The reference to rehabilitation is particularly interesting, because it is not found in the corresponding provision of the ICESCR.[16] The fact that rehabilitation of health is expressly mentioned in the right-to-health article of the CRC can be explained by the fact that childhood ill health can affect a child's development and consequently have long-term or permanent effects.[17] Also of relevance to the question of rehabilitation of health is Article 39 CRC, which will be analysed below.

The second sentence of Article 24(1) obliges States Parties to strive to 'ensure that no child is deprived of his or her right of access to such health care services'. The *travaux préparatoires* of the CRC show that the purpose of this provision was to ensure that no child would be deprived of his or her right of access to health care because of an inability to pay.[18] However, a broader contemporary interpretation of the right of access to health care is given by the Com. RC. Thus, General Comment No. 15 provides that access to health care encompasses not only economic accessibility but also non-discrimination, physical accessibility, and information accessibility.[19]

Article 24(2) sets out the measures a State Party must take to pursue the full implementation of the right of the child to health. Article 24(2)(b) establishes that States Parties must ensure 'the provision of necessary medical assistance and health care to all children with emphasis on the development of primary health care'. There are two aspects to this obligation: first, the provision of necessary medical assistance and health care; and second, the development of primary health care. The wording makes clear that the second is a necessary but not sufficient condition for the first. The most comprehensive definition of primary health care is provided in the Declaration of Alma Ata on Primary Health Care 1979.[20] This Declaration establishes that primary health care is 'primary' in the sense of being essential health care, the first level of contact with the national health system and the first element of a continuing health care process. Primary health care addresses the main health problems in the community, providing promotive, preventive, curative and rehabilitative

---

15 Com. RC, General Comment No. 15, *op. cit*, para. 25.
16 However, the Com. ESCR does consider rehabilitation to be an integral part of the general right to health. Com. ESCR, General Comment 14, 'The right to the highest attainable standard of health', UN Doc. E/C.12/2000/4 (2000), para. 17.
17 On this point, see A. Eide and W. Barth Eide, *A Commentary on the United Nations Convention on the Rights of the Child, Article 24, The Right to Health*, Leiden/Boston: Martinus Nijhoff Publishers, 2006, para. 31.
18 *Ibid.*, para. 32.
19 Com. RC, General Comment No. 15, *op. cit.*, para. 114.
20 International Conference on Primary Health Care, Alma-Ata, USSR, 6–12 September 1978. Endorsed by UN General Assembly Resolution 34/43 of 19 November 1979. Reinforced by the World Health Assembly, 'Primary health care, including health systems strengthening', *Document A62/8*, 2009.

services accordingly. It includes *at least*, among other services, child health care. As to what, other than primary health care, constitutes *necessary* medical assistance and health care can be identified by a process of elimination. The emphasis placed on primary health care suggests that resources should not be spent on tertiary health care (i.e. high-tech, high-cost institutions, which are highly equipped and staffed but which benefit only a small number of people).[21] What remains is secondary health care by a hospital or physician following referral by a primary health care worker and emergency hospital treatment. Where such health care is 'necessary', it falls within the parameters of Article 24(2)(b).

Moving now to Article 39 CRC, which obliges States to promote the physical and psychological recovery and reintegration of a child victim of various types of ill-treatment. Apart from the novelty of this provision in international law, Article 39 is interesting because of the way it conceives of recovery and reintegration. States Parties are obliged to 'take all appropriate measures to promote physical and psychological recovery and reintegration [...] in an environment which fosters the health, self-respect and dignity of the child'. Two aspects of this are noteworthy. First, the *psychological* as well as physical recovery and reintegration of the child is required. Hence, the mental-health aspect of recovery and reintegration is placed on a par with the physical aspect, with obvious implications for the provision of psychological services, counselling and so forth. Second, in line with the broad understanding of the right to health discussed above, Article 39 CRC adopts a holistic, as distinct from a strictly 'sickness', approach to recovery and reintegration. Thus, States Parties are required to take *all appropriate measures* – including but not confined to medical ones – to promote recovery and reintegration. Moreover, the recovery and reintegration must take place in an environment that fosters the health, self-respect and dignity of the child. This holistic approach recognises the fact that the psycho-social well-being of the child is as important to recovery and reintegration as is medical intervention. It also recognises the linkages between recovery and the right of the child to an adequate standard of living, i.e. one that promotes self-respect and dignity. In this regard, it is interesting to note that the CRC provides in Article 27(1) that the child has a right to a standard of living 'adequate for the child's physical, mental, spiritual, moral and social development'. Therefore, the right of the child to rehabilitation and recovery in Article 39 CRC is likely to be frustrated if the right to an adequate standard of living as defined in Article 27(1) CRC is not fulfilled.[22] This linkage will be taken up in the next section.

---

21 On this point, see A. Eide and W. Barth Eide, *op. cit.*, para. 58.
22 The Com. RC made this link in its Concluding Observations to Lithuania in 2006, *UN Doc. CRC/C/LTU/CO/2*, when it recommended the State Party at § 8 to '[t]ake urgent measures to further improve the reception conditions for families and in particular children seeking asylum in Lithuania by, *inter alia*, providing psychosocial and recovery services for

In sum, the normative content of the right of the child to health comprises the fulfillment of the underlying determinants of health as well as a right to health care. The right to health care covers preventive, curative and rehabilitative health services, with an emphasis on primary health care. No child should be denied access to such health care services. Furthermore, the right of the child victim of various types of ill-treatment to recovery and reintegration requires States to take positive and holistic measures to facilitate that recovery and reintegration.

The 'core content' of the right

Having discussed the normative content of the right of the child to health, it is necessary to identify the 'core content' of the right, the term 'core' being understood as the essence of the right that is impervious to resource constraints and hence immediately realisable. According to General Comment 3 of the Com. ESCR on the nature of States Parties obligations, every socio-economic right contains two 'core' obligations: the immediate duty to 'take steps' towards the goal of full realisation thereby ensuring minimum essential levels of the right; and the undertaking to guarantee the right without discrimination.

I. THE MINIMUM ESSENTIAL OBLIGATION

In its General Comment 3 on the nature of States Parties obligations, the Com. ESCR states that the undertaking in Article 2(1) ICESCR 'to take steps' is not qualified or limited by other considerations.[23] Thus, while the full realisation of the relevant rights may be achieved progressively, steps towards that goal must be taken immediately. These steps correspond to the minimum essential obligation. Although the term 'measures' rather than steps is used in corresponding Article 4 CRC, it is submitted that there is no practical difference between the terms.[24] Both make a distinction between what have become known as 'obligations of conduct' and 'obligations of result'.[25]

In terms of the right of the child to health, it is clear that Article 24(1) corresponds to the obligation of result and that Article 24(2) corresponds to the obligation of conduct. Accordingly, pursuant to Article 24(2)(b), immediate

---

traumatized children and children arriving from armed conflicts *as well as* by improving the environment of the reception facilities'. Emphasis added.

23 Com. ESCR, General Comment 3, *op. cit.,* para. two.

24 Indeed, in the Spanish version of the ICESCR, the obligation in Article 2(1) 'to take steps' is 'a adopter medidas' (to adopt measures).

25 The distinction between obligations of conduct and result was first articulated by Robert Ago, Special Rapporteur on State Responsibility to the International Law Commission and the concept finds expression in the ILC's Articles on The Responsibility of States for Internationally Wrongful Acts, adopted by General Assembly resolution 56/83 of 12 December 2001.

steps must be taken 'to ensure the provision of necessary medical assistance and health care to all children with emphasis on the development of primary health care'. Since the emphasis must be placed on the latter, the provision of primary health care constitutes the minimum core of the right of the child to health. Hence, the Com. RC has stated that '[e]nsuring universal coverage of quality primary health services, including prevention, health promotion, care and treatment and essential drugs [and providing] an adequate response to the underlying determinants of children's health' form part of the core obligations under children's right to health.[26] This is also the position adopted by the Com. ESCR in relation to the general right to health. Thus, General Comment No. 3 provides that:

> [a] minimum core obligation to ensure the satisfaction of, at the very least, minimum essential levels of each of the rights is incumbent upon every State Party. Thus for example, a State Party in which any significant number of individuals is deprived of essential foodstuffs, of *essential primary health care*, of basic shelter and housing, or of the most basic forms of education is, *prima facie*, failing to discharge its obligations under the Covenant.[27]

Similarly, General Comment 14 of the Com. ESCR on the right to health states that the Alma-Ata Declaration on Primary Health Care provides 'compelling guidance' on the core obligations arising from the right to health, which include at least the obligation '[t]o ensure reproductive, maternal (pre-natal as well as post-natal) and *child health care*'.[28] Consequently, it is not permissible to limit the right of the child to health below the level of primary health care in all its promotive, preventive, curative and rehabilitative dimensions.

As regards Article 39 CRC on the right of the child to rehabilitation and recovery, since this right is *sui generis* in international human rights law, it is inappropriate to classify it according to the civil and political/economic, social and cultural dichotomy. Consequently, Article 4 CRC relating to the progressive realisation of socio-economic rights in the Convention does not apply with the result that Article 39 is immediately realisable. Therefore, it is necessary to analyse the terms of Article 39 itself to establish whether it permits of limitation. In this regard, it is noteworthy that the language relating to the obligation ('States Parties shall take') is one of the strongest formulations used in international human rights law. These words constitute, according to Price Cohen, 'emphatic words of universal scope' and place 'the strongest possible obligation upon States Parties'.[29] This is so notwithstanding the fact that

---

26 Com. RC, General Comment No. 15, *op. cit.*, para. 73.
27 Com. ESCR, General Comment 3, *op. cit.*, para. 10 (emphasis added).
28 Com. ESCR, General Comment 14, *op. cit.*, para. 44 (emphasis added).
29 C. Price Cohen, *op. cit.*, p. 76.

some degree of latitude is given to States in deciding on what are 'appropriate measures'. However, even this discretion is qualified by the absolute requirement that '[s]uch recovery and reintegration *shall* take place in an environment which fosters the health, self-respect and dignity of the child'. Accordingly, there is little scope for limitation of the right.

II. THE PROHIBITION OF DISCRIMINATION

Any limitation on the right of the child to health, in addition to respecting the minimum essential obligation, must not be discriminatory. A prohibition of discrimination is part of the normative content of the right of the child to health. This is evident from two clauses of Article 24 CRC. The second sentence of Article 24(1) provides that 'States Parties shall strive to ensure that *no child is deprived of his or her right of access* to such health care services', while Article 24(2)(b) requires States Parties to 'ensure the provision of necessary medical assistance and health care to *all children*'. Furthermore, Article 2 CRC establishes a prohibition of discrimination as a cross-cutting general principle of the Convention, providing:

1   States Parties shall respect and ensure the rights set forth in the present Covenant to each child within their jurisdiction without distinction of any kind, irrespective of the child's or his or her parent's or legal guardian's race, color, sex, language, religion, political or other opinion, national, ethnic or social origin, property, disability, birth or other status.
2   States Parties shall take all appropriate measure to ensure that the child is protected against all forms of discrimination or punishment on the basis of the status, activities, expressed opinions, or beliefs of the child's parents, legal guardians or family members.

The first paragraph of Article 2 CRC is a standard 'auxiliary' non-discrimination provision, prohibiting discrimination in relation to other rights in the Convention, like the right to health. Like other such provisions in international human rights law, it prohibits discrimination on a number of grounds, including 'other status'. Following the initiative of other treaty monitoring bodies,[30] and indeed the ECtHR in relation to Article 14 ECHR,[31] 'other status' has been interpreted by the Com. RC as extending to nationality and even

---

30   Com. ESCR, General Comment 20, 'Non-discrimination in economic, social and cultural rights (art. 2, para. 2 of the International Convenant on Economic, Social and Cultural Rights)', *UN Doc E/C.12/GC/20 (2009)*, para. 30; Committee on the Elimination of Racial Discrimination, General Recommendation 30, 'Discrimination against Non-citizens', *UN Doc CERD/C/64/Misc 11/rev. 3 (2004)*, particularly paras. 29 and 36 which relate to discrimination in relation to the right to health; Human Rights Committee, General Comment 15, 'The position of aliens under the Covenant', *UN Doc. HRI/Gen/Rev.1 at 18 (1994)*, para. 2.
31   ECtHR, *Gaygusuz v Austria*, Appl. No. 17371/90, Judgment of 16 September 1996.

protection status. Thus, the Committee has stated that '[t]he principle of non-discrimination [...] prohibits any discrimination on the basis of the status of a child as being unaccompanied or separated, or being a refugee, asylum seeker or migrant'.[32] Interestingly, Article 2(2) CRC is an 'autonomous' non-discrimination provision, prohibiting discrimination or punishment in any matter (including but not limited to the enjoyment of Convention rights) on the basis not only of the status but also, *inter alia*, of the *activities* of the child's parents, legal guardians or family members.[33]

Hence, discrimination against or between children seeking or enjoying international protection is clearly prohibited. However, this does not mean that every difference in health treatment between, for example, children seeking and children enjoying international protection, or either of those groups and national children, offends against the prohibition of discrimination. There is a well-established international legal 'formula' for assessing claims of discrimination, which contains a number of hurdles that have to be overcome before a distinction will be branded as discrimination. This formula starts from the premise that not every difference in treatment amounts to discrimination because, in the words of ECtHR, 'the competent national authorities are frequently confronted with situations and problems which, on account of difference inherent therein, call for different legal solutions; moreover, certain legal inequalities tend only to correct factual inequalities'.[34] Consequently, the alleged victim of discrimination must show that he/she is less favorably treated as compared with similarly situated persons. If this hurdle is overcome and a *prima facie* case of discrimination is made out, the burden of proof shifts to the State to show that the differential treatment is justified. The Com. ESCR has stated in General Comment 20 on non-discrimination in economic, social and cultural rights that:

> Differential treatment on prohibited grounds will be viewed as discriminatory unless the justification for differentiation is reasonable and objective. This will include an assessment as to whether the aim and effects of the measures or omissions are legitimate, compatible with the nature of the Covenant rights and solely for the purpose of promoting the general welfare in a democratic society. In addition, there must be a clear and reasonable relationship of proportionality between the aim sought to be realized and the measures of omissions and their effects.[35]

---

32 Com. RC, General Comment No. 6, *op. cit.*, para. 18.
33 For analysis of this innovative provision in international law, see S. Besson, 'The principle of non-discrimination in the Convention on the Rights of the Child', *International Journal of Children's Rights* 13, 2005, 433–461.
34 ECtHR, *Belgian Linguistics* case, Appl. Nos. 1474/62; 1677/62; 1691/62; 1769/63; 1994/63; 2126/64, Judgment of 23 July 1968, para. 10.
35 Com. ESCR, General Comment 20, *op. cit.*, para. 13.

In sum, the question of whether the child seeking or benefiting from international protection is discriminated against in the enjoyment of his/her right to health turns on a comparator test and thereafter on whether the difference in treatment is justifiable. This cannot be determined in the abstract but requires a contextual assessment, which will be undertaken below.

Phase One CEAS: Compliance with the right of the child to health

Having set out the normative and core content of the right of the child to health, this sub-section explores whether the RCD and the QD are consistent with both, or at least with the minimum standard. Given the complexity of the provisions on health care in each directive, it is convenient to devote a subsection to each directive.

The Reception Conditions Directive

Article 15 of the RCD relating to health care provides as follows:

1   Member States shall ensure that applicants receive the necessary health care which shall include, at least, emergency care and essential treatment of illness.
2   Member States shall provide necessary medical or other assistance to applicants who have special needs.

Hence, a general standard of health care is established in paragraph 1, while a specific standard is established in paragraph 2 regarding persons with special needs. Taking the general standard first, it can be observed that paragraph 1 actually sets two different standards: a higher standard, i.e. *necessary* health care, which implies access to the full range of primary health care services as well as access to secondary health care services where they are needed; and a lower standard, i.e. *emergency* care and *essential* treatment of illness, which suggests emergency hospital and curative care. It can be observed that while the higher standard conforms to both the normative and the core content of the right of the child to health, the lower standard conforms to neither.

The effect of paragraph 2 is to insulate applicants who have special needs from the lower standard established in paragraph 1, since such applicants must be provided with *necessary* medical or other assistance. But there is confusion about the scope of paragraph 2 *ratione personae*. Who are persons who have special needs? Some light is shed on this question in Chapter IV on Provisions for Persons with Special Needs. This chapter includes an article on minors (Article 18), unaccompanied minors (Article 19) and victims of torture and violence (Article 20). It establishes a 'general principle' in Article 17 for dealing with 'vulnerable persons', according to which Member States are required to take the specific situation of such persons into account in the national legislation implementing the provisions relating to material reception conditions and health care. An illustrative list of such persons is provided and includes minors and unaccompanied minors alongside other groups such as persons who have been subjected to torture, rape or other serious forms of psychological, physical or sexual violence. But the general principle only applies if such persons are 'found to have special needs after an individual evaluation of their situation'. It is unclear whether this provision mandates an individual screening process to identify persons with special needs, or whether the absence of such screening at the national level could vitiate the obligation. Related to this, it is unclear whether being a minor or unaccompanied minor *per se* is enough to qualify a child as being a person with special needs, or whether some further vulnerability must be demonstrated. The Commission evaluation of the RCD reflects these ambiguities.[36]

Chapter III RCD is also relevant to the question of the level of health care provision. It allows for the reduction, withdrawal and even outright refusal of reception conditions in certain situations in an effort to counteract perceived abuse of the reception system. Article 16(1) provides that where the asylum seeker abandons the place of residence, fails to comply with reporting duties or requests for information, fails to appear for personal interview, has already lodged a previous application or has concealed financial resources, the Member State may reduce or withdraw reception conditions. Pursuant to Article 16(2), Member States may refuse (outright) reception conditions 'where an asylum seeker has failed to demonstrate that the asylum claim was made as soon as reasonably practicable after arrival in that Member State'. However, Article 16(4) establishes that 'Member States shall under all circumstances ensure access to emergency health care'. Consequently, it is not possible to refuse the right to health care outright, or reduce or withdraw it beyond this minimum level. Nevertheless, the level is considerably below the 'core content' of the right of the child to health, namely, access to the full range of primary health care services.

Article 16(4) further provides that '[d]ecisions shall be based on the particular situation of the person concerned, especially with regard to persons covered by Article 17 [i.e. the general principle on persons with special needs], taking into account the principle of proportionality'. This provision establishes that minors and unaccompanied minors are not exempted from having their health

---

36 Thus, according to the evaluation, '[a]lthough the majority of Member States recognize [persons with special needs] by listing all the groups mentioned in the Directive or by using an open clause, some do not cover the full list in Article 17 or do not address persons with special needs at all (SK, FR, HU, LT, MT, PL, LV, EE and some regions of AT). Furthermore, in some Member States (UK, DE, BE, LU, EL, IT, SK, SI) no identification procedure is in place'. 'Report from the Commission to the Council and to the European Parliament on the Application of Directive 2003/9/EC of 27 January 2003 Laying Down Minimum Standards for the Reception of Asylum Seekers', *COM (2007) 745 final*, §. 3.5.1, p. 9. Hereinafter, 'Commission evaluation of the RCD'.

care under the directive reduced or withdrawn, although their special needs must be taken into account in assessing proportionality. This raises the question of whether such treatment could ever be proportionate when the object of the treatment is a child. The normative content of the right of the child to health draws attention to the vulnerability of the child to ill health and its attendant consequences for development.[37] Children seeking international protection are widely regarded as being more vulnerable than children in the host population.[38] This double vulnerability means that the impact of reduced health care on the child is likely to be more profound than in respect of someone who does not have special needs. In this context, it is submitted that Article 16(4) of the directive is unworkable and bound to be defeated by its own requirement of proportionality.

Furthermore, where, as in the case of derived rights, the child's access to health care is reduced, withdrawn or refused because of the parents' 'abuse' of the reception system, this falls foul of the prohibition of discrimination in Article 2(2) CRC, which forbids 'all forms of discrimination *or punishment* on the basis of the status, *activities*, expressed opinions, or beliefs of the child's parents, legal guardians or family members'.[39]

To sum up, the main provision on health care in the RCD, namely Article 15(1), contains two possible standards of health care, the lower of which conforms to neither the normative nor core content of the right of the child to health. This is mitigated somewhat by the reference to necessary medical assistance for persons with special needs, but it is unclear whether minors or unaccompanied minors automatically fall within the personal scope of this provision. Furthermore, Chapter III RCD allows for the reduction and withdrawal of health care, subject to the floor of emergency health care. This minimum level offends against the core content of the right of the child to health.

Turning now to the right of the child victim of ill treatment to recovery and reintegration under Article 39 CRC, two articles of the RCD are of note. Article 20 on the victims of torture and violence provides that 'Member States shall ensure that, if necessary, persons who have been subjected to torture, rape and other serious acts of violence receive the necessary treatment of damages caused by the aforementioned acts'. The rather redundant use of the words 'if necessary' aside, it should be noted that this provision also applies to minor victims of torture and sexual and other violence.

---

37 In this regard, the Com. RC notes in General Comment No. 13 that '[a]t a universal level all children aged 0–18 years are considered vulnerable until the completion of their neural, psychological, social and physical growth and development'. *Op. cit.*, para. 72(f), p. 27.
38 The Com. RC has identified refugee and asylum-seeking young children (of pre-school age) and adolescents experiencing all types of migration as vulnerable groups. See, respectively, Com. RC, General Comment No. 7, 'Implementing child rights in early childhood', *UN Doc. CRC/C/GC/7/Rev.1 (2006)*, para. 24 and Com. RC, General Comment No. 4, *op. cit.*, para. 38.
39 Emphasis added.

But of even greater significance, Article 18 RCD relating to minors provides:

> Member States shall ensure access to rehabilitation services for minors who have been victims of any form of abuse, neglect, exploitation, torture or cruel, inhuman and degrading treatment, or who have suffered from armed conflicts, and ensure that appropriate mental health care is developed and qualified counseling is provided when needed.

The RCD is the only CEAS instrument to contain a provision specifically directed to 'incorporating' Article 39 CRC. The inclusion of this provision in the directive, with its specific reference to appropriate mental health care and qualified counselling, is praiseworthy. However, it does not accurately reflect the terms of Article 39 CRC. Notably, the references to 'all appropriate measures' and to 'an environment which fosters the health, self-respect and dignity of the child' are omitted. This is not a question of squabbling over wording; these omissions are significant. The holistic approach advanced in Article 39 CRC is essential in the context of traumatised child asylum seekers, in which it is well established that the medical or 'sickness' model of rehabilitation is a limited one.[40] First, the medical model pathologises responses to trauma rather than understanding such responses as normal reactions to situations of extreme stress. Second, it flounders on the almost inevitable under-funding of mental health care and consequent shortage of mental health professionals and qualified counselling. In this regard, it is unsurprising that the Commission evaluation of the RCD found that 'adequate access to health care has its limitations, e.g. no effective access to medical care, lack of specific care (in particular for victims of torture and violence) and insufficient cost cover'.[41] And third, it fails to recognise that a contributory factor to a child's trauma is his/her current living conditions.

A further problem with Article 18 RCD is that it fails to provide a mechanism for identifying minors who have been victims of the listed ill treatment, an obligation arguably implicit in Article 39 CRC. Thus, the Com. RC has referred to the duty to identify such children in its General Comment No. 6[42] and in a number of concluding observations made to States Parties in relation

---

40 See, for example, M. E. Kalverboer, A. E. Zijlstra and E. J. Knorth, 'The developmental consequences for asylum-seeking children living with the prospect for five years or more of enforced return to their home country', *European Journal of Migration and Law* 11, 2009, 41–67, and M. McCallin, 'The Convention on the Rights of the Child as an instrument to address the psychosocial needs of refugee children', *International Journal of Refugee Law* 3, 1991, 82–99.
41 § 3.5.2, p. 9.
42 Com. RC, General Comment No. 6, *op. cit.* Paragraph 47 provides that in ensuring the access of separated and unaccompanied children to facilities for the treatment of illness and rehabilitation of health, 'States must *assess* and address the particular plight and vulnerabilities of such children' (emphasis added).

to asylum-seeking children.[43] The lack of a mechanism for identifying persons with special needs in general has already been commented on.

In sum, the right of the child victim of various types of ill treatment to recovery and reintegration is reflected in the RCD, albeit imperfectly.

The Qualification Directive

The QD establishes five distinct 'streams' of access to healthcare.

First, Article 29(1) provides that beneficiaries of international protection have access to health care under the same eligibility conditions as nationals. Thus, equal access to the full range of health care services available to nationals is implied.

Second, however, an exception is crafted in Article 29(2) in respect of beneficiaries of subsidiary protection, whose right to health care may be limited to 'core benefits', which must nevertheless be provided 'at the same levels and under the same eligibility conditions as nationals'.

Third, Article 29(3) provides that 'adequate health care' under the same eligibility conditions as nationals must be provided to beneficiaries of international protection who have special needs. It provides an illustrative list of persons with special needs, which includes 'minors who have been victims of any form of abuse', although not minors or unaccompanied minors *per se*. By contrast, Article 20, which establishes general rules relating to the rights of refugees and beneficiaries of subsidiary protection provides in paragraph 3 that Member States shall 'take into account' the specific situation of vulnerable persons such as minors and unaccompanied minors when implementing such rights. However, paragraph 4 clarifies that this applies 'only to persons found to have special needs after an individual evaluation of their situation'. This formulation raises the same confusion as discussed above in relation to Article 17 of the RCD. The relationship between Article 29(3) and Article 20 QD is unclear.

Fourth, as regards family members of beneficiaries of international protection, the general rule established under the principle of family unity in Article 23 is that family members 'are entitled to claim the benefits referred to in Articles 24–34'. These benefits include the right to health care in Article 29. However, again, an exception is crafted regarding family members of beneficiaries of subsidiary protection status: per Article 23(2), 'Member States may define the conditions applicable to such benefits [as health care]'.

---

43 For example, in its Concluding Observations to Norway in 2010, the Committee expressed its concern 'at the cursory identification of children affected by armed conflict'. *UN Doc. CRC/C/NOR/CO/4*, para. 50. Similarly in its Concluding Observations to Finland in 2000, the Committee recommended 'that the State Party ensure that every effort is made to identify [asylum-seeking and refugee] children who require special support upon their arrival in the State Party, as well as consider providing adequate psychological assistance to them and their parents'. *UN Doc. CRC/C/15/Add.132,* para. 54.

Finally, Article 20, which establishes the general rules regarding the rights of refugees and beneficiaries of subsidiary protection, provides in paragraphs 6 and 7 that where a refugee or beneficiary of subsidiary protection obtained that status 'on the basis of activities engaged in for the sole or main purpose of creating the necessary conditions for being recognized', Member States may reduce such rights, albeit within the limits set out by the Geneva Convention and international obligations of Member States, respectively. In respect of the Geneva Convention, it should be noted that no provision of that Convention relates to health care. However, in respect of the international obligations of Member States, this clearly includes obligations under the right to health articles of the CRC. Consequently, the Article 20 'good faith' requirement is not as punitive as it first appears.

In sum, under the QD, refugees and their family members are entitled to the *full range of public health care services* available to nationals; beneficiaries of SP are entitled, at a minimum, to *core benefits*, while *conditions* may be imposed on their family members' access to health care; persons with special needs, which may or may not include minors and unaccompanied minors, are entitled to *adequate health care*; and persons who gained recognition in bad faith may have their right to health care *reduced*, but within the limits set by international refugee and human rights law.

There are two major problems with these various streams of access to health care from the point of view of the right of the child to health. First, the terminology (e.g. 'core benefits', 'conditions', 'adequate', 'reduced') does not map easily onto the terminology used in Article 24 CRC, making it difficult to assess whether the various streams conform to either the normative or core content of the right of the child to health. Second, the permitted differential treatment of different groups raises the question of discrimination and consequently of whether there is a violation of the core content of the right of the child to health. Of particular concern is the differential treatment of refugees as compared with beneficiaries of subsidiary protection, and of family members of refugees as compared with family members of beneficiaries of subsidiary protection. The extent to which Member States do actually differentiate between these groups is hard to ascertain from the Commission evaluation of the QD.[44] Nevertheless, on principle, it is worth exploring whether this treatment constitutes discrimination. The reasoning pursued here follows the international legal 'formula' for assessing claims of discrimination.

First, on the issue of comparability, it is hard to sustain the charge that children from different protected groups are incomparable to one another.

---

44 'Report from the Commission to the European Parliament and the Council on the Application of Directive 2004/83/EC of 29 April 2004 on Minimum Standards for the Qualification and Status of Third Country Nationals or Stateless Persons as Refugees or as Persons Who Otherwise Need International Protection and the Content of the Protection', *COM (2010) 314 final*, see, in particular, § 5.5.1.2, p. 14. Hereinafter, 'Commission evaluation of the QD'.

Of course, as Westen observes, the determination of whether two people are alike for purposes of the equality principle flounders on the truism that no two people are alike in every respect and all people are alike in some respect.[45] To have meaning, the comparator principle must refer to people who are alike in respect of a right requiring certain treatment. Therefore, the purpose of comparison is to establish whether there is a *relevant* difference between, for example, a child beneficiary of subsidiary protection and a child refugee vis. à vis. the right to health. Since all children are vulnerable to ill health and its attendant consequences for their development, it is submitted that there is no relevant difference between the groups.

Second, on the issue of the legitimate aim, economic justifications or justifications relating to protection status are arguably harder to make out when the child is the subject of equality. As for economic justifications, the Com. ESCR has underlined the fact that 'even in times of severe resources constraints whether caused by a process of adjustment, or economic recession, or by other factors the vulnerable members of society can and indeed must be protected'.[46] Similarly, the Com. RC has stated that (even scarce) economic resources must be mobilised to meet the rights of particularly vulnerable children, such as separated and unaccompanied children.[47] Equally, children enjoying international protection (whether accompanied or unaccompanied) can be regarded as a vulnerable group, as has already been argued.

As for justifications relating to protection status, one can anticipate, for example, an argument that child beneficiaries of subsidiary protection have an inherently temporary status and consequently it is justifiable to limit their health care accordingly. A number of counter-arguments can be made. First, there is no correlation between temporariness as it corresponds to stability of status and temporariness in the temporal sense. Indeed, it is well known that beneficiaries of subsidiary protection may require indefinite protection, depending on the situation in the country of origin.[48] Indeed, all or a large part of a childhood can be spent under a supposedly temporary status. Second,

---

45 P. Westen, 'The empty idea of equality', *Harvard Law Review* 95, 1982, 537–596. For a succinct analysis of the difficulties in using comparability to assess claims of discrimination, see A. Baysfsky, 'The principle of equality or non-discrimination in international law', *Human Rights Law Journal,* 11, 1990, 1–34.
46 Com. ESCR, General Comment 3, *op. cit.*, para. 12.
47 Com. RC, General Comment No. 6, *op. cit.*, para. 16.
48 Indeed the Commission has noted in this regard: 'When subsidiary protection was introduced, it was assumed that this status was of a temporary nature. As a result, the Directive allows Member States the discretion to grant them a lower level of rights in certain respects. However, practical experience acquired so far has shown that this initial assumption was not accurate.' 'Explanatory Memorandum to the Proposal for a Directive of the European Parliament and of the Council on minimum standards for the qualification and status of third country nationals or stateless persons as beneficiaries of international protection and the content of the protection granted', *COM (2009) 551*, p. 8.

given that children are in the critical process of developing, even a temporary diminution in health care can be critical.

This segues with the third part of the international legal 'formula' for assessing discrimination – the question of proportionality. The reader is referred back to the discussion on proportionality in the analysis of the RCD, where it was argued that a diminution in health care can never be proportionate where the object of the treatment is a child. Accordingly, it is submitted that the 'streams' of entitlement to health care in the QD constitute discrimination and thus are contrary to the core content of the right of the child to health.

As regards the right of the child victim of ill-treatment to recovery and reintegration, the QD refers, in Article 29(3) on health care, to 'minors who have been victims of any form of abuse, neglect, exploitation, torture, cruel, inhuman and degrading treatment or who have suffered from armed conflict' – a list that is clearly derived from Article 39 CRC. However, rather than establishing a right to recovery and reintegration of children in such situations, Article 29(3) requires Member States to provide such children (along with other beneficiaries of international protection with special needs), with more generic assistance, namely 'adequate health care'. Furthermore, unlike the RCD, the QD does not contain any general provision on victims of torture or violence. Both omissions are regrettable.

To conclude, some, at least, of the different streams of access to health care provided for in the QD offend against the minimum essential obligation inherent in the right of the child to health and against the prohibition of discrimination. Therefore, the core content of the right of the child to health is not consistently met in the QD. The directive also fails to secure the right of the child victim of various forms of ill treatment to recovery and reintegration, *pace* Article 39 CRC.

Phase Two CEAS: Prospects for enhanced compliance

The recast Reception Conditions Directive

Article 19 of the recast RCD on health care provides:

1 Member States shall ensure that applicants receive the necessary health care which shall include at least emergency care and essential treatment of illness or of serious mental disorders.
2 Member States shall provide necessary medical or other assistance to applicants who have special reception needs, including appropriate mental health care where needed.

Compared to Article 15 of the existing directive, the reference in paragraph 1 to mental disorders and in paragraph 2 to appropriate mental health care for applicants with special reception needs is an advance. However, the reference to serious mental disorders, with its suggestion of grave psychiatric illness, contrasts negatively with the amended Commission proposal for a recast RCD, which referred to post-traumatic disorders.[49] Moreover, the reference to mental health care for applicants who have special reception needs 'where needed' suggests a double test: first, that an applicant is an applicant with special reception needs and second, that he/she needs appropriate mental health care. This returns us to the vexed issue of the identity and identification of persons with special needs.

Chapter IV, now re-named 'Provisions for vulnerable persons', reiterates in Article 21 the general principle that Member States must take into account the specific situation of vulnerable persons such as minors and unaccompanied minors in the national implementing legislation. However, the provision expressly limiting the scope of the principle to persons found to have special needs after an individual evaluation of their situation is omitted. Rather, Article 22(1) provides that '[i]n order to effectively implement Article 21, Member States *shall assess* whether the applicant is an applicant with special reception needs. Member States *shall also indicate* the nature of such needs'.[50] Hence, although these provisions stop short of designating minors and unaccompanied minors *per se* as persons with special reception needs, they do establish that, as vulnerable persons, minors and unaccompanied minors must be assessed for special reception needs.[51] That said, if Article 22 is interpreted, as it should be, in light of the obligation in Article 20 CRC relating to the right of the child temporarily or permanently deprived of his or her family environment to special protection and assistance (see Chapter 5 above), it is hard to conceive how unaccompanied minors could ever be assessed *not* to have special reception needs. Indeed, it is submitted that all child applicants for international protection are, *prima facie*, persons with special reception needs. In this regard, the need for an additional bureaucratic and potentially exclusionary layer is regrettable. On the other hand, the establishment of a clear legal obligation to assess minors and unaccompanied minors for special needs is an improvement on the existing directive. In terms of the right to health, children designated as applicants with special reception needs are not susceptible to the problematic lower standard of health care in Article 19(1)

---

49 The die had already been cast during negotiations of the recast QD. In the Commission proposal for a recast of that directive, the reference was to mental health care. This was replaced by the phrase 'treatment of mental disorders' during negotiations. See Proposal for a Directive of the European Parliament and of the Council on minimum standards for the qualification and status of third country nationals or stateless persons as beneficiaries of international protection and the content of the protection granted, *COM (2009) 551*, Article 30(2). Unsurprisingly, negotiations of the recast RCD went the same way.
50 Emphasis added. Of concern, little guidance is provided on the conduct of the assessment and it is stated that the assessment need not take the form of an administrative procedure.
51 This interpretation is reinforced by Article 22(3) which states that 'only vulnerable persons in accordance with Article 21 may be considered to have special reception needs and thus benefit from the specific support provided in accordance with this directive'.

but are brought squarely within the scope of the higher standard of health care in Article 19(2), which, in turn, conforms to the normative content of the right of the child to health.

Chapter III relating to reduction or withdrawal of reception conditions subsists in the recast, but with two important amendments. First, whereas the original directive provides that emergency health care must be provided even in cases of reduction, withdrawal or refusal of reception conditions, the recast effectively insulates the right to health care from the scope of application of Chapter III. Thus, new Article 20(5) provides that 'Member States shall *under all circumstances* ensure access to health care' in accordance with Article 19, the health care article.[52] Second, and this is something of a moot point in light of the foregoing, the possibility of refusing outright reception conditions where the applicant did not make the application as soon as reasonably practicable after arrival is deleted.

Finally, whereas the original RCD makes no reference to the right to health care of applicants in detention, new Article 11 of the recast, relating to the detention of vulnerable persons and persons with special needs, provides in paragraph 1:

> The health, including mental health, of applicants in detention who are vulnerable persons shall be of primary concern to national authorities.
> Where vulnerable persons are detained, Member States shall ensure regular monitoring and adequate support taking into account their particular situation, including their health.

Further provisions that relate to the detention of minors and unaccompanied minors will be critiqued in Chapter 7. Although new Article 11(1) is an improvement on the existing directive, it is a retrograde step from the amended Commission proposal for a recast RCD, which predicated the detention of vulnerable persons on their state of health and implicitly provided for their release in the event of a significant deterioration of their health.[53]

The provision of the recast RCD on victims of torture and violence (Article 25, which corresponds to Article 20 of the present directive) contains two innovations. In addition to the 'necessary treatment of damages', paragraph 1 adds that victims of torture and violence are entitled to receive 'in particular access to appropriate medical and psychological treatment or care'. The reference to psychological treatment is particularly noteworthy. A new second paragraph establishes a training and confidentiality requirement for those working with victims of torture, rape or other serious acts of violence. Regrettably, however, the recast makes no attempt to align better the provision

---

52 Emphasis added.
53 Amended proposal for a Directive of the European Parliament and of the Council laying down minimum standards for the reception of asylum seekers, *COM (2011) 320 final*, Article 11(1).

on the right of the child victim of various forms of ill-treatment to recovery and reintegration with the more holistic wording of Article 39 CRC.[54]

In short, the recast RCD, as it relates to the right of the child to health, is an improvement on the current directive in several respects and is consistent with the core content of the right of the child to health. Despite some enduring misgivings, it can also be considered to be broadly consistent with the normative content of the right of the child to health.

The recast Qualification Directive

As regards the recast QD, the major question is whether it removes the confusing plethora of streams of entitlement to health care sanctioned in the original directive. Some important improvements should be noted in this regard.

First, Article 30(1) reiterates that beneficiaries of international protection have access to health care under the same eligibility conditions as nationals. Second, the exception in the original directive providing that the health care entitlements of beneficiaries of subsidiary protection may be limited to core benefits is deleted. Thus, there is no distinction in the level of health care afforded to refugees and beneficiaries of subsidiary protection. Third, Article 30(2) reiterates the obligation to provide 'adequate health care' to beneficiaries of international protection who have special needs, but adds a stipulation that this includes the 'treatment of mental disorders when needed'. The reference to mental disorders has already been critiqued in the analysis of the recast RCD. The general rules on the content of international protection in Article 20(3), which obliges Member States to 'take into account' the situation of vulnerable persons such as minors and unaccompanied minors in the national implementing legislation, is still subject to the limitation, now in Article 20(4), that this only applies to 'persons found to have special needs after an individual evaluation of their situation'. However, unlike in the recast RCD, there is no express obligation to conduct such an evaluation. Fourth, as regards family members of beneficiaries of subsidiary protection, it is no longer open to Member States to define the conditions applicable to their derived rights. Consequently, such persons are entitled to health care under the same eligibility conditions as nationals. Finally, the provisions of the original directive authorising Member States to reduce the rights of refugees and beneficiaries of subsidiary protection who obtained their status in bad faith is deleted.

In sum, the various streams of access to health care are removed in the recast QD, bringing the health care provisions broadly into line with the normative content of the right of the child to health. However, it is still unclear whether minors or unaccompanied minors are persons with special needs, and thereby entitled to 'the treatment of mental disorders'. This could be significant if

---

54 Article 18(2) of the current directive is reproduced without amendment in Article 23(4) of the recast.

such treatment is not generally provided to nationals. Moreover, the recast QD fails to add a provision corresponding to Article 39 CRC or any specific provision on victims of torture or violence.

Standard of living

The right of the child to an adequate standard of living

Article 27 CRC provides, *inter alia*:

1. States Parties recognize the right of every child to a standard of living adequate for the child's physical, mental, spiritual, moral and social development.
2. The parent(s) or others responsible for the child have the primary responsibility to secure, within their abilities and financial capacities, the conditions of living necessary for the child's development.
3. States Parties, in accordance with national conditions and within their means, shall take appropriate measures to assist parents and others responsible for the child to implement this right and shall in case of need provide material assistance and support programmes, particularly with regard to nutrition, clothing and housing.

Article 27 CRC is based on, but goes significantly beyond, a comparable provision in Article 11 ICESCR.[55] A number of regional human rights instruments also address the right to an adequate standard of living.[56]

The normative content of the right

Article 27(1) sets out an obligation of result: the right of the child to a standard of living adequate for the child's physical, mental, spiritual, moral and social development. In order to understand the meaning of this provision, it

---

55 Article 11(1) ICESCR provides, *inter alia*: 'The States Parties to the present Covenant recognise the right of everyone to an adequate standard of living for himself and his family, including adequate food, clothing and housing, and to the continuous improvement of living conditions. The States Parties will take appropriate steps to ensure the realisation of this right.' Furthermore, Article 10(1) of the Covenant is also of relevance: 'The widest possible protection and assistance should be accorded to the family, which is the natural and fundamental group unit of society, particularly for its establishment and while it is responsible for the care and education of dependent children.'

56 Article 17 of the Revised European Social Charter and Article 34 of the Charter of Fundamental Rights of the EU. Issues relating to the right to an adequate standard of living may also arise under various articles of the ECHR, notably Articles 6, 8 and P1-1 in conjunction with Article 14. In extreme cases Article 3 ECHR may be of relevance. See ECtHR, *MSS v Belgium and Greece*, Appl. No. 30696/09, Judgment (GC) of 21 January 2011 and ECtHR, *Rahimi v Greece*, Appl. No. 8687/08, Judgment of 5 April 2011.

is useful first to examine the 'template' right to an adequate standard of living set out in the ICESCR. Article 11(1) of the Covenant provides, *inter alia*, '[t]he States Parties to the present Covenant recognise the right of everyone to an adequate standard of living for himself and his family, including adequate food, clothing and housing, and to the continuous improvement of living conditions'. The reference to adequate food, clothing and housing establishes that the right to an adequate standard of living is aimed at fulfilling the most basic human needs. However, the Com. ESCR has stressed that this does not mean that the normative content of the right is a minimal one. Thus, in its General Comment 4 on the right to adequate housing, the Committee states that 'the right to housing should not be interpreted in a narrow or restrictive sense which equates it with, for example, the shelter provided by merely having a roof over one's head, or views shelter exclusively as a commodity. Rather it should be seen as the right to live somewhere in security, peace and dignity'.[57] Similarly, in its General Comment 12 on the right to adequate food, the Committee notes that:

> The right to adequate food is realized when every man, woman and child, alone or in community with others, has physical and economic access at all times to adequate food or means for its procurement. The right to adequate food shall therefore not be interpreted in a narrow or restrictive sense which equates it with a minimum package of calories, proteins and other specific nutrients.[58]

Nevertheless, the definition of the right to an adequate standard of living in terms of such basic commodities as food, clothing and housing does indicate that the right is rather narrow in scope. By contrast, Article 27 CRC does not limit the right to physical determinants of well-being, but rather refers to a standard of living adequate for the 'child's physical, mental spiritual, moral and social development'. Thus, Asbjorn Eide observes that '[t]he right of the child to an adequate standard of living goes beyond the purely material aspects of living such as food and housing. [...] It goes beyond the right of the child to survive by having the basic needs safeguarded. The child is entitled to enjoy conditions which facilitate its development into a fully capable and well functioning adult person'.[59] Hence, economic adequacy – in the sense of having enough (income) to secure material well-being – is a necessary but not

---

57 Com. ESCR, General Comment 4, 'The right to adequate housing', *UN Doc E/1992/23 (1991), annex III at 114*, para. 7.
58 Com. ESCR, General Comment 12, 'The right to adequate food', *UN Doc E/C.12/1999/5 (1999)*, para. 6.
59 A. Eide, *Article 27, The Right to an Adequate Standard of Living, A Commentary on the United Nations Convention on the Rights of the Child*, Leiden/Boston:Martinus Nijhoff Publishers, 2006, 17.

sufficient condition for the attainment of the right of the child to an adequate standard of living. What the further conditions are is not clear from the text of Article 27 itself and, in attempting to attribute meaning to the right, commentators have attempted to link Article 27 to anti-poverty concepts from the social sciences, such as the concept of social exclusion, which understands poverty as a relative, as opposed to an absolute phenomenon.[60] This appears also to be the position of the Com. RC, which notes in General Comment No. 7 that '[g]rowing up in relative poverty undermines children's well-being, social inclusion and self-esteem and reduces opportunities for learning and development'.[61]

Furthermore, the Com. RC links the right to an adequate standard of living with a host of other rights in the Convention, such as the right of the child to social security (Article 26), the right of the child to such care and protection as are necessary for well-being (Article 3(2)), the right of the child to development (Article 6(2)), the right of the child to health (Article 24), the right of the child to education (Article 28) and the right of the child to 'rest and leisure, to engage in play and recreational activities appropriate to the age of the child and to participate freely in cultural life and the arts' (Article 31).[62] In this regard, it may be observed that the rights in the CRC are truly (as opposed to rhetorically) indivisible and interdependent, and consequently, it is not possible to address the child's right to an adequate standard of living in isolation from these other rights.

In sum, therefore, the right of the *child* to an adequate standard of living is broader and more comprehensive than the right to an adequate standard of living in general human rights law. However, a distinction must be made between the State's obligation and the parents' obligation regarding the right of the child to an adequate standard of living. It is clear from paragraphs 2 and 3 of Article 27 that the primary responsibility to secure for the child an adequate standard of living falls to the child's parents, with the State assuming a secondary responsibility. This delineation of responsibility provides further insight into the normative content of the right. Commenting on Article 18 of the CRC, which also deals with the respective responsibilities of parents and the State, Detrick observes that the term 'primary responsibility' was intended to achieve two aims: to protect parents against excessive State intervention and, conversely, to establish that parents should not expect the State always to intervene. 'That being said' according to Detrick, 'the use of the term "primary responsibility" [...] implies that a secondary responsibility to secure the conditions of living necessary for a child's development lies with the State'.[63]

---

60 See, for example, G. Redmond, 'Child poverty and child rights: Edging towards a definition', *Journal of Children and Poverty* 14, 2008, 63–82.
61 Com. RC, General Comment No. 7, *op cit.*, para. 26.
62 *Ibid.*, para. 10.
63 S. Detrick, *A Commentary on the United Nations Convention on the Rights of the Child*, The Hague/Boston/London: Martinus Nijhoff Publishers, 1999, 459.

It is worth pointing out that the division of responsibility between the parents and the State is redundant in the context of unaccompanied minors, where there are no parents. In such situations, the primary responsibility to secure the child's right to an adequate standard of living falls entirely to the State. Thus, the Com. RC notes that '*States* should ensure that separated and unaccompanied children have a standard of living adequate for their physical, mental, spiritual and moral development'.[64]

As for the secondary responsibility of the State, the precise contours of this responsibility are set out in Article 27(3), according to which the State has a positive obligation, firstly, to take appropriate measures to assist parents in discharging their duty, and secondly, 'in case of need [to] provide material assistance and support programmes, particularly with regard to nutrition, clothing and housing'. As regards the duty to assist parents in discharging their duty, the Com. RC recommends indirect interventions such as taxation and benefits, adequate housing and health services as well as more direct interventions such as parenting education, parent counselling and other parent and family supports.[65] The Committee also observes that:

> Situations which are most likely to impact negatively on young children include [...] parenting under acute material or psychological stress or impaired mental health; [...] The Committee urges States Parties to take all necessary steps to ensure that parents are able to take primary responsibility for their children; to support parents in fulfilling their responsibilities, including by reducing harmful deprivations, disruptions and distortions in children's care.[66]

This observation has a particular resonance in the asylum context, as a growing body of research shows that asylum-seeking families tend to be more dysfunctional and the parents in such families at greater risk of suffering from mental health problems than families even in deprived sections of the host population.[67] This is considered to be due to past trauma coupled with current living conditions and uncertainty about status. Consequently, the State's duty to assist parents in providing an adequate standard of living for their children has important ramifications for the *parents'* right to an adequate standard of living and associated rights. Thus, the Committee observes that 'realising children's rights is in large measure dependent on the well-being and resources available to those with responsibility for their care. Recognising these

---

64 Com. RC, General Comment No. 6, *op. cit.*, para. 44 (emphasis added).
65 Com. RC, General Comment No. 7, *op. cit.*, para. 20.
66 *Ibid.* at para. 18.
67 See, for example, Kalverboer, Zijlstra and Knorth, *op. cit.*

interdependencies is a sound starting point for planning assistance and services to parents, legal guardians and other caregivers'.[68]

As regards material assistance and support in case of need, whether a family seeking or enjoying international protection is needy in this sense will depend on whether the adults are able to work (i.e. eligible to work, capable of working and successful in finding work) and receive adequate remuneration. Where they are not, the State must provide the material aspects of living. Furthermore, in such situations, arguably the delineation of responsibility between the parents and the State shifts, with the State becoming primarily responsible for securing the child's standard of living. Thus, the Com. ESCR underlines that 'States Parties are obliged to fulfil (provide) a specific right contained in the Covenant when individuals or groups are unable for reasons *beyond their control* to realise the right themselves by the means at their disposal'.[69]

In sum, the right of the child to an adequate standard of living is pitched higher than the corresponding right in general human rights law. However, the right is primarily to be met by the child's parents, with the State exercising a secondary responsibility. The State's responsibility involves supporting parents in discharging their responsibility (which raises the issue of the parents' right to an adequate standard of living) and providing material assistance and support in cases of need.

The 'core content' of the right

I. THE MINIMUM ESSENTIAL OBLIGATION

Being a socio-economic right, the right of the child to an adequate standard of living is subject to resource constraints per Article 4 CRC. Indeed, the issue of resource constraints is expressly factored into the obligation of conduct in Article 27(3), which obliges States to act 'in accordance with national conditions and within their means'. In this context, the question arises as to the content of the minimum absolute obligation.

Recalling that the minimum obligation corresponds with the duty to take steps towards the full realisation of the right, it can be observed that Article 27(3) envisages two steps: 1) to take appropriate measures to assist parents to implement the right; and 2) to provide, in case of need, material assistance and support programmes, particularly with regard to nutrition, clothing and housing. As regards the first, the term 'appropriate' leaves a large measure of discretion to States Parties about which measures they take to assist parents. Nevertheless, demonstrable measures must be taken. As regards the second, there is no leeway (cf. 'shall in case of need provide'). Consequently, States

---

68 Com. RC, General Comment No. 7, *op. cit.*, para. 20.
69 Com. ESCR, General Comment 13, 'The right to education', *UN Doc. E/C.12/1999/10 (1999)*, para. 47 (emphasis added).

Parties are under an obligation to provide for basic human needs. Any erosion of the right beyond this level would be incompatible with human dignity. This is consistent with the approach of the Com. ESCR, which states in General Comment No. 3:

> [a] minimum core obligation to ensure the satisfaction of, at the very least, minimum essential levels of each of the rights is incumbent upon every State Party. Thus for example, a State Party in which any significant number of individuals is deprived of *essential foodstuffs*, of essential primary health care, *of basic shelter and housing*, or of the most basic forms of education is, *prima facie*, failing to discharge its obligations under the Covenant.[70]

This is also consistent with the approach of the ECtHR in two recent cases in which the Court found a violation of Article 3 ECHR because the respondent State failed to ensure the most basic standard of living for the applicant asylum seekers, with the result that there were homeless and destitute. In *M.S.S. v Belgium and Greece*, the Court revised its earlier case-law that Article 3 EHCR does not entail any general obligation to give refugees financial assistance to enable them to maintain a certain standard of living.[71] The Court seemed to consider that because Greece is bound by the minimum standards of the RCD, this brought the issue of a minimum standard of living within the material scope of Article 3 ECHR.[72] It follows that the minimum standard of living in the RCD must itself be compatible with Article 3 ECHR. In *Rahimi v Greece*, the Court found that the abandonment by the State of a fifteen-year-old unaccompanied minor until he happened to be taken care of by a local NGO constituted a violation of Article 3 ECHR.[73] In both cases the Court noted the extreme vulnerability of the applicants as members of an 'underprivileged and vulnerable population', an observation that applied *a fortiori* to the unaccompanied minor.[74]

---

70 *Ibid.*, para. 10 (emphasis added).
71 ECtHR, *M.S.S. v Belgium and Greece*, Appl. No. 30696/09, Judgment of 21 January 2011.
72 *Ibid.* See, in particular, para. 250 of the judgment.
73 ECtHR, *Rahimi v Greece*, Appl. No. 8687/08, Judgment of 5 April 2011.
74 A number of decisions of the European Committee of Social Rights are worth mentioning here. In *Defence for Children International (DCI) v the Netherlands*, the Committee found that children unlawfully present in the Netherlands: a) came within the personal scope of Article 31(2) of the Revised ESC relating to the right to shelter despite the express wording of the Charter limiting its scope to lawful residents; and b) had been denied their right to shelter. What is interesting about this case from our perspective is not the jurisdictional issue (the rights in the CRC applying, per Article 2, to every child within the jurisdiction of a State Party), but to the role of human dignity (and vulnerability to violations of human dignity) in ring-fencing a core content of rights that can neither be excluded *ratione personae* nor – it follows logically – limited. European Committee of Social Rights, Complaint No. 47/2008, Decision on the merits, 29 October 2009. A similar decision was reached in *Defence for Children International (DCI) v Belgium*, Complaint No. 69/2011, Decision on the

In conclusion, the minimum essential obligation inherent in the right of the child to an adequate standard of living is the duty to assist parents in their fulfilment of the obligation and, in cases of need, to provide for basic levels of nutrition, clothing and housing. Anything less than this is likely to constitute inhuman and degrading treatment.

II. THE PROHIBITION OF DISCRIMINATION

Unlike the right to health, the right to an adequate standard of living does not contain an express prohibition of discrimination. However, the two concepts are intimately connected. The prohibition of discrimination is designed to tackle relative as opposed to absolute deprivation, as is clear from the first part of the 'formula' for assessing discrimination, namely, the question of whether the alleged victim is less favourably treated as compared with similarly situated persons. Similarly, the right to an adequate standard of living is interpreted as countering social exclusion, which focuses on relative as well as absolute poverty. In any event, a prohibition of discrimination is part of the 'core content' of each and every right in the CRC as a result of the general principle of non-discrimination in Article 2.

Phase One CEAS: Compliance with the right of the child to an adequate standard of living

The Reception Conditions Directive

Article 13 RCD establishes general rules on material reception conditions and health care. Material reception conditions are defined as including 'housing, food and clothing, provided in kind, or as financial allowances or in vouchers, and a daily expenses allowance'.[75] Article 13(2) provides that:

> Member States shall make provisions on material reception conditions to ensure a standard of living *adequate for the health of applicants and capable of ensuring their subsistence*. Member States shall ensure that *that* standard of living is met in the specific situation of persons who have special needs, in accordance with Article 17.[76]

Article 17, in turn, obliges Member States to 'take into account the specific situation of vulnerable persons such as minors [and] unaccompanied minors [...] in

---

Merits, 23 October 2012. The CJEU also referred to the concept of human dignity, which finds expression in Article 1 of the EU Charter of Fundamental Rights, in its judgment in *Cimade and GISTI*, noting that 'the [Reception Conditions] directive aims in particular to ensure full respect for human dignity'. Case C-179/11, Judgment of 27 September 2012, para. 42.
75 Article 2(j).
76 Emphasis added.

the national legislation implementing the provisions [...] relating to material reception conditions and health care'. However, according to the second paragraph of Article 17, this 'shall apply only to persons found to have special needs after an individual evaluation of their situation'. The obliqueness of this caveat has previously been discussed. Hence, there is an awareness that concepts such as health and subsistence have a subjective, variable dimension and that in order to meet the minimum standard of living, more may need to be done for minors and unaccompanied minors. Nevertheless, the objective standard established in the directive is the same for everyone. Thus, once a minor can subsist and his/her health is adequate, the standard is reached. While the standard may conform to the right to an adequate standard of living in general human rights law, it does not properly reflect the more robust right of the child to an adequate standard of living in the CRC, namely, one adequate for the child's physical, mental, spiritual, moral and social development.

Article 14 RCD elaborates on the standard of living established in the directive. It relates to 'modalities for material reception conditions' – standards that must be met when housing is provided in kind (i.e. direct provision). It sets out the possible types of housing and the rights applicants have in such housing, which include protection of their family life and family unity of minor children with their parents. However, it contains a derogation provision in paragraph 8, according to which Member States are permitted in four situations, including when the asylum seeker is in detention or confined to border posts, to 'exceptionally set modalities for material reception conditions different from those provided in this Article, for a reasonable period, which shall be as short as possible'.[77] In such cases, the different conditions 'shall cover in any case basic needs'. Of course, Article 14 is still subject to the general rule in Article 13 requiring Member States to ensure a standard of living 'adequate for the health of applicants and capable of ensuring their subsistence'. Hence, basic needs are regarded as being not incompatible with an adequate standard of living – an interesting insight into the meaning of the latter term. It seems clear that 'basic needs' correspond to the core but not the normative content of the right of the child to an adequate standard of living.

There is no corollary to Article 14 on how material reception conditions are to be met in situations other than direct provision.[78] Article 13(5) does stipulate that '[w]here Member States provide material reception conditions in the form of financial allowances or vouchers, the amount thereof shall be

---

77 The other three situations are: 1) when an initial assessment of the specific needs of the applicant is required; 2) when the types of accommodation outlined in the article are not available in a certain geographical area; 3) when housing capacities normally available are temporarily exhausted.
78 A case concerning the standards that apply under the RCD when material support is provided in the form of financial allowances has been referred to the CJEU: *Saciri*, Case C-79, Request for a preliminary ruling lodged on 15 February 2013.

determined in accordance with the principles set out in this Article'. In other words, the minimum standard of living established in the directive applies. However, no benchmarks are established regarding the amount of financial allowances or vouchers. Nor is any reference made to a right to social security. In light of the fact that under Article 11 of the directive Member States can (and according to the Commission evaluation, do) prohibit access to the labour market for a period of at least one year and thereafter can impose conditions on asylum seekers' access to the labour market, this is a significant omission.[79] Unsurprisingly, the Commission found in its evaluation of the RCD that:

> The main problems concerning application of the Directive were discovered in Member States where asylum seekers are given financial allowances. These allowances are very often too low to cover subsistence (CY, FR, EE, AT, PT, SI). The amounts are only rarely commensurate with the minimum social support granted to nationals, and even when they are, they might still not be sufficient, as asylum seekers lack family and/or other informal kinds of support.[80]

The standard of living that results from Article 13(5) suggests that neither component of the core content of the right of the child to an adequate standard of living is met when asylum seekers are given financial allowances or vouchers. Thus, it seems that the minimum essential obligation is not adequately met (i.e. material assistance in case of need and support to parents) *and* asylum-seeking children are discriminated against as compared with similarly situated national children (i.e. national children dependent on State assistance).

Chapter III of the RCD relating to the reduction or withdrawal (and refusal) of reception conditions is also relevant to the question of the right to an adequate standard of living. As previously outlined, Article 16 allows for the reduction and withdrawal of reception conditions in certain situations in an effort to counteract perceived abuse of the reception system and even for the outright refusal of reception conditions if the applicant failed to lodge his/her application as soon as reasonably practicable after arrival. Persons with special needs, such as minors and unaccompanied minors, are fully susceptible to the operation of Article 16, although their particular situation must be taken into account in assessing the proportionality of the measure. The only 'floor' established in reducing, withdrawing or refusing reception conditions relates to access to emergency health care. Two objections to this chapter of the RCD were made in the section on the right of the child to health, namely, that the proportionality requirement is bound to be defeated in the case of

---

79 Commission evaluation of the RCD, *op. cit.*, § 3.4.3.
80 *Ibid.*, p. 6. A similar finding was made by the Asylum Information Database project in its annual report 2012/13, 'Not there yet: An NGO perspective on challenges to a fair and effective Common European Asylum System'.

children and that to reduce, withdraw or refuse reception conditions to a child on the basis of the parents' behaviour offends against Article 2(2) CRC, which forbids 'all forms of discrimination or *punishment* on the basis of the status, *activities*, expressed opinions, or beliefs of the child's parents, legal guardians or family members'.[81] These arguments apply equally here, and another can be added. Since the only floor relates to health care, this means that all other reception conditions can conceivably be reduced to a level well below not only the normative content of the right of the child to an adequate standard of living, but also the core content of the right, and indeed, can be withdrawn or refused altogether, resulting in an outright violation of the right and in treatment that is inhuman or degrading.

Overall, therefore, it cannot be said that the right of the child to an adequate standard of living is met in the RCD. The general standard of living in the directive is pitched at the standard in general, but not child-specific, human rights law. Moreover, while the core of the child-right seems to be met when asylum seekers are in direct provision, it is unmet when asylum seekers are given financial allowances or vouchers. The option to reduce, withdraw or refuse reception conditions without limitation in certain cases could constitute an outright violation of the right of the child to an adequate standard of living and possibly amount to a violation of Article 3 ECHR.

The Qualification Directive

The QD does not establish a general minimum standard of living, the inference being that the rights afforded to beneficiaries of international protection (e.g. access to employment, education, social assistance, health care, accommodation and integration facilities) imply a reasonable standard of living. However, given the restrictions on many of the rights of beneficiaries of subsidiary protection, this inference is questionable. Thus, Member States are permitted to impose restrictions on access to employment, social assistance, health care and integration facilities when it comes to beneficiaries of subsidiary protection. For example, whereas refugees are entitled to necessary social assistance on the same basis as nationals, Member States may limit the social assistance granted to beneficiaries of subsidiary protection to 'core benefits', which must then be provided at the same levels and under the same eligibility conditions as to nationals.[82] However, some insight into the question of the minimum standard of living for beneficiaries of subsidiary protection can be gleaned from the entitlements of their family members. Article 23 provides for the concept of derived rights for family members of beneficiaries of international protection, subject to the exception that, in respect of family members of beneficiaries of subsidiary protection, Member States 'may define

---

81 Emphasis added.
82 Article 28(2).

the conditions applicable to such benefits'. However, '[i]n these cases, Member States shall ensure that any benefits provided guarantee an adequate standard of living'. *A fortiori*, this standard must be met in respect of beneficiaries of subsidiary protection themselves. To the extent that this standard is less than the standard of living afforded to refugees, it can be regarded as discriminatory according to the same logic used earlier to analyse the compliance of the QD with the right to health. As such, it is contrary to the core content of the right of the child to an adequate standard of living.

Phase Two CEAS: Prospects for enhanced conformity

The recast Reception Conditions Directive

The recast RCD contains a number of important amendments of relevance to the right of the child to an adequate standard of living. The general standard of living, set out in Article 17 of the recast, is still established as one adequate for health and subsistence, but health is said to encompass physical *and* mental health. Again, that standard must be met in the specific situation of vulnerable persons, but the procedures for identifying such persons are somewhat improved, as previously discussed.

Moreover, a number of important new provisions are added to the article on minors (now Article 23). First and of greatest importance, paragraph 1, in addition to specifying the best-interests obligation, provides that 'Member States shall ensure a standard of living adequate for the minor's physical, mental, spiritual, moral and social development'. This brings the recast RCD into line with the CRC as regards the right of the child to an adequate standard of living. Interestingly, if this provision is interpreted, as it should be, in the light of Article 27 CRC, this is likely to have a knock-on effect on the standard of living of the parents of accompanied children, given the intimate connection between the child's and the parents' standard of living.

Second, paragraph 3 obliges Member States to 'ensure that minors have access to leisure-activities, including play and recreational activities appropriate to their age within [direct provision] premises and accommodation centres'. This provision, which reflects the terms of Article 31 CRC, is a welcome addition.[83] Unfortunately, it does not extend to children in private houses, flats, hotels or

---

[83] Article 31 CRC provides in para. 1: 'States Parties recognise the right of the child to rest and leisure, to engage in play and recreational activities appropriate to the age of the child and to participate freely in cultural life and the arts.' The Com. RC has emphasised that 'States Parties shall take all appropriate measures to ensure that all children have the opportunity to realise their rights under article 31 without discrimination of any kind [...]. Particular attention should be given to addressing the rights of certain groups of children, including [...] asylum-seeking and refugee children'. General Comment No. 17, 'The right of the child to rest, leisure, play, recreational activities, cultural life and the arts (art. 31)', *UN Doc CRC/C/GC/17 (2013)*, para. 16.

other premises adapted for housing applicants. While it is accepted that the State could not guarantee such a right in privately-sourced accommodation, this argument does not apply when such accommodation is provided by the State. Therefore, if a distinction is to be introduced, it should be between State-sourced and privately-sourced accommodation, not between *types* of accommodation.

Third, the right of minors to family unity with their parents or adult responsible for them is moved from the article on modalities for material reception conditions (i.e. the direct provision article) to Article 23 on minors. The consequence of this move is that it is no longer subject to the derogation provision in the former article. Furthermore, the right to family unity is made subject to a best-interests assessment.

As regards the article on modalities for material reception conditions (now Article 18), a new paragraph 3 provides that 'Member States shall take into consideration gender and age-specific concerns and the situation of vulnerable persons in relation to applicants within the premises and accommodation centres', but again, with the regrettable exception of private houses, flats, hotels or other premises adapted for housing applicants. Article 18 is still subject to derogation (per paragraph 6), but the grounds are reduced from four to two and the derogation can only be resorted to in 'duly justified cases'.[84] The existing requirement that, in such situations, the reception conditions 'shall in any event cover basic needs' subsists.

As regards reception conditions in situations other than direct provision, a new provision (Article 17(5)) provides:

> Where Member States provide material reception conditions in the form of financial allowances or vouchers, the amount thereof shall be determined on the basis of the level(s) established by the Member States concerned either by law or by the practice to ensure adequate standards of living for nationals. Member States may grant less favourable treatment to applicants compared with nationals in this respect, in particular where material support is partially provided in kind or where those level(s), applied for nationals, aim to ensure a standard of living higher than that prescribed for applicants under the Directive.

The first sentence of this provision is a modified version of that in the amended Commission proposal for a recast RCD, which, in turn, was a whittled-down version of the original Commission proposal. The latter squarely pegged the value of material reception conditions to the amount of social welfare assistance granted to nationals, while the former referred to social welfare assistance as an

---

84 The grounds for derogating from Article 18 in the recast are: when an initial assessment of the specific needs of the applicant is required and when housing capacities normally available are temporarily exhausted.

example of the level established to ensure an adequate standard of living for nationals.[85] Both versions specified that any differences in treatment had to be 'duly justified'. Seen in this light, the obligation in the first sentence of Article 17(5) is relatively weak. This is compounded by the second sentence which permits differential treatment, *inter alia*, where the national level of support aims to ensure a higher standard of living than under the Directive. The reasoning here is entirely circular: the level of support in the directive should be determined on the basis of the national level unless the national level is higher than the level in the directive. The sub-national standard of material support, where that support is provided in the form of financial allowances or vouchers, means that the problem of discrimination subsists in the recast.

However, the problem is mitigated somewhat by new rules regarding access to the labour market. New Article 15 obliges Member States to grant access to the labour market no later than nine months after lodging an application, if a first instance decision has not been taken and the delay cannot be attributed to the applicant. This is both a retreat and an advance on the amended Commission proposal for a recast RCD, which established a lower time-limit of six months but stated that this could be extended to a year in cases where the first instance procedure was delayed either because of the large number of applicants at a given time or due to obstruction on the part of the applicant.[86] Member States may still impose conditions on access to the labour market according to their national law, but these conditions cannot impede effective access to the labour market.

Finally, the provisions of Chapter III relating to the reduction or withdrawal of reception conditions remain largely intact. No exemption for minors or unaccompanied minors is introduced. However, the provision relating to the outright refusal of reception conditions when an asylum seeker fails to make a claim as soon as reasonably practicable after arrival is deleted.

In sum, the revised article on minors establishes a standard of living for children that is consistent with – indeed, based on – Article 27 CRC. The article relating to accommodation in kind is also improved from a child-rights perspective. However, the article on reception conditions in situations other than direct provision is still arguably discriminatory when compared with the situation of similarly-situated national children, and it remains possible to reduce or withdraw reception conditions of minors in cases of perceived abuse of the asylum system. These provisions are inconsistent with the provision that pitches the standard of living for minors at the level established in the CRC. It remains to be seen how the inconsistency will be ironed out in the jurisprudence.

---

85 Proposal for a directive of the European Parliament and of the Council laying down minimum standards for the reception of asylum seekers, *COM (2008) 815 final*, Article 17(5) and *COM (2011) 320 final, op. cit.*, Article 17(5).
86 *COM (2011) 320 final, ibid.*, Article 15(1).

The recast Qualification Directive

The recast QD also contains a number of amendments that impact on the implicit standard of living established in the directive. These amendments are geared towards a greater equalisation of treatment of refugees and beneficiaries of subsidiary protection. Thus, beneficiaries of subsidiary protection are to be granted access to employment, health care and integration facilities on the same basis as refugees. Moreover, the provision on access to employment-related education is enhanced, and a new article (28) is devoted to access to procedures for recognition of qualifications – the lack of which hitherto constituted a significant practical barrier to access to employment. However, the distinction between refugees and beneficiaries of subsidiary protection is retained in terms of the right to social welfare: the social welfare entitlements of beneficiaries of subsidiary protection may still be limited to 'core benefits' under Article 29.[87] Hence the recast QD constitutes a modified improvement on the QD in terms of the right of the child to an adequate standard of living.

Conclusion

This chapter explored the extent to which the CEAS in both phases complies with two key socio-economic rights of the child: the right to health and the right to an adequate standard of living. It was posited that the CEAS instruments should generally conform to the normative content of these rights, but where the instruments allow for Member State flexibility in the form of discretionary and derogation provisions, they should conform at least to the core content of the rights.

As regards the right to health, neither the RCD nor the QD was found to conform clearly to either the normative or the core content of the right. The essential problem in the RCD is that although the general standard of health it establishes must be levelled up in the case of persons with special needs, it is uncertain whether minors and unaccompanied minors fall into this category. Furthermore, the directive allows for the reduction and withdrawal of health care to a minimum level that is less than the core content of the right of the child to health. However, the RCD does provide for rehabilitation and recovery for child victims of various types of ill treatment, although identification of such children remains a problem and the relevant provision is not an accurate reflection of the corresponding right in the CRC. In the recast, most of these various problems are addressed, such that it can be considered to conform broadly to both the core and the normative content of the right of the child to health. As regards the QD, the essential problem is that it fails to establish one basic standard of health care for everyone, but rather creates different

---

87 This provision was deleted in the Commission proposal but the European Parliament reinstated the limitation during negotiations with the result that it reappears in the recast QD.

streams of entitlement. This offends against the prohibition of discrimination and therefore violates the core content of the right of the child to health. Furthermore, the directive fails to establish a right of the child victim of various forms of ill treatment to recovery and reintegration. The first but not the second problem is addressed in the recast QD.

As regard the right of the child to an adequate standard of living, the normative content of the right is not met in the RCD because the standard of living in the directive is pitched at the standard in general, not child-specific, human rights law. As regards the 'core content' of the right, this is unmet when asylum seekers are given financial allowances and where Member States avail of the option to reduce, withdraw or refuse reception conditions. As for the recast, a new provision establishes a separate, and child-rights compliant, standard of living for minors, but the other problems persist and it is unclear, in the mix, whether the right of all children to an adequate standard of living will be met. As regards the QD, while the right of the child refugee to an adequate standard of living appears to be secured, the right of the child beneficiary of subsidiary protection may be limited. As this offends against the prohibition of discrimination, it follows that the core content of the right is unmet. In the recast QD, some rights relating to the standard of living of beneficiaries of subsidiary protection are levelled up, but there is still a differentiation in the matter of social welfare. Consequently, the recast QD does not fully comply with the core content of the right of the child to an adequate standard of living.

7 The right of the child to liberty

Introduction

This chapter explores the compliance of the CEAS with the right of the child to liberty.[1] Unfortunately, a great many children seeking international protection in the EU – both accompanied and unaccompanied – are detained.[2] Sometimes the detention is said to be justified on the grounds that it is protective detention.[3] But generally, detention of children is regarded as inimical to the protection and care of children. For this reason, the CRC has developed stringent standards for the detention of minors to ensure that they are protected *from* detention and, if detained, that they are protected *in* detention. This chapter follows the structure of previous chapters, albeit in simplified form, since just one right is involved. Thus, the first section sets out the right of the child to liberty in its various dimensions; the second section scrutinises

---

1 The author would like to thank Koninklijke Brill NV for permission to reproduce here some of the same material as is contained in the following article: C. Smyth, 'Is the Right of the Child to Liberty Safeguarded in the Common European Asylum System?', *European Journal of Migration and Law* 15, 2013, 111–136.
2 Accurate statistics for minor asylum seekers in detention are hard to come by. However, in its evaluation of the RCD, the Commission found that 'most of [the Member States] authorize the detention of minors and many of them even authorize the detention of unaccompanied minors'. 'Report from the Commission to the Council and to the European Parliament on the application of Directive 2003/9/EC of 27 January 2003 laying down minimum standards for the reception of asylum seekers', *COM (2007) 745 final*, § 3.5.2, p. 9. Hereinafter, 'Commission evaluation of RCD'. The Asylum Information Database (AIDA) annual report for 2012/13 provides that of the fourteen EU Member States surveyed, eight detain unaccompanied minors, although some only in border or transit zones. AIDA, 'Not there yet: An NGO perspective on challenges to a fair and effective Common European Asylum System', 2013.
3 For example, in the Explanatory Memorandum to the amended Commission proposal for a recast RCD, it is stated that '[d]iscussions in the Council revealed that in certain circumstances it is in the best interests of unaccompanied minors to be kept in detention facilities, in particular to prevent abductions which reportedly do occur in open centers'. Amended proposal for a Directive of the European Parliament and of the Council laying down standards for the reception of asylum seekers (recast), *COM (2011) 320 final*, § 3.1.2, p. 6.

whether the relevant Phase One instruments comply with the right of the child to liberty; the final section assesses the prospects for better compliance in Phase Two. The relevant CEAS instruments are the Reception Conditions Directive (RCD) and the APD.

The right of the child to liberty

The administrative detention of asylum seekers is situated at the juncture of international human rights and international refugee law. On the one hand, refugee law establishes a presumption against the detention of asylum seekers,[4] while on the other, human rights law, while not prohibiting such detention outright, subjects it to a series of criteria and safeguards in view of the importance of liberty. Thus, at the international level, Articles 9 and 10 of the International Covenant on Civil and Political Rights (ICCPR) relate, respectively, to safeguards against arbitrary or unlawful detention and minimum standards regarding conditions of detention.[5] At the regional level, Article 5 of the ECHR, while it permits in paragraph 1(f) administrative detention to prevent unauthorised entry and to effect deportation, requires that such detention must be lawful and amenable to judicial review.[6] In cases where the conditions of detention are very poor, Article 3 ECHR may also be

---

4 See Article 31, 1951 Convention relating to the Status of Refugees, UNHCR Excom. Conclusion No. 44 (XXXVII) 1986, 'Detention of Refugees and Asylum Seekers', and UNHCR, 'Guidelines on Applicable Standards and Criteria relating to the Detention of Asylum Seekers', 1999. A question has been referred to the CJEU on the meaning of Article 31 of the 1951 Convention, and it will be interesting to see whether the Court reformulates the question as pertaining to the CEAS or declines to answer it for lack of jurisdiction: *Qurbani*, Case C-481/13, Reference for a preliminary ruling lodged on 9 September 2013.
5 Article 9 ICCPR provides, *inter alia*: '1. Everyone has the right to liberty and security of person. No one shall be subjected to arbitrary arrest or detention. No one shall be deprived of his liberty except on such grounds and in accordance with such procedures as are established by law. 2. Anyone who is arrested shall be informed, at the time of arrest, of the reasons for his arrest and shall be promptly informed of any charges against him. [...] 4. Anyone who is deprived of liberty by arrest or detention shall be entitled to take proceedings before a court, in order that the court may decide without delay on the lawfulness of his detention and order his release if the detention is not lawful.' Article 10(1) ICCPR provides: 'All persons deprived of their liberty shall be treated with humanity and with respect for the inherent dignity of the human person.'
6 Article 5 ECHR provides in relevant part: '1. Everyone has the right to liberty and security of person. No one shall be deprived of his liberty save in the following cases and in accordance with a procedure proscribed by law: [...] (f) the lawful arrest or detention of a person to prevent his effecting the unauthorized entry into the country or of a person against whom action is being taken with a view to deportation or extradition. 2. Everyone who is arrested shall be informed promptly, in a language which he understands, of the reasons for his arrest and of any charge against him. [...] 4. Everyone who is deprived of his liberty by arrest or detention shall be entitled to take proceedings by which the lawfulness of his detention shall be decided speedily by a court and his release ordered if the detention in not lawful.'

engaged.[7] Finally, Article 6 of the EU Charter of Fundamental Rights establishes a right to liberty and security.[8]

The detention of minor asylum seekers is more problematic than that of adults, because the impact of detention on a child's rights are more profound – the right of the child to development, family unity and education being cases in point – and the child is more susceptible to abuse, victimisation and violation of his/her protection rights while in detention than adults are generally. For this reason, a number of specific criteria and guarantees apply to the detention of minors under Article 37(b)–(d) CRC, which provides:

b   No child shall be deprived of his/her liberty unlawfully or arbitrarily. The arrest, detention or imprisonment of a child shall be in conformity with the law, used only as a measure of last resort and for the shortest appropriate period of time.
c   Every child deprived of liberty shall be treated with humanity and respect for the inherent dignity of the human person and in a manner which takes into account the needs of persons of his/her age. In particular, every child deprived of liberty shall be separated from adults, unless it is considered in the child's best interests not to do so and shall have the right to maintain contact with his/her family through correspondence and visits, save in exceptional circumstances.
d   Every child deprived of his/her liberty shall have the right to prompt access to legal and other appropriate assistance, as well as the right to challenge the legality of the deprivation of his/her liberty before a court or other competent independent and impartial authority and to a prompt decision on any such action.

In short, Article 37(b) relates to permissible detention, Article 37(c) to conditions of detention and Article 37(d) to procedural protection. The subsequent analysis proceeds under these headings.

Permissible detention

Let us consider first Article 37(b), which deals with the situations in which a child may legitimately be deprived of his or her liberty. The first sentence encapsulates the dual requirements of lawfulness and non-arbitrariness that are common to most prohibitions of deprivation of liberty in international human rights law.

---

7   For a full discussion of the relevant case-law, see the sub-section on Conditions of detention below.
8   Article 6 reads: 'Everyone has the right to liberty and security of person.' According to the Explanations Relating to the Charter of Fundamental Rights, Article 6 corresponds to Article 5 ECHR and has the same meaning and scope as the latter: *2007/C 303/02*, Explanation on Article 6.

The requirement of lawfulness is the most straightforward, pertaining to the need for detention to be prescribed by law, in the sense of having a legal basis that is accessible, precise and foreseeable. The case-law of the ECtHR on the question of lawfulness is instructive. In *Amuur v France*, the Court rejected the contention that a number of disparate administrative decrees and circulars provided a legal basis for the detention of a group of Somali asylum seekers in the international transit zone of an airport for twenty days.[9] Among the problems with the various documents was that they failed to contain any due process guarantees, permit judicial review, place time-limits on detention or make provision for legal, humanitarian or social assistance. In *Abdolkhani and Karimnia v Turkey*, the Court held that a law that required non-nationals without valid travel documents to reside at designated places did not provide a sufficiently clear legal basis for the detention of non-nationals pending deportation.[10] The Court noted that:

> These provisions do not refer to a deprivation of liberty in the context of deportation proceedings. They concern the residence of certain groups of foreigners in Turkey, but not their detention. Nor do they provide any details as to the conditions for ordering and extending detention with a view to deportation, or set time-limits for such detention. The Court therefore finds that the applicants' detention [...] did not have a sufficient legal basis.[11]

In *Lokpo and Touré v Hungary*, the Court held that the authorities' failure to release asylum applicants from detention 'was not incarnated by a decision, accompanied by a reasoning or susceptible to a remedy', and was therefore incompatible with the requirement of lawfulness.[12] Hence, in order to be lawful, the administrative detention must be explicitly provided for by law, as must the permitted length of detention and the rights of detainees associated with judicial review.

The requirement of arbitrariness is more complicated, and in this regard two different approaches to the question of arbitrariness can be discerned in international human rights law. On the one hand, there is the approach of the Human Rights Committee under Article 9 of the ICCPR. In considering whether a detention is arbitrary, the Committee will inquire into whether the individual detention is justified, in the sense of being reasonable, necessary

---

9 ECtHR, *Amuur v France*, Appl. No. 19776/92, Judgment of 25 June 1996.
10 ECtHR, *Abdolkhani and Karimnia v Turkey*, Appl. No. 30471/08, Judgment of 22 September 2009.
11 *Ibid.* at para. 133.
12 ECtHR, *Lokpo and Touré v Hungary*, Appl. No. 10816/10, Judgment of 20 September 2011, para. 24. See further, *Said and Said v Hungary*, Appl. No. 13457/11, Judgment of 23 October 2012 and *Abdelhakim v Hungary*, Appl. No. 13058/11, Judgment of 23 October 2012.

and proportionate in the circumstances of the particular case.[13] Detention will be considered to be arbitrary if an alternative to detention could have been used in the case.[14] Consequently, mandatory immigration detention will always be found to be arbitrary, as it does not allow for an individualised assessment of arbitrariness. As regards the detention of minors, the Committee will consider the best interests of the child in its individualised assessment of arbitrariness.[15] In this regard, the Committee is facilitated by Article 24(1) ICCPR, which provides that 'Every child shall have, without any discrimination [...] the right to such measures of protection as are required by his status as a minor', a provision the Committee has interpreted as encompassing the best-interests principle.[16]

By contrast, Article 5 ECHR does not contain any express prohibition of arbitrariness, but rather contains an exhaustive list of permissible grounds of detention, including ground (f) – the lawful arrest or detention of a person to prevent his effecting an unauthorised entry into the country, or of a person against whom action is being taken with a view to deportation or extradition. If the detention does not fall under one of the permissible grounds, it is *prima facie* considered to be arbitrary. Conversely, if the detention does fall under one of the permissible grounds, it will be presumed not to be arbitrary. Although the Court has 'read down' a proportionality requirement in respect of some of the grounds of detention foreseen by Article 5(1), it has traditionally declined to do so in respect of Article 5(1)(f). Thus, states are not required to show that the detention was necessary, reasonable or proportionate in the individual circumstances of the case.[17] Detention must be reasonably justified *in general terms*, detention with a view to deportation must proceed with 'due diligence'[18] and detention to prevent unauthorised entry, including of asylum

---

13 Human Rights Committee, *A v Australia*, Communication No. 560/1993, UN Doc CCPR/C/59/D/560/1993 (1997), Views of 3 April 1997. The Committee stated that 'remand in custody could be considered arbitrary if it is not necessary in all the circumstances of the case, for example to prevent flight or interference with evidence: the element of proportionality becomes relevant in this context'. At para. 9.2.
14 Human Rights Committee, *C v Australia*, Communication No. 900/1999, UN Doc CCPR/C/76/D/900/1999, Views of 28 October 2002. The Committee held that 'the State Party has not demonstrated that, in the light of the author's particular circumstances, there were not less invasive means of achieving the same ends, that is to say, compliance with State Party's immigration policies, by, for example, the imposition of reporting obligation, sureties or other conditions'. At para. 8.2. According to UNHCR, alternatives to detention include monitoring requirements, provision of a guarantor/surety, release on bail and the use of open centres. UNHCR, *op. cit.*, Guideline 4.
15 See Human Rights Committee, *Bahktiyari v Australia*, CCPR, Communication No. 1069/2002, Views of 6 November 2003, para. 9.6 and Human Rights Committee, *Samba Jollah v the Netherlands*, CCPR, Communication No. 794/1998, Views of 15 April 2002.
16 *Ibid (Bakhtiyari v Australia)*.
17 ECtHR, *Chahal v the United Kingdom*, Appl. No. 22414/93, Judgment (GC) of 15 November 1996.
18 ECtHR, *Conka v Belgium*, Appl. No. 51564/99, Judgment of 5 February 2002.

seekers, must be closely connected to the purpose of preventing unauthorised entry and should not be unreasonably prolonged.[19] But no individualised assessment is required.[20] When followed to its logical conclusion, this approach does not permit a best-interests assessment to be factored into the question of the permissibility of detaining a child *per se*, although it may feature, as we shall see, in the assessment of the conditions of detention – but this is a separate issue.

The question is, which approach to the question of arbitrariness is taken in Article 37(b) CRC? Here, the second sentence of Article 37(b) is instructive. The fact that detention can be used only as a measure of last resort and for the shortest appropriate period of time clearly indicates that an individual assessment of arbitrariness is required, *per* the ICCPR and *pace* the ECHR. Put differently, it would be impossible to show that detention was a measure of last resort if alternatives to detention for the particular individual had not been explored; and it would be impossible to show that detention was for the shortest appropriate period of time, if appropriateness were not assessed in relation to the individual. Consequently, Article 37(b) implicitly prohibits the mandatory detention of children and requires an individualised assessment of the need for detention in each case. Since the best interests of the child is a general principle of relevance to the interpretation and application of all the rights in the Convention, including Article 37(b), the individualised assessment must encompass a best-interests assessment.

When applied to the asylum context, Article 37(b) establishes a strong presumption against the administrative detention of asylum-seeking children. Accordingly, UNHCR considers that minors should not, as a general rule, be detained. In the case of accompanied minors, '[c]hildren and their primary caregivers should not be detained unless this is the only means of maintaining family unity',[21] and in the case of unaccompanied minors '[w]here possible they should be released into the care of family members who already have residency within the asylum country'.[22] Where this is not possible, UNHCR advocates that alternative care arrangements, comprising adequate accommodation and appropriate supervision, should be made

---

19 ECtHR, *Saadi v UK*, Appl. No. 13229/03, Judgment (GC) of 29 January 2008.
20 The recent case of *Suso Musa v Malta* may signal a softening of the Court's position. The Court referred to Recommendation *Rec (2003) 5* of the Committee of Ministers, which states that measures of detention of asylum seekers should be applied only after a careful examination of their necessity in each individual case. In this regard, the Court noted that it had 'reservations' as to the government's good faith in applying an across-the-board detention policy to asylum seekers. However, this was not the basis for the Court's finding a violation of Article 5(1)(f). Furthermore, the judgment is not yet final, pending a request for referral to the Grand Chamber. Appl. No. 42377/12, Judgment of 23 July 2013, para. 100.
21 UNHCR, *op. cit.*, p. 10.
22 *Ibid.*

by the competent child care authorities. Similarly, the Com. RC has stipulated that:

> [U]naccompanied or separated children should not, as a general rule, be detained. Detention cannot be justified solely on the basis of the child being unaccompanied or separated, or on their migratory or residence status, or lack thereof. [Where detention is exceptionally justified under Article 37(b)] all efforts, including acceleration of relevant processes, should be made to allow for the immediate release of unaccompanied or separated children from detention and their placement in other forms of appropriate accommodation.[23]

The combined influence of Articles 37(b) and 3 CRC has begun to make itself felt in the approach of the ECtHR to Article 5(1)(f) ECHR. In the groundbreaking case of *Rahimi v Greece*, which involved the detention prior to expulsion of a fifteen-year-old unaccompanied Afghan boy, the Court reiterated its established position that detention does not have to be reasonably considered necessary in the circumstances of the case, but then went on to reprimand the Greek authorities for automatically applying the law on detention to the boy without taking into consideration his particular situation as an unaccompanied minor.[24] The Court noted the requirements of Articles 3 and 37 CRC and the fact that the best interests principle is reiterated in the RCD, which the impugned domestic law transposed. The Court further noted that it had already recognised in its Article 8 jurisprudence that there is a wide consensus that in all decisions concerning children the best interests of the child must be a primary consideration. Consequently, it held:

> Or, en l'occurrence, en ordonnant la mise en détention du requérant les autorités nationales ne se sont aucunement penchées sur la question de son intérêt superieur en tant que mineur. De plus, elles n'ont pas recherché si le placement du requérent dans le centre de détention [...] était

---

23 Com. RC, General Comment No. 6, 'Treatment of unaccompanied and separated children outside their country of origin', *UN Doc CRC/GC/2005/6*, p. 18. The immigration detention of minors has been a consistent theme of the Com. RC in its concluding observations to States Parties that are EU Member States. See Com. RC, Concluding Observations to Greece in 2002, *UN Doc. CRC/C/15/Add.170*, paras. 68 and 69; to the United Kingdom in 2002, *UN Doc. CRC/C/15/Add.188*, para. 50; to the Czech Republic in 2003, *UN Doc. CRC/C/15/Add.201*, para. 56; to Italy in 2003, *UN Doc. CRC/C/15/Add.198*, para. 45; to Romania in 2003, *UN Doc. CRC/C/15/Add.199*, para. 55; to the Netherlands in 2004, *UN Doc. CRC/C/15/Add.227*, para. 54; to Latvia in 2006, *UN Doc. CRC/C/LVA/CO/2*, para. 53; to Lithuania in 2006, *UN Doc. CRC/C/LTU/CO/2*, § 8; to the United Kingdom in 2008, *UN Doc. CRC/C/GBR/CO/4*, para. 71; to Spain in 2010, *UN Doc. CRC/C/ESP/CO/3-4*, para. 59; and to Belgium in 2010, *UN Doc. CRC/C/BEL/CO/3-4*, paras. 76 and 77.
24 ECtHR, *Rahimi v Greece*, Appl. No. 8687/08, Judgment of 5 April 2011.

une mesure de dernier ressort et si elles pouvaient lui substituer une autre mesure moins radicale afin de garantir son expulsion. Ces éléments suscitent des doutes aux yeux de la Cour, quant à la bonne foi des autorités lors de la mise en oeuvre de la mesure de détention.[25]

In finding a violation of Article 5(1)(f), the Court effectively established an exception for unaccompanied minors to its established position that no proportionality test is required by sub-paragraph (f).[26] In the subsequent case of *Popov v France*, the Court extended the exception for unaccompanied minors to minors who are accompanied by their parents.[27] These developments bring the approach of the ECtHR on the permissibility of detaining minors into line with the approach of the CRC.[28]

In sum, the international legal position is now that mandatory immigration detention of children is not permitted. Detention of minors can only follow an individualised assessment, including a best-interests assessment, and must comply with the principle of last resort. Hence liberty is the rule, with detention as the (exceptional) exception.

Conditions of detention

International human rights law establishes strict requirements regarding conditions of detention, which have been expanded on in various soft-law documents.[29] Thus, explicit criteria relating to conditions of detention are established in Article 10 ICCPR,[30] and while no equivalent criteria are

---

25 *Ibid.*, para. 109.
26 This new position of the Court was already signalled in *Mayeka Mitunga v Belgium*, a case which involved the detention of a five-year-old unaccompanied minor. The Court stated that 'in the absence of any risk of the second applicant's seeking to evade the supervision of the Belgian authorities, her detention in a closed centre for adults was unnecessary. Other measures could have been taken that would have been more conducive to the higher interest of the child guaranteed by Article 3 of the Convention on the Rights of the Child. These included her placement in a specialized center or with foster parents'. Appl. No. 13178/03, Judgment of 12 October 2006 at para. 83. The Court confirmed the *Rahimi* exception in *Housein v Greece*, Appl. No.71825/11, Judgment of 24 October 2013.
27 ECtHR, *Popov v France*, Appl. Nos. 39472/07 and 39474/07, Judgment of 19 January 2012. See, in particular, paras. 119 and 120.
28 For critical commentary on this development, see M. Bossuyt, 'The Court of Strasbourg acting as an asylum court', *European Constitutional Law Review* 8, 2012, 203–245.
29 See, for example: 'UN Standard Minimum Rules on the Treatment of Prisoners', adopted in 1955, approved by the Economic and Social Council in Resolution *663 C (XXIV)* of 31 July 1957, and Resolution *2076 (LXII)* of 13 May 1977; 'Body of Principles for the Protection of All Persons Under Any Form of Detention or Imprisonment', *GA Res. 43/173*, 9 December 1988; 'United Nations Rules for the Protection of Juveniles Deprived of their Liberty', *GA Res. 45/113* of 14 December 1990.
30 Article 10 ICCPR comprises three paragraphs, of which only the first relates to detention generally, as opposed to detention in the criminal justice context. Article 10(1) provides:

specified in Article 5 ECHR, the ECtHR deals with the issue as part of the requirement of lawfulness in Article 5(1)(f).[31] Very poor conditions of detention may also constitute inhuman or degrading treatment contrary to Article 3 ECHR.[32] These basic criteria establish that persons deprived of their liberty should be treated with humanity and with respect for their dignity. This is also the point of departure of Article 37(c) CRC, but with the additional requirements that treatment in detention must take into account: a) the needs of persons of his/her age; b) that every child deprived of liberty must be detained separate from adults unless this is contrary to the child's best interests; and c) that the child has the right to maintain contact with his/her family through correspondence and visits 'save in exceptional circumstances'.

Taking first the requirement that every child deprived of liberty must be treated in accordance with the needs of persons of his/her age, Sax, in his commentary on Article 37 CRC, considers that this 'conveys the message that children should not be regarded as one homogenous group but instead that the conditions and the treatment of the young persons have to be constantly monitored and flexibly adapted due to their personal developments'.[33] Thus, for example, conditions of detention that are adequate for older teenagers may not be suitable for younger children. Moreover, age cannot be the only determining criterion in this regard, since the general principle of the best interests of the child must a primary consideration. The individualised assessment of best interests allows factors such as degree of maturity, stage of development and personal circumstances to be taken into account in determining whether the conditions of detention are appropriate. It follows that, at a minimum, the conditions of detention of young children cannot be the same as conditions of detention of adults.

A trilogy of ECHR cases involving Belgium speak clearly to this last requirement. In *Mayeka Mitunga v Belgium*, ECtHR held that the detention of a five-year-old unaccompanied minor for nearly two months in a closed centre for adults constituted inhuman or degrading treatment contrary to Article 3 ECHR and a violation of the requirement under Article 5(1)(f) that the detention be lawful.[34] In arriving at its decision the Court took note of the

---

'All persons deprived of their liberty shall be treated with humanity and with respect for the inherent dignity of the human person.'

31 For example, the Court stated in *Mayeka Mitunga v Belgium* that 'the fact that the second applicant's detention came within paragraph (f) of Article 5§1 does not necessarily mean that it was lawful within the meaning of this provision, as the Court's case-law requires that there must be some relationship between the ground of permitted deprivation of liberty relied on and the place and conditions of detention'. *Op. cit.*, para. 102.

32 *Ibid.*

33 W. Schabas and H. Sax, *A Commentary on the United Nations Convention on the Rights of the Child, Article 37, Prohibition of Torture, Death Penalty, Life Imprisonment and Deprivation of Liberty*, Leiden/Boston: Martinus Nijhoff Publishers, 2006, 89.

34 *Op. cit.*

applicant's extreme vulnerability and in particular of the fact that she was detained in a centre that had initially been designed for adults, that no one was assigned to look after her even though she was unaccompanied by her parents, and that no measures were taken to ensure that she received proper counselling and educational assistance from qualified personnel specially mandated for that purpose.

The Court applied the same reasoning and reached the same conclusions in *Muskhadzhiyeva v Belgium*, a case concerning the detention for one month of four children all under the age of six, at least two of whom were shown to be suffering from post-traumatic stress disorder, in the same detention centre as in the *Mitunga* case but accompanied by their mother.[35] The Court declined to attach any significance to the fact that they were accompanied, holding, 'cet élément ne suffit pas à exempter les autorités de leur obligation de protéger les enfants et d'adopter des mesures adéquates au titre des obligations positives découlant de l'article 3 de la Convention'.[36]

The Court confirmed its decision in *Muskhadzhiyeva* and extended its scope in *Kanagaratnam and Others v Belgium*, a case in which three children were detained with their mother in the same detention centre as in the previous two cases.[37] The Court was not persuaded by the government's argument that the children were older than those in the *Muskhadzhiyeva* case and that no evidence had been submitted regarding their psychological state. In view of the principle of the best interests of the child in Article 3 CRC, the Court held that the State should have operated on the assumption that the children were vulnerable *qua* children and because of their personal history as asylum seekers. The Court also noted the comparatively long period of detention – four months. By contrast, in *Rahimi*, the Court held that the detention of a fifteen-year-old unaccompanied minor in an overcrowded detention centre for adults, with 'deplorable' hygiene standards, no contact with the outside world and no possibility of fresh air or leisure, even though the detention was only for two days, constituted a violation of Article 5(1)(f) and Article 3 ECHR.[38]

Another way of stating the requirement in Article 37(c) that every child deprived of liberty must be treated in accordance with the *needs* of persons of his/her age, is that every child detainee must be treated in accordance with his/her *rights* as established in the CRC, since a reliable indication of the needs of the child are his/her rights. Thus, the detained child is entitled to all the Convention rights, with the exception of those few that are incompatible with detention itself, such as the right to liberty, freedom of movement or freedom of association and assembly. In this regard, the majority of rights in the CRC

---

35 ECtHR, *Muskhadzhiyeva v Belgium*, Appl. No. 41442/07, Judgment of 19 January 2010.
36 *Ibid.*, para. 58.
37 ECtHR, *Kanagaratnam and Others v Belgium*, Appl. No. 15297/09, Judgment of 13 December 2011.
38 ECtHR, *Rahimi v Greece*, *op. cit.* See further, ECtHR, *Popov v France*, *op. cit.*

apply regardless of whether the child is in detention or at liberty. Consider, for example, the right of the child deprived of his/her family environment to special protection and assistance, including alternative care; the right of the child seeking or enjoying refugee status to *appropriate* protection and humanitarian assistance; the right of the child to family unity; the right of the child to education; the right of the child to health care; the right of the child to rest, leisure, play and recreation; and the right of the child who has been victim of any sort of violence or abuse to recovery and reintegration. Such rights are not placed in abeyance because the child is in detention.

Indeed, many of the 'protection' rights in the Convention are of particularly urgent application in the context of detention, such as the right of the child in Article 19 CRC to protection from all forms of physical or mental violence, injury or abuse, neglect or negligent treatment, maltreatment or exploitation, including sexual abuse. Various soft-law instruments establish how, precisely, effect should be given to these rights in situations of detention.[39] But the most important point to establish here is that detained children are entitled to these rights on an equal basis to non-detained children. Any denial of these rights to a child who is in detention is likely to offend against the non-discrimination provision in Article 2(1) CRC, a general principle of the Convention which provides, 'States Parties shall respect and ensure the rights set forth in the present Convention to each child within their jurisdiction without discrimination of any kind, irrespective of the child's or his or her parent's or legal guardian's [...] status'. The status of relevance here is the child's detention status.

Next, there is the requirement that every child deprived of liberty be separated from adults, 'unless it is considered in the child's best interests not to do so'. Sax, referring to the 1957 UN Standard Minimum Rules for the Treatment of Prisoners, notes that the norm that children should be kept separately from adults ranks among the oldest of UN standards in the field of criminal justice.[40] Indeed, two similar provisions relating to accused and convicted juvenile offenders are contained in Article 10(2) and (3) ICCPR, respectively.[41] The purpose in the criminal justice context is two-fold: to prevent criminal contagion and to protect the minor from exploitation and abuse by adults. While the latter consideration applies equally to immigration detention, the former is an additional argument for not detaining asylum-seeking children in prison accommodation. Notably, the only exception to the rule requiring

---

39 The most comprehensive soft-law instrument in this regard is the 'UN Rules for the Protection of Juveniles Deprived of their Liberty', *op. cit.*
40 W. Schabas and H. Sax, *op. cit.*
41 Article 10(2)(b) ICCPR reads: 'Accused juvenile persons shall be separated from adults and brought as speedily as possible for adjudication.' Article 10(3) ICCPR provides, *inter alia*: 'Juvenile offenders shall be segregated from adults and be accorded treatment appropriate to their age and legal status.'

segregation of children and adults in detention is where such segregation is not in the best interests of the child. Accordingly, any failure to separate child detainees from adults due to other considerations, such as a lack of space or resources, will offend against Article 37(c).

A related point, but one that does not receive specific mention in the context of Article 37, is the question of detention of accompanied children and their right not to be separated from their parents against their will, as established in Article 9(1) CRC.[42] As was discussed in Chapter 5 above, Article 9(1) establishes the best-interests principle as the paramount – indeed, the only – consideration in separating a child from his/her parents. Moreover, in determining the best interests of the child, only considerations personal to the child and his or her relationship with the parents are determinative; extraneous considerations relating to the interests of the State or the rights of the others are immaterial. It follows that children who are accompanied by their parents and who are placed in detention must be detained together with their parents in all but the most exceptional circumstances. However, this is not to suggest that detention of children for the purposes of family unity with their parents dispenses with the need for a rigorous assessment of the justification of the detention of the minor under Article 37(b). In fact, if the detention of the child cannot be justified under Article 37(b), then Article 9(1) poses a compelling argument for the release of the whole family.[43]

This contention is supported by a recent judgment of the ECtHR. In *Popov v France,* a six-month-old baby and three-year-old infant were detained with their parents in the 'family zone' of a detention centre for fifteen days prior to expulsion.[44] The family zone amounted to a wing reserved for families and single women, which nevertheless had barred and barbed-wire windows, no facilities for leisure or education, no access to the open air, no children's furniture and few toys. Furthermore, announcements were made over a tannoy, the general atmosphere was described as anguished and stressed, and the behaviour of the inmates was characterised by promiscuity and tension. Unsurprisingly,

---

42 Article 9(1) CRC reads: 'States Parties shall ensure that a child shall not be separated from his or her parents against their will, except when competent authorities subject to judicial review determine, in accordance with applicable law and procedures, that such separation is necessary for the best interests of the child. Such determination may be necessary in a particular case such as one involving abuse or neglect of the child by the parents, or one where the parents are living separately and a decision must be made as to the child's place of residence.'

43 Thus, in its Concluding Observations to Belgium in 2010, the Com. RC expressed 'concern that in spite of a decision by the Minister of Migration Policy and Asylum that families with children would no longer be detained in closed centers as of 1 October 2008, some children and their parents are still being detained in precarious conditions in facilities unsuitable for children'. The Com. RC urged 'the State party to put an end to the detention of children in closed centers [and] to create alternatives to detention for asylum seeking families'. *UN Doc. CRC/C/BEL/CO/3-4,* paras. 76 and 77.

44 ECtHR, *Popov v France, op. cit.*

the court found that the conditions of detention were contrary to Articles 3 and 5(1)(f) ECHR in the case of the children. However, in an unprecedented move, the Court went on to find a violation of Article 8 ECHR in the case of the whole family, holding that:

> [E]lle est d'avis que l'intérêt supérieur de l'enfant ne peut se limiter à maintenir l'unité familiale mais que les autorités doivent mettre en oeuvre tous les moyens nécessaires afin de limiter autant que faire se peut la détention de familles accompagnées d'enfants et préserver effectivement le droit à une vie familiale.[45]

In particular, the State failed to explore thoroughly whether alternatives to detention for the family, who were not a flight risk, were possible.

As to the final provision of Article 37(c), namely, the right of the child to maintain contact with his/her family through correspondence and visits, save in exceptional circumstances, the Com. RC has elaborated on this obligation in the context of unaccompanied minors, providing that detention 'facilities should not be located in isolated areas where culturally appropriate community resources and access to legal aid are unavailable. Children should have the opportunity to make regular contact and receive visits from friends, relatives, religious, social and legal counsel and their guardian'.[46]

To sum up, Article 37(b) CRC relating to conditions of detention requires that the child detainee must be treated in accordance with the needs/rights of persons of his/her age, must be separated from adults unless this is contrary to the child's best interests, must be kept together with his/her family if the family is detained and must be allowed to communicate with relatives if the child is separated or unaccompanied.

Procedural protection

Article 37(d) establishes the right of the child who is detained to prompt access to legal and other appropriate assistance, and the right to challenge the legality of the detention and to a prompt decision on any such action. The right to mount a legal challenge to detention is also established under Article 9(4)

---

45 *Ibid.*, para. 147. *Popov* signals a development on *Muskhadzhiyeva*, previously discussed, in which the Court found no violation of Article 8 ECHR on the basis that the mother and the children had been detained together. However, the Court did find a violation of Articles 3 and 5(1)(f) in respect of the conditions in which the children were detained. Therefore, *Muskhadzhiyeva* already hints that release of the entire family is the only way to avoid both a violation of Article 8 and Articles 3 and 5(1)(f) ECHR. For commentary, see 'Case Comment, *Muskhadzhiyeva v Belgium* (Application No. 41442/07): Detention of asylum seekers – accompanied minors', *European Human Rights Law Review* 3, 2010, 338–342.

46 Com. RC, General Comment No. 6, *op. cit.*, p. 19.

ICCPR[47] and Article 5(4) ECHR,[48] and both the Human Rights Committee and the ECtHR have developed a sophisticated jurisprudence on safeguards relating to judicial review of detention. These include the requirement that the review be: clearly prescribed by law, by an independent and impartial judicial body, of sufficient scope and possessed of sufficient powers to be effective, consistent with standards of due process and prompt.[49] These requirements also follow from Article 37(d) CRC. However, what is unique about Article 37(d) is the explicit reference to the right to legal and other appropriate assistance. While the ECtHR has found that access to legal advice may, depending on the facts of the case, be necessary in order that the detention meet the requirement of legality,[50] Article 37(d) establishes that access to legal and other appropriate assistance is a requirement in each case. In the context of unaccompanied minors, the Comm. RC has interpreted the reference to legal *and* other appropriate assistance in Article 37(d) as mandating the assignment of a legal representative as well as a guardian or adviser tasked with ensuring the child's best interests.[51]

Finally, one omission from Article 37(d) should be noted. Whereas Article 9 ICCPR and Article 5(2) ECHR provide that anyone who is arrested must be informed promptly of the reasons for the arrest, Article 37 is silent on the issue. However, such an obligation is implicit in the right to challenge the legality of the detention in Article 37(d) and in Article 12(1) CRC, a general principle of the Convention, which provides that the child has the right to express views freely in all matters affecting the child. This latter right presupposes that the child has access to information about his/her situation. Interestingly, the ECtHR has held that the right to be informed must not only be in a language that the person understands – an explicit requirement of Article 5(2) ECHR – but must also be in a form that takes account of his/her level of education.[52] Implicitly, this establishes a requirement that information be provided to detained minors in an age-appropriate manner.

---

47 'Anyone who is deprived of liberty by arrest or detention shall be entitled to take proceedings before a court, in order that the court may decide without delay on the lawfulness of his detention and order his release if the detention is not lawful.'
48 'Everyone who is deprived of his liberty by arrest or detention shall be entitled to take proceedings by which the lawfulness of his detention shall be decided speedily by a court and his release ordered if the detention is not lawful.'
49 For an outline of the case-law of the ECtHR establishing these requirements, see EU Fundamental Rights Agency, *Handbook on European law relating to asylum, borders and immigration*, 2013, Chapter 6.
50 For example, ECtHR, *Öcalan v Turkey*, Appl. No. 46221/99, Judgment (GC) of 12 May 2005, para. 70.
51 Committee RC, General Comment No. 6, *op. cit.*, para. 36.
52 ECtHR, *Nasrulloyev v Russia*, Appl. No. 656/06, Judgment of 11 October 2007, para. 77. Strangely, in *Rahimi v Greece*, while the Court reprimanded the Greek authorities for providing written information in Arabic to a fifteen-year-old Afghan unaccompanied minor who spoke only Farsi, the Court omitted to address the fact that the boy was illiterate and,

In brief, in addition to the usual procedural guarantees to which a detained person is entitled under general human rights law, detained children are entitled to legal assistance and the assistance of a guardian or adviser. Furthermore, the child detainee must be informed of the reasons for his/her detention in a manner appropriate to his/her age.

Phase One CEAS: Compliance with the right of the child to liberty

Just two of the Phase One CEAS instruments contain provisions relating to detention: the RCD and the APD. While both directives were subject to a Commission impact evaluation, only the provisions of the RCD relating to detention were reported on;[53] unhelpfully, the provisions of the APD relating to detention did not feature in the evaluation of that directive.[54]

Permissible detention

In terms of when detention of asylum seekers is permissible, Article 7 of the RCD (Residence and freedom of movement) provides in paragraph 3 that, '[w]hen it proves necessary, for example for legal reasons or reasons of public order, Member States may confine an applicant to a particular place in accordance with their national law'. Although the title of the article and the wording of paragraph 3 give the impression that (mere) restrictions on freedom of movement are envisaged, later provisions, which are dealt with below, relate more explicitly to detention. This suggests that Article 7 is actually an oblique reference to detention. Article 18 of the APD (Detention) provides in paragraph 1 that, 'Member States shall not hold a person in detention for the sole reason that he/she is an applicant for asylum'. A *contrario*, Article 18 implicitly establishes that detention is permissible if there is any other reason for it.

Neither directive contains a provision exempting minors or unaccompanied minors from detention, with the resulting inference that both minors and unaccompanied minors are fully susceptible to detention. This interpretation is reinforced by Article 35 of the APD, which relates to border procedures. Article 35(3), which relates to a border-entry procedure that Member States may maintain on the basis of a stand-still clause, provides in sub-paragraph (f) for the right of an unaccompanied minor who is being dealt with in such a

---

consequently, would not have understood the written information even if it had been in his own language. *Op. cit.*, paras. 8 and 120.
53 Commission evaluation of the RCD, *op. cit.*
54 'Report from the Commission to the European Parliament and the Council on the Application of Directive 2005/85/EC of 1 December 2005 on Minimum Standards on Procedures in Member States for Granting and Withdrawing Refugee Status', *COM (2010) 465 final*. Hereinafter, 'Commission evaluation of the APD'.

procedure to a representative. This provision implicitly establishes that unaccompanied minors are subject to such a procedure. At a minimum, border-entry procedures involve restrictions on freedom of movement. However, as the case-law of the ECtHR makes clear, the dividing line between restrictions on freedom of movement and detention is a question of fact, depending on such issues as the length of the deprivation of liberty and the conditions in which the person is confined.[55] In this regard, Article 35(4) envisages a time-limit of four weeks. Such a length clearly corresponds to detention.[56] The applicability of border-entry procedures to unaccompanied minors confirms that the latter are indeed susceptible to detention. Are these provisions compatible with the requirements of Article 37(b) CRC? Recall that Article 37(b) encompasses a requirement of lawfulness and non-arbitrariness.

On the requirement of lawfulness, it is doubtful that the provisions of Article 7(3) of the RCD or Article 18(1) of the APD, taken alone or together, meet the requirement of lawfulness. Article 7(3) of the RCD, which permits detention if it 'proves necessary […] for legal reasons or reasons of public order', is entirely circular: detention is legal if there is a legal reason for it. It tells us nothing about the type of legal reasons or reasons of public order that might give rise to a need for detention in the asylum context. Moreover, the euphemistic clause permitting Member States to 'confine an applicant to a particular place' falls foul of the judgment of the ECtHR in *Abdolkhani and Karimnia v Turkey*.[57] As for Article 18(1) APD, which prohibits detention on the sole ground of being an asylum seeker, it can be observed that this article tacitly sanctions the detention of asylum seekers for any other immigration-related or, indeed, non immigration-related reason. A typical example of an immigration-related reason for detention is: entering or attempting to enter the State irregularly or without the proper documentation. Therefore, the minimum standards established in the directives do not appear to conform to the requirement that the law on detention be 'accessible, precise and foreseeable'. Indeed, the ECtHR found as much in *Lokpo and Touré v Hungary*, in which the State sought to justify a vague detention provision of national law on the basis that it was enacted to ensure compliance with Article 18 of the APD. The Court accepted that the 'reasons underlying the applicants' detention may well be those referred to by the Government, that is, to comply with European Union standards', but nevertheless went on to find the deprivation of liberty unlawful.[58]

---

55 ECtHR, *Abdolkhani and Karimnia v Turkey*, op. cit.
56 In the *Saadi* case, it was not disputed that the applicant, who had been held in a closed 'reception centre' for seven days to facilitate a fast-track asylum process, had been deprived of his liberty. ECtHR, *Saadi v UK*, op. cit.
57 *Op. cit.*
58 *Op. cit.*, para. 24. See further *Said and Said v Hungary* and *Abdelhakim v Hungary*, op. cit.

On the requirement of non-arbitrariness, the key issue is whether the provisions mandate an individualised assessment of the need for detention. In this regard, it is interesting to note that, in its evaluation of the RCD, the Commission states that, '[g]iven that according to the Directive detention is an exception to the general rule of free movement, which might be used only when "it proves necessary", automatic detention without any evaluation of the situation of the person in question is contrary to the Directive'.[59] It is submitted that this is a rather reaching interpretation by the Commission of the wording of Article 7(3) RCD, since it is open to Member States to define the legal reasons or reasons of public order for detention at a broad level of generality. Unsurprisingly, the Commission evaluation reports that:

> Detention is foreseen by all Member States on numerous grounds (from exceptional circumstances – Germany – to the general practice of detention of all asylum seekers illegally entering the Member State except for those with special needs – Malta). Similarly, the length of detention varies from 7 days (PT) to 12 months (MT, HU) or even an undefined period (UK, FI).[60]

As for the APD, the Article 18(1) prohibition of detention on the sole ground of being an applicant for asylum does not infer an individualised assessment, since detention could conceivably apply, for example, to all asylum applicants who enter or attempt to enter the State irregularly or without the proper documentation, as indicated above.

Finally, neither Article 7(3) RCD nor Article 18(1) APD states that detention of minors is a measure of last resort and for the shortest appropriate period of time. However, in its evaluation of the RCD, the Commission seems to consider that various *other* provisions of the directive establish this requirement, such as the best-interests requirement, the classification of minors as vulnerable persons or the right of the unaccompanied minor to alternative care.[61] Again, however, it is submitted that it is expecting rather too much of Member States to join the dots in this way, in the absence of an explicit statement of the principle of last resort. In this regard, it comes as no surprise that the Commission found in its evaluation of the RCD that 'most of [the Member States] authorize the detention of minors and many of them even authorize the detention of unaccompanied minors'.[62]

In conclusion, the provisions of the RCD and APD relating to detention do not conform to standards established in Article 37(b) CRC regarding when the detention of minors is permissible.

---

59 Commission evaluation of the RCD, *op. cit.*, § 3.4.1, p. 7.
60 *Ibid.*
61 *Ibid*, § 3.5.2, p. 10.
62 *Ibid.*, § 3.5.2, p. 9.

Conditions of detention

The APD is silent on conditions of detention. However, Article 13(2) RCD is relevant to the issue of conditions of detention, providing:

> Member States shall make provision on material reception conditions to ensure a standard of living adequate for the health of applicants and capable of ensuring their subsistence. Member States shall ensure that that standard of living is met in the specific situation of persons who have special needs [...] as well as in relation to the situation of persons who are in detention.

Futhermore, Article 14 RCD, which relates to modalities for material reception conditions (i.e. accommodation and associated rights), contains a number of potentially useful provisions. Paragraph 2 provides that where applicants are provided with housing-in-kind, they must be assured protection of their family life and the possibility of communicating with relatives, legal advisers, representatives of UNHCR and recognised NGOs. It further establishes that 'Member States shall pay particular attention to the prevention of assault within the premises and accommodation centres'. Paragraph 3 obliges Member States, 'if appropriate', to lodge minor children with their parents or responsible adult family members. However, Member States are permitted to derogate temporarily from their obligations under Article 14 when the asylum seeker is in detention or confined to border posts.[63]

Are these provisions consistent with Article 37(c) CRC, which mandates that: 1) detained minors be treated in a manner that takes account of the needs (and implicitly rights) of persons of their age; 2) that they be separated from adults unless this is contrary to their best interests; 3) that accompanied children should not be separated from their parents while in detention; and 4) that unaccompanied children should have contact with their relatives?

The absence of any specific guarantees relating to the detention of minors, coupled with the express permission to derogate from the obligation to prevent assault and from such rights as family unity and the right to communicate with relatives etc., strongly indicates that the requirements of Article 37(c) are not met. In this context, the broad *proviso* in Article 13(2) of the RCD – that Member States must ensure that the minimum standard of living established in the directive is met in detention – is of limited benefit, since it relates only to health and subsistence and fails to encompass the myriad other rights of the child that are implicated by detention, such as the right to education or the right of the child to protection from all forms of ill treatment or violence. In any event, the minimum standard of living alluded to in Article 13(2) falls well short of the minimum standard of living to which the

---

63 Article 14(8).

child is entitled – regardless of whether he is at liberty or in detention. Thus, as outlined in Chapter 6 above, Article 27 CRC entitles the child to a standard of living adequate for his/her *physical, mental, spiritual, moral and social development*.

It is hardly surprising that 'serious problems' were reported by the Commission in its evaluation of the RCD in terms of the applicability of the directive in all premises hosting asylum seekers. It found that as many as seven Member States do not apply the directive in detention centres, while other Member States do not apply it in transit zones. Since, as the Commission rightly noted, the level of reception conditions in detention inevitably drops, 'it is hard to imagine how the special needs of vulnerable persons (especially minors) might be met' in detention.[64] More specifically, the Commission found that only a few Member States recognise the right of detained asylum-seeking children to education in their transposing legislation, and that many Member States deny detained minors access to education or make it impossible or very limited in practice.[65]

In sum, therefore, the few provisions of the RCD that relate to conditions of detention do not conform to the requirements of Article 37(c) CRC.

Procedural protection

Article 7(3) of the RCD, which tacitly sanctions detention, contains no provision for procedural protection. However, Article 21 on appeals is of utmost relevance in this regard, providing:

1   Member States shall ensure that [...] decisions taken under Article 7 which individually affect asylum seekers may be the subject of an appeal within the procedures laid down in the national law. At least in the last instance the possibility of an appeal or review before a judicial body shall be granted.
2   Procedures for access to legal assistance in such cases shall be laid down in national law.

Paragraph 1 establishes that detention decisions must be amenable to some sort of appeal but does not establish any requirements regarding the appeal body (except at last instance), the scope of the appeal, due process guarantees or time-frame. While Paragraph 2 appears to mandate the provision of some sort of legal assistance to detainees, this is tempered by the fact that restrictions may be placed on access to places of detention by legal representatives. Thus, as previously noted, the right in Article 14(2) of applicants who are provided with housing-in-kind to communicate with legal advisers, and the obligation in Article 14(7) to grant legal advisors access to accommodation centres and

---

64   Commission evaluation of the RCD, *op cit.*, § 3.5.2, p. 9.
65   *Ibid*, § 3.4.4, p. 8.

housing facilities, can be derogated from under Article 14(8) when the asylum seeker is in detention or confined to border posts.

As for the APD, Article 18(2) provides that '[w]here an applicant for asylum is held in detention, Member States shall ensure that there is a possibility of speedy judicial review'. Thus, the appeal body (a court) and timeframe (speedy) are specified. However, no standards are established regarding the scope of the judicial review or due-process guarantees. Although Article 18 is silent on the right to legal assistance for the purpose of challenging the legality of detention, other articles of the directive may be of relevance. Notably, Article 10(1) establishes a right to information, to the services of an interpreter and to communication with UNHCR, while Articles 15 and 16 establish a right to legal assistance and representation. Moreover, Article 16(2) guarantees that 'the legal adviser or other counsellor who assists or represents an applicant for asylum has access to closed areas, such as detention facilities and transit zones, for the purpose of consulting the applicant'. However, when interpreted in their context, these rights appear to be guaranteed only with respect to the asylum application.

It can be observed that the interplay of the provisions of the RCD and the APD on detention leads to rather a bizarre outcome. Under the RCD, a detainee has some sort of right to legal assistance in order to challenge the detention, but no guarantee that the legal adviser will be granted access to the place of detention; while under the APD, the legal adviser must be granted access to the place of detention but the detainee has no express right to legal assistance for the purposes of challenging the detention. This inconsistency does not sit well with the right of the child under Article 37(d) to legal assistance. Moreover, while both directives provide for the appointment of a representative to the unaccompanied minor, neither directive has anything to say about the role of the representative when the unaccompanied minor is in detention.[66]

Therefore, it can be concluded that both directives only partially conform to the requirements of Article 37(d) CRC. Regrettably, the issue of procedural protection while in detention is not addressed in the Commission's evaluation of either directive.

Phase Two CEAS: Prospects for enhanced compliance

The recast RCD contains four entirely new and detailed articles relating to the detention of applicants for international protection, covering grounds of detention (Article 8), guarantees for detained persons (Article 9), conditions

---

66 Article 19(1) RCD and Article 17(1) APD. Article 19(1) RCD is silent on the role of the representative, but Article 17(1) APD provides that the role of the representative is to 'represent and/or assist the unaccompanied minor with respect to the examination of the application', which suggests that the representative has no role regarding the detention of the minor.

of detention (Article 10) and detention of vulnerable persons and persons with special needs (Article 11). These provisions are cross-referenced in the recast APD[67] and are either substantially mirrored or cross-referenced in the recast DR, which provides for the first time for the detention of applicants who are subject to a Dublin transfer and who are considered to be at risk of absconding.[68] Since the recast RCD is the lead instrument on detention, the analysis below is of its provisions.

Permissible detention

Article 8 of the recast RCD provides that detention of applicants for international protection must be provided for by law and outlines six broad but exhaustive grounds on which such detention may be permitted under national law.[69] It states that detention must only be resorted to when it proves necessary on an individual basis, and if alternatives to detention, which must be laid down in national law, cannot be applied effectively. Article 9 provides that detention must be for as short a period as possible. Of utmost importance, Article 11 establishes particular rules for the detention of vulnerable persons and persons with special reception needs, such as minors and unaccompanied minors. Article 11(2), which relates to minors, states *inter alia*:

> Minors shall only be detained as a measure of last resort and after it having been established that other less coercive measures cannot be applied effectively. Such detention shall be for the shortest period of time and all efforts shall be made to release the detained minors and place them in accommodation suitable for minors.
> [...]
> The minor's best interests [...] shall be a primary consideration.

---

67 Article 26.
68 Article 27.
69 The grounds in Article 8 are: '(a) in order to determine or verify [the applicant's] identity or nationality; (b) in order to determine those elements on which the application for international protection is based which could not be obtained in the absence of detention, in particular where there is a risk of absconding of the applicant; (c) in order to decide, in the context of a procedure, on the applicant's right to enter the territory; (d) when [the applicant] is detained subject to a return procedure under Directive 2008/115/EC of the European Parliament and of the Council on common standards and procedures in Member States for returning illegally staying third-country nationals in order to prepare the return and/or carry on the removal process, and the Member State can substantiate on the basis of objective criteria, including that he/she already had the opportunity to access the asylum procedure, that there are reasonable grounds to believe that he/she is making the application for international protection merely in order to delay or frustrate the enforcement of the return decision; (e) when protection of national security or public order so requires; (f) in accordance with Article 28 of the [recast DR]'.

Article 11(3), which relates to unaccompanied minors, provides that '[u]naccompanied minors shall be detained only in exceptional circumstances. All efforts shall be made to release the detained unaccompanied minors as soon as possible'.

Article 11(2) relating to the detention of minors is a retrograde step from the text of the amended Commission proposal in 2011, which subjected the decision to detain minors to an individualised best-interests assessment.[70] By contrast, in the recast the reference to best interests is located in a separate sub-paragraph, which has the apparent effect of disengaging the best-interests assessment from the decision to detain. Article 11(3) relating to the detention of unaccompanied minors is a double retrograde step: first, from the text of the amended Commission proposal in 2011, which provided that unaccompanied minors could only be detained in 'particularly exceptional cases', and second, from the text of the original Commission proposal in 2008, which exempted unaccompanied minors from detention altogether.[71] These claw-backs, insisted on by the Council, are to be regretted. Nevertheless, it is submitted that the provisions of the recast conform broadly to the requirements of Article 37(b) CRC as regards lawfulness, the principle of last resort and brevity of detention.

Conditions of detention

Article 10 of the recast RCD lays down minimum standards relating to conditions of detention. It establishes in paragraph 1 that detention should, as a rule, take place in specialised detention facilities, but that, where this is not possible, Member States may resort to prison accommodation. However, Article 11(3) establishes that unaccompanied minors 'shall never be detained in prison accommodation', but rather, 'as far as possible', in institutions provided with personnel and facilities which take account of the needs of persons of their age. In the absence of such institutions or space therein, it is unclear where unaccompanied minors should be accommodated *in lieu* of prison. By contrast, accompanied minors are susceptible to prison detention on the same basis as adults. The failure to exempt all minors in all circumstances from prison detention must be regarded as falling foul of the injunction in Article 37(c) CRC to treat the minor detainee in a manner that takes account of his/her age. In this regard, it is highly questionable whether administrative detention *in prison* is appropriate for anyone under the age of eighteen years.

As regards the rights of the minor detainee, including the right not to be discriminated against in the enjoyment of his/her rights vis a vis non-detained children, there is no express statement of equality of treatment or full applicability of the rights established in the directive generally to situations of

---

70 Amended Proposal for a Directive of the European Parliament and of the Council laying down minimum standards for the reception of asylum seekers (recast), *COM (2011) 320 final*.
71 *Ibid.*; Proposal for a Directive of the European Parliament and of the Council laying down minimum standards for the reception of asylum seekers (recast), *COM (2008) 815 final*.

detention.⁷² However, Article 11(2) does introduce an obligation that detained minors be given the possibility to engage in leisure activities, including play and recreational activities appropriate to their age. This provision, which reflects Article 31 CRC, is an important innovation in the recast.⁷³ Unfortunately, however, it is subject to derogation in Article 11(6), 'in duly justified cases and for a reasonable period that shall be as short as possible', when the asylum seeker is detained at a border post or transit zone other than as part of an accelerated or admissibility procedure. Surprisingly, in view of the finding in the Commission evaluation of the RCD that many Member States deny detained minors access to education or make it impossible or very limited in practice,⁷⁴ no mention is made of the right to education. It is submitted that the partial nature of the commitment to child rights while in detention signals a deviation from the requirements of Article 37(c).

As for the right of detained children to be separated from adults unless contrary to their best interests, and to be kept together with their parents unless contrary to their best interests, Article 11(3) provides that '[w]here unaccompanied minors are detained, Member States shall ensure that they are accommodated separately from adults', while Article 11(4) establishes that detained families must be accommodated separately in conditions guaranteeing them adequate privacy. However, the latter provision is subject to the derogation provision in Article 11(6), previously outlined. In the light of the judgment of the ECtHR in *Popov v France*, it seems highly likely that any derogation from the right to family life while in detention would fall foul of Article 8 ECHR.⁷⁵ In this regard, the recast RCD has already been overtaken by developments in human rights law.

Finally, Articles 10(3) and (4) provide that UNHCR, legal advisors and family members have the right to communicate with and be granted access to detained applicants. This is consistent with the right in Article 37(c) CRC to maintain contact with family members and others.

Overall, the recast RCD contains some improvements in the conditions of detention of minors, but these are piecemeal and often subject to derogation and consequently do not fully reflect the requirements of Article 37(c) CRC.

---

72 On the other hand, Article 3 (Scope) does not exclude places of detention from the material scope of the directive. In *CIMADE and Gisti*, the Court held that 'it follows from Articles 2 and 3 of [the RCD] that the directive provides for only one category of asylum seekers, comprising all third-country nationals or stateless persons who make an application for asylum'. This suggests that persons in detention come fully within the personal scope of the directive. CJEU, Case C-179/11, Judgment of 27 September 2012, para. 40.
73 Article 31 CRC provides in paragraph 1: 'States Parties recognize the right of the child to rest and leisure, to engage in play and recreational activities appropriate to the age of the child and to participate freely in cultural life and in the arts.'
74 *Op. cit.*, § 3.4.4, p. 8.
75 *Op. cit.*

Procedural protection

It will be recalled that, pursuant to Article 37(d) CRC, minors have a right to legal and other appropriate assistance in challenging their detention, while the jurisprudence of the ECtHR establishes a requirement that information relating to the detention and how to challenge it should be in a format appropriate to the particular detainee.

Article 9 of the recast RCD establishes guarantees for detained persons, including rights relating to judicial review of the detention and legal assistance for that purpose. However, a distinction is drawn between judicial review of detention that is ordered by administrative authorities and judicial review of detention that is ordered by judicial authorities. The first type of judicial review must be speedy (Article 9(3)) and attracts a right to legal assistance and representation (Article 9(6)), albeit subject to numerous limitations such as monetary and time restrictions (Article 9(6) *et seq.*). The second type of judicial review is less onerous. It must be 'at reasonable intervals of time' (Article 9(5)) and attracts no right to legal assistance and representation.[76] While one can readily appreciate the intent behind more stringent judicial review of detention ordered by administrative authorities (for example, at the border), it can nevertheless be observed that the lesser form of judicial review does not conform to the requirements of Article 37(d) CRC.

On the issue of a representative for the unaccompanied minor in detention, although the provisions on detention in the recast RCD are silent on the role of the representative in the detention context, a revised definition of the representative in Article 2(j) states that the role of the representative is 'to assist and represent an unaccompanied minor in procedures provided for in this Directive with a view to ensuring the best interests of the child'. Since Article 11(2) establishes that the best interests of the child must be a primary consideration in the detention context, it follows that the representative has an important role to play when the unaccompanied minor is in detention.

Finally, as regards the requirement of age-appropriate information, Article 9(4) stipulates that detained applicants must be immediately informed in writing, in a language they understand or are reasonably supposed to understand, of the reasons for the detention and the procedures laid down in national law for challenging the detention. Although this provision can be criticised for failing to establish that the information should be clear, in a language that the applicant actually does understand and, preferably, in an age-appropriate form, it is nonetheless preferable to the position that holds under the original directive.

---

76 Article 9(4) does provide that detained applicants (in general) must be immediately informed of 'the *possibility* to request free legal assistance and representation' (emphasis added). Furthermore, Article 9(10) establishes that 'Procedures for access to legal assistance and representation shall be laid down in national law'. However, the only *right* to such legal assistance and representation under the directive is in the context of detention ordered by administrative authorities.

In sum, while the general procedural guarantees for applicants in detention in the recast RCD are a clear advance on the current directive, there are no child-specific procedural guarantees with the exception of a more clearly defined role for representatives of unaccompanied minors in detention.

Conclusion

This chapter explored whether the relevant CEAS instruments conform to the right of the child to liberty. The right was delineated along three main lines, all suggested by the wording of Article 37(b)–(d) CRC: permissible detention, conditions of detention and procedural protection. It was found that the relevant Phase One CEAS instruments do not fully conform to *any* of the elements of the right of the child to liberty. Thus, the directives fail to establish any general, much less child-specific, criteria relating to the lawfulness or non-arbitrariness of detention. They contain weak provisions relating to the conditions of detention, which fail to acknowledge that where children are detained they must be detained in conditions appropriate to their age and, indeed, rights. The directives also contain insubstantial procedural guarantees for challenging the legality of detention, which do not appear to conform with the right of the detained child to legal assistance. Phase Two is a clear improvement on Phase One in one area: establishing that the detention of minors is only permitted in exceptional circumstances, subject to the principle of last resort. In the area of conditions of detention, some improvements can be noted, but these neither apply to all minors nor are absolute. The provisions relating to procedural protection are a general improvement on the current situation but fail to contain any child-specific guarantees. Consequently, while some important advances are contained in the Phase Two recasts, these stop short of being fully in conformity with the right of the child to liberty.

Conclusion

This book has attempted to identify the rights of the child in the CRC that are most relevant to the asylum context, to ascribe meaning to those rights in the asylum context and to examine systematically whether the provisions of the CEAS instruments (Phases One and Two) comply with those rights. In so doing, a reasonably clear picture has emerged. Phase One CEAS reflects some rights of the child but not others, and of those it reflects, the level of protection it affords is not necessarily commensurate with the standards of international child-rights law. Put differently, the EU legislator has selected among the rights of the child that are relevant to the asylum context, legislating for some but not others, and of the chosen rights, has selected among the attributes of the rights, legislating for some attributes but not others. The prospects for enhanced compliance with the rights of the child in Phase Two CEAS are good. Notable improvements are made to the provisions of the recasts that impact, directly or indirectly, on all the rights of the child under scrutiny. However, there is a difference between *enhanced* compliance, which is a relative question, and *full* compliance, which is an absolute question. Despite all the changes in Phase Two CEAS, some of which are quite far-reaching, there is still not a single right of the child that is fully and accurately reflected in every instrument in which it arises.

It is apt, therefore, to conclude this book by commenting on possible factors which inhibit full compliance with the rights of the child. Two possible causes are discussed: the fact that the child-rights agenda is overwhelmed by the larger migration-control agenda that drives the CEAS; and the fact that the EU legislator may lack the child-rights capacity necessary to integrate a child-rights perspective into the CEAS effectively. Nevertheless, this chapter ends on a positive note, drawing attention to the potential of the best-interests principle, cited in all the CEAS instruments in both phases, to correct any apparent discrepancies between the CEAS and the rights of the child.

The policy decision by the EU legislator to integrate the rights of the child into the CEAS has not occurred in a vacuum. Rather, it is a sub-policy within the broader policy agenda that has driven the creation and development of the CEAS. That broader policy agenda is complex, and justice cannot be done here to its many facets. It is, however, well established that the broader policy agenda has a significant deterrent component, whereby the aim is to harmonise policy to a standard that is just high enough to comply with the requirements of general human rights law, but still low enough to make the asylum process unpleasant and unfruitful, to encourage asylum seekers to seek protection in the region of origin, to discourage secondary movements of refugees from those regions and to detect and punish 'abuse' of the asylum system.[1] When the child-rights policy agenda is situated in this broader policy context, it is easy to see how the former becomes compromised. In this book, the compromise is seen in two key ways.

First, it is seen in the act of giving to the child asylum seeker/refugee with one hand and taking from asylum seekers/refugees generally with the other, such that the latter action cancels out the former. The recast APD is probably the starkest illustration of this. On the one hand, the recast reiterates the guarantee that the personal interview of the unaccompanied minor (where one takes place) must be conducted by a person with the necessary knowledge of the special needs of minors, and that the decision by the determining authority must be prepared by a similarly knowledgeable official. Furthermore, the recast adds to these guarantees by establishing higher, and in some cases child-specific, standards in relation to staff competence and training, the examination of the applications and the personal interview. On the other hand, the recast retains or introduces possibilities to derogate, directly or indirectly, from these standards in a host of circumstances. The derogations are sweeping – not directed at minors *per se*, but taking in minors nonetheless. The net result is that there is no necessary improvement to the situation of minors.

Second, the compromise is seen in an ambivalent attitude towards the child, whereby the legislation variously constructs an image of the child as needy and vulnerable, and prioritises the child's status as a child over and above his/her migration status; and an image of the child as being just an adult in miniature, possibly even an adult in fact, and prioritises the child's migration status over and above his/her status as a child. The first image is apparent in the many additional guarantees in the CEAS relating to the care of unaccompanied minors, and the increasing tendency to designate minors as 'persons with special needs', alongside persons with a disability and persons who have been subjected to psychological, physical or sexual violence. It is apparent in the references to the 'special needs' of unaccompanied minors, and

---

1 For a cross-section of the considerable scholarly literature on this subject, see: C. Costello, 'The Asylum Procedures Directive and the proliferation of safe country practices: Deterrence, deflection and the dismantling of international protection?', *European Journal of Migration and Law* 7, 2005, 35–69; C. Teitgen-Colly, 'The European Union and asylum: An illusion of protection', *Common Market Law Review* 34, 2006, 1303–1566; H. Lambert, 'The EU Asylum Qualification Directive, Its impact on the jurisprudence of the United Kingdom and international law', *International and Comparative Law Quarterly* 55, 2006, 161–192; and J. Pirjola, 'European asylum policy – inclusions and exclusions under the surface of universal human rights language', *European Journal of Migration and Law* 11, 2009, 347–366.

in the assumption that accompanied minors lack the capacity to make an asylum application in their own right, making it justifiable to subsume their claims to protection into those of their parents. The second image is apparent in the equivocation about the dividing line between childhood and adulthood. Thus, in the case of the accompanied child, the recast RCD and the recast QD still impose various restrictions on the married child, the sub-text being that marriage makes a child an adult. In the case of the unaccompanied child, the lack of any mechanism in the directives for identifying such children reveals an assumption that unaccompanied minors will self-present, just like adults do. Moreover, the provisions in the recast APD on age assessment, although an improvement on the current provisions, signal that there are real doubts about whether unaccompanied minors are actually minors at all. Even when age is not in dispute, certain provisions of the directives betray an assumption that older unaccompanied minors can legitimately be treated like adults. Thus, the recast APD retains the derogation from the obligation to appoint a representative in situations in which the unaccompanied minor is likely to 'age out' and the recast RCD retains the derogation from the obligation to provide a special placement in cases when the unaccompanied minor is over the age of sixteen, albeit subject to the best interests of the child. This tendency to blur the line between minority and adulthood has been noted in the literature as creating situations 'when a child is not a child'.[2]

This contradictory image of the child (needy and vulnerable versus able and knowing) may also reflect a less-than-full understanding of the tensions within child-rights law. As outlined in Chapter 2, the CRC attempts to maintain a delicate balance between acknowledging and providing for the special developmental and protection needs of the child, on the one hand, and the fact that the child is a rights-bearer, a decision-maker, an agent, on the other. This so-called welfare-agency dichotomy is part and parcel of child-rights law and, moreover, is not simply a question of balancing competing rights, but also of balancing the dichotomy within rights. The challenge for any legislator is to maintain this balance, accommodating the child's agency *and* providing for the child's protection, without the child's agency being used as an excuse for diminished protection. As Bhabha vividly puts it, 'there is an acute tension between the infantilization of autonomous youth making decisions in suboptimal situations and the dereliction of duty towards exceedingly vulnerable child populations liable to severe abuse'.[3] It is evident from this book that the EU legislator has struggled with this challenge, oscillating between paternalism and scepticism. This calls into question the capacity of the EU legislator in the complex area of child-rights law.

2 H. Crawley, 'When is a child not a child? Asylum, age disputes and the process of age assessment', ILPA Research Report, 2007.
3 J. Bhabha, 'Arendt's children: Do today's migrant children have a right to have rights?', *Human Rights Quarterly* 31, 2009, 410–451, 439.

There is also a question of rigour, of whether the rights of the child have been systematically and thoroughly integrated into the relevant provisions of the CEAS instruments. Most provisions of the instruments are 'age-neutral'. But these provisions are neutral only formally, in the sense that they are not explicitly addressed to any particular age cohort. Being implicitly geared towards adults, such provisions often have a disproportionately negative impact on children. The provisions of the recast RCD on conditions of detention illustrate this point. By contrast, some provisions of the instruments are child-specific, being directed explicitly to children. However, on closer scrutiny, the child-specific provisions of the instruments in both phases are often geared not to all children, but only to a particular sub-set of children, namely, unaccompanied minors. Of course, the situation of unaccompanied minors is particularly perilous and demands special safeguards and guarantees. Nevertheless, the distinct impression created in both phases of the CEAS is that the EU legislator has fastened onto the theme of unaccompanied minors to the detriment of accompanied minors. Thus, accompanied minors are not necessarily entitled to lodge an asylum application on their own behalf, are not entitled to a representative, are more susceptible to detention, are more likely to be detained under conditions contrary to the needs/rights of a child and are not exempt from any of the extraordinary asylum procedures or the safe country concepts.

Furthermore, the child-specific provisions of the directive are not necessarily guided by rights-based considerations. For example, the recast APD exempts unaccompanied minors from some (but not all) of the grounds for acceleration/manifestly unfounded; from a finding of inadmissibility on the grounds of coming from a safe third country where this is not in the child's best interests; and from the first country of asylum concept, but only when conducted as part of a border procedure. While perhaps lamenting the narrow scope of these exemptions compared with what was proposed by the Commission, no child-rights advocate would quibble with these exemptions *per se*. But what is the underlying principle? It cannot be the principle that exceptional procedures are not suitable for unaccompanied minors, since unaccompanied minors remain fully susceptible to the admissibility procedure on grounds other than safe third country; the procedure for subsequent applications; and the re-introduced European safe third country procedure. Focusing on the (partial) exemption from the safe third country concept, this cannot be based on a principled objection to applying safe-country concepts to unaccompanied minors, since they are still susceptible to the first country of asylum concept when conducted other than as part of a border procedure; the European safe third country concept; and, indeed, the DR. Finally, the exemptions cannot be based on the principle that such procedures are in some way contrary to the rights of the child (which Chapter 4 of this book has shown them to be) since only unaccompanied minors are (partially) exempted. One is forced to conclude that the exemptions are *ad hoc*, random and lacking in transcendent principle.

It appears, therefore, that the EU is not effectively 'mainstreaming' the rights of the child into relevant legislation, contrary to stated policy.[4] It has not been the work of this book to probe the mechanisms by which the EU legislator attempts to integrate the rights of the child into EU legislation generally, or the CEAS in particular. Suffice to note that child-rights are mainstreamed into EU legislation by way of the regular Charter mainstreaming processes but that there is no *separate* child-rights mainstreaming methodology.[5] This is problematic because the rights of the child are *lex specialis*. The specialist nature of children's rights is most apparent in the child-specific protection rights that make up roughly one-third of the rights in the CRC (recall the typology in Chapter 3). But the exploration of the meaning of various civil and political and socio-economic rights of the child in this book has highlighted the distinct content of these rights too, at least in the asylum context. The right of the child to be heard and the right of the child to an adequate standard of living are cases in point, being qualitatively different from corresponding rights in general human rights law. Assimilating the rights of the child to general human rights standards risks obscuring the specificity and uniqueness of the rights of the child. This raises the more profound question of the appropriateness of mainstreaming as a method of integrating the rights of the child into law and policy. Mainstreaming is based on the premise that integration, as opposed to segregation, is the best way to ensure compliance with rights for the target group. However, it cannot be ruled out that a better way to ensure compliance with the rights of the child in the CEAS would be to establish a parallel, but separate, regime for children, possibly in the form of a discrete directive. This idea, which is only beginning to be considered in the literature, is worthy of further research in the context of Phase Three CEAS.[6] However, given the negotiation fatigue associated with Phase Two CEAS, coupled with

---

4 The seminal Commission Communication, 'Towards an EU strategy on the rights of the child', identifies a key objective as 'mainstreaming children's rights in EU actions'. *COM (2006) 367 final*. As follow-up to this outline strategy, the Commission published in early 2011 'An EU Agenda for the Rights of the Child', the purpose of which was 'to reaffirm the strong commitment of all EU institutions and of all Member States to promoting, protecting and fulfilling the rights of the child in all relevant EU policies and to turn it into concrete results'. *COM (2011) 60 final*, p. 3.
5 On the part of the Commission, see Commission Staff Working Paper, 'Operational guidance on taking account of fundamental rights in Commission impact assessments', *SEC (2011) 567 final*; on the part of the European Parliament, see 'Report on the Situation of Fundamental Rights in the European Union (2009) – Effective Implementation After the Entry into Force of the Treaty of Lisbon', *2009/2161(INI)*; on the part of the Council, see 'Guidelines on methodological steps to be taken to check fundamental rights compatibility at the Council's preparatory bodies', *10140/11*, 18 May 2011.
6 E. Drywood, '"Child-proofing" EU law and policy: Interrogating the law-making processes behind European asylum and immigration provision', *International Journal of Children's Rights* 19, 2011, 405–428.

the dominant migration-control agenda in the EU, the political will for such a course of action may well be lacking.

In this context, the role of ensuring that the CEAS complies with the rights of the child is likely to fall to the courts – the national courts of the Member States and the CJEU. Here, the potential of the principle of the best interests of the child comes sharply into focus. As outlined in Chapter 2, this principle requires that in all actions concerning children, the best interests of the child be a primary consideration. As to the meaning of 'best interests', it is apt to recall that the concept is inherently a rights-based one: relevant rights of the child imbue the concept with meaning, rendering it *contra legem* to promote a course of action as being in the best interests of the child if it runs counter to a relevant right of the child. The EU legislator is to be congratulated for the fact that all the CEAS instruments in both phases commit Member States to adhere to the principle, even if some provisions of the CEAS themselves are not in the best interests of children.[7] This raises the question of how Member States can reconcile the provisions of the instruments that are apparently contrary to the rights of the child with the best-interests principle. Given the primacy of the principle, it is submitted that, in such a scenario, the best-interests principle could have a potentially transformative effect, informing (i.e. constraining) the transposition, implementation and interpretation of contrary provisions of the CEAS instruments and their application to any given child. The making of strategic requests for preliminary rulings to the CJEU could help realise this potential. It is hoped that this book, to the extent that it charts the distance between certain provisions of the CEAS instruments and the rights of the child, will help with this task.

---

7 Although some of the instruments in both phases purport to limit the scope of the best-interests principle to particular articles or chapters therein, in light of the Court's judgment in *M.A., B.T. & D.A* it seems likely that the best-interests principle applies to all provisions of the CEAS whenever the applicant is a child. CJEU, Case C-648/11, Judgment of 6 June 2013.

Index

1951 Convention Relating to the Status of Refugees 8, 12, 99, 138, 188; Article 1A(2) 25, 72, 74n54, 75, 76n62, 78, 82–3, 84n87, 105n42, 123n106, 156n50; Article 1C 87, 94; Article 1E 88n95; Article 1F 88, 89, 94, 156n50; Article 22 64n30; Article 31 210n4; Article 33(1) 39; Article 63 10n17; Article 64 10n17; contains no child-specific provisions 27, 63–4; humanitarian instrument 39, 56–7; outline of regime 6–7; reasons for persecution 76

Abdolkhina and Karimnia v. Turkey 212, 224
accelerated/manifestly unfounded procedure 23, 60, 62–3, 112, 122, 123, 124, 126–7, 132, 134, 135, 136, 237
accommodation 149, 165–7, 204–5, 206, 226, 227–8 *see also* detention; housing
accompanied child/minor: access to international protection procedure 57–8, 59, 94–5; detention of 214, 218, 220, 226, 230, 237; in care of relative 155; later application for protection 60, 61, 62–3; negative procedural consequences 33; protection and care 140–53; representative at a hearing 104, 117, 118, 119, 129, 136, 137
acquis on asylum 11
'acting in the scope of', member states and EU law 52–3

administrative detention *see* detention
admissibility procedure 23, 60, 63, 109, 112–13, 127, 132, 134, 237
age assessment 155–6, 162–3, 236
age neutrality of provisions of instruments 17, 27, 48, 237
age specificity of provisions of instruments 27, 28, 237
Ago, Robert 179n25
Ahmed, T. 50n92
Alma-Ata Declaration on Primary Health Care 180
alternative care 37–8, 85, 158–60, 165–7, 169–70 *see also* unaccompanied child/minor
Amuur v. France 212
appeal/appeals procedure 23, 24, 114–15, 120, 127–8, 133, 136, 137, 227, 228
'appropriate bodies', reference in Returns Directive 62
Archard, D. 29n4
Arend, A. C. 64n32
Aries, P. 37n39, 66n44
armed conflict 79–80 *see also* child soldiers
Arneil, B. 29n4
arrest, right to be informed of reason 222–3
Asylum Procedures Directive (APD) 21–4; Article 2 164, (recast) 129; Article 4 111, 118n87, 119–20, (recast) 130, (recast) 131–2; Article 5 51n95, (recast) 51n95; Article 6 59n16, 59–60, 110, 145, 147n27, 162n69&71, (recast) 168n83;

//
Index

Article 7 (recast) 61, 62; 114; Article 8 119, 120, 130, (recast) 168n83; Article 9 59n16; Article 10 118, (recast) 130–1, (recast) 132, (recast) 133, 228; Article 12 110–12, 113, 115, 119, 120, 121n96, 122nn98&99, 131; Article 13 117, 119, 120, (recast) 131; Article 14 (recast) 126n115, (recast) 132–3; Article 15 (recast) 127n122, (recast) 131, (recast) 132, 228; Article 16 (recast) 115n80, (recast) 131, (recast) 132, 228; Article 17 59, 61, 116–17, 118, 120, 129, 162–3, 228n66; Article 18 223, 224, 225, 228; Article 20 111n66, 115n79, (recast) 63n28, (recast) 128n123; Article 23 60, 109n56, 111n66, 115n79, 122nn97,98&99, 124–5, 128n125; Article 24 109n57, 117, 120, (recast) 167n81; Article 25 60n18, 109n55, 111n66, 112–13, 122nn99&100, (recast) 126n117, (recast) 127n119, (recast) 128, 129, (recast) 132nn134,136&137, (recast) 134nn139,140,141,143&145, (recast) 135n149; Article 26 124 (recast) 229n67; Article 27 123; Article 28 109n56, 122n98, 124; Article 29 122n99; Article 31 (recast) 62, 122, (recast) 126n116, (recast) 128n125, (recast) 135; Article 32 60n18, 109n58; Article 33 109n58, 115n79, 128n125, (recast) 134n144; Article 34 109n58, 122n97, (recast) 127n120; Article 35 109n59, 111n66, 117n84, (recast) 134, 223, 224; Article 36 109n59, 134, (recast) 134; Article 37 109n60; Article 38 109n60, 113, (recast) 134; Article 39 109n61, 114, (recast) 134–5; Article 40 (recast) 62nn24,25,&26, (recast) 63n27, (recast) 127n121; Article 41 (recast) 62n24; Article 42 (recast) 62n24; Article 43 (recast) 131–2; Article 46 (recast) 127–8; classification of procedures 108–10; derived rights 145, 147; detention 223–9; identification 162–3; overview of 21–4; Recitals (recast) 43–5, 132; right to be heard 108–37
'asylum shopping' 9
automatic negative credibility inferences 107–8, 120, 124–5, 133, 136
available resources 41, 172, 173, 174

Backstrom, K. 74n57
Barth Eide, W. 177n17, 178n21
Battjes, H. 12n29
Baysfsky, A. 189n45
Beck, R. J. 64n32
Besson, S. 33n25, 182n33
best interests assessment/obligation/principle 18, 19, 20, 21, 22, 24, 26, 27, 33–6, 44, 45, 47, 48–9, 63, 91, 103, 104, 113, 129, 132, 134, 140, 142–4, 147, 148, 149, 151, 152–3, 155, 156–8, 159, 163, 165–6, 167, 169–70, 171, 204, 205, 213, 214, 215–16, 217, 218, 219–20, 221, 222, 226, 229–30, 231, 232, 234, 236, 237, 239
Bhabha, J. 27, 31n18, 64n32, 77n65, 105n42, 107n50, 143n17, 236
bias in refugee law, civil and political rights 37, 66, 70, 71, 72
Bierwirth, C. 141n13
Boccardi, I. 9n15
Bossuyt, M. 157n56, 216n28
Brownlie, I. 84n85
Bulterman, M. 51n97
burden of proof 25, 107, 121–5, 133–5; later application of accompanied child 60, 63
Byrne, R. 11nn21&24

Campbell, T. 29n6, 30n9
capacity; presumption of 97–9, 102, 110; to make asylum application 59, 61–2, 236
cessation 6, 87–8, 93–4
Chandhi, P.R. 39n43, 57n6
Charlesworth, H. 64n32
child, definition of in CRC 142
child soldiers 76, 89, 91, 94
child-specific persecution 74
child-specific rights 59–60, 71, 238

child victims 175; health care under QD 187, 190; health care under RCD 185–6, (recast) 192–3; right to recovery and reintegration 185–7
Chinkin, C. 64n32
civil rights and freedoms 37
'classic' civil and political rights 37, 41
Coady, C.A.J. 30
Cohen, C. Price 180
Committee on the Rights of the Child (Com. RC) 32; EU Member States and 43, 45; General Comment No. 1 31n16; General Comment No. 4 146–7, 176n12, 185n38; General Comment No. 5 40n47, 97n2, 98n9; General Comment No. 6 33n24, 34n27, 36n36, 41n54, 42n58, 57n9, 65n34,75n61, 104n38, 139n3, 154n43, 155nn45&48, 156n51, 157, 158n58, 160n62, 173n6, 182n32, 186n42, 189n47, 197n64, 215n23, 221n46; General Comment No. 7 34n30, 185n38, 196n61, 197n65, 198n68; General Comment No. 8 35n32; General Comment No. 12 37n38, 98nn10&11, 102n30, 103nn33&37, 105nn41&43, 106n48; General Comment No. 13 36n37, 185n37; General Comment No. 14 4nn27&28, 35n33, 36n35, 41n52; General Comment No. 15 176n12, 177nn15&19, 180n26; General Comment No. 17 42n59, 204n83
Common European Asylum System (CEAS) 9–27; Asylum Procedures Directive (APD) 21–4; communitarisation of asylum 10–11; compliance with right to adequate standard of living 200–7; compliance with right to be heard 108–36; compliance with right to family unity 145–53; compliance with right to health 183–94; compliance with right to liberty 223–33; compliance with right to seek international protection 58–63; compliance with right of unaccompanied and separated child to special protection and assistance 160–70; compliance with rights of child 234; complicated political landscape 11–12; conforms to EU Charter of Fundamental Rights 44; Dublin Regulation (DR) 17–19; eligibility for international protection 72–94; evolution of 9–16; important substantive changes 14–15; integration of rights of child into 237; negotiation of instruments difficult 15–16; overview of key instruments 16–27; Phase One 9–13; Phase Two 13–16; Qualification Directive (QD) 24–7; Reception Conditions Directive (RCD) 19–21; references to various rights of child in 48–9; right to seek international protection 58–61; Third Phase 16
communication with legal advisors and UNHCR, right to 228, 231
comparability, right to health 188–9
'competent authorities' 111, 143–4
complementary protection 8–9, 10, 12, 65
Convention for the Protection of Human Rights and Fundamental Freedoms *see* European Convention on Human Rights (ECHR)
Convention on the Elimination of all Forms of Discrimination Against Women: Article 5 28n2; Article 16 147n26
Convention on the Rights of Persons with Disabilities: Article 6 28n2
Costello, C. 12n29, 109n54, 110n62, 235n1
Court of Justice of the European Union (CJEU) 15, 45, 46, 48–9, 73, 81–2, 92, 93, 94, 98, 100, 103, 104, 113, 115, 121, 122, 123–4, 135, 239; *Abdulla* case 87–8; exclusion/inclusion 90–1
Crawley, H. 64n31, 156n50, 236n2
criminal responsibility, age of 89

de Jesús Butler, I. 50n92
De Schutter, O. 51–2
de Zwann, J.W. 12n31

Index 243

Denman, D. 50n92
derived rights 38, 141–2, 145–8, 151–2, 170–1, 185, 203–4
derogation: alternative care 165–6, 169–70, 236; conduct of hearing 119–20, 131–2, 133; detention conditions 226, 227–8, 231, 235; EU fundamental rights 52–3; family unity 148, 149, 152; none in CRC 45; none in public emergency 42, 70; obligation to appoint representative 117, 118, 129, 236 persecution and non-derogable rights 72–3, 80; socio-economic rights 174, 201, 205, 207
detention 209–33; arbitrariness of permissible detention 212–14; conditions of 216–21, 226–7, 230–1; health care in 192; permissible 211–16, 223–5, 229–30; procedural protection 221–3, 227–8, 232–3; Reception Conditions Directive 19, 21; right to liberty 210–11; separation from adults in 217, 219–21, 231
Detrick, S. 196
development, standard of living and 194–7
direct provision, accommodation 201, 203, 204
discrimination: right to health 181–3, 188, 190; right to standard of living 200, 203
documentation, improper 224, 225
Doek, J. 143–4, 155n47
Dolgin, J. 33n26
Donnelly, J. 30n10
Douglas-Scott, S. 50n92
Drywood, E. 13n32, 46n72, 50n93, 98n7, 238n6
Dublin Regulation (DR) 11–12, 108, 123–4, 131, 140, 148, 152, 229, 237; Article 2 (recast) 152n38; Article 3 58n14; Article 4 150n35; Article 6 49n84; Article 27 (recast) 229n68; Article 28 (recast) 229n69; Article 33 18n60; overview of 17–19; *see also* safe third country (STC)
'due weight', right to be heard 106–8, 121, 124, 133, 135, 137

Eaton, J. 84n87
economic migrants 65
economic, social and cultural rights 38, 41, 65, 66, 70, 71, 73, 74, 91, 172–208
education 38; right of detained children to 227, 231
Edwards, A. 64n33
Eekelaar, J. 30n7
Eide, A. 177n17, 178n21, 195
El-Enany, N. 12n31
Elgafaji case 57, 81, 92
employment 207 *see also* labour market
Enenajor, A. 161n66
Engel, C. 51n96
Errera, R. 82n83
ERT line of cases 52, 53
Espinosa, A. 30n8
'EU Agenda for the Rights of the Child' 49
EU Charter of Fundamental Rights 18, 43–5, 46, 49, 50, 73, 97; Article 1 200n74; Article 6 211n8; Article 18 55n1; Article 19 57; Article 24 28n2, 44–5, 49n84, 97n3, 102n32, 103, 104, 138n1, 140n9; Article 34 194n56; Article 35 175n10; Article 42 100; Article 47 97n4, 101n27; Article 51 44n64, 49n84, 51n94, 52n100, 53; Article 52 45n68, 46, 173n4
EU-fundamental rights nexus, complications in 43, 50–4
EURODAC Regulation 12n25
European asylum law, channelling rights of child into 42–50; Article 3(3) TEU 48; Charter of Fundamental Rights 43–5; European Convention on Human Rights (ECHR) 46–8; general principle of respect for fundamental rights in EU law 46; policy commitments to the rights of the child 49–50; references in CEAS 48–9
European Asylum Support Office (EASO) 14, 130
European Commission, policy commitment to child rights 49–50
European Convention on Human Rights (ECHR) 39, 46–8, 73, 92; Article 2

Index

48n81, 175n10; Article 3 7, 8, 47, 57n7, 65n40, 81, 82n80, 84–5, 99, 100, 121, 125, 154, 157, 164, 175n10, 194n56, 199, 203, 211, 216, 217, 218, 221n45; Article 5 8n11, 47n76, 210n6, 211n8, 213, 214n20, 215, 216, 217, 218, 221n45, 222; Article 6 47–8, 97n4, 99, 101, 194n56; Article 8 8n12, 47n77, 140n7, 142, 143n18, 194n56, 221n45, 231; Article 13 97n4, 99n17, 112n70, 114, 125; Article 14 33, 181, 194n56; Article 15 72; Protocol 1 Article 2 48, Protocol 4 Article 4 8n13

European Court of Human Rights (ECtHR) 7, 33, 46, 47, 48, 81, 84, 97–8, 99, 114, 115, 121, 124, 125, 128, 135, 142, 181, 182, 199, 212, 215, 216, 217, 220, 222, 224, 231, 232

European Parliament v. Council 46

European STC *see* safe third country

Evans Cameron, H. 125n114

exclusion 6, 88–91, 94

family: environment and alternative care 37–8; protection of family life in detention 226; understanding of term in CRC 141–2

family members: definition of term in RCD and QD 146–7, 150; definition of term in recast RCD and QD 151–2; right to communication with 226, 231

family unity 17, 91; concept of derived rights 141–2, 151–2; health care under QD 187; prohibition of separating child from parents 142–4, 148–50, 152–3; right of child to 140–4, 145–8; standard of living under recast RCD 205

Feller, E. 64n33, 84n87

female genital mutilation 70, 71, 74

feminist scholars 64

Ferguson, L. 31n17

financial allowances/vouchers 200, 201–2, 203, 205–6

fingerprints *see* EURODAC Regulation

first country of asylum (FCA) 122, 124, 132, 134, 237

food 195, 199

Foster, M. 84n87

free legal assistance and representation 128

freedom of movement *see* liberty

Freeman, M. 30n7, 31n16, 66n42

fundamental rights: ambiguity in the extent to which member states are bound 52–4; assessing whether EU law complies with 50–2; general principle of respect for in EU law 46; *see also* EU Charter of Fundamental Rights

Gallagher, M. 89n96

gender-specific persecution 74

Geneva Convention *see* 1951 Convention Relating to the Status of Refugees

Geneva Conventions of 1949: Common Article 3 80n76

Gil-Bazo, M. 55n1

Gomien, D. 141n10

Goodwin-Gill, G. 38, 71n49, 77, 139n2

Goudappel, F.A.N.J. 12n31

Grahl-Madsen, A. 77

Griffey, B. 174n7

Groussot, X. 53n102, 173n4

guardianship 116–17, 155, 156–8, 163–5

Guggenheim, M. 29n5

Gutierrez, F. 106n46

Hafen, B. 29n5

Hague European Council 2004 14

Halvorsen, K. 156n50

Hathaway, J. 7n2, 84n87

health, right to 175–93, 196; core content of right 179–83; minimum essential obligation 179–81; normative content of right 176–9; prohibition of discrimination 181–3; Qualification Directive 187–90, 193–4; Reception Conditions Directive 183–7, 190–3; *see also* mental health care

hearing, right of the child to a 36–7, 96–137, 238; adaptation of the hearing 104–6, 118–20, 129–33; burden of proof 25, 107, 121–5, 133–5; conduct of the hearing 103–8, 116–18, 129; evaluation of child's views 106–8, 120–5, 133–6; negative credibility inferences 107–8, 120, 135–6; right to a hearing 99–103, 110–15, 125–8; right to a representative 103–4, 116–18, 129
HID, BA case 122, 124
Hodgkin, R. 102n32
Houlgate, L. 102n32
housing 148, 152, 195, 201, 226, 227–8
humanitarian instruments 39, 56–7, 138
Hunt Federle, K. 29n4, 30n12

Iglesias Sánchez, S. 50n92
I. M. v. France 100
inadmissibility procedure 112–13, 127, 237
indirect channelling, child rights into EU law 43–50
indiscriminate violence 81–2
indivisibility, doctrine of 70, 172–3
information, right to in detention 228
internal flight *see* internal protection
internal protection 25, 84–7, 93
International Covenant on Civil and Political Rights (ICCPR) 39, 42, 57, 71, 214; Article 2 28n1, 97n4; Article 7 7, 57n7; Article 9 8n11, 210n5, 212, 221–2; Article 10 8n11, 210n5, 216n30, 219n41; Article 13 8n13; Article 14 97n4; Article 17 8n12, 140n7; Article 24 28n2, 153n39, 213
International Covenant on Economic, Social and Cultural Rights (ICESCR): Article 2 41n53, 173nn4,5&6, 179n24; Article 10 28n2, 194n55; Article 11 194n55, 195; Article 12 175; Article 13 176; General Comment 3 of Com. ESCR 179, 180; General Comment 4 195; General Comment 12 195; General Comment 14 177, 180; General Comment 20 182
international human rights law, relevance for asylum law 7–9
international protection 55–95; CEAS Phase I compliance 58–61; CEAS Phase II compliance 61–3; cessation 87–8, 93–4; content in Qualification Directive 26; eligibility for 63–72; exclusion 88–91, 94; internal protection 84–7, 93; refugee definition 72–9, 91–2; right to seek 56–8; 'serious harm'; definition 79–82, 92; sources of harm and protection 82–4, 93; *see also* complementary protection; subsidiary protection
interpreter, right to services of 228

judicial review 144, 228, 232

Kalverboer, M. 94n110, 186n40, 197n67
Kanagaratnam and Others v. Belgium 218
Kaunert, C. 16n48
Keselman, O. 105n44
Klug, F. 30n14
Knorth, E. 94n110, 186n40, 197n67
Kosar, D. 91n104
Krappmann, L. 101n28

labour market 202, 206
Lambert, H. 82n82, 235n1
later application *see* accompanied child
Leary, V. 176n14
legal and other appropriate assistance, right to 221–3, 227–8, 232–3
legal capacity, access to asylum procedure 59, 61–2
leisure activities, obligation to provide 204–5, 231
Leonard, S. 16n48
liberty, right of child to 210–33; conditions of detention 216–21, 226–7, 230–1; permissible detention 211–16, 223–5, 229–30; procedural protection 221–3, 227–8, 232–3
life, survival and development, right to 36

limitation clauses 41, 45 *see also* derogation
Lisbon Treaty 14, 48
Lokpo and Touré v. Hungary 212, 224
Lücker-Babel, M. 102n32

McAdam, J. 9n14, 63n29
McCallin, M. 186n40
McGillivray, A. 29n6
McGlynn, C. 45n67
McGoldrick, D. 173n5
Machel, Graça 80n75
Macleod, C. 29n4
'mainstreaming' rights of child into relevant legislation 49–50, 238–9
Margulies, P. 58n11
marital status of minor 59, 62, 145–8, 150, 151–2, 236
material reception conditions 20, 21, 200–1, 205, 226 *see also* standard of living
Mayeka Mitunga v. Belgium 157, 217
medical examinations 162–3
medical model of rehabilitation 186
mental health care 178, 186, 190–1, 204
migration-control approach to asylum 11, 234, 239
military service 74–5 *see also* child soldiers
Mink, J. 52n99
Minow, M. 30n11
M.M. case 100, 121, 122
Mnookin, R. 33n26
MSS v. Belgium and Greece 124, 135
Mullally, S. 160n61
Muskhadzhiyeva v. Belgium 218

NA v. The United Kingdom 81
name and nationality, right to *see* civil rights and freedoms
negative credibility inferences 107–8, 120, 124–5, 133, 135–6
Neulinger and Shuruk v. Switzerland 47
Newell, P. 102n32
Nicholson, F. 64n33, 84n87
Noll, G. 11nn21&24, 121n94
non-discrimination 32–3, 40, 67, 139, 177, 181–2, 200, 219 *see also* discrimination

non-refoulement 2, 6–9, 39, 44, 55, 57, 65, 123–4; Article 3 of UN Convention Against Torture 7; Article 3 of European Convention on Human Rights 7–8
non-state actors of protection 82–4, 93
non-verbal forms of communication 102–3
N.S. and M.E. cases 53, 123

Ochaita, E. 30n8
O'Donnell, D. 107n49
Olsen, F. 30n11, 64n32
O'Neill, O. 30nn13&15, 76n63
O'Nions, H. 12n29
'other status', interpretation by Com. RC 33, 181–2

parents: discrimination in health care on basis of 185; standard of living obligation 196; *see also* accompanied child; derived rights
Parker, S. 33n26
Pech, L. 53n102, 173n4
Peers, S. 15n45, 45n68, 50n93
persecution: acts of 72–5, 91; non-state actors 25, 78–9; 82, 84, 92–3; reasons for 76–9, 92
personal interview 18, 22, 24, 61, 110–15, 116, 117, 118, 119, 120, 122, 125–8, 130–3, 184, 235; admissibility procedure 112–13; appeals procedure 114–15; fitness for interview 126; problematic grounds for omission 112; withdrawal of refugee status 113–14
Pirjola, J. 12n29, 235n1
political opinion, ground for persecution 76–9
Popov v. France 216, 220, 231
poverty, standard of living and 196
pregnant women, derived rights and 146
Price Cohen, C. 31n16, 41n51, 42n57, 180
primary health care 177–8
prison accommodation 230 *see also* detention
private and family life, right to 8, 47, 140 *see also* family unity

prohibition of collective expulsion of aliens 8
proportionality: withdrawal of healthcare 184–5, 190; withdrawal of standard of living 202–3
protection and care, right of child to 138–71; EU Charter of Fundamental Rights 44; family unity 140–53; 'protection' rights urgent in detention 219; rights in CRC 37–8; unaccompanied child 153–70
protection, non-state actors 83, 95
protection status, limitation of health care and 189–90
Protocol II Additional to the Geneva Convention 1977: Article 1 80n76
psychological treatment or care, victims of torture and violence 192–3 *see also* mental health care
Purdy, L. 29n6

qualification criteria, international protection 55
Qualification Directive (QD): access to health care 187–90, 193–4; adoption of recast 15; Article 1 24n75; Article 2 72, 79, 88, 146, 147n28, 150, 161n65; Article 3 51n95, (recast) 51n95; Article 4 121n93; Article 6 77–8, 82, 93, (recast) 93; Article 7 82–4, 93; Article 8 84, 86–7, 93, (recast) 93; Article 9 72–5, 78–9, 80, 91, (recast) 91, (recast) 92, 123n106; Article 10 76–8, (recast) 92n106; Article 11 87n92, 93–4; Article 12 75, 88–91, 94, (recast) 94; Article 13 58n15; Article 14 113; Article 15 79–82, 85, 92, (recast) 92; Article 18 58n15; Article 20 146, 187, 188, (recast) 193; Article 23 145, 150, 151, 187, 203–4, (recast) 151; Article 28 203n82 (recast) 207; Article 29 187,190; Article 30 164, 167, (recast) 193; Article 31 (recast) 170n88; overview of 24–7; Recital 12 91; Recital 18 (recast) 91, 170; Recital 24 79; Recital 26 81; Recital 27 78, 93; standard of living 203–4, 207

qualifications, recognition of 207
Quennerstedt, A. 66n43, 71n48

Rabinovici, I. 100n23
Rahimi v. Greece 47, 157, 199, 215, 218
Reception Conditions Directive (RCD): Article 2 146, 147n28, 150, (recast) 151n36, 161, (recast) 169, 200n75, (recast) 232; Article 3 145n23, 162n67, (recast) 167n80, (recast) 231n72; Article 4 51n95, (recast) 51n95; Article 7 149n33, 223, 224, 225, 227; Article 8 (recast) 21n67, 148, 152, (recast) 228, (recast) 229n69; Article 9 (recast) 21n67, (recast) 228, (recast) 229, (recast) 232n76; Article 10 (recast) 21n67, (recast) 229, (recast) 230, (recast) 231; Article 11 (recast) 21n67, (recast) 192, 202, (recast) 229–30, (recast) 231, (recast) 232; Article 12 (recast) 152; Article 13 200, 201–2, 226; Article 14 148, 149, 201, 226n63, 227–8; Article 15 183, 185, 190, (recast) 206; Article 16 184, 185, 202–3; Article 17 146, 183, 184n36, 187, 200–1, (recast) 204, (recast) 205–6; Article 18 149, 166, 169, 186–7, 193n54, (recast) 205n84; Article 19 161–2, 164, 165–7, 169, 183, (recast) 190, (recast) 191–2, 228n66; Article 20 (recast) 63n28, 183, 185, (recast) 192; Article 21 (recast) 191n51, 227; Article 22 (recast) 167n81, (recast) 191n51; Article 23 (recast) 152–3, (recast) 170, (recast) 193n54, (recast) 204–5; Article 24 (recast) 169–70; Article 25 (recast) 192; Commission evaluation of 227; derived rights 145–8, 151–2; family unity under 148–50, 152–3; overview of 19–21; Recital 22 151; right to health care 183–7, 190–3; standard of living 200–3, 204–6; unaccompanied minors 161–70
Redmond, G. 196n60
refoulement 100, 123 *see also* non-refoulement

refugee, definition 6, 72–9, 91–2
refugee-relevant, rights of child as 63–72
'refugees in orbit' 9
Reneman, M. 114n76
representative, unaccompanied minor's: care and protection 166–7, 169; lodging asylum application 60–1, 62; minor in detention 232; obligation to appoint 162, 163–5; right to at hearing 103–4, 116–18, 129
resource constraints, socio-economic rights and 41–2, 172–4, 189, 198–9
Returns Directive 62
Revised European Social Charter 153–4; Article 7 28n2; Article 11 175n10; Article 13 175n10; Article 17 28n2, 154n40, 194n56; Article 31 199n74
rights of the child, relationship between European Asylum Law and 42–54
Rodham, H. 102n32

safe country of origin (SCO) 112, 122–3, 133–4
safe third country (STC) 17, 23, 24, 112, 113, 122, 123–4, 126, 132, 133–5, 237; Dublin Regulation 17–19
Sarmiento, D. 50n92
Sax, H. 217, 219
Schabas, W. 217n33, 219n40
Schuurman, M. 48n83
separating child from parents, prohibition on *see* family unity
serious harm: definition 79–82, 92; internal protection from 84–7, 93; sources of 82–4, 93
Sharpston, A. G. 77n64
Sicilianos, Judge 47n77
Smith, C. 97n5
Smith, G. 105n44
Smyth, C. 47n79, 209n1
social group, ground for persecution 76, 92
social welfare assistance 205–6 *see also* standard of living
socio-economic rights 172–208; health 175–93; resource constraints and 41–2, 172–4, 189, 198–9; standard of living 194–207
special needs: adaptation of hearing 118–20; QD and right to health care 187–90, 193–4; RCD and right to health care 183–7, 190–3
special protection/assistance 38–9, 153–70; alternative care 158–60, 165–7, 169–70; compliance of CEAS 160–70; identification 154–6, 161–3, 167–9; oversight 156–8, 163–5, 169
staff competence/training 105–6, 118–19, 130–1, 166–7, 170
Stalford, H. 48n83, 98n7
standard of living 194–208; broad right 196; CEAS phase 1 compliance 200–4; CEAS phase 2 conformity 204–7; core content of right 198–200; minimum essential obligation 198–200; normative content of right 194–8; parent/state responsibilites 196–7; prohibition of discrimination 200; provision for in detention 226–7
States Parties' periodic reports 40, 43
Stevens, D. 140n8
Storey, H. 12n30
subsidiary protection 24, 25–6, 79–80; derived rights 145; equalisation of protection statuses 207; limit of social assistance 203–4; right to health care 187–90, 193

Taefi, N. 74
Teitgen-Colly, C. 11n22, 80n74, 235n1
'theory gap', children as rights holders 29–31
Thielemann, E. 12n31
'Towards an EU Strategy on the Rights of the Child' 49
trafficking 74
Trajkovska, Judge Lazarova 47n77
Treaty Establishing the European Community (TEC): Article 63 9–10, 11, 14; Article 67 10, 14n40; Article 68(1) 10
Treaty of Amsterdam 9, 10

Treaty on European Union (TEU):
  Article 3(3) 48; Article 6
  44nn63,64&66; 46, 48
Treaty on the Functioning of the EU
  (TFEU): Article 78 14, 15n41;
  Article 267 49n85
Tridimas, T. 101n26
Türk, V. 64n33, 84n87

UN Convention Against Torture 7, 39,
  57n7, 175n11
UN Convention on the Rights of the
  Child (CRC) 28–9, 234–9; 3Ps
  scheme classification of rights 66;
  Article 1 142; Article 2 32, 40, 139,
  181–2, 185, 199n74, 200, 203, 219;
  Article 3 33, 35n34, 66n42, 106,
  113, 138n1, 141n12, 143, 156n51,
  157, 160, 196, 215, 216n26, 218;
  Article 4 39–40, 41, 97n2, 172–3,
  179, 198; Article 5 104, 141n12;
  Article 6 36, 73n53, 196; Article 7
  40n49, 140, 142; Article 8, 140,
  155, 163; Article 9 37, 40n49, 140,
  142–3, 144n22, 148, 149, 150, 152,
  153, 220; Article 10 40n49, 140;
  Article 12 36–7, 96–137, 144, 222;
  Article 14 141n12; Article 16 140,
  142; Article 18 141, 156–7, 196;
  Article 19 35n32, 159, 219; Article
  20 38, 41–2, 83, 153, 154, 155,
  156, 158, 159, 160, 163, 165–6,
  191; Article 22 7n1, 32, 39, 40n49,
  56–8, 61–2, 101, 113, 138, 140,
  144n22, 153,154, 172; Article 23
  141n12; Article 24 42n59, 141n12,
  175, 176–83, 188, 196; Article 25
  144; Article 26 141n12, 196; Article
  27 141n12, 178, 194–200, 204,
  206, 227; Article 28 196; Article 31
  42n59, 196, 204–5, 231; Article 32
  159n60; Article 33 159n60; Article
  34 159n60; Article 35 73n53, 74,
  159n60; Article 36 159n60; Article
  37 47, 73n53, 165n76, 211–16,
  217, 218, 220, 221–3, 224, 225,
  226, 227, 228, 230, 231, 232, 233;
  Article 38 75; Article 39 83, 89,
  175, 178, 180–1, 185- 7, 190, 193,
  194; Article 40 73n53; Article 42
  97n2; Article 44 97n2; best interests
  of child 33–6; civil rights and
  freedoms 37; disability, basic health
  and welfare 38; education, leisure and
  cultural activities 38; EU not party
  to 43; family environment and
  alternative care 37–8; General
  Comments see Committee on the
  Rights of the Child (Com. RC);
  general principles 32–7; legal
  obligation 39–42; lex specialis
  character of CRC obligations 42;
  non-derogable rights 42, 45, 70;
  non-discrimination 32–3; optional
  protocols 31, 40, 98; overview 31–9;
  right to be heard 36–7; right to life
  36; special protection measures 38–9;
  typology of rights 66–72
UN Standard Minimum Rules for the
  Treatment of Prisoners 219
unaccompanied child/minor 22, 24, 26,
  126–7; access to international
  protection procedure 57–8; definition
  of 147, 151, 161; detention of
  214–16, 217–18, 221, 223–4, 228,
  230, 232; evaluation of child's views
  134, 135–6; identification of child
  entitled to special protection and
  assistance 154–6, 161–3, 167–9;
  internal protection and 85–6, 93;
  oversight of care and protection
  156–8, 163–5, 169; provision of
  alternative care 158–60, 165–7,
  169–70; right to representative at
  hearing 104, 116–17; right to special
  protection and assistance 153–70;
  role of representative 60–1, 62;
  standard of living obligation 197
United Nations High Commissioner
  for Refugees (UNHCR) 7; burden of
  proof in child cases 107–8;
  detention of minors 214, 226, 228,
  231; evaluation of child's views at
  hearing 107–8, 123; exclusion
  analysis 89–90; membership of a
  particular social group test 76;
  refugee law bias 71; typology of
  rights 71, 74, 76

Universal Declaration of Human Rights: Article 14 55n1
unmarried minors, later application by 62–3, 127, 145 *see also* accompanied child/minor; unaccompanied child/minor

Van Bueren, G. 66n42
Vander Lugt, R. D. 64n32
Vedsted-Hansen, J. 11nn21&24
Veerman, P. 31n16
victims *see* child soldiers; child victims; persecution
Vienna Convention on the Law of Treaties 1969: Article 27 40n46

Wachauf line of cases 52, 53
war crimes 75, 89 *see also* child soldiers; child victims

Ward, A. 45n68
welfare-agency dichotomy 236
well being 176, 178, 195–6 *see also* standard of living
Westen, P. 189
withdrawal: reception conditions 20, 184, 192, 202–3, 206; refugee status 23, 113–14, 120, 127, 133
Wolff, S. 12n31
Wouters, K. 7n6, 65n38
Wright, S. 64n32

Young, W. 105n42, 143n17

Zarraga v. Pelz 103, 104
Zermatten, J. 138n1
Zijlstra, A. 94n110, 186n40, 197n67
Zschirnt, E. 13n32, 165n76